Liberal and Conservative:
Issues for college students

Liberal
and
Conservative

Issues for college students

Edited by
Eugene K. Garber
University of Iowa
and
John M. Crossett
Grinnell College

Scott, Foresman and Company

Library of Congress Catalog Card No. 68-17215
Copyright © 1968 by Scott, Foresman and Company, Glenview, Illinois 60025.
All Rights Reserved. Printed in the United States of America.
Regional offices of Scott, Foresman and Company are located in
Atlanta, Dallas, Glenview, Palo Alto, and Oakland, N.J.

ACKNOWLEDGMENTS

Permission to reprint the following is gratefully acknowledged. Credits for selections are cited in the order they appear in the book.

THE PHILOSOPHICAL CONTINUITY.   From Protagoras' Fragments, *The Pre-Socratic Philosophers* (a companion to Diels, *Fragmente der Vorsokratiker*), by Kathleen Freeman (Oxford: The Oxford University Press, 1949).   From *Protagoras*, by Plato, Jowett translation, 4th ed. (Oxford: The Clarendon Press, 1964), pp. 145-148; reprinted by permission of the publisher.   From the "Politics," *The Philosophy of Aristotle*, edited by Renford Bambrough and translated by J. L. Creed and A. E. Wardman, pp. 387-389; copyright © 1963 by Renford Bambrough; reprinted by arrangement with The New American Library, Inc.   From *The Ethics of Aristotle*, translated by J. A. K. Thomson, condensed and adapted from pp. 126-128; copyright 1953 by George Allen & Unwin Ltd.; reprinted by permission of Barnes & Noble, Inc.   From *Tamburlaine* and *The Tragical History of Doctor Faustus*, in *The Complete Plays of Christopher Marlowe*, edited by Irving Ribner, pp. 75, 171-172; copyright © 1963 by The Odyssey Press, Inc.; reprinted by permission.   From *Troilus and Cressida*, in *The Complete Works of Shakespeare*, edited by Hardin Craig (Glenview, Ill.: Scott, Foresman and Company, 1951), p. 870; reprinted by permission of the editor.   "Jefferson to Adams," *The Adams-Jefferson Letters: The Complete Correspondence Between Thomas Jefferson and Abigail and John Adams*, Vol. II, edited by Lester J. Cappon (Chapel Hill: University of North Carolina Press, 1851), pp. 388-392; reprinted by permission of the publisher, for the Institute of Early American History and Culture.   From "Discourses on Davila," *The Works of John Adams*, notes and illustrations by his grandson, Charles Francis Adams (Boston: Charles C. Little and James Brown, 1951), Vol. XI, pp. 274-281.   From *The Good Society*, by Walter Lippmann, pp. 203-234; reprinted by permission of Atlantic-Little, Brown and Co.; copyright 1936, 1937, 1943, by Walter Lippmann.   From *Reinhold Neibuhr on Politics*, edited by Harry R. Davis and Robert C. Good, pp. 12-25; condensed and reprinted with the permission of Charles Scribner's Sons; copyright © 1960 Charles Scribner's Sons.

THE ISSUES. RELIGION.   From *Reason in Religion*, by George Santayana, pp. 3-14; reprinted with the permission of Charles Scribner's Sons.   From "The Lost Dimension in Religion," by Paul Tillich, *The Saturday Evening Post* (June 14, 1958), pp. 29, 76, 78; reprinted by permission of the author's estate.   From *Systematic Theology*, by Paul Tillich, Vol. III, pp. 130-134; copyright © 1963 by The University of Chicago Press; reprinted by permission of The University of Chicago Press.   From *Radical Theology and the Death of God*, by William Hamilton and Thomas J. J. Altizer, pp. ix-xiii, 41-50; copyright © 1966 by Thomas J. J. Altizer and William Hamilton; reprinted by permission of The Bobbs-Merrill Company, Inc.   From "The Vitality of the Old Testament," by James Alvin Sanders, *Union Seminary Quarterly* (January, 1966), pp. 173-181; reprinted with permission of the *Union Seminary Quarterly*, 2031 Broadway, New York, N. Y. 10027. From *The Doors of Perception*, by Aldous Huxley, abridgment of pp. 9-21, 52-79; copyright 1954 by Aldous Huxley; reprinted by permission of Harper & Row, Publishers and Chatto & Windus Ltd.   From *Mysticism Sacred and Profane*, by R. C. Zaehner (Oxford: The Clarendon Press, 1957), condensed and adapted from pp. xi-27; reprinted by permission of The Clarendon Press, Oxford.

LAW.   From *Law and the Modern Mind*, by Jerome Frank, pp. 3-20; copyright 1930, 1933, 1949 by Coward-McCann, Inc., copyright 1930 by Brentano's, Inc., Anchor Book's edition, 1963; copyright renewed in 1958 by Florence K. Frank; reprinted by arrangement with the estate of Barbara Frank Kristein.   From "Natural Law and the Public Consensus," by John Courtney Murray, S. J., from *Natural Law and Modern Society*, edited by John Cogley, pp. 62-71; copyright © 1962, 1963 by The Fund for the Republic, Inc.; reprinted by permission of The World Publishing Company.   From *Political Power and Personal Freedom*, by Sidney Hook, pp. 86-100; copyright © 1959 by S. G. Phillips, Inc.; reprinted by permission of S. G. Phillips, Inc.   "Opposing the Opinion of the Supreme Court," by Eugene Cook and William I. Potter, *American Bar Association Journal* (April, 1956), Vol. XLII, pp. 313-391; copyright 1956 by the *American Bar Association* and reprinted with their permission.   From "The Cultural Context of Sex Censorship," by Eric Larrabee; reprinted with permission from a symposium, "Obscenity and the Arts," appearing in *Law and Contemporary Problems* Vol. XX, No. 4 (Autumn, 1955), (Durham, North Carolina: Duke University School of Law), pp. 672-688; copyright 1955, by Duke University. Condensed from *The Smut Peddlers*, by James Jackson Kilpatrick, pp. 229-241; copyright © 1960 by James Jackson Kilpatrick; reprinted by permission of Doubleday & Company, Inc.

FOREWORD

This is a book of reasoned controversy. The confrontation that it presents—liberal versus conservative—is ubiquitous; men necessarily adopt liberal or conservative positions whenever they take a stand on issues important to their well-being. It has been impossible, of course, to cover the many particular subjects about which liberals and conservatives argue, but we believe that the ones we have chosen are basic: philosophy, religion, law, education, and politics. The final section, "Literature of the Liberal and Conservative Imagination," presents the conflict artistically. Thus, the book moves from the general to the particular, from the philosophical basis for the controversy to the rich texture of life reflected in literature created in the liberal and conservative traditions. Similarly, each section under "The Issues" begins with a discussion of the basic liberal and conservative tenets applicable to the issue and then proceeds to an application of these principles to particular questions.

The criteria for the choice of each selection were relevance and excellence. We have not been much influenced by the reputation of the writer. Whether he is generally considered liberal or conservative has not been so important as his expression of a liberal or conservative opinion about a particular issue. This principle of selection explains both the occasional appearance of a figure on an unexpected side of a fence (Robert M. Hutchins as a conservative) and the omission of such important historians as Clinton Rossiter and Russell Kirk, whose writings, though invaluable to us, never precisely fitted our polemical needs.

We have tried to preserve for the book a distinctly American character except where, in "The Philosophical Continuity," such an aim would have been clearly perverse. For the only other departure—Professor R. C. Zaehner—we plead grounds of his singular competence and pertinence.

The Afterword will, we hope, be useful to the reader in observing and exploring those relationships between selections which, though remote from each other in the book, are nevertheless profoundly linked.

The questions which follow the Afterword can be used in several ways: for discussion in class, projects in research, and topics for themes or speeches. They are suggestive rather than exhaustive.

CONTENTS

Part III: **Literature of the Liberal and Conservative Imagination**

Part I: **The Philosophical Continuity**

The oldest, simplest, and most lucid expressions for kinds of government were invented by the Greeks: government by the one, the few, or the many. Later Greek political thinkers, notably Plato and Aristotle, distinguished between good and bad kinds of each. Thus a good one-man rule was a monarchy, a bad one a tyranny; a good government by the few was an aristocracy, a bad one an oligarchy; a good ruling majority was a polity or timocracy, a bad one a democracy.

Today we have returned to simplistic terminology, for we use the one word *dictator* to denote one-man rule; *elite* to denote rule by the few; and *democracy* for rule by the many. Since both we and our political enemies call our governments democracies and since dictators may be either fascistic or communistic, we find ourselves in a semantic turmoil as dangerous as that described by Thucydides in his *History of the Peloponnesian War* (III. 82), when war and revolution confounded institutions and language alike.

Behind all of these terms, however, two prevailing attitudes can be discerned, to which we today give the names *liberal* and *conservative*. Of course, even here the corruption of language is apparent, as the variety of synonyms for both words reveals. The liberal thinks of himself as kind and generous, progressive and advanced, broad-minded and unprejudiced, democratic; the conservative thinks of the liberal as licentious (as in Shakespeare's phrase "liberal villain"), radical, socialistic, and even communistic. Conversely, the conservative thinks of himself as safe and moderate, traditional and sound, aristocratic; his liberal opponent calls him oligarchical, reactionary, and even fascistic. When we add to this complex polarity the fact that men take overlapping and even contradictory positions, we see that some effort needs to be made to clarify these two terms, which still have power to move men's minds and hearts.

Although the political sense of the word *liberal* originates, surprisingly, in eighteenth-century Spain, liberalism itself, like conservatism, stretches back to ancient Greece, as Professor Eric Havelock has undertaken to show in his book the *Liberal Temper in Greek Politics* (New Haven, 1957). Hence we have chosen to open our selection of liberal and conservative writings with a section entitled "The Philosophical Continuity" and within that section to start with Greek expositors of the two views. The meaning of the suffix *-ism* most relevant to this collection is "adherence to a body of doctrine," but the mere existence of such a collection as this may suggest that even this meaning is far from comprehensive. After all, if liberalism and conservatism were truly bodies of doctrine, we would need only to print their credos, their articles of faith. But they are not so much bodies of doctrine as certain attitudes, commitments, and assumptions.

The opening section is at once philosophical and historical; it consists of four sets of polar analyses, taken from antiquity, the Renaissance, the Age of Enlightenment, and our own century: Protagoras and Aristotle, Marlowe and Shakespeare, Jefferson and Adams, Walter Lippmann and Reinhold Niebuhr. The writings have been selected in order to show the most basic and profound expressions of the liberal and conservative beliefs, as they were in their unlabeled origins and as they are now in an age of historical self-consciousness. In the head-note for each author, we shall try, briefly, to place him in his historical context and to indicate the relationship of his selection both to its companion piece and to the whole tradition.

This section is not intended to survey the entire historical development of these two movements. Thus we have passed over the Middle Ages as if they were darker than some still think they were. Yet the writings of such men as Marsiglio of Padua and William of Occam contain the germ of much modern liberal theory—the belief in popular sovereignty; while on the other hand, the writings of Dante and John of Salisbury exhibit a reverence for hierarchy that is instinct with conservatism.

For further information, the reader may wish to consult such works as the six-volume *History of Medieval Political Theory of the West* edited by R. W. and A. J. Carlyle (New York, 1936) or the handier two-volume *Medieval Political Ideas* edited by Ewart Lewis (New York, 1954). More glaringly, we have omitted the nineteenth century, during which the very words *liberalism* and *conservatism* were domesticated in the English political vocabulary. The infinite riches of thinkers like Arnold, Disraeli, Coleridge, Gladstone, Bright, Macaulay, Ricardo—to name only English figures—simply would not fit in our little room. It is possible, however, to find in our choices, selective as they are, the essential tenets and attitudes of these two movements as they have been expressed in historical periods that all will agree are seminal.

Man Is the Measure
Protagoras / from Fragments and Plato's *Protagoras*

Protagoras (480?–411? B.C.) belonged to that famous group of Greek thinkers and educators which has been known, ever since Plato, as the "Sophists." Other prominent members were Gorgias, Hippias, Prodicus, and Thrasymachus —sometimes known as the "Elder Sophists." The writings of the Sophists exist only in fragments, and for their views we must rely, all too often, on the accounts given by their enemies, like Plato. The movement that they represented can be reconstructed sufficiently to enable us to classify them as the founders of what we today call liberalism, *for in their reported views and extant writings we can find the principal tenets of liberalism. Stated in their most rigorous form, these are religious skepticism, embracing a divorce of church and state and ranging from complete tolerance to outright atheism; moral relativism, with a consequent anthropocentric concern, whether humanistic, as in Mill, or scientific, as in Lenin; and political egalitarianism, extending from realistic recognition that all men are equal in the eyes of the law to idealistic faith that all men are brothers and that each individual psyche is sacrosanct. (For the basic tenets of conservatism, see the headnote for Aristotle.)*

Thus, in the two most famous fragments of Protagoras—quoted below— are found the germs of religious skepticism and moral relativism. The third selection is taken from Plato's dialogue Protagoras, *and though some scholars, notably Professor Havelock in the* Liberal Temper in Greek Politics, *doubt the fairness or accuracy of Plato's representation, we can find in the speech which Plato gives to Protagoras a mythical explanation of political egalitarianism. The use of myth is a clear sign that Protagoras, despite his religious skepticism, was willing to exploit the traditional form of Greek religious pedagogic technique for his anthropocentric ends.*

As with all the selections in this anthology, the reader should, of course, examine the dramatic and historical context of the speech.

/from Fragments

"Man is the measure of things. . . ."
"As for the gods, I do not know whether they exist or not."

/from Plato's *Protagoras*

Once upon a time there were gods only, and no mortal creatures. But when the appointed time came that these also should be created, the gods fashioned them out of earth and fire and various mixtures of both elements in the interior of the earth; and when they were about to bring them into the light of day, they ordered Prometheus and Epimetheus to equip them, and to distribute to them severally their proper qualities. Epimetheus said to Prometheus: 'Let me distribute, and do you inspect.' This was agreed, and

Epimetheus made the distribution. There were some to whom he gave strength without swiftness, while he equipped the weaker with swiftness; some he armed, and others he left unarmed; and devised for the latter some other means of preservation. Upon those whom he clothed in diminutive bodies, he bestowed winged flight or subterranean habitation: those which he aggrandized with magnitude, he protected by their very size: and similarly with the rest of his distribution, always compensating. These devices he used as precautions that no race should be destroyed. And when he had provided against their destruction by one another, he contrived also a means of protecting them against the seasons of heaven; clothing them with close hair and thick skins sufficient to defend them against the winter cold, yet able to resist the summer heat, and serving also as a natural bed of their own when they wanted to rest; also he furnished them with hoofs and hair and hard and callous skins under their feet. Then he gave them varieties of food,—herb of the soil to some, to others fruits of trees, and to others roots, and to some again he gave other animals as food. And some he made to have few young ones, while those who were their prey were very prolific; and in this manner the race was preserved. Thus did Epimetheus, who, not being very wise, forgot that he had distributed among the brute animals all the qualities which he had to give,—and when he came to man, who was still unprovided, he was terribly perplexed. Now while he was in this perplexity, Prometheus came to inspect the distribution, and he found that the other animals were quite suitably furnished, but that man was naked and shoeless, and had neither bed nor arms of defence. The appointed hour was approaching when man in his turn was to emerge from earth into the light of day; and Prometheus, not knowing how he could devise his salvation, stole the mechanical arts of Hephaestus and Athene, and fire with them (they could neither have been acquired nor used without fire), and gave them to man. Thus man had the wisdom necessary to the support of life, but political wisdom he had not; for that was in the keeping of Zeus, and the power of Prometheus no longer extended to entering into the citadel of heaven, where Zeus dwelt, who moreover had terrible sentinels; but he did enter by stealth into the common workshop of Athene and Hephaestus, in which they used to practise their favourite arts, and carried off Hephaestus' art of working by fire, and also the art of Athene, and gave them to man. And in this way man was supplied with the means of life. But Prometheus is said to have been afterwards prosecuted for theft, owing to the blunder of Epimetheus.

Now man, having a share of the divine attributes, was at first the only one of the animals who had any gods, because he alone was of their kindred; and he would raise altars and images of them. He was not long in inventing articulate speech and names; and he also constructed houses and clothes and shoes and beds, and drew sustenance from the earth. Thus provided, mankind at first lived dispersed, and there were no cities. But the consequence was that they were destroyed by the wild beasts, for they were utterly weak in comparison of them, and their practical attainments were only sufficient to provide them with the means of life, and did not enable them to carry on war against the animals: food they had, but not as yet the art of government, of which the art of war is a part. After a while the desire of self-preservation gathered them into cities; but when they were gathered together, having no art of government, they evil entreated one another, and were again in process of dispersion and destruction. Zeus feared that the entire race would be exterminated, and so he sent Hermes to them, bearing reverence and justice to be the ordering principles of cities and the bonds of friendship and conciliation. Hermes asked Zeus how he should impart justice and reverence among men:—Should he distribute them as the arts are distributed; that is to say, to a favoured few only, one skilled individual having enough of medicine or of any other art for many unskilled ones? 'Shall this be the manner in which I am to distribute justice and reverence among men, or shall I give them to all?' 'To all,' said Zeus; 'I should like them all to have a share; for cities cannot exist, if a few only share in the virtues, as in the arts. And further, make a law by my order, that he who has no part in reverence and justice shall be put to death, for he is a plague of the state.'

And this is the reason, Socrates, why the Athenians and mankind in general, when the question relates to carpentering or any other mechanical art, allow but a few to share in their deliberations; and when anyone else interferes, then, as you say, they object, if he be not of the favoured few; which, as I reply, is very natural. But when they meet to deliberate about political virtue, which proceeds only by way of justice and wisdom, they are patient enough of any man who speaks of them, as is also natural, because they think that every man ought to share in this sort of virtue, and that states could not exist if this were otherwise. Such, Socrates, is the reason of this phenomenon. . . .

The Class Society and The Golden Mean
Aristotle / from the *Politics* and the *Ethics*

Aristotle (384–322 B.C.) was the most systematically profound of Greek thinkers, and although he was a polymath, his works in all fields remain fundamental texts. The pupil of Plato, Aristotle saw the end of the polis, *the city-state, which reached its flowering in Athenian culture; as private tutor to Alexander the Great, he witnessed the beginning of the form which replaced it, the* cosmopolis, *or world-state.*

In the Politics, *which he regarded as the culmination of his great work on ethics, Aristotle reveals the dominating civic-mindedness of antiquity and its attendant analysis of social structure. More clinical, less prescriptive than his master Plato, and without his master's unorthodoxly conservative belief in communism of property, Aristotle confronted the problem of superior and inferior men with analytical candor.*

The first selection, from the Politics, *presents Aristotle's cool justification of slavery, an indispensable element in the great social and cultural structures of antiquity. Although as a formal institution, slavery has been eradicated from the modern world, it remains in subtler ways—as in economic subservience, political disenfranchisement, and class consciousness. But Aristotle argues* (Politics, *I. 6) that a slave is better off than an independent worker or artisan because a slave is part of a family and is thus more organically connected with the social structure. Once we set aside the modern antipathy aroused by the word* slavery, *Aristotle's arguments stand as the fundamental justification for all societies in which there is a marked division of classes.*

Because human superiority and inferiority were grounded in nature, which was for Aristotle divine, men are not equal and henceforth should not be treated as equal, even in the eyes of the law. Here lies the basis for Aristotle's theory of proportional justice, a moral absolutism not colored simple-mindedly in black and white but tempered to the color of the famous "golden mean." This view and its arguments are expressed in the second selection, taken from the Ethics. *Here Aristotle deals with the kind of justice appropriate to a class-society; the use of mathematical terms in the argument—a predilection shared by all theorists, conservative as well as liberal—marks at once the logic and impersonality of his mind.*

Although Aristotle, like Socrates, seems to have been suspected, and even accused, of impiety, he was philosophically a profoundly religious man, as the reader will find by studying both his poetry and the famous analysis of God's nature in the Metaphysics *(XII. 7), recently and finely translated by H. G. Apostle (Bloomington, Ind., 1966).*

We can find, then, in his writings the three basic tenets of conservatism, rigorously polar to those of liberalism as described in the headnote for Protagoras: religious orthodoxy, which ranges historically from Protestant latitudinarianism to the Catholic Inquisition; moral absolutism, based on a theory of proportional justice which is, ideally, aristocratic but which all too often, in practice, turns out to be oligarchical; and political hierarchy, extending from Cicero's idea of political harmony among recognized classes (concordia ordinum) to a rigid caste system, as manifested theoretically in Plato's Republic *and historically in the feudal system.*

/from the *Politics*

We must now see whether there is such a person as a slave by nature, and whether it is good and just for some people to be slaves or not—whether all slavery is contrary to nature. It is not hard to get the answer either by reasoning philosophically or by working from the facts.

Ruling and being ruled are not only necessary, they are also expedient. From birth onwards, the difference is noticeable; some tend to be ruled, others to rule. There are many kinds of rulers and subjects. (It is always the case that the better the subject, the higher the rule: rule over men is higher than rule over beasts. The function achieved by higher things is itself higher in the scale; and there is such a function when there is a combination of ruler and subject.)

To resume: in cases in which we are dealing with composites, made up of several parts that form a single common whole—whether the parts are continuous or separate—a ruler and a subject can always be found. This is by nature an essential characteristic of animate things; even in things that are inanimate there is a sort of ruling principle, as with harmony in music.

This is, however, more suitable for a less rigorous kind of study. The prime elements of living things are soul and body, of which the former is by nature the ruler, the latter the subject. We should study what is true by nature, taking things that are in a state of nature, and not corrupted; we should examine the person who is in the best state of both soul and body. In him, the truth of our view is made clear. In the case of bad men, or of those who are in a bad state, it will often strike one that the body is ruler over the soul, simply because such people are in a bad state, a state contrary to nature.

At any rate, animate creatures are the first cases where we can see the authority of a master and the rule of a statesman. Soul rules over body like a master; and mind rules over appetite like a statesman or king. This makes it clear that it is natural and expedient for the body to be ruled by the soul, and for the emotional part to be ruled by the mind and by the part that has reason. When both are equal, or the natural relation is reversed, all these functions are impaired.

What is true of man is also true of other living creatures. Domesticated animals are superior in nature to untamed animals; it is better for all the former to be ruled by man, since in this way they obtain security.

Also, as regards male and female, the former is superior, the latter inferior; the male is ruler, the female is subject. It must also be that the same is true for the whole of mankind. Where there is a difference between people, like that between soul and body, or between man and mere animal (this being the condition of people whose function is to use their bodies, manual labor being the best service they can give, for such people are by nature slaves), it is better for the lower ones to be ruled, just as it is for the subjects mentioned above. A man is a slave by nature if he *can* belong to someone else (this is why he does in fact belong to someone else) or if he has reason to the extent of understanding it without actually possessing it. Animals other than man do not obey reason, but follow their instincts. There is only a slight difference between the services rendered by slaves and by animals: both give assistance with their bodies for the attainment of the essentials of living.

Nature tries to make a difference between slave and free, even as to their bodies—making the former strong, with a view to their doing the basic jobs, and making the free people upright, useless for servile jobs but suitable for political life, which is divided into the tasks of war and of peace. The opposite, however, often turns out to be the case: it happens that some have the physique of free men, whereas others have the souls. It is quite obvious that if people showed their differences in their mere physique, as the statues of the gods show the difference between gods and men, everyone would say that the inferior ones ought to be slaves of the others.

If this is true of the body, it is even more just for the distinction to apply to the soul. But it is not so easy to see the beauty of the soul as the beauty of the body. It is clear, then, that people are by nature free men or slaves, and that it is expedient and just for those who are slaves to be ruled. . . .

/from the *Ethics*

Since the unjust man is a man who is not content to have an equal share with others, and since the unjust thing is the unequal thing, it is obvious that there must be a mean between the greater and the less inequality. This is the equal. In whatever action we find a greater and a less there must be an equal. If then the unjust is the unequal, the just is the equal; everyone accepts this conclusion without demanding a reason for it. But, since the equal is the mean, the just must also be a mean. Now equality cannot be stated in less than two terms. From this certain consequences naturally flow. *First,* the just is both a mean and an equal. *Second,* in its character as mean it must have extremes between which it lies.[1] *Third,* in its character of equal its equality must be expressed in two equal parts of what is shared. *Fourth,* in its character of just there must be certain persons to whom it is just. Here then is a minimum of four terms in which justice finds expression—two *persons* and two *shares.* And the equality of the second pair will be reflected in the equality of the first. The ratio will be the same in the one case as in the other, because, if the persons are not equal, their shares will not be equal. As a matter of fact when quarrels and complaints arise, it is when people who are equal have not got equal shares, or *vice versa.*

We see the same result when we look at the practice followed in awarding shares according to merit. It is admitted on all hands that in distributing shares justice must take some account of merit. By 'merit,' however, people do not all mean the same thing. Men of democratic sympathies measure degrees of merit by degrees of freedom, oligarchs by degrees of wealth, others judge by good birth, those who believe in the rule of the 'best' go by moral and intellectual qualifications. Justice, then, is the expression of a proportion. For proportion is not merely a property of numerical quantity, but of quantity as such. It is in fact an equality of ratios. And, as we saw, it involves four terms at least.[2] If you look at the diagram [A:B::B:C] before you, you will see the equation. As the line representing the first term (1) is to the line representing the second (2), so is (2) to the line representing the third term (3). Thus (2) is mentioned twice. Therefore, if it is counted in twice, there will be four proportionals.

The just, then, like the equal requires a minimum of four terms for its complete expression. Also the ratio between the two sets of terms is the same. Here is another diagram. [See note 3, p. 10.] Observe that the line representing the persons is divided in the same proportion as the line representing the shares. Then, as the first term is to the second, so is the third to the fourth. Hence by alternation as the first is to the second, so is the second to the fourth. Therefore as the first term is to the second, so is the sum of the first and third to the sum of the second and fourth. This is the combination which is produced in a fair division, and the combination is fair if sharers and

---

[1]The greater, namely, and the less.
[2]It is open to inspection that a discrete—that is a discontinuous—proportion is in four terms. But this is equally true of a continuous proportion, for it treats one term as two by repeating it.

shared are connected in this way. In this manner we get 'distributive' justice, which results from the conjunction of the first term of a proportion with the third, and of the second with the fourth; and such justice is a mean between the two extremes of more and less of what is fair. In a word the just is the proportionate. [If $A:B::C:D$, then $A+C:B+D::A:B$][3]

We see, then, that the just, by which is here meant the expression of distributive justice, can be stated as a proportion, and the unjust in this sense is a violation of proportion. What is unjust, therefore, is what is either too much or too little. One sees this happen. When some good is at stake the man who acts unjustly is the man who takes too much; the man who suffers the injustice gets too little. The position is reversed when the matter at stake is an evil. In that case the lesser evil is reckoned as a good in comparison with the greater, because of two evils the lesser is more desirable than the greater, and the desirable is good, the degree of goodness being measured by its desirability. . . .

---

[3]This is the kind of proportion which Greek mathematicians call 'geometrical,' being one in which the sum of the first and third terms is in the same ratio to the sum of the second and fourth as one term to the other in either of the two pairs. On the other hand distributive justice is not a continuous proportion, the reason being that its second and third terms, consisting as they do in a sharer and a share, do not make a single term.

Faustian Man

Christopher Marlowe/from *Tamburlaine* and *The Tragical History of Doctor Faustus*

Christopher Marlowe (1564–1593) presents, in the "high astounding" verse that he wrote, views polar in attitude, yet equal in dynamic vibrancy, to the great Renaissance expressions of order. Shakespeare turned to Homer, Milton to the Old Testament, to find dramatic voices for their faith in order, but Marlowe turned to such exotic figures as Tamerlane and Faust. The doctrine of degree (hierarchy) had been shaken in the Renaissance—notably by the discovery of new stars, a revelation which caused anxiety in those thinkers who based their justification of social and civic order on the immaculate and eternal order of the heavens. Although hierarchy remained the dominant principle of the age, rumblings of doubt and skepticism began to be heard. In Tamburlaine, *the first selection from Marlowe, we find the hero of his play using heavenly order—which Shakespeare's Ulysses uses to sanction hierarchy—as an image for anthropocentric relativism and as an argument for the infinite right of man's mind to quest for knowledge and happiness wherever he wills.*

In the second selection, Marlowe's greatest dramatic hero, Doctor Faustus, specifically and systematically analyzes the various degrees on the ladder of being, only to reject them one by one as unable to fulfill his human aspirations. The Faust theme continues to fascinate the liberal-minded artists of Europe, as exemplified in the figures created by Goethe and Thomas Mann; in our own day the theme provides the explanation of John Hersey's recent novel, Too Far to Walk. *In Marlowe's tumbling and condensed lines, we find modern Europe's initial dramatic exposition of the conflict between man's craving for complete freedom and God's insistence on obedience to principles, both natural and theological.*

Marlowe is, as might be expected, one of the central figures in Hiram Haydn's book The Counter-Renaissance *(New York, 1950), in which Haydn, editor of* The American Scholar, *argues that liberalism and anthropocentric humanism are the dominant attitudes of the Renaissance. His book is an attempt to answer the more orthodox views embodied in such works as Douglas Bush's influential volume of the new* Oxford History of English Literature *(Oxford, 1945; revised 2nd ed. 1962).*

/from *Tamburlaine*

    TAMBURLAINE. The thirst of reign and sweetness of a crown,
That caused the eldest son of heavenly Ops
To thrust his doting father from his chair,
And place himself in the imperial heaven,   15
Moved me to manage arms against thy state.

13-14. **eldest . . . chair,** Jupiter, the son of Saturn and Ops, with his mother's aid deposed his father and made himself king of the gods.   15. **imperial,** the 1590 'Emperiall' may be read also as 'empyreal.' There seems to have been little distinction in Marlowe's time between the two words.

What better precedent than mighty Jove?
Nature, that framed us of four elements
Warring within our breasts for regiment,
Doth teach us all to have aspiring minds.   20
Our souls, whose faculties can comprehend
The wondrous architecture of the world
And measure every wandering planet's course,
Still climbing after knowledge infinite,
And always moving as the restless spheres,   25
Wills us to wear ourselves and never rest,
Until we reach the ripest fruit of all,
That perfect bliss and sole felicity,
The sweet fruition of an earthly crown.

/from *The Tragical History of Doctor Faustus*

    FAUSTUS. Settle thy studies, Faustus, and begin
To sound the depth of that thou wilt profess.
Having commenced, be a divine in show;
Yet level at the end of every art,
And live and die in Aristotle's works.   5
Sweet Analytics, 'tis thou hast ravished me!
Bene disserere est finis logices.
Is to dispute well logic's chiefest end?
Affords this art no greater miracle?
Then read no more; thou hast attained that end.   10
A greater subject fitteth Faustus' wit!
Bid *On cay mae on* farewell; Galen come.
Seeing *ubi desinit philosophus ibi incipit medicus,*
Be a physician, Faustus; heap up gold,
And be eternized for some wondrous cure.   15
Summum bonum medicinae sanitas.
The end of physic is our body's health.
Why, Faustus, hast thou not attained that end?
Is not thy common talk sound aphorisms?
Are not thy bills hung up as monuments,   20
Whereby whole cities have escaped the plague,
And divers desperate maladies been cured?
Yet art thou still but Faustus and a man.
Couldst thou make men to live eternally,
Or, being dead, raise them to life again,   25

---

    3. **commenced,** taken a degree.   4. **level,** aim.   7. **Bene . . . logices,** The end of logic is to dispute well. This notion is part of the anti-Aristotelian system of Petrus Ramus, introduced at Cambridge while Marlowe was a student there.   12. **On cay mae on,** Aristotle's being or not being (as Bullen seems to be the first to have perceived). **Galen,** a Greek physician regarded throughout the Middle Ages as a medical authority.   13. **ubi . . . medicus,** Where the philosopher stops the doctor begins.   20. **bills,** medical prescriptions.

Then this profession were to be esteemed.
Physic, farewell! Where is Justinian?
Si una eademque res legatus duobus,   [*He reads.*]
Alter rem, alter valorem rei, etc.
A petty case of paltry legacies!   30
Exhæreditare filium non potest pater nisi—   [*He reads.*]
Such is the subject of the Institute
And universal body of the law.
This study fits a mercenary drudge
Who aims at nothing but external trash,   35
Too servile and illiberal for me.
When all is done, divinity is best.
Jeromè's Bible, Faustus, view it well:
Stipendium peccati mors est. Ha! *Stipendium, etc.*   [*He reads.*]
The reward of sin is death. That's hard.   40
Si peccasse negamus, fallimur   [*He reads.*]
Et nulla est in nobis veritas.
If we say that we have no sin,
We deceive ourselves, and there's no truth in us.
Why then belike we must sin,   45
And so consequently die.
Ay, we must die an everlasting death.
What doctrine call you this? *Che serà, serà:*
What will be, shall be! Divinity, adieu!
These metaphysics of magicians   50
And necromantic books are heavenly.
Lines, circles, signs, letters, and characters—
Ay, these are those that Faustus most desires.
O, what a world of profit and delight,
Of power, of honor, of omnipotence   55
Is promised to the studious artisan!
All things that move between the quiet poles
Shall be at my command. Emperors and kings
Are but obeyed in their several provinces,
Nor can they raise the wind or rend the clouds,   60
But his dominion that exceeds in this
Stretcheth as far as doth the mind of man.
A sound magician is a demi-god.
Here try thy brains to get a deity!

---

27. **Justinian,** Roman emperor of Constantinople (527-565) responsible for assembling the
Roman law; he was famous throughout the Middle Ages as a jurist.   28-29. **Si . . . rei, etc.** If the
same object is willed to two persons, let one have the thing itself and the other its value, etc. This
is an incorrect version of one of the rules in Justinian's *Institutes.*   31. **Exhæreditare . . . nisi,**
The father cannot disinherit the son except (another of Justinian's rules, roughly paraphrased).
38. **Jerome's Bible,** the Vulgate, translated by St. Jerome.   39. **Stipendium . . . est,** Romans,
VI,23.   41-42. **Si . . . veritas,** St. John, I,8.

The Doctrine of Degree

William Shakespeare / from *Troilus and Cressida*

Shakespeare (1564–1616) presents in his works expositions of nearly all possible views on man, nature, and society, all given dramatic and verbal forms that make them classic both in their completeness and in their objectivity. Here, in the famous speech of Ulysses from Troilus and Cressida, *we find a full and yet compact elaboration of that doctrine enunciated first by Homer: "let there be one king, one ruler, to whom Zeus has given the sceptre" (Iliad II. 204-206). Homer, no less than the Bible, was cited by the proponents of the "divine right of kings."*

The doctrine of degree appeals to the order of heaven and the order of nature for its justification of social classes. The tradition can be traced steadily from Homer through Plato and Aristotle, Cicero and Aquinas, Hooker and Burke, Kirk and even Niebuhr. By putting the speech in the mouth of Ulysses, in a play designed for a Christian audience, Shakespeare links the traditional views of antiquity and the Middle Ages, and at the same time reveals how dominant and pervasive this tradition was even in that humanistic period called the Renaissance.

Ulysses' speech has been quoted out of context so often as a locus classicus *that one almost forgets its dramatic source—a play that is the most bitter and obscure of Shakespeare's tragedies. One should read it in its context, keeping in mind especially the character and speeches of Thersites, who is the most cynical man to speak in Homer's* Iliad. *Whatever ironic construction may be put upon the play as a whole, however, the interior solidity and tightness of the speech make it a legitimately self-contained excerpt.*

ULYSSES. Troy, yet upon his basis, had been down,
And the great Hector's sword had lack'd a master,
But for these instances.
The specialty of rule hath been neglected:
And, look, how many Grecian tents do stand
Hollow upon this plain, so many hollow factions.   80
When that the general is not like the hive
To whom the foragers shall all repair,
What honey is expected? Degree being vizarded,

---

78. **specialty of rule,** particular rights of supreme authority (Johnson).   80. **Hollow,** empty, groundless, unnecessary.   83. **Degree,** here the equivalent of authority. Below (l. 86) the word has a more cosmological import, where it reflects the Renaissance belief (inherited from Plato) that the world achieved its stability by means of the gradation of all created things. The social and political implication of this conception is that human beings are born to a designated station or degree to which they must adhere with mutual respect and the responsibilities of which they must accept if society and government are to remain stable. Renaissance writers were fond of pointing out analogies between the civil organization and any natural or cosmological manifestations of some kind of order or degree. This passage (ll. 85-134) is not only Shakespeare's fullest and most eloquent statement of the concept, but also one of the most distinguished in all Renaissance literature.

The unworthiest shows as fairly in the mask.
The heavens themselves, the planets and this centre
Observe degree, priority and place,
Insisture, course, proportion, season, form,
Office and custom, in all line of order;
And therefore is the glorious planet Sol
In noble eminence enthroned and sphered   90
Amidst the other; whose medicinable eye
Corrects the ill aspects of planets evil,
And posts, like the commandment of a king,
Sans check to good and bad: but when the planets
In evil mixture to disorder wander,
What plagues and what portents! what mutiny!
What raging of the sea! shaking of earth!
Commotion in the winds! frights, changes, horrors,
Divert and crack, rend and deracinate
The unity and married calm of states   100
Quite from their fixure! O, when degree is shaked,
Which is the ladder to all high designs,
The enterprise is sick! How could communities,
Degrees in schools and brotherhoods in cities,
Peaceful commerce from dividable shores,
The primogenitive and due of birth,
Prerogative of age, crowns, sceptres, laurels,
But by degree, stand in authentic place?
Take but degree away, untune that string,
And, hark, what discord follows! each thing meets   110
In mere oppugnancy: the bounded waters
Should lift their bosoms higher than the shores
And make a sop of all this solid globe:
Strength should be lord of imbecility,
And the rude son should strike his father dead:
Force should be right; or rather, right and wrong,
Between whose endless jar justice resides,
Should lose their names, and so should justice too.
Then every thing includes itself in power,
Power into will, will into appetite;   120
And appetite, an universal wolf,
So doubly seconded with will and power,
Must make perforce an universal prey,
And last eat up himself. Great Agamemnon,
This chaos, when degree is suffocate,

---

85. **this centre,** the earth.   87. **Insisture,** steady continuance in their path.   91. **medici-nable,** healing.   92. **aspects,** relative positions of the heavenly bodies as they appear to an observer on the earth's surface at a given time, and the influence attributed thereto.   95. **mixture,** conjunction.   99. **deracinate,** uproot.   101. **fixure,** stability.   102. **ladder ... designs,** means by which all lofty purposes are realized.   105. **dividable,** separated.   113. **sop,** pulp. 114. **imbecility,** weakness.

Follows the choking.
And this neglection of degree it is
That by a pace goes backward, with a purpose
It hath to climb. The general's disdain'd
By him one step below, he by the next,   130
That next by him beneath; so every step,
Exampled by the first pace that is sick
Of his superior, grows to an envious fever
Of pale and bloodless emulation:
And 'tis this fever that keeps Troy on foot,
Not her own sinews. To end a tale of length,
Troy in our weakness stands, not in her strength.

Natural Aristocracy

Thomas Jefferson / from *The Adams-Jefferson Letters*

Thomas Jefferson (1743–1826) was at once the most radical and the most deliberate of eighteenth-century American liberals—radical in speculation, deliberate in action. Although he never wrote any single work embodying his principles, as the iconoclastic Thomas Paine did in the famous Rights of Man, *Jefferson's views are clear in his miscellaneous writings. Far less doctrinaire than Paine, who did not have to deal with the practical realities of politics, Jefferson was, surprisingly, more philosophically speculative. The magnificent opening of the Declaration of Independence, regarded by many liberals as a more important document than the Constitution—in which Jefferson had no hand—testifies to the scope of his political vision; the famous change of the phrase "life, liberty, and property" to "life, liberty, and the pursuit of happiness" illuminates a fundamental difference between conservatives and liberals.*

Although Jefferson and Adams were polar figures geographically, politically, and even personally, they were friends; their friendship, forged during the Revolution, broke when Jefferson became President but was later renewed. In the famous Adams-Jefferson letters, we find these two great Americans writing extensively, profoundly, and personally to each other on matters ranging from Greek accents to moral philosophy. The letter below starts with their mutual concern for Greek literature and then moves to an analysis of what constitutes an aristocracy. Here we find Jefferson agreeing with Adams that a natural aristocracy exists but sharply distinguishing his natural aristocracy from that upheld by New Englanders and conservatives. The distinction derives from a principle which Jefferson expressed to Madison in a letter written from France in 1789; and according to Jefferson's editors, "In later life Jefferson never wavered" from this principle.[1] The principle, taken directly from Richard Gem, an English Francophile and revolutionary sympathizer, is this: "The earth belongs in usufruct to the living." Jefferson defends it thus:

> . . . it may be proved that no society can make a perpetual constitution, or even a perpetual law. The earth belongs always to the living generation. They may manage it then, and what proceeds from it, as they please, during their usufruct. They are masters too of their own persons, and consequently may govern them as they please. . . . Every constitution, then, and every law naturally expires at the end of 19. years. If it be enforced longer, it is an act of force and not of right.

To support the peculiar precision of "19. years," Jefferson indulges in some mathematics as abstruse as those employed by many ancient philosophers— from Plato on—betraying that passion for systematic precision which separates the theorist from the pragmatist. Since the number nineteen is so close to twenty, we may regard this letter as explaining Jefferson's more famous dictum —repeated often in his writings—that the tree of liberty must be refreshed every twenty years by the blood of patriots and martyrs.

---

[1] *The Papers of Thomas Jefferson*, ed. Julian P. Boyd (Princeton, N.J., 1958) XV, 390.

Thus Jeffersonian aristocracy, like the liberty that it refreshes, must be renewed in each generation. It is not to derive its sanction from birth or wealth but from virtue, talents, and from the rational ability of the citizenry to recognize an aristocrat and elevate him to leadership—an aristocracy, in short, very different from the more hereditary or, at least, traditional kind desired by Adams.

Jefferson to Adams

Monticello Oct. 28. 13.

Dear Sir

According to the reservation between us, of taking up one of the subjects of our correspondence at a time, I turn to your letters of Aug. 16. and Sep. 2.

The passage you quote from Theognis, I think has an Ethical, rather than a political object. The whole piece is a moral *exhortation*, παραινεσις, and this passage particularly seems to be a reproof to man, who, while with his domestic animals he is curious to improve the race by employing always the finest male, pays no attention to the improvement of his own race, but intermarries with the vicious, the ugly, or the old, for considerations of wealth or ambition. It is in conformity with the principle adopted afterwards by the Pythagoreans, and expressed by Ocellus in another form. Περὶ δὲ τῆς ἐκ τῶν ἀλλήλων ἀνθρώπων γενέσεως etc.—οὐχ ἡδονῆς ἕνεκα ἡ μίξις. Which, as literally as intelligibility will admit, may be thus translated. 'Concerning the interprocreation of men, how, and of whom it shall be, in a perfect manner, and according to the laws of modesty and sanctity, conjointly, this is what I think right. First to lay it down that we do not commix for the sake of pleasure, but of the procreation of children. For the powers, the organs and desires for coition have not been given by god to man for the sake of pleasure, but for the procreation of the race. For as it were incongruous for a mortal born to partake of divine life, the immortality of the race being taken away, god fulfilled the purpose by making the generations uninterrupted and continuous. This therefore we are especially to lay down as a principle, that coition is not for the sake of pleasure.' But Nature, not trusting to this moral and abstract motive, seems to have provided more securely for the perpetuation of the species by making it the effect of the oestrum implanted in the constitution of both sexes. And not only has the commerce of love been indulged on this unhallowed impulse, but made subservient also to wealth and ambition by marriages without regard to the beauty, the healthiness, the understanding, or virtue of the subject from which we are to breed. The selecting the best male for a Haram of well chosen females also, which Theognis seems to recommend from the example of our sheep and asses, would doubtless improve the human, as it does the brute animal, and produce a race of veritable ἄριστοι ["aristocrats"]. For experience proves that the moral and physical qualities of man, whether good or evil, are transmissible in a certain degree from father to son. But I suspect that the equal rights of men will rise up against this privileged Solomon, and oblige us to continue acquiescence under the

Ἀμαύρωσις γένεος ἀστῶν ["the degeneration of the race of men"] which Theognis complains of, and to content ourselves with the accidental aristoi produced by the fortuitous concourse of breeders. For I agree with you that there is a natural aristocracy among men. The grounds of this are virtue and talents. Formerly bodily powers gave place among the aristoi. But since the invention of gunpowder has armed the weak as well as the strong with missile death, bodily strength, like beauty, good humor, politeness and other accomplishments, has become but an auxiliary ground of distinction. There is also an artificial aristocracy founded on wealth and birth, without either virtue or talents; for with these it would belong to the first class. The natural aristocracy I consider as the most precious gift of nature for the instruction, the trusts, and government of society. And indeed it would have been inconsistent in creation to have formed man for the social state, and not to have provided virtue and wisdom enough to manage the concerns of the society. May we not even say that that form of government is the best which provides the most effectually for a pure selection of these natural aristoi into the offices of government? The artificial aristocracy is a mischievous ingredient in government, and provision should be made to prevent it's ascendancy. On the question, What is the best provision, you and I differ; but we differ as rational friends, using the free exercise of our own reason, and mutually indulging it's errors. *You* think it best to put the Pseudo-aristoi into a separate chamber of legislation where they may be hindered from doing mischief by their coordinate branches, and where also they may be a protection to wealth against the Agrarian and plundering enterprises of the Majority of the people. I think that to give them power in order to prevent them from doing mischief, is arming them for it, and increasing instead of remedying the evil. For if the coordinate branches can arrest their action, so may they that of the coordinates. Mischief may be done negatively as well as positively. Of this a cabal in the Senate of the U.S. has furnished many proofs. Nor do I believe them necessary to protect the wealthy; because enough of these will find their way into every branch of the legislation to protect themselves. From 15. to 20. legislatures of our own, in action for 30. years past, have proved that no fears of an equalisation of property are to be apprehended from them.

I think the best remedy is exactly that provided by all our constitutions, to leave to the citizens the free election and separation of the aristoi from the pseudo-aristoi, of the wheat from the chaff. In general they will elect the real good and wise. In some instances, wealth may corrupt, and birth blind them; but not in sufficient degree to endanger the society.

It is probable that our difference of opinion may in some measure be produced by a difference of character in those among whom we live. From what I have seen of Massachusetts and Connecticut myself, and still more from what I have heard, and the character given of the former by yourself, [vol. I, pa. III.][1] who knew them so much better, there seems to be in those two states a traditionary reverence for certain families, which has rendered the offices of the government nearly hereditary in those families. I presume that from an early period of your history, members of these families happen-

---

[1] TJ's note referring to JA's *Defence.*

ing to possess virtue and talents, have honestly exercised them for the good of the people, and by their services have endeared their names to them.

In coupling Connecticut with you, I mean it politically only, not morally. For having made the Bible the Common law of their land they seem to have modelled their morality on the story of Jacob and Laban. But altho' this hereditary succession to office with you may in some degree be founded in real family merit, yet in a much higher degree it has proceeded from your strict alliance of church and state. These families are canonised in the eyes of the people on the common principle 'you tickle me, and I will tickle you.' In Virginia we have nothing of this. Our clergy, before the revolution, having been secured against rivalship by fixed salaries, did not give themselves the trouble of acquiring influence over the people. Of wealth, there were great accumulations in particular families, handed down from generation to generation under the English law of entails. But the only object of ambition for the wealthy was a seat in the king's council. All their court then was paid to the crown and it's creatures; and they Philipised in all collisions between the king and people. Hence they were unpopular; and that unpopularity continues attached to their names. A Randolph, a Carter, or a Burwell must have great personal superiority over a common competitor to be elected by the people, even at this day.

At the first session of our legislature after the Declaration of Independance, we passed a law abolishing entails. And this was followed by one abolishing the privilege of Primogeniture, and dividing the lands of intestates equally among all their children, or other representatives. These laws, drawn by myself, laid the axe to the root of Pseudo-aristocracy. And had another which I prepared been adopted by the legislature, our work would have been compleat. It was a Bill for the more general diffusion of learning. This proposed to divide every county into wards of 5. or 6. miles square, like your townships; to establish in each ward a free school for reading, writing and common arithmetic; to provide for the annual selection of the best subjects from these schools who might receive at the public expense a higher degree of education at a district school; and from these district schools to select a certain number of the most promising subjects to be compleated at an University, where all the useful sciences should be taught. Worth and genius would thus have been sought out from every condition of life, and compleatly prepared by education for defeating the competition of wealth and birth for public trusts.

My proposition had for a further object to impart to these wards those portions of self-government for which they are best qualified, by confiding to them the care of their poor, their roads, police, elections, the nomination of jurors, administration of justice in small cases, elementary exercises of militia, in short, to have made them little republics, with a Warden at the head of each, for all those concerns which, being under their eye, they would better manage than the larger republics of the county or state. A general call of ward-meetings by their Wardens on the same day thro' the state would at any time produce the genuine sense of the people on any required point, and would enable the state to act in mass, as your people have so often done, and with so much effect, by their town meetings. The law for religious freedom, which made a part of this system, having put down the aristocracy of the clergy, and restored to the citizen the freedom of the mind, and those of entails and descents nurturing an equality of condition among them, this on Education would have raised the mass of the people to the high ground of moral respectability necessary to their own safety, and to orderly government; and would have compleated the great object of qualifying them to select the veritable aristoi, for the trusts of government, to the exclusion of the Pseudalists: and the same Theognis who has furnished the epigraphs of your two letters assures us that 'οὐδεμίαν πω, Κύρν, ἀγαθοὶ πόλιν ὤλεσαν ἄνδρες ["Curnis, good men have never harmed any city"]'. Altho' this law has not yet been acted on but in a small and inefficient degree, it is still considered as before the legislature, with other bills of the revised code, not yet taken up, and I have great hope that some patriotic spirit will, at a favorable moment, call it up, and make it the key-stone of the arch of our government.

With respect to Aristocracy, we should further consider that, before the establishment of the American states, nothing was known to History but the Man of the old world, crouded within limits either small or over-charged, and steeped in the vices which that situation generates. A government adapted to such men would be one thing; but a very different one that for the Man of these states. Here every one may have land to labor for himself if he chuses; or, preferring the exercise of any other industry, may exact for it such compensation as not only to afford a comfortable subsistence, but wherewith to provide for a cessation from labor in old age. Every one, by his property, or by his satisfactory situation, is interested in the support of law and order. And such men may safely and advantageously reserve to themselves a wholsome controul over their public affairs, and a degree of freedom, which in the hands of the Canaille of the cities of Europe, would be instantly perverted to the demolition and destruction of every thing public and private. The history of the last 25. years of France, and of the last 40. years in America, nay of it's last 200. years, proves the truth of both parts of this observation.

But even in Europe a change has sensibly taken place in the mind of Man. Science had liberated the ideas of those who read and reflect, and the American example had kindled feelings of right in the people. An insurrection has consequently begun, of science, talents and courage against rank and birth, which have fallen into contempt. It has failed in it's first effort, because the mobs of the cities, the instrument used for it's accomplishment, debased by ignorance, poverty and vice, could not be restrained to rational action. But the world will recover from the panic of this first catastrophe. Science is progressive, and talents and enterprize on the alert. Resort may be had to the people of the country, a more governable power from their principles and subordination; and rank, and birth, and tinsel-aristocracy will finally shrink into insignificance, even there. This however we have no right to meddle with. It suffices for us, if the moral and physical condition of our own citizens qualifies them to select the able and good for the direction of their government, with a recurrence of elections at such short periods as will enable them to displace an unfaithful servant before the mischief he meditates may be irremediable.

I have thus stated my opinion on a point on which we differ, not with a view to controversy, for we are both too old to change opinions which are the result of a long life of inquiry and reflection; but on the suggestion of a former letter of yours, that we ought not to die before we have explained ourselves to each other. We acted in perfect harmony thro' a long and perilous contest for our liberty and independance. A constitution has been acquired which, tho neither of us think perfect, yet both consider as competent to render our fellow-citizens the happiest and the securest on whom the sun has ever shone. If we do not think exactly alike as to it's imperfections, it matters little to our country which, after devoting to it long lives of disinterested labor, we have delivered over to our successors in life, who will be able to take care of it, and of themselves.

Of the pamphlet on aristocracy which has been sent to you, or who may be it's author, I have heard nothing but thro' your letter. If the person you suspect[2] it may be known from the quaint, mystical and hyperbolical ideas, involved in affected, new-fangled and pedantic terms, which stamp his writings. Whatever it be, I hope your quiet is not to be affected at this day by the rudeness of intemperance of scribblers; but that you may continue in tranquility to live and to rejoice in the prosperity of our country until it shall be your own wish to take your seat among the Aristoi who have gone before you. Ever and affectionately yours.

Th: Jefferson

P.S. Can you assist my memory on the enquiries of my letter of Aug. 22.?

The Equilibrium of Power
John Adams / from *Discourses on Davila*

John Adams (1735–1826) was the first Vice-President and the second President of the United States; his son, John Quincy Adams, was also President; and his grandson, Charles Francis Adams, was Vice-President. If America has any aristocracy at all, it is the "aristocracy of the intellect"—a phrase that John Adams coined—and the Adams family has given America its greatest intellectual aristocrats.

A selection from Adams' long and thoughtful work on political philosophy, Discourses on Davila, *is more appropriate here than one taken from Edmund Burke's more famous* Reflections on the Revolution in France, *for three reasons. First, Adams is an American and hence in keeping with the general scope of this anthology. Second, he was naturally polar to Jefferson, since both men were lifelong friends and foes and both held the same high office of the Presidency. Third, the* Discourses *appeared before the worst excesses of the French Revolution; consequently, Adams was at once more temperate and more prophetic than Burke. Also, Adams' prose, though it can be rhetori-*

---
[2]John Taylor of Caroline.

cally stinging, is tighter and more analytical than that of Burke, whose rhetorical gifts sometimes, under the pressure of indignation, led him into floridity.

　　For the title pages of his two longest political works, Adams chose quotations from Alexander Pope's conservative poem Essay on Man. *One of the couplets on the title page of the* Discourses *is a verse-capsule of Adams' position:*

> Till jarring interests of themselves create
> Th' according music of a well-mix'd state.

Adams argues that although a passion for distinction is a universal characteristic of man, the operation of reason is not. The desire for esteem, for reputation, for emulation "is as real a want of nature as hunger. . . . It is a principal end of government to regulate this passion. It is the only adequate instrument of order and subordination in society, and alone commands effectual obedience to laws, since without it neither human reason, nor standing armies, would ever produce that great effect" (Discourse II).

　　Clearly Adams had no faith in the mere power of reason to achieve a good society; here he differed sharply with Jefferson, who brought back from France just such a faith in reason. When Adams annotated the Discourses *in 1813, some twenty-four years after its composition, he included an appendix in which he singled out Napoleon as the inventor of the political term* ideology— *a verbal acuteness confirmed by the* Oxford English Dictionary. *The government of France from 1789 to 1799, says Adams, coining a mocking word of his own, was an "ideocracy," a government by theory rather than by nature. Madison replied to Jefferson's "ideocratic" notion that 'the earth belongs to the living' (see headnote for Jefferson)—with dubious politeness; one would like to have seen Adams comment on the idea. The selection that follows will provide a basis for reconstructing such a reply.*

On government

> First follow nature; and your judgment frame
> By her just standard, which is still the same.　　　Pope.

The world grows more enlightened. Knowledge is more equally diffused. Newspapers, magazines, and circulating libraries have made mankind wiser. Titles and distinctions, ranks and orders, parade and ceremony, are all going out of fashion. This is roundly and frequently asserted in the streets, and sometimes on theatres of higher *rank*. Some truth there is in it; and if the opportunity were temperately improved, to the reformation of abuses, the rectification of errors, and the dissipation of pernicious prejudices, a great advantage it might be. But, on the other hand, false inferences may be drawn from it, which may make mankind wish for the age of dragons, giants, and fairies. If all decorum, discipline, and subordination are to be destroyed, and universal Pyrrhonism, anarchy, and insecurity of property are to be introduced, nations will soon wish their books in ashes, seek for darkness and ignorance, superstition and fanaticism, as blessings, and follow the standard of the first mad despot, who, with the enthusiasm of another Mahomet, will endeavor to obtain them.

Are riches, honors, and beauty going out of fashion? Is not the rage for them, on the contrary, increased faster than improvement in knowledge? As long as either of these are in vogue, will there not be emulations and rivalries? Does not the increase of knowledge in any man increase his emulation; and the diffusion of knowledge among men multiply rivalries? Has the progress of science, arts, and letters yet discovered that there are no passions in human nature? no ambition, avarice, or desire of fame? Are these passions cooled, diminished, or extinguished? Is the rage for admiration less ardent in men or women? Have these propensities less a tendency to divisions, controversies, seditions, mutinies, and civil wars than formerly? On the contrary, the more knowledge is diffused, the more the passions are extended, and the more furious they grow. Had Cicero less vanity, or Cæsar less ambition, for their vast erudition? Had the King of Prussia less of one than the other? There is no connection in the mind between science and passion, by which the former can extinguish or diminish the latter. It, on the contrary, sometimes increases them, by giving them exercise. Were the passions of the Romans less vivid in the age of Pompey than in the time of Mummius? Are those of the Britons more moderate at this hour than in the reigns of the Tudors? Are the passions of monks the weaker for all their learning? Are not jealousy, envy, hatred, malice, and revenge, as well as emulation and ambition, as rancorous in the cells of Carmelites as in the courts of princes? Go to the Royal Society of London. Is there less emulation for the chair of Sir Isaac Newton than there was, and commonly will be, for all elective presidencies? Is there less animosity and rancor, arising from mutual emulations in that region of science, than there is among the most ignorant of mankind? Go to Paris. How do you find the men of letters? united, friendly, harmonious, meek, humble, modest, charitable? prompt to mutual forbearance? unassuming? ready to acknowledge superior merit? zealous to encourage the first symptoms of genius? Ask Voltaire and Rousseau, Marmontel and De Mably.

The increase and dissemination of knowledge, instead of rendering unnecessary the checks of emulation and the balances of rivalry in the orders of society and constitution of government, augment the necessity of both. It becomes the more indispensable that every man should know his place, and be made to keep it. Bad men increase in knowledge as fast as good men; and science, arts, taste, sense, and letters, are employed for the purposes of injustice and tyranny, as well as those of law and liberty; for corruption, as well as for virtue.

Frenchmen! Act and think like yourselves! confessing human nature, be magnanimous and wise. Acknowledging and boasting yourselves to be men, avow the feelings of men. The affectation of being exempted from passions is inhuman. The grave pretension to such singularity is solemn hypocrisy. Both are unworthy of your frank and generous natures. Consider that government is intended to set bounds to passions which nature has not limited; and to assist reason, conscience, justice, and truth, in controlling interests, which, without it, would be as unjust as uncontrollable.

Americans! Rejoice, that from experience you have learned wisdom; and instead of whimsical and fantastical projects, you have adopted a promising essay towards a well-ordered government. Instead of following any foreign example, to return to *the legislation of confusion,* contemplate the means of restoring decency, honesty, and order in society, by preserving and completing, if any thing should be found necessary to complete the balance of your government. In a well-balanced government, reason, conscience, truth, and virtue, must be respected by all parties, and exerted for the public good. Advert to the principles on which you commenced that glorious self-defence, which, if you behave with steadiness and consistency, may ultimately loosen the chains of all mankind. If you will take the trouble to read over the memorable proceedings of the town of Boston, on the twenty-eighth day of October, 1772, when the Committee of Correspondence of twenty-one persons was appointed to state the rights of the colonists as men, as Christians, and as subjects, and to publish them to the world, with the infringements and violations of them,[1] you will find the great principles of civil and religious liberty for which you have contended so successfully, and which the world is contending for after your example. I could transcribe with pleasure the whole of this immortal pamphlet, which is a real picture of the sun of liberty rising on the human race; but shall select only a few words more directly to the present purpose.

"The first fundamental, positive law of all commonwealths or states is the establishment of the legislative power." Page 9.

"It is absolutely necessary in a mixed government like that of this province, that a *due proportion* or *balance* of power should be established among the several branches of the legislative. Our ancestors received from King William and Queen Mary a charter, by which it was understood by both parties in the contract, that such a proportion or balance was fixed; and, therefore, every thing which renders any one branch of the legislative more independent of the other two than it was originally designed, is an alteration of the constitution."

Americans! in your Congress at Philadelphia, on Friday, the fourteenth day of October, 1774, you laid down the fundamental principles for which you were about to contend, and from which it is to be hoped you will never depart. For asserting and vindicating your rights and liberties, you declared, "That, by the immutable laws of nature, the principles of the English constitution and your several charters or compacts, you were entitled to life, liberty, and property; that your ancestors were entitled to all the rights, liberties, and immunities of free and natural born subjects in England; that you, their descendants, were entitled to the exercise and enjoyment of all such of them as your local and other circumstances enabled you to exercise and enjoy. That the foundation of English liberty and of all free governments, is a right in the people to participate in their legislative council. That you were entitled to the common law of England, and more especially to the great and inestimable privilege of being tried by your peers of the vicinage, according to the course of that law. *That it is indispensably necessary*

---

[1] This Boston pamphlet was drawn by the great James Otis. J. A. [John Adams] 1813. Vol. VI.

to good government, and rendered essential by the English constitution, that the constituent branches of the legislature be independent of each other." These among others you then claimed, demanded, and insisted on, as your indubitable rights and liberties. These are the principles on which you first united and associated, and if you steadily and consistently maintain them, they will not only secure freedom and happiness to yourselves and your posterity, but your example will be imitated by all Europe, and in time, perhaps, by all mankind. The nations are in travail, and great events must have birth.

"The minds of men are in movement from the Boristhenes to the Atlantic. Agitated with new and strong emotions, they swell and heave beneath oppression, as the seas within the polar circle, at the approach of spring. The genius of philosophy, with the touch of Ithuriel's spear, is trying the establishments of the earth. The various forms of prejudice, superstition, and servility, start up in their true shapes, which had long imposed upon the world, under the revered semblances of honor, faith, and loyalty. Whatever is loose must be shaken; whatever is corrupted must be lopped away; whatever is not built on the broad basis of public utility must be thrown to the ground. Obscure murmurs gather and swell into a tempest; the spirit of inquiry, like a severe and searching wind, penetrates every part of the great body politic; and whatever is unsound, whatever is infirm, shrinks at the visitation. Liberty, led by philosophy, diffuses her blessings to every class of men; and even extends a smile of hope and promise to the poor African, the victim of hard, impenetrable avarice. Man, as man, becomes an object of respect. Tenets are transferred from theory to practice. The glowing sentiment, the lofty speculation, no longer serve 'but to adorn the pages of a book.' They are brought home to men's business and bosoms; and what, some centuries ago, it was daring but to think, and dangerous to express, is now realized and carried into effect. Systems are analyzed into their first principles, and principles are fairly pursued to their legitimate consequences."[2]

This is all enchanting. But amidst our enthusiasm, there is great reason to pause and preserve our sobriety. It is true that the first empire of the world is breaking the fetters of human reason and exerting the energies of redeemed liberty. In the glowing ardor of her zeal, she condescends, Americans, to pay the most scrupulous attention to your maxims, principles, and example. There is reason to fear she has copied from you errors which have cost you very dear. Assist her, by your example, to rectify them before they involve her in calamities as much greater than yours, as her population is more unwieldy, and her situation more exposed to the baleful influence of rival neighbors. Amidst all their exultations, Americans and Frenchmen should remember that the perfectibility of man is only human and terrestrial perfectibility. Cold will still freeze, and fire will never cease to burn; disease and vice will continue to disorder, and death to terrify mankind. Emulation next to self-preservation will forever be the great spring of human actions, and the balance of a well-ordered government will alone be able to

---

[2]This was a summary of the language of the world in 1790, in newspapers, pamphlets, and conversation. In 1813 we can judge of it, as the author of these discourses judged of it then, to the destruction of all his popularity.

prevent that emulation from degenerating into dangerous ambition, irregular rivalries, destructive factions, wasting seditions, and bloody, civil wars.

The great question will forever remain, *who shall work?* Our species cannot all be idle. Leisure for study must ever be the portion of a few. The number employed in government must forever be very small. Food, raiment, and habitations, the indispensable wants of all, are not to be obtained without the continual toil of ninety-nine in a hundred of mankind. As rest is rapture to the weary man, those who labor little will always be envied by those who labor much, though the latter in reality be probably the most enviable. With all the encouragements, public and private, which can ever be given to general education, and it is scarcely possible they should be too many or too great, the laboring part of the people can never be learned. The controversy between the rich and the poor, the laborious and the idle, the learned and the ignorant, distinctions as old as the creation, and as extensive as the globe, distinctions which no art or policy, no degree of virtue or philosophy can ever wholly destroy, will continue, and rivalries will spring out of them. These parties will be represented in the legislature, and must be balanced, or one will oppress the other. There will never probably be found any other mode of establishing such an equilibrium, than by constituting the representation of each an independent branch of the legislature, and an independent executive authority, such as that in our government, to be a third branch and a mediator or an arbitrator between them. Property must be secured, or liberty cannot exist. But if unlimited or unbalanced power of disposing property, be put into the hands of those who have no property, France will find, as we have found, the lamb committed to the custody of the wolf. In such a case, all the pathetic exhortations and addresses of the national assembly to the people, to respect property, will be regarded no more than the warbles of the songsters of the forest. The great art of lawgiving consists in balancing the poor against the rich in the legislature, and in constituting the legislative a perfect balance against the executive power, at the same time that no individual or party can become its rival. The essence of a free government consists in an effectual control of rivalries. The executive and the legislative powers are natural rivals; and if each has not an effectual control over the other, the weaker will ever be the lamb in the paws of the wolf. The nation which will not adopt an equilibrium of power must adopt a despotism. There is no other alternative. Rivalries must be controlled, or they will throw all things into confusion; and there is nothing but despotism or a balance of power which can control them. Even in the simple monarchies, the nobility and the judicatures constitute a balance, though a very imperfect one, against the royalties.

Let us conclude with one reflection more which shall barely be hinted at, as delicacy, if not prudence, may require, in this place, some degree of reserve. Is there a possibility that the government of nations may fall into the hands of men who teach the most disconsolate of all creeds, that men are but fireflies, and that this *all* is without a father? Is this the way to make man, as man, an object of respect? Or is it to make murder itself as indifferent as shooting a plover, and the extermination of the Rohilla nation as innocent as the swallowing of mites on a morsel of cheese? If such a case should happen, would not one of these, the most credulous of all believers, have reason to pray to his eternal nature or his almighty chance (the more absurd-ity there is in this address the more in character) *give us again the gods of the Greeks; give us again the more intelligible as well as more comfortable systems of Athanasius and Calvin; nay, give us again our popes and hierarchies, Benedictines and Jesuits, with all their superstition and fanaticism, impostures and tyranny.* A certain duchess of venerable years and masculine understanding, said of some of the philosophers of the eighteenth century, admirably well,—"On ne croit pas dans le Christianisme, mais on croit toutes les sottises possibles." [One does not believe in Christianity, but one believes all possible stupidities.]

The Good and Great Society
Walter Lippmann / from *The Good Society*

Walter Lippmann (1889–   ) is generally considered, by the public and by his fellow columnists alike, to be the most erudite and philosophical of modern American political journalists. In very recent years, it has become fashionable, although only among younger liberals, to consider Lippmann a conservative; nevertheless, his name produces strong reactions from any orthodox conservative. His career spans all that is modern in the United States, for it starts in 1913, the year when Woodrow Wilson assumed office as President and when the income tax, hitherto declared unconstitutional, became part of the American way of life. It was then that what is now called "big government" began.

In a series of books and articles starting in 1913 (A Preface to Politics), *Lippmann has embodied his views and informed the public of them, in a prose which is lucid and elegant yet which breathes with a passion for human rights that is the spirit of liberalism. The selection chosen here comes from his book* The Good Society *(1937); perhaps one sign of its vital contemporaneity is the fact that in it Lippmann uses the term and the idea of the "Great Society," now—nearly thirty years later—popularized as the slogan of a Democratic administration.*

In the preface to the 1943 edition, Lippmann singles out two sentences from the book as expressive of its central theme. The first "affirmation," as he calls the two, is that "the politics, law, and morality of the Western world are an evolution from the religious conviction that all men are persons and that the human person is inviolable." This he rightly regards as the more fundamental of the two affirmations. The second is that the industrial revolution "which still engages the whole of mankind and poses all the great social issues of the epoch in which we live, arises primarily from the increasing division of labor in ever-widening markets; the machine, the corporation, the concentration of economic control and mass production are secondary phenomena."

In the first affirmation, we hear and see the voice of the whole liberal tradition; in the second, we see that tradition coming to grips with the modern world. The tension between the two affirmations calls for action, and in the selection printed here, from the chapter entitled "The Agenda of Liberalism," Lippmann outlines the liberal program for performing that action. It would be difficult to find any similar statement which is at once as passionate and temperate, as comprehensive and detailed, as complex and clear. The chapter follows a full analysis of the history of liberalism, for Lippmann never works without the light of history. Perhaps it is his historical astuteness and perspective that have made some younger liberals—the young often are impatient with history—call him a conservative. As the companion piece by Reinhold Niebuhr will show, no conservative can think of Lippmann in this way.

The agenda of liberalism

1. The inexorable law of the industrial revolution

The debacle of liberalism in the nineteenth century occurred when the thinking of liberals was arrested by their misunderstanding of laissez-faire and of the classical economics. It is a case of a great scientific movement suddenly inhibited by intellectual error, and it is by no means the first or the only instance of its kind in history. The progress of ancient science appears to have been halted in the fourth century B.C. by an analogous deflection of the Hellenic mind from a progressive examination of experience to circular, metaphysical speculation. Liberal thinking was inhibited in the metaphysics of laissez-faire, and the effect was to make the political philosophy of liberalism a grand negation, a general non possumus, and a complacent defense of the dominant classes. It was inhibited no less completely in the circular dialectics of the classical economics. The effect here was to shut off the minds of the liberals from the study of social readjustment, and to close their imaginations and their sympathies to the crying need for reform. . . .

To the debacle of liberal science can be traced the moral schism of the modern world which so tragically divides enlightened men. For the liberals are the inheritors of the science which truly interprets the progressive principle of the industrial revolution. But they have been unable to carry forward their science; they have not wrested from it a social philosophy which is humanly satisfactory. The collectivists, on the other hand, have the zest for progress, the sympathy for the poor, the burning sense of wrong, the impulse for great deeds, which have been lacking in latter-day liberalism. But their science is founded on a profound misunderstanding of the economy at the foundation of modern society, and their actions, therefore, are deeply destructive and reactionary. So men's hearts are torn, their minds are divided, they are offered impossible choices. They are asked to choose between the liberals who came to a dead stop—but stopped on the right road up to wealth and freedom and justice—and the collectivists who are in furious movement—but on a road that leads down to the abyss of tyranny, impoverishment, and general war.

Yet this impossible choice exists only in the minds of men, in their doctrines and their prejudices, and not in the nature of things. The impasse in which men find themselves is subjective. It is the consequence of human error and not of fate. There is no reason to think that the time has come when the social order cannot adapt itself to the economy brought into being by the industrial revolution, and that, therefore, men must destroy the new economy. For that would mean that the industrial revolution itself had come to a dead end. It would mean that the new mode of production which underlies all social systems and all institutions and all public policies can no longer be tolerated by mankind. It would mean that men must dismantle and reverse the industrial revolution itself—as the autarchists are doing in Germany—and that by painful steps they must retrace the path back to isolated communities practising a relatively low degree of division of labor.

That is why such momentous conclusions hang upon the question of whether the debacle of liberalism was due to the error of the liberals or, as the collectivists believe, to some kind of inescapable historic necessity. In raising the question I am certainly not concerned to rehabilitate the word "liberalism," which is now a battered ornament that evokes the most equivocal sentiments. But I am concerned with the substance. And that substance, as I see it, is that men cannot undo the consequences of the industrial revolution, that they are committed to the new mode of production, to the division of labor among interdependent communities and individuals. This is the truly inexorable historic necessity. They can no more reverse the industrial revolution by an act of will and by political coercion than they could return from manufacture to handicraft, from settled agriculture to a pastoral economy. Nor do men wish to do this. Nor would they willingly consent. . . .

A free choice between a liberal and a collectivist order does not exist in fact. That is to say, it does not exist for ordinary men who wish to maintain and to improve their standard of life. There is no choice because men are committed to the division of labor, and it is as impossible for them to live by any other means as it was for their ancestors in the villages clustered around regional market towns to exist without a high degree of self-sufficiency. The *apparent* choice between a liberal and a collectivist order exists only in the mind, only *until* collectivism is put fully into practice, only in the realm of hopes and projects where men discuss what they think they would like to do. The choice does not exist when they come to find out what they can do. For there is no way of practising the division of labor, and of harvesting the fruits of it, except in a social order which preserves and strives to perfect the freedom of the market. This is the inexorable law of the industrial revolution, and while men may disobey that law, the price of their disobedience is the frustration of all their hopes. . . .

But the truth will prevail. When I say that the renascence of liberalism is assured, I do not mean, of course, that it must come in our own time, or that it will come before mankind has gone through the disaster which the descent into collectivism has prepared. I do not know whether the disaster is avoidable by intelligence and resolute action. But I do believe that there is no escape from the disaster and no way of restoring the civilization which it would shatter except by a social philosophy which obeys the law of the industrial revolution. Either men will find this social philosophy by their intelligence, or they will learn it by bitter experience when, as in Russia, they have passed through ordeal by fire. But learn it they will. For they must. It is the condition of their survival as civilized men.

2. The social problems

I have suggested that the "frictions" and "disturbances" which the classical economists recognized—only to neglect them—were, in fact, the social problems which should have been, and in a society practising the division of labor must always be, the paramount concern of enlightened men. For the frictions and disturbances mark the points at which the social order is in conflict with the economy. They are the points where for one reason or another men fail to adapt themselves successfully to the way in which mankind earns its living. The causes of the maladaptation are numerous and mixed; it is certain that they cannot all be traced, as socialists think, to the single fact that the residual legal titles to property in the means of production are vested in private persons and not in the state. The maladaptation arises from the fact that a revolution in the mode of production has occurred. Since it is proceeding among men who have inherited a radically different way of life, the readjustment required must necessarily take place throughout the social order. It must almost certainly continue as long as the industrial revolution itself continues. There can be no moment at which "the new order" is in being. A dynamic economy must in the nature of things inhabit a progressive social order.

The real problems of modern societies arise where the social order is not consistent with the requirements of the division of labor. A survey of all the current problems would be a catalogue of these inconsistencies. The catalogue would begin with the pre-natal endowment of human stock, would traverse all customs, laws, institutions, and policies, and would not be complete until it had included man's conception of his destiny on earth and his valuation of his soul and of the souls of all other men. For where there is conflict between the social heritage and the manner in which men must earn their living, there will be disorder in their affairs and division in their spirits. When the social heritage and the economy do not form a seamless web, there must be rebellion against the world or renunciation of the world. That is why in epochs like our own, when society is at odds with the conditions of its existence, discontent drives some to active violence and some to asceticism and other-worldliness. When the times are out of joint some storm the barricades and others retire into a monastery. Thus it is that the greater part of the literature of our time is in one mood a literature of revolution and in another, often completely fused with it, a literature of escape.[1]

3. The field of reform

This malaise of the spirit reflects, like the discomfort of a badly fitted shoe, the maladjustment of men to the way they must obtain a living. There are those who are born handicapped; by the deterioration of the stock from which they spring they are without the capacity to make their way. Others grow up handicapped by disease in childhood, by malnutrition and neglect. Others are the casualties of a vicious or stupid family life, carrying with them forever the scars of inferiority and perversion. They do not adapt themselves easily. Then there are those who have been broken by the poverty and squalor of their youth, and who never do obtain an equal opportunity to develop their faculties. There is the whole unresolved task of educating great populations, of equipping men for a life in which they must specialize, yet be capable of changing their specialty. The economy of the division of labor requires, and the classical economics assumes, a population in which these eugenic and educational problems are effectively dealt with. But they are not yet dealt with. Nor do they settle themselves, as the dogma of laissez-faire supposes. And so they must take their place upon the agenda of liberal policy. . . .

But there is required no less, and again the classical economics takes this for granted, the conservation of the land and of all natural resources, and their progressive improvement by clearing, reclamation, and fertilization. The land and what is under it, the seas and the highways, are the patrimony of all the generations to come, and all rights of private property in this patrimony must, therefore, be subject to the condition that this natural

---

[1]e.g., Mr. Stuart Chase's alternating admiration for the machine technic and Mexican primitivism, his simultaneous disgust at industrialism and his enchanting vision of an engineering Utopia. Or the fascination exerted by D. H. Lawrence—who fled from reality into sexual sensation with the fanaticism of an ascetic—upon so many ardent sympathizers with Marxian socialism.

inheritance will not be wasted or destroyed, that it will, on the contrary, be enriched. Since it would be as impossible for the new economy to produce wealth in an exhausted land as it is for a Chinese peasant to eke out a decent living on an eroded hillside, the conclusion is undeniable that conservation, in its broadest sense, including the zoning of urban and agricultural land, is a paramount obligation of a liberal state. That anyone who thought he was preserving the system of free enterprise should have persuaded himself to believe that the law must leave men free to destroy the patrimony of their children is one of the curiosities of human unreason.

The system requires not only great adaptability in men, but an even higher degree of mobility in capital. On the whole, the machines must come to the men rather than men to the machines. A civilized life is impossible for nomads who settle nowhere and do not put down deep roots in a particular place. For men who have just arrived and will soon depart tend to be crudely acquisitive. They are transients who have no permanent stake in any community, and there are no ties, other than the cash nexus, between them and their neighbors. They live only in the present, having no ancestral tradition fixed on any place and no care for posterity. The good life finds little encouragement where men do not feel themselves to be links in a chain from the past into the future, where they live from day to day without deep associations and long memories and more than personal hopes. There is no doubt that the industrial revolution decivilized great masses of men when it drew them out of their ancestral homes and gathered them together in great, bleak, anonymous, congested slums.

It follows that if the necessities of a civilized life are to be accommodated with the new economy, the stipulation of the classical economics, that labor and capital must both be perfectly mobile, has to be modified. Capital has to be more mobile than labor, sufficiently more mobile to compensate for the inevitable and desirable human resistance to a migratory existence. This is not to say that all the generations must remain forever rooted in the place where they happen to be. But it does mean that the tides of population must move slowly if old communities are not to be devitalized by emigration and new communities overwhelmed by unassimilable immigration. It should, therefore, be the aim of policy to mitigate this human evil by using social controls to induce inanimate capital, rather than living men to achieve high mobility. It should be the aim of educational policy to make most men versatile and adaptable in the place where they were born, and of economic policy to make capital mobile. . . .

But that is not all. If capital is to achieve the necessary mobility, it must not become entrenched, uneconomically bottled up, in certain favored corporate structures. This is what happens when the managers are permitted to retain the profits, over and above sinking funds and working reserves, and to reinvest them, without submitting to the test of the competitive capital market. The effect of this is to aggrandize certain corporations beyond their true economic worth, and to cause a congestion of capital at the wrong places. No one who really believes in the principle of a free market as the regulator of the economy can, I think, fail to see that the limited-liability corporation must be deprived of the right to retain profits and invest them, not according to the judgment of the market but at the discretion of the managers. For the retention of the profits immobilizes capital, whereas the economy of the division of labor requires that capital shall move readily to the places and to the men who make the highest bids for it.

Furthermore, although the separation of ownership from management is necessary to the operation of the economic order, the separation of control from management is not. The development of holding companies, that is to say, of corporations which own the control of the management of other corporations, is an exceedingly dubious innovation. They establish industrial empires within which planning and administrative discretion supplants the market as the regulator of enterprise. Their size is often mistaken for evidence of their economic success, but actually they suffer from the same vices which are inherent in any administered economy. There is no true ascertainment of costs and prices within the corporate empire. The constituent enterprises deliver goods to each other, not at the cost which would be set in a free market, but at a cost fixed by the supreme management. Thus the management of a giant corporation which dominates dozens of distinct industrial operations is, in the economic sense, irrational. It does not really know whether its rolling mills are subsidizing its captive coal mines or are being exploited by them. It has no true economic criterion to determine whether its investments in blast furnaces or in railroads should be increased or retarded. I am talking, of course, of big business, which is big because it controls many separate enterprises, and not of separate enterprises which have grown big. The two are often confused, though they are wholly distinct: the little business which has grown big by making more and more of the product it makes is a success by the test of the market; but the business which has been made big by use of the holding company, or by some other corporate device, or by community of financial control, is the result of a deliberate attempt to evade the test of the market. . . .

Obviously, it is the duty of a liberal society to see that its markets are efficient and honest. But under the laissez-faire delusion it was supposed that good markets would somehow organize themselves or, at any rate, that the markets are as good as they might be. That is not true. The improvement of the markets must be a subject of continual study in a liberal society. It is a vast field of necessary reform. In its first phase it is merely the elaboration of a principle universally accepted from earliest times, that it is the function of government to see that weights and measures are honest. Applied to the complexities of the modern exchange economy, where goods are made by technical processes which only experts understand, the principle of honest weights and measures must mean a drastic modification of the old rule, caveat emptor. The buyer is no longer able to judge the technological honesty of the goods he is offered in the market. He does not know whether they are what they are advertised to be. So it becomes necessary to make the seller liable for an untruthful presentation of his wares, to make it unlawful to sell harmful products, to stipulate that only goods of the same quality shall bear the same label, to provide the purchaser with effective means of finding out whether he is getting the best that can be had for the money. . . .

Still we have not come to the end of our survey of the fields in which liberal policy must operate in order to adapt the social order to the exchange economy. By its very nature the economy is dynamic—that is to say, the technic and the localization of production is in continual change. Industries die and others are born, and within industries some enterprises are growing and others declining. Industries which were established in one place are replaced by industries in another place, sometimes halfway around the world. In the long view this is industrial progress, but in the close view its human evil is tragic. At no point, perhaps, were the latter-day liberals more insensitively doctrinaire than in the complacency with which they accepted the human costs of industrial progress.

Yet there is nothing whatever in the necessities of the new economy which compels society to be indifferent to the human costs. There is no reason whatever why some part of the wealth produced should not be taken by taxation and used to insure and indemnify human beings against their personal losses in the progress of industry. If technological improvement increases wealth,—and, of course, it does,—if society as a whole is richer when an industry moves from a place where costs are high to one where they are lower, then some part of that increased wealth can be used to relieve the victims of progress. It can be used to tide them over while they are changing their occupations, to reëducate them for new occupations, to settle them in new places if they have to move. . . .

It will be seen that the agenda of liberalism is long and yet I should make no claim that mine is complete. The adaptation of the social order to the division of labor is of necessity an immense undertaking since it is the finding of a new way of life for mankind. In all its ramifications it must, therefore, transcend the understanding of any man who lives in the midst of it, or the programme of any party, or the reforming energies of any one generation. I have sought only to indicate the more urgent and obvious points at which modern society is maladjusted to its mode of production, and then to illustrate the unfinished mission of liberalism. The agenda refute the notion that liberalism is the sterile apologetic which it became during its subjection to the dogma of laissez-faire and to the misunderstanding of the classical economists. The agenda demonstrate, I believe, that liberalism is not the rationalization of the status quo, but the logic of the social readjustment required by the industrial revolution.

If, now, we consider the agenda as a whole, we shall see, I think, that they imply a different distribution of incomes from that which now obtains in most organized societies. For one thing the effect of these reforms would be drastically to reduce the opportunities for making money by necessitous bargains and by levying tolls through the exercise of legal privileges. These reforms strike at the source of the big incomes which arise from the various kinds of monopoly, from exclusive rights in land and natural resources, from bad markets in which the ignorant and the helpless are at a disadvantage. Income arising from these inequalities of opportunity and legal status are unearned by the criterion of the exchange economy. They are parasitical upon it, not integral with it, and if the actual world corresponded with the theory of the classical economists, these unearned incomes would not be obtained. They are not the wages of labor or management, the interest on capital, or the profits of enterprise, as determined in free and efficient markets, but tolls levied upon wages, interest, and profits by the subversion or the manipulation of the market price for goods and services.

The reformers of liberalism must aim, therefore, at correcting the conditions under which such unearned incomes arise, and in so far as the reforms are thoroughgoing and effective the unearned incomes will not arise. Now the correction of the conditions involves, as we have seen, large social expenditure on eugenics and on education; the conservation of the people's patrimony in the land and natural resources; the development of the people's estate through public works which reclaim land, control floods and droughts, improve rivers and harbors and highways, develop water power, and establish the necessary facilities for transporting and exchanging goods and services; providing the organization of markets by information, inspection, and other services; insurance and indemnification against the risks and losses of technological and economic change; and many other things, such as providing the opportunities for recreation which would not otherwise exist in specialized and congested communities.

These public investments and social services are, of course, expensive, and the process of financing them is a redistribution of income. In a society in which there was no unearned income, the taxation to pay for them would be in effect a form of forced saving for investment in the people's estate, diverting a part of the income spent on private consumption to such forms of social consumption as schools, playgrounds, museums, and the like. But in society as it now is, where a progressive proportion of most of the larger incomes is unearned, the primary cost of the public investments and social services can be properly charged in a graduated scale against the larger incomes. If the science of taxation were highly developed, and the methods of public budgeting were refined, the cost of reform, as distinguished from the support of government and of social consumption, could be fixed with a nice discrimination, not on the size of an income, but on the unearned portion of all incomes. And in the higher refinements of a just system of taxation, that part of an unearned income now spent for private consumption by the possessor would be completely expropriated. It would be recognized that while an unearned income which is reinvested replenishes the capital goods of the whole society, unearned income spent on consumable goods is sheer privilege. These refinements of public finance are still beyond our knowledge of the science of taxation, and above all beyond the present competence of officials to administer them. They indicate, however, the direction in which reformers can work. In the practical present a cruder policy is unavoidable: one which redistributes large incomes by drastic inheritance and steeply graduated income taxes.

There need be no reluctance in the avowal that a greater equalization of incomes, *if brought about in the way outlined here,* is the necessary objective of a liberal policy. I stress the manner because a mere leveling of incomes by taking from the rich and giving doles to the poor would defeat itself and would merely paralyze and impoverish the whole economy. The equalization must be effected by measures which promote the efficiency of the markets as regulators of the division of labor; they must strike, therefore, not at the profits of successful competition but at the tolls of monopoly.

The taxes levied on the rich must be spent not on doles to the poor but on the reform of the conditions which made the poor. The dole, by which I mean cash given by the government directly to the poor, is a relief of, but not a remedy for, their poverty, whereas money spent on public health, education, conservation, public works, insurance, and indemnification is both a relief and a remedy. It improves the productive capacity both of the individual and of the national patrimony from which he must earn his living. By improving the marginal productivity of labor, it raises the minimum wage of all labor out of an increased national dividend. This is equivalent to saying that some portion of the national dividend must be invested, in order to conserve and improve the foundations of the economy, in the people and in the national estate from which they earn their living.

The returns on these investments are real enough. But they are imponderable and deferred. Values created by the schools in educating the next generation, by public works to preserve the fertility of the soil, do not have a market price and would, therefore, not be undertaken by ordinary private enterprise. This is the realm of investment by public authority which does not have to pay its way and show returns measured in money within a short span of time. For the most farsighted private investment cannot look much beyond one generation; only the exceptionally prudent plant trees for their children. But a society, as Burke so eloquently said, comprehends the dead, the living, and the unborn. And as the living inherited the national estate from their ancestors so they must transmit it to their posterity. This carries with it the obligation to plough back some portion of the current income into the foundations of the social economy. . . .

The earlier economists could not foresee this because in their time the private demand for capital was so urgent. They assumed that it would always be urgent. But they underestimated the productivity of the new economy and they overestimated the acquisitiveness of human nature. Gradually we have learned to see that men do not care to go on accumulating wealth ad infinitum. When they attain a middle-class standard of life the wants of most men are sated; they do not have the tastes for spending a lot more money. To earn it is not worth the trouble; to spend it is more trouble than it seems when in the abstract they envy the very rich. To be sure, the middle-class standard of life rises. But it is not true, as someone has said, that wealth must go on increasing until the last Hottentot lives like a millionaire. At least it is not true that the last Hottentot would wish to work hard enough to be a millionaire, or would care to devise ways of spending a millionaire's income. Long before that point is reached in the actual world the profit motive loses its incentive, and men prefer leisure, security, and intangible values to further economic gains. The acquisitive psychology of the nineteenth-century economic man is no longer the psychology of real men who have reached the slowly rising level of middle-class comfort. . . .

. . . Since the time of Aristotle it has been recognized by the wise that extremes of riches and poverty, that spectacular differentials of income, are dangerous and pernicious in any society. The enlargement of the middle class as against the poor and the rich must, therefore, be sought by anyone who wishes a society to live soundly and endure long. For the great inequalities do not represent the true inequalities in men's native endowment, or in their characters and their diligence; thus the inequalities obscure and distort the whole moral conception of income as the reward of useful work, of poverty as the punishment for laziness and imprudence. Because to-day it cannot be said sincerely that wealth is the reward of virtue, the very notion that man must earn his living by his own effort is gravely discredited. And inasmuch as the maldistribution of income causes capital to accumulate excessively in the presence of destitution and want, we have the paradox of poverty in the midst of plenty which makes the whole economy appear irrational and unjust.

4. The radical conservatism of liberal reform

These agenda are not to be taken as a definitive and comprehensive outline of liberal social reform. If, as I am arguing, it is the mission of liberalism to discern the guiding principles of the transition from the primitive way of life in relatively self-contained communities to a way of life in a Great Society of interdependent specialists, then liberalism is concerned with nothing less than a readaptation of the human race to a new mode of existence. . . .

The Soft Utopia
Reinhold Niebuhr / from *Reinhold Niebuhr on Politics*

Reinhold Niebuhr (1892–   ) is one of the very few native and contemporary American theologians—perhaps the only one—who can claim intellectual equality with European theologians; but even he, like most American theologians, has directed much of his energy to social questions. His piece below, entitled "The Soft Utopians: Liberalism," is in one sense not a true companion piece to Lippmann's "Agenda for Liberalism," because it does not contain any program of action for conservatives. Instead it dissects what Niebuhr, and most conservatives, regard as the sentimentality and impracticality of liberal thinkers, their curious amalgamation of theory and emotionalism. Niebuhr sees in liberalism an excessive faith in rationalism, together with a failure to remember and live by the dark lessons of history. Such rationalism is most directly subsumed under the liberal position labeled "religious skepticism," though it also pervades the two other principal liberal tenets, moral relativism and political egalitarianism. In Niebuhr's theological eye, neither the nature of man nor his history sanctions any belief in natural progress, in automatic and gradual emancipation from impulse, prejudice, and sin.

Since conservatism arises, as a conscious philosophy, not from its nature but instead as a response to the attacks of liberals, who wish to transform the society which the conservative seeks to preserve, it was thought best to show the counterattacking quality of conservative thought by using Niebuhr's piece. Liberals are "soft Utopians," who "expect perfection to emerge out of the ongoing process of history." All that is needed is a continued appeal to love, justice, goodwill, and brotherhood; for man is by nature good, a belief justifying the liberal's faith that by developing his powers of reason, man will become reasonable. But such a faith becomes a rationalistic fanaticism when it fails to recognize that the finiteness of particular men is not adequate to their imagined paradigms.

Liberals often use the child as a symbol for the kind of adult they wish to father, and all too often the social changes they advocate derive from this ideal. Nowhere does Niebuhr differ from liberalism more sharply than on this point: for him, maturity is qualitatively more complex than childhood, and that qualitative difference lies precisely in a full awareness of history and the way in which it renders rational schematization suspect. The culmination of liberal sentimentality comes, for Niebuhr, in liberal Christianity, which has united with secular liberalism in an evasion of life's "tragic realities." By emphasizing the tragic quality of human life, Niebuhr strikes at the foundations of all liberal dreams for a great, or even a good, society.

The soft utopians: liberalism

It would have been difficult for generations of the twentieth century to survive the hazards and to face the perplexities of our age in any event, since every problem of human existence had been given a wider scope than known in previous ages. But our perplexities became the more insoluble and the perils to which we were exposed became the more dangerous because the men of this generation had to face the rigors of life in the twentieth century with nothing but the illusions of the previous two centuries to cover their spiritual nakedness. There was nothing in the creeds and dogmas of these centuries which would have enabled modern men either to anticipate or to understand the true nature of the terrors and tumults to which they would be exposed.[1]

I. Two forms of utopianism

This is why there is a curious pathos in the conflict between the Western and the Russian world. The Western world, though partly Christian, is primarily informed by the secular religion of faith in progress. The Russian world is animated by the secular creed of faith in redemption through revolution. The conflict is of course something more than an ideological one. But insofar as the conflict is ideological, each side is involved in a situation for which its creed offers no source of understanding.

The liberal creed of progress assumes that men are progressing toward higher and higher forms of social life and more and more inclusive loyalties. The Nazi rebellion against a world community was difficult to explain in terms of this faith and as we shall see was usually put down as a mysterious reversion to barbarism, which would not finally impede the onward march of humanity toward world community. Now the liberal world is confronted not by a cynical, but by a utopian foe, who also believes in world community, not by evolution but by revolution.[2]

For Marxism believes that the revolution will usher in an idyllic society of brotherly love, in which each would give according to his ability and take

---

[The footnotes refer to writings from which Niebuhr's editors have assembled and arranged this section.]

[1]*Faith and History*, p. 1.

[2]"Two Forms of Utopianism," *Christianity and Society*, Vol. 12 (Autumn, 1947), p. 6.

according to his need. If a period of dictatorship intervenes no one will have to worry, since the whole state apparatus will wither away with the victory of its cause and the universal abolition of property.[3]

In other words two secular religions of world redemption are in conflict with one another. One cannot deny that there is a special pathos in a conflict in the world community between two political forces each of which underestimates the complexities of history and both of which fail to understand the tragic character of human history. The communist creed of world redemption is the more dangerous because it is informed by a hard utopianism, while the liberal world is informed by soft utopianism. *Hard utopianism* might be defined as the creed of those who claim to embody the perfect community and who therefore feel themselves morally justified in using every instrument of guile or force against those who oppose their assumed perfection. *Soft utopianism* is the creed of those who do not claim to embody perfection, but expect perfection to emerge out of the ongoing process of history. The liberal soft utopians are obviously not as dangerous and fanatic as the communist hard utopians; but they are at a disadvantage in their conflict with the hard utopians because they do not understand that history makes the problems of man's togetherness more, rather than less, complex.[4]

II. The several varieties of liberalism

We have been using the term, liberal, in a special sense. In the broadest sense, liberalism is rightly identified with the rise of a modern technical society availing itself of democratic political forms and of capitalistic economic institutions. This "liberal society" came to birth in Britain, France and America in opposition to the feudal aristocratic culture of the European past. Liberalism in the broadest sense is therefore synonymous with democracy. Its strategy is to free the individual from the traditional restraints of a society, to endow the governed with the power of the franchise, to establish the principle of the "consent of the governed" as the basis of political society, to challenge all hereditary privileges and traditional restraints upon human initiative, particularly in the economic sphere, and to create the mobility and flexibility which are the virtues and achievements of every liberal society as distinguished from feudal ones.

But liberalism has more distinct connotations. One of these connotations arises out of the history of technical societies; the other arises out of the peculiar philosophy of the Renaissance and the French Enlightenment. In the first instance, the narrower connotation of liberalism is identified with the peculiar and unique ethos of middle-class life. But since the middle classes soon found the laboring classes to the left of them, liberalism soon ceased to be the exclusive philosophy of democracy. Even without the rise of labor as a political power, modern democracies, as they developed from commercialism to industrialism, found that the freeing of economic initiative from political restraint was only one side of the problem of justice. The other side was the placing of restraints upon initiative in the interest of security and justice.

---

[3]"The Sickness of American Culture," *Nation*, Vol. 166 (March 6, 1948), p. 268.
[4]"Two Forms of Utopianism," *op. cit.*, p. 7.

Thus in every modern industrial nation the word liberalism achieved two contradictory definitions. It was on the one hand the philosophy which insisted that economic life was to be free of any restraint. In this form it was identical with the only conservatism which nations such as our own, who had no feudal past, could understand. It was the philosophy of the more successful middle classes who possessed enough personal skill, property or power to be able to prefer liberty to security. On the other hand the word was also used to describe the political strategy of those classes which preferred security to absolute liberty and which sought to bring economic enterprise under political control for the sake of establishing minimal standards of security and welfare. It has been rather confusing that both of these strategies go by the name of liberalism. . . .[5]

Though there appeared variations in this philosophy (differentiations for instance between secular and religious liberals) there developed nevertheless a pretty sharply defined credo which holds all liberalism together. Some of the articles in the credo are:

a. That injustice is caused by ignorance and will yield to education and greater intelligence.

b. That civilization is becoming gradually more moral and that it is a sin to challenge either the inevitability or the efficacy of gradualness.

c. That the character of individuals rather than social systems and arrangements is the guarantee of justice in society.

d. That appeals to love, justice, good-will and brotherhood are bound to be efficacious in the end. If they have not been so to date we must have more appeals to love, justice, good-will and brotherhood.

e. That goodness makes for happiness and that the increasing knowledge of this fact will overcome human selfishness and greed.

f. That wars are stupid and can therefore only be caused by people who are more stupid than those who recognize the stupidity of war.[6]

What then is the liberal creed? It is primarily faith in man; faith in his capacity to subdue nature, and faith that the subjection of nature achieves life's final good; faith in man's essential goodness, to be realized either when man ceases to be spiritual and returns to nature (romanticism), or when he ceases to be natural and becomes rational; and finally, faith in human history which is conceived as a movement upward by a force immanent within it. Whether this faith rests upon Darwin or upon Hegel (that is, whether nature is believed to guarantee progress or whether progress is conceived of as man's "gradual spiritualization" and his emancipation from natural impulses, prejudices and parochial attachments) the optimistic conclusion is the same.[7]

Liberalism is in short a kind of blindness to which those are particularly subject who imagine that their intelligence or the eneluctable processes of history have emancipated them from all the stupidities of the past. It is a blindness which does not see the perennial difference between human actions and aspirations, the perennial source of conflict between

---

[5]"Liberalism: Illusions and Realities," *New Republic,* Vol. 133 (July 4, 1955), pp. 11-12.
[6]"The Blindness of Liberalism," *Radical Religion,* Vol. 1 (Autumn, 1936), pp. 4-5.
[7]"Ten Years That Shook My World," *Christian Century,* Vol. 56 (April 26, 1939), p. 543.

life and life, the inevitable tragedy of human existence, the irreducible irrationality of human behavior, and the tortuous character of human history.[8] To sum up, liberalism is based upon illusions as to the nature of man and of history.[9]. . .

Harmless Man

Almost every version of liberal culture has some futile and fatuous scheme for lifting men from selfish purposes as painlessly as possible. The simplest idea of all is that which underlies the *laissez faire* social philosophies of the eighteenth and nineteenth centuries. According to these philosophies all conflicting interests in human society, and all competing egoistic drives, would result in harmony rather than conflict if they were only left alone. If political society did not interfere with economic process, economic life would achieve a natural harmony. This idea, which obviates the necessity of either moral or political control upon selfish impulses, was a nice device for eating your cake and having it too. It justified unrestrained selfishness without justifying egoism morally; for it gave the assurance that "each man seeking his own would serve the commonweal." The only difficulty with the idea is that it is not true. The one element of truth in it is that there are indeed certain automatic harmonies in the economic process, and it is wise to maintain them. But on the whole, history, unlike nature, has no natural balances of power. Where power is disproportionate, power dominates weakness and injustice results.[10]. . .

The theory of the harmlessness of natural man, if only he is not controlled and regulated, is usually compounded with another theory, which is a little more profound. It is the theory that ignorant selfishness is dangerous to society, but that a wise and prudent selfishness knows how to relate the interests of the self to the interests of the whole; so that a wise egoist while seeking his own pleasure, will finally serve "the greatest good of the greatest number." The confidence in the essential virtue of the intelligent man takes various forms. Sometimes intelligence supposedly restrains egoism in its narrow form and broadens it to include the interests of others. Sometimes it is assumed that the intelligence preserves a nice balance between egoistic and altruistic impulses. And sometimes reason throws the weight of its authority on the side of altruism as against egoism.[11]

The French Enlightenment assigned reason the primary function of discerning the "laws of nature" and of destroying man's abortive efforts to circumvent these laws. It was assumed that increasing rationality would gradually destroy the irrational (primarily religious) justifications of special privilege. Or that increasing reason would gradually prompt all men to grant their fellow men justice, the power of logic requiring that the interests of each individual be brought into a consistent scheme of value.[12]

Of course, the Enlightenment was not entirely wrong, either in what it opposed or in what it affirmed. It rightly opposed the obscurantism to

---

[8]"The Blindness of Liberalism," *op. cit.,* p. 5.
[9]"Liberalism: Illusions and Realities," *op. cit.,* p. 12.
[10]"A Faith for History's Greatest Crisis," *Fortune,* Vol. 26 (July 1942), pp. 122, 125.
[11]"A Faith for History's Greatest Crisis," *op. cit.,* p. 125.
[12]*Faith and History,* p. 5.

which an authoritarian religion is inevitably tempted when it seeks to trans-
mute the symbols of its faith into adequate descriptions of detailed historical
occurrences. A religion which has discovered the limits of human knowledge
does not improve the inadequacies of this knowledge if it seeks to shackle
culture by religious dogma. Such dogmatism invariably leads to a religious
sanctification of the viewpoints of a particular age and the morality of a
particular class. A genuine passion for humanity animated the Enlightenment in its opposition to divisive dogmatisms which had leagued God with a
particular cultural viewpoint or social position.[13]

Nor was the Enlightenment entirely wrong in what it affirmed. Reason,
inasfar as it is able to survey the whole field of life, analyzes the various
forces in their relation to each other and, gauging their consequences in
terms of the total welfare, it inevitably places the stamp of its approval
upon those impulses which affirm life in its most inclusive terms. Practically
every theory, whether utilitarian or intuitional, insists on the goodness of
benevolence, justice, kindness and unselfishness. It is fair, therefore, to
assume that growing rationality is a precondition of man's growing morality.

For the measure of our rationality determines the degree of vividness
with which we appreciate the needs of other life, the extent to which we
become conscious of the real character of our own motives and impulses, the
ability to harmonize conflicting impulses in our own life and in society,
and the capacity to choose adequate means for approved ends. In each instance a development of reason may increase the moral capacity.

The ability to consider, or even prefer, the interests of others to our
own, is not dependent only upon the capacity for sympathy. Harmonious
social relations depend upon the sense of justice as much as, or even more
than, upon the sentiment of benevolence. This sense of justice is a product
of the mind and not of the heart. It is the result of reason's insistence upon
consistency.[14]

But the Enlightenment was also productive of dangerous errors. For a
consistent rationalism makes human reason God. Reason becomes the
universal value which is set above all particular values and is made the criterion of all morality. It is by human reason that all history is to be judged.
The fatal error of rationalism is its failure to recognize that reason is universal
only in purely formal terms. Logic and mathematics may be universal; but
no judgment which fills logical forms with material content is universal. A
rationalism which does not recognize this fact invariably mistakes its particular judgments for genuinely universal judgments, failing to see how it has in-
sinuated its partial and finite perspectives into its supposedly universal
standards.

Rationalism, in other words, forgets the finiteness and creatureliness of
man. It does not subject human righteousness to a transcendent righteousness, the righteousness of God. Thus it tempts men to "go about establishing
their own righteousness" and finally degenerates into a fanaticism more griev-
ous than that of dogmatic religion. The logic of the decay of modern culture
from universalistic humanism to nationalistic anarchy may be expressed

---

[13]*Beyond Tragedy*, pp. 232-233.
[14]*Moral Man and Immoral Society*, pp. 27-29.

as follows: Men seek a universal standard of human good. After painful effort they define it. The painfulness of their effort convinces them that they have discovered a genuinely universal value. To their sorrow, some of their fellow men refuse to accept the standard. Since they know the standard to be universal the recalcitrance of their fellows is a proof, in their minds, of some defect in the humanity of the non-conformists. Thus a rationalistic age creates a new fanaticism. The non-conformists are figuratively expelled from the human community.[15]

Insofar as human reason really frees the human spirit from the necessities and contingencies of nature it creates the possibility of moral action. Insofar as this emancipation is never complete and rationality is never discarnate, it accentuates the disharmonies of nature. Thus the same human reason which, on the one hand, regards differences of race as accidents of nature, as contingencies to be discounted and defied in the name of rational brotherhood, also gives these differences a spiritual significance, which they do not have in nature. Race pride and prejudice are just as much the fruits of rational freedom as is inter-racial brotherhood. In a word, the very reason, which modern culture has regarded as God, as the principle of universality and as the guarantor of goodness, is really a part of man's problem and not his answer to the problem.[16]

The tragic realities of contemporary history have fully revealed the illusory elements in this confidence in human rationality as the guarantor of increasing social peace and justice. The late Professor Einstein came to the despairing conclusion that if he had to live his life again he would want to be a plumber or a peddler and not a scientist. He based his pessimistic thought upon the fact that scientific freedom was in danger through government restrictions upon science, occasioned by the relation of physics to the whole development of nuclear weapons.

But one may suspect that a deeper problem than that of freedom was agitating the conscience of Einstein. It was the problem of the uneasy conscience of a once "pure" scientist, who had become involved in the guilt and moral perplexities of an atomic age.

Einstein once believed that if he could only get two per cent of the population to disavow war he might succeed in abolishing it. How deeply ironic that this very man should have been the one to write the letter of introduction to President Roosevelt for a group of physicists, whose visit to the President initiated the whole process that finally gave us the hydrogen bomb.

This is a case in which the pure rationalism of another age stumbles upon, and becomes involved in, the perennial problem of sin and guilt. The rationalists had dismissed the problem, which meanwhile reached the monstrous proportions of our atomic age. Furthermore, it was not merely the problem of guilt attendant upon a conscious wrong. It was the guilt in which we became involved even when we were trying to do what is right. Here is the moral dilemma of a civilization which once believed in "progress" and now finds all technical advances to be morally ambiguous.[17]

---

[15]*Beyond Tragedy*, pp. 236-237.
[16]*Ibid.*, pp. 241-242.
[17]"Einstein and the World Situation," *Messenger*, Vol. 19 (December 14, 1954), p. 6.

IV. Redemptive history

We have defined the error that underlies all the optimistic illusions of our liberal culture as a too-simple confidence in man, particularly in rational man, and as a too-simple hope in the progressive achievement of virtue in history, by reason of the progressive extension of intelligence. This confidence that human history ultimately answers all its unsolved problems and overcomes all its earlier insecurities, that history is itself a kind of process of redemption, has gained such a strong hold upon modern man because it is actually partly true and because all the tremendous advances of science, technology, and intelligence seemed to justify the belief.[18]

The conception of a redemptive history informs the most diverse forms of modern culture. The French physiocrats believed that progress would be assured by the removal of the irrelevancies of historical restraints from the operation of the laws of nature. Comte on the other hand thought it would be achieved by bringing social process under the control of an elite of social scientists. But this contrast between determinism and voluntarism (which is, incidentally, never composed in modern culture) had no influence upon the shared belief in progress. There is only a slight difference in optimism between the deterministic thought of Herbert Spencer and the modern voluntarism of John Dewey.

Even Karl Marx, who introduced a provisional historical catastrophism to challenge the optimism of bourgeois life, did not shake the modern conception of a redemptive history basically. He saw in the process of historical development certain "dialectical" elements not observed in bourgeois theories. He knew that there is disintegration as well as increasing integration in history; that there is death as well as growth. But he also believed that a new life and a new age would rise out of the death of an old one with dialectical necessity. Catastrophe was the certain prelude of redemption in his scheme of salvation. The ultimate similarity between Marxist and bourgeois optimism, despite the provisional catastrophism of the former, is, in fact, the most telling proof of the unity of modern culture. It is a unity which transcends warring social philosophies, conflict between which contributed to the refutation of a common hope.

The goal toward which history was presumably moving was variously defined. The most unreflective forms of historical optimism in the nineteenth century assumed that increasing physical comfort and well-being were the guarantee of every other form of advance. . . .[19]

There were experiences in previous centuries which might well have challenged this unqualified optimism. But the expansion of man's power over nature proceeded at such a pace that all doubts were quieted, allowing the nineteenth century to become the "century of hope" and to express the modern mood in its most extravagant terms. History, refusing to move by the calendar, actually permitted the nineteenth century to indulge its illusions into the twentieth. Then came the deluge. Since 1914 one tragic experience has followed another, as if history had been designed to refute the vain delusions of modern man.[20]

---

[18]"A Faith for History's Greatest Crisis," *op. cit.,* p. 126.
[19]The quotation is from Edmund Noble, *Purposive Evolution,* p. 418.
[20]*Faith and History,* pp. 3-7.

There is always progress in history in the sense that it cumulates wisdom, perfects technics, increases the areas of human cooperation, and extends the human control over nature. But this cannot be regarded as moral progress. There are morally ambiguous elements in human history on every new level of achievement. We ought to have known that. A person progresses from childhood to maturity, but it is not easy to compare the virtue of maturity with the innocency of a child, because mature life achieves higher unities and is subject to greater complexities than child life. It is in fact irrelevant to measure mature virtue with childish innocency because they are incommensurate. So it is with the history of mankind. . . .

. . . History cannot be the answer to our problems, for history is itself our problem. History is, in short, an inadequate god. We have failed to gauge every contemporary problem in its true depth because of this false faith in history. Previous civilizations only made the mistake of misjudging their own history and estimating their own security too highly. We went one step beyond them in pride and pretension. We thought no evil could befall us because we trusted not "Roman civilization" nor medieval culture, but history itself. Yet our error was greater than previous errors, precisely because we believed that history's development of all human potencies also guaranteed the elimination of all human insecurities. The very opposite is the truth. A highly dynamic technical society is more destructive in its decay than a simple agrarian society. Destruction dumped from the skies is more awful than the lethal power of a bow and arrow.[21] The possession of a phenomenal form of destructive power in the modern day has proved to be so fruitful of new fears that the perennial ambiguity of man's situation of power and weakness became more vividly exemplified, rather than overcome. Thus a century which was meant to achieve a democratic society of world-scope finds itself at its half-way mark uncertain about the possibility of avoiding a new conflict of such proportions as to leave the survival of mankind, or at least the survival of civilization, in doubt.

The tragic irony of this refutation by contemporary history of modern man's conception of history embodies the spiritual crisis of our age.[22] We thought that life's meaning was guaranteed by the historical process. We believed in progress. Now we find that an atomic bomb stands at the end of the technical development. And at the end of the hoped for rational-moral progress we find little statesmen, representing little nations, drawing pretensions of omniscience from their military omnipotence, and playing with the powder which might blow up the world.[23]

V. Liberalism and Christianity

One reason why the whole of modern liberal Christianity has become infected with the illusions of soft utopianism is because the modern idea of progress seemed to reinforce all the hopes for the progressive triumph of pure love which the soft utopians cherished. The spread of the pacifist movement in modern liberal Christianity, particularly in the Anglo-Saxon

---

[21]"A Faith for History's Greatest Crisis," *op. cit.*, p. 128.
[22]*Faith and History*, p. 8.
[23]"Which Question Comes First for the Church?" *Christianity and Crisis*, Vol. 5 (November 12, 1945), p. 1.

countries, to the point where it seemed that the perfectionist hopes of the small sectarian churches would be shared by the whole of Protestantism, was undoubtedly due primarily to the substitution of the idea of progress in liberal Christianity for the truth of the Gospel. In the words of a typical exponent of the American "social gospel," "the new social order will be based not on fighting but on fraternity . . . not simply because the cooperative fraternal life is the highest ideal of human living but because the spirit and method of cooperation is the scientific law of human progress."[24]. . .

Furthermore the liberal church, preaching in a catastrophic age in which the communal life of man is torn by a thousand hatreds, in which the newly won freedom of India is almost drowned in the blood of fratricidal strife, in which conflicting rights of Jews and Arabs reveal how terribly complex problems of justice are, and in which the vicious circle of mutual fear between two great centers of power in the community of nations threatens to tear the world apart, blandly advises men and nations to love one another if they would escape disaster. There is in this preaching no understanding either of the complex problems of the justice which is required to preserve a tolerable peace among nations, races and groups which do not love each other, nor yet of the agony of rebirth required if the individual would turn from self-love to love.[25]

Liberal Christianity and modern secular liberalism have become united in the errors and sentimentalities of a soft utopianism, which manages to evade the tragic realities of life and to obscure the moral ambiguity in all political positions. These evasions are achieved by hoping for a progressive alteration of the character of human history. This soft utopianism is free of the sin of fanaticism but it is not without its dangers. The recent encounter of the democratic world with tyrannical Nazism might have proved fatal to civilization had not the common sense of "the children of this world" outweighed the illusions of "the children of light." For the soft utopians were prepared to meet malignant evil with non-resistance, hoping that kindness would convert the hearts of tyrants.[26]

VI. Liberalism and Nazism

The fact is that the tragic realities in which Western civilization is involved are really striking refutations of our characteristic liberal credos. It is particularly significant that millions of rational and "idealistic" people refused to take seriously the monstrous perils of Nazi totalitarianism. We talked about it as a "reversion to barbarism" which meant that we could imagine evil in history only as a return to a primitive past. We could not imagine that a mature civilization would produce in its decay, not the evils of nature nor of primitive society, but terrible evils that are relevant to, and possible only in, maturity. We did not understand the difference between nature and history. In nature, beasts of prey lie down to go to sleep when their maws are crammed. In human history, no hunger is ever perfectly satisfied and grows by what it feeds on. Just as the desires of man are in-

---

[24]*Faith and History*, p. 207.
[25]"The Reunion of the Church through the Renewal of the Churches," *Christian Century*, Vol. 7 (November 24, 1947), p. 5.
[26]*Faith and History*, p. 208.

finite so also are the possibilities for good and evil in history. But the possibilities for evil keep abreast of the possibilities for good. The delicate balances of a mature mind are more easily subject to disarrangement (insanity) than the simple psychic processes of a child; and a complex technical society can fall into more utter confusion than a simple agrarian economy. The cruelty of the Nazis was no more like "barbarism" than insanity is childishness. The persistent inclination of modern culture to minimize the monstrous evils against which we must contend, and to interpret them as reversions to nature or to a primitive past, reveals a false estimate of human history and a false confidence in its securities. The conflicts and catastrophes of our era have been the more terrible because we had no philosophy by which we could anticipate them, or understand them when they were upon us.[27]

In a sense, Nazi philosophy had in every case taken neglected portions of the total truth about man and history and fashioned them into perverse but potent instruments against a civilization that did not understand the nature and history of man. For the liberal faith in reason, Nazism substituted the romantic faith in vitality and force. For the simple faith that right creates its own might, it substituted the idea that might makes right. For the hope of liberal democracy that history was in the process of eliminating all partial, national and racial loyalties and creating a universal community of mankind, it substituted a primitive loyalty to race and nation as the final end of life. In place of the sentimental idea that men could easily combine devotion to their own interests with loyalty to universal justice, it proclaimed the cynical idea that there is no justice but that which serves "my" or "our" purpose and interest.

It is wrong to worship force and to make power self-justifying. But such an error could not have arisen in a civilization that had not made the opposite mistake and assumed that men were in the process of becoming purely rational. It is perverse to make the interests of our nation the final end of life. But this error could not have achieved such monstrous proportions if our culture had not foolishly dreamed and hoped for the development of "universal" men, who were bereft of all loyalties to family, race, and nation. It is monstrous to glorify war as the final good. But that error could not have brought us so close to disaster if a comfortable civilization had not meanwhile regarded peace as a final good, and had not expected perfect peace to be an attainable goal of history. It is terrible to conduct the diplomacy and military strategy of nations upon the basis of "all or nothing" policies. But the fury expressed in such policies would not have come so close to success if it had not been met by the illusions of comfortable and fat nations in which the love of ease had been compounded with the caution of prudence, and the two together had resulted in an inability to act. If the lies embodied in the Nazi creed did not contain a modicum of truth and if that modicum of truth had not been directed against our weakness and our illusions, we would not have come so close to disaster.[28]

So the tragic events of modern history have negated practically every presupposition upon which modern culture was built. History does not

---

[27] "A Faith for History's Greatest Crisis," *op. cit.*, pp. 100, 122.
[28] *Ibid.*, p. 126.

move forward without catastrophe, happiness is not guaranteed by the multiplication of physical comforts, social harmony is not easily created by more intelligence, and human nature is not as good or as harmless as had been supposed. We are thus living in a period in which either the optimism of yesterday has given way to despair, or in which some of the less sophisticated moderns try desperately to avoid the abyss of despair by holding to credos which all of the facts have disproved.[29]

---

[29]*Christianity and Power Politics*, p. 188.

Part II: **The Issues**

Liberals, we argued earlier, are committed to religious skepticism, conservatives to religious orthodoxy. For liberals, religion is at best a part of life; for conservatives, religion permeates life. Although liberals tend to regard religion's claim to ultimacy as metaphysical mysticism, they do not—in their most humanistic moments—deny the psychological need for religious experience. Once the anthropologists and psychologists had demonstrated that mankind needs some form of religious awareness, the liberal mind was ready to sanction religious commitment, provided that it was kept subject to humanistic and humanitarian ends. But such tolerance, no matter how generous and rational, constitutes religious skepticism. The content of religious commitment, for a liberal, is apt to be dubious.

Not all conservatives, of course, insist on the metaphysical authenticity of religion; for some, like Cicero, the primary value of religion is its contribution to political stability. In fact, the orthodoxy of conservative religious commitment is so bound up with the question of political stability that one is often unable to separate or even distinguish the two.

We have chosen for spokesmen of liberal and conservative views on religion two men of intelligent good will: George Santayana, whose philosophy is characterized by a pragmatic aestheticism and by a materialistically religious attitude, treated religion with tender and poetic understanding. Paul Tillich, although he took a nonformalistic and noncreedal religious stance, was a theologian of genuine piety and conviction, for whom the religious experience was paramount and architectonic.

The two men present a striking pattern of paradoxical similarity. Both were born in Europe in the latter half of the nineteenth century. They grew up speaking no English, yet both spent their mature years developing philosophical positions that spoke to and for their adopted country, America. Santayana, Spanish-born, Boston-bred, and Catholic-trained, displays Mediterranean playfulness; he saw in religion little more than a poetic symbolism which could be used, by a refined liberal intelligence, to enhance men's immediate response to a rational life of pleasure. Tillich, German-born and Protestant-trained, represents Nordic earnestness; throughout his life he sought to find a *via media* between traditional forms of fundamentalism—seen at its most sophisticated in the writings of Karl Barth—and the growing "religionless Christianity" made vulgarly eloquent in recent years under the slogan "God is dead." Santayana provides a *via media* for culturally sophisticated atheists and skeptics; Tillich has become the religious man's philosopher, the philosopher's theologian. Santayana has postulated an "animal faith"—to use one of his most pregnant phrases; Tillich has used the existential psychology of the twentieth century to provide for a faithful animal, a Cartesian soul, functioning on the principle of *dubito, ergo credo*.

The Life of Reason

George Santayana / from *Reason in Religion*

George Santayana (1863–1952) was one of the cluster of distinguished philosophers, including William James and Josiah Royce, who taught at Harvard at the turn of the century. Born in Spain, he came to the United States at the age of nine. In later life, after several years of teaching at Harvard, he returned to Europe, where he lived his life in travel and reflection. His closing years were spent in a hospital managed by Roman Catholic sisters.

His two major works were The Life of Reason *and* Realms of Being. *In these, as in many other books and essays, he surveyed the world philosophically, with an Epicurean tranquility that showed itself in the nature of his prose: limpid, calm, graceful, urbane, with all of Pater's felicity and none of his preciosity.*

Santayana's religious attitude is liberal and humanistic, as the title, The Life of Reason, *shows. From the third volume of that work,* Reason in Religion, *the opening chapter, provocatively entitled "How Religion May Be an Embodiment of Reason," is reprinted here. For Santayana, the Life of Reason is "the seat of all ultimate values." Consequently, he views religion not as the end of life but as a means to a rational life of pleasure, a life that is an end in itself. The failure of traditional religions, whose aims often correspond to those of the Life of Reason, derives from their reliance on imagination. In short, religion is only a form of poetry. And it is a defective one at that, for religion perverts itself into literalism, but poetry is a pure "liberal imaginative exercise." Once the reasoning mind sees that religion is "merely symbolic and thoroughly human," it can exploit the inherent advantages of religion's beautiful symbolism to enhance that reasonable life of man which is its own end. Religions will be "better or worse, never true or false" precisely in accordance with their ability to make the essentially aesthetic and material end of reasonable life more or less attainable.*

Santayana's opening exposition leads him to the conclusion reached in Chapter XI that the spiritual part of reason's life is a consciousness that seeks to enhance instinct's natural desire to react to the immediate sensation. "I know not what army of microbes evidently invaded from the beginning the soul's physical basis and devoured its tissues, so that sophistication and bad dreams entirely obscured her limpidity." There can be few things more complexly paradoxical than the notion of a materialistic soul invadable by microbes and subject to the disease of sophistication.

Spirituality is, nevertheless, the fundamental mode of life for man, in Santayana's eyes. He argues that the most ideal human passion is love, a passion at once animal and transient. Hence awareness of the immediate facts of sensation becomes for him an end in itself: "Sucking and blinking are ridiculous processes, perhaps, but they may bring a thrill and a satisfaction no less ideal than the lark's inexhaustible palpitations." In developing this notion, Santayana argues that "in comparison with the worldling's mental mechanism and rhetoric, the sensualist's soul is a well of wisdom." Of course, Santayana is too intelligent to mean a mere sensualist, a debauchee or a poet without art or a mystic without discipline. Yet one can see in his theories the germs of both the religious issues discussed: "God is Dead" theology and the religious use of chemicals.

How religion may be an embodiment of reason

Experience has repeatedly confirmed that well-known maxim of Bacon's, that "a little philosophy inclineth man's mind to atheism, but depth in philosophy bringeth men's minds about to religion." In every age the most comprehensive thinkers have found in the religion of their time and country something they could accept, interpreting and illustrating that religion so as to give it depth and universal application. Even the heretics and atheists, if they have had profundity, turn out after a while to be forerunners of some new orthodoxy. What they rebel against is a religion alien to their nature; they are atheists only by accident, and relatively to a convention which inwardly offends them, but they yearn mightily in their own souls after the religious acceptance of a world interpreted in their own fashion. So it appears in the end that their atheism and loud protestation were in fact the hastier part of their thought, since what emboldened them to deny the poor world's faith was that they were too impatient to understand it. Indeed, the enlightenment common to young wits and worm-eaten old satirists, who plume themselves on detecting the scientific ineptitude of religion—something which the blindest half see—is not nearly enlightened enough: it points to notorious facts incompatible with religious tenets literally taken, but it leaves unexplored the habits of thought from which those tenets sprang, their original meaning, and their true function. Such studies would bring the sceptic face to face with the mystery and pathos of mortal existence. They would make him understand why religion is so profoundly moving and in a sense so profoundly just. There must needs be something humane and necessary in an influence that has become the most general sanction of virtue, the chief occasion for art and philosophy, and the source, perhaps, of the best human happiness. If nothing, as Hooker said, is "so malapert as a splenetic religion," a sour irreligion is almost as perverse.

At the same time, when Bacon penned the sage epigram we have quoted he forgot to add that the God to whom depth in philosophy brings back men's minds is far from being the same from whom a little philosophy estranges them. It would be pitiful indeed if mature reflection bred no better conceptions than those which have drifted down the muddy stream of time, where tradition and passion have jumbled everything together. Traditional conceptions, when they are felicitous, may be adopted by the poet, but they must be purified by the moralist and disintegrated by the philosopher. Each religion, so dear to those whose life it sanctifies, and fulfilling so necessary a function in the society that has adopted it, necessarily contradicts every other religion, and probably contradicts itself. What religion a man shall have is a historical accident, quite as much as what language he shall speak.

In the rare circumstances where a choice is possible, he may, with some difficulty, make an exchange; but even then he is only adopting a new convention which may be more agreeable to his personal temper but which is essentially as arbitrary as the old.

The attempt to speak without speaking any particular language is not more hopeless than the attempt to have a religion that shall be no religion in particular. A courier's or a dragoman's speech may indeed be often unusual and drawn from disparate sources, not without some mixture of personal originality; but that private jargon will have a meaning only because of its analogy to one or more conventional languages and its obvious derivation from them. So travellers from one religion to another, people who have lost their spiritual nationality, may often retain a neutral and confused residuum of belief, which they may egregiously regard as the essence of all religion, so little may they remember the graciousness and naturalness of that ancestral accent which a perfect religion should have. Yet a moment's probing of the conceptions surviving in such minds will show them to be nothing but vestiges of old beliefs, creases which thought, even if emptied of all dogmatic tenets, has not been able to smooth away at its first unfolding. Later generations, if they have any religion at all, will be found either to revert to ancient authority, or to attach themselves spontaneously to something wholly novel and immensely positive, to some faith promulgated by a fresh genius and passionately embraced by a converted people. Thus every living and healthy religion has a marked idiosyncrasy. Its power consists in its special and surprising message and in the bias which that revelation gives to life. The vistas it opens and the mysteries it propounds are another world to live in; and another world to live in—whether we expect ever to pass wholly into it or no—is what we mean by having a religion.

What relation, then, does this great business of the soul, which we call religion, bear to the Life of Reason? That the relation between the two is close seems clear from several circumstances. The Life of Reason is the seat of all ultimate values. Now the history of mankind will show us that whenever spirits at once lofty and intense have seemed to attain the highest joys, they have envisaged and attained them in religion. Religion would therefore seem to be a vehicle or a factor in rational life, since the ends of rational life are attained by it. Moreover, the Life of Reason is an ideal to which everything in the world should be subordinated; it establishes lines of moral cleavage everywhere and makes right eternally different from wrong. Religion does the same thing. It makes absolute moral decisions. It sanctions, unifies, and transforms ethics. Religion thus exercises a function of the Life of Reason. And a further function which is common to both is that of emancipating man from his personal limitations. In different ways religions promise to transfer the soul to better conditions. A supernaturally favoured kingdom is to be established for posterity upon earth, or for all the faithful in heaven, or the soul is to be freed by repeated purgations from all taint and sorrow, or it is to be lost in the absolute, or it is to become an influence and an object of adoration in the places it once haunted or wherever the activities it once loved may be carried on by future generations of its kindred. Now reason in its way lays before us all these possibilities:

it points to common objects, political and intellectual, in which an individual may lose what is mortal and accidental in himself and immortalise what is rational and human; it teaches us how sweet and fortunate death may be to those whose spirit can still live in their country and in their ideas; it reveals the radiating effects of action and the eternal objects of thought.

Yet the difference in tone and language must strike us, so soon as it is philosophy that speaks. That change should remind us that even if the function of religion and that of reason coincide, this function is performed in the two cases by very different organs. Religions are many, reason one. Religion consists of conscious ideas, hopes, enthusiasms, and objects of worship; it operates by grace and flourishes by prayer. Reason, on the other hand, is a mere principle or potential order, on which, indeed, we may come to reflect, but which exists in us ideally only, without variation or stress of any kind. We conform or do not conform to it; it does not urge or chide us, nor call for any emotions on our part other than those naturally aroused by the various objects which it unfolds in their true nature and proportion. Religion brings some order into life by weighting it with new materials. Reason adds to the natural materials only the perfect order which it introduces into them. Rationality is nothing but a form, an ideal constitution which experience may more or less embody. Religion is a part of experience itself, a mass of sentiments and ideas. The one is an inviolate principle, the other a changing and struggling force. And yet this struggling and changing force of religion seems to direct man toward something eternal. It seems to make for an ultimate harmony within the soul and for an ultimate harmony between the soul and all the soul depends upon. So that religion, in its intent, is a more conscious and direct pursuit of the Life of Reason than is society, science, or art. For these approach and fill out the ideal life tentatively and piecemeal, hardly regarding the goal or caring for the ultimate justification of their instinctive aims. Religion also has an instinctive and blind side, and bubbles up in all manner of chance practices and intuitions; soon, however, it feels its way toward the heart of things, and, from whatever quarter it may come, veers in the direction of the ultimate.

Nevertheless, we must confess that this religious pursuit of the Life of Reason has been singularly abortive. Those within the pale of each religion may prevail upon themselves to express satisfaction with its results, thanks to a fond partiality in reading the past and generous draughts of hope for the future; but any one regarding the various religions at once and comparing their achievements with what reason requires, must feel how terrible is the disappointment which they have one and all prepared for mankind. Their chief anxiety has been to offer imaginary remedies for mortal ills, some of which are incurable essentially, while others might have been really cured by well-directed effort. The Greek oracles, for instance, pretended to heal our natural ignorance, which has its appropriate though difficult cure, while the Christian vision of heaven pretended to be an antidote to our natural death, the inevitable correlate of birth and of a changing and conditioned existence. By methods of this sort little can be done for the real betterment of life. To confuse intelligence and dislocate sentiment by gratuitous fictions is a short-sighted way of pursuing happiness. Nature is soon avenged. An unhealthy exaltation and a one-sided morality have to be followed by regrettable reactions. When these come, the real rewards of life may seem vain to a relaxed vitality, and the very name of virtue may irritate young spirits untrained in any natural excellence. Thus religion too often debauches the morality it comes to sanction, and impedes the science it ought to fulfil.

What is the secret of this ineptitude? Why does religion, so near to rationality in its purpose, fall so far short of it in its texture and in its results? The answer is easy: Religion pursues rationality through the imagination. When it explains events or assigns causes, it is an imaginative substitute for science. When it gives precepts, insinuates ideals, or remoulds aspiration, it is an imaginative substitute for wisdom—I mean for the deliberate and impartial pursuit of all good. The conditions and the aims of life are both represented in religion poetically, but this poetry tends to arrogate to itself literal truth and moral authority, neither of which it possesses. Hence the depth and importance of religion become intelligible no less than its contradictions and practical disasters. Its object is the same as that of reason, but its method is to proceed by intuition and by unchecked poetical conceits. These are repeated and vulgarised in proportion to their original fineness and significance, till they pass for reports of objective truth and come to constitute a world of faith, superposed upon the world of experience and regarded as materially enveloping it, if not in space at least in time and in existence. The only truth of religion comes from its interpretation of life, from its symbolic rendering of that moral experience which it springs out of and which it seeks to elucidate. Its falsehood comes from the insidious misunderstanding which clings to it, to the effect that these poetic conceptions are not merely representations of experience as it is or should be, but are rather information about experience or reality elsewhere—an experience and reality which, strangely enough, supply just the defects betrayed by reality and experience here.

Thus religion has the same original relation to life that poetry has; only poetry, which never pretends to literal validity, adds a pure value to existence, the value of a liberal imaginative exercise. The poetic value of religion would initially be greater than that of poetry itself, because religion deals with higher and more practical themes, with sides of life which are in greater need of some imaginative touch and ideal interpretation than are those pleasant or pompous things which ordinary poetry dwells upon. But this initial advantage is neutralised in part by the abuse to which religion is subject, whenever its symbolic rightness is taken for scientific truth. Like poetry, it improves the world only by imagining it improved, but not content with making this addition to the mind's furniture—an addition which might be useful and ennobling—it thinks to confer a more radical benefit by persuading mankind that, in spite of appearances, the world is really such as that rather arbitrary idealisation has painted it. This spurious satisfaction is naturally the prelude to many a disappointment, and the soul has infinite trouble to emerge again from the artificial problems and sentiments into which it is thus plunged. The value of religion becomes equivocal. Religion remains an imaginative achievement, a symbolic representation of moral reality which may have a most important function in vitalising the mind and in transmitting, by way of parables, the lessons of experience. But it becomes at the same time a continuous incidental deception; and this deception, in proportion as it is strenuously denied to be such, can work indefinite harm in the world and in the conscience.

On the whole, however, religion should not be conceived as having taken the place of anything better, but rather as having come to relieve situations which, but for its presence, would have been infinitely worse. In the thick of active life, or in the monotony of practical slavery, there is more need to stimulate fancy than to control it. Natural instinct is not much disturbed in the human brain by what may happen in that thin superstratum of ideas which commonly overlays it. We must not blame religion for preventing the development of a moral and natural science which at any rate would seldom have appeared; we must rather thank it for the sensibility, the reverence, the speculative insight which it has introduced into the world.

We may therefore proceed to analyse the significance and the function which religion has had at its different stages, and, without disguising or in the least condoning its confusion with literal truth, we may allow ourselves to enter as sympathetically as possible into its various conceptions and emotions. They have made up the inner life of many sages, and of all those who without great genius or learning have lived steadfastly in the spirit. The feeling of reverence should itself be treated with reverence, although not at a sacrifice of truth, with which alone, in the end, reverence is compatible. Nor have we any reason to be intolerant of the partialities and contradictions which religions display. Were we dealing with a science, such contradictions would have to be instantly solved and removed; but when we are concerned with the poetic interpretation of experience, contradiction means only variety, and variety means spontaneity, wealth of resource, and a nearer approach to total adequacy.

If we hope to gain any understanding of these matters we must begin by taking them out of that heated and fanatical atmosphere in which the Hebrew tradition has enveloped them. The Jews had no philosophy, and when their national traditions came to be theoretically explicated and justified, they were made to issue in a puerile scholasticism and a rabid intolerance. The question of monotheism, for instance, was a terrible question to the Jews. Idolatry did not consist in worshipping a god who, not being ideal, might be unworthy of worship, but rather in recognising other gods than the one worshipped in Jerusalem. To the Greeks, on the contrary, whose philosophy was enlightened and ingenuous, monotheism and polytheism seemed perfectly innocent and compatible. To say God or the gods was only to use different expressions for the same influence, now viewed in its abstract unity and correlation with all existence, now viewed in its various manifestations in moral life, in nature, or in history. So that what in Plato, Aristotle, and the Stoics meets us at every step—the combination of monotheism with polytheism—is no contradiction, but merely an intelligent variation of phrase to indicate various aspects or functions in physical and moral things. When religion appears to us in this light its contradictions and controversies lose all their bitterness. Each doctrine will simply represent the moral plane on which they live who have devised or adopted it. Religions will thus be better or worse, never true or false. We shall be able to lend ourselves to each in turn, and seek to draw from it the secret of its inspiration.

The Life of Faith

Paul Tillich/from "The Lost Dimension in Religion" and *Systematic Theology*

Paul Tillich (1886–1966) was born and educated in Germany. He taught at the universities of Berlin, Marburg, Dresden, and Leipzig before coming to the United States, where he was professor at Union Theological Seminary for many years. He later taught at Harvard and the University of Chicago. His works are numerous, both technical—like his three volumes of Systematic Theology, *and popular—like* The Courage to Be. *As if in answer to the foreboding title of Santayana's only novel,* The Last Puritan, *Tillich sought to revive American Protestantism by assimilating the newer movements in psychology, existentialism, and linguistic philosophy.*

No one would care to argue that Tillich was an accomplished stylist; yet it is paradoxical that his Germanic English should have contributed to the popular vocabulary of America much more than Santayana's analytical elegance. Many who have never read Tillich use such phrases as "ultimate concern" and "ground of being." Yet Tillich's popularity should not mislead readers to undervalue the quality of his mind; his classical and Germanic training gave his diction profound etymological impact. Much of Tillich's success as a theologian is attributable to his vitalizing contemporary diction with an ontological significance at once classical and Christian. A word like ultimate *for him means exactly what it says; it is never a sloppy synonym for* important *or* urgent.

In his autobiographical sketch, On the Boundary, *Tillich asserts that he is theologically a liberal; and yet later in the brief book he rejects liberal dogmatics. Such apparent inconsistencies should caution the reader about Tillich's use of the word* liberal *in theological discussions. In Christianity, a liberal theologian is one who believes in a historical rather than a revealed or divine Jesus, and Tillich states flatly that "the foundation of Christian belief is the biblical picture of Christ, not the historical Jesus." By labeling himself "liberal," Tillich means that he rejects the "intellectual Pharisaism" of "orthodoxy," of what he calls "heteronomy." The word* heteronomy *means "a law laid down by others," and for Tillich the chief sinners in this category are the orthodoxies of Roman Catholicism and Karl Barth. The antonym is* autonomy, *a law unto oneself. Though for Tillich, autonomy is better than heteronomy, the proper mediation between these two antithetical states is* theonomy, *the law of God, whose roots lie in the complex existential and essential being of man.*

Because Tillich uses and emphasizes traditional concepts like "faith" and "sin" and "God," he is profoundly conservative. Paradoxically, the so-called "God-is-dead" theologians claim to derive from Tillich. Yet in his last lecture, delivered on the day he suffered a fatal heart attack, Tillich, like Niebuhr, carefully rejects this new school of theology. Although Tillich uses the newer vocabularies of psychology and existentialism, he sees in their historical limitations universal and fundamental principles. It seems fair, then, to use him as the spokesman for the conservative side in religion. Where Santayana finds proof in the bewildering variety of religious experience that it has only a poetic and imaginative validity, Tillich finds, in that same variety, material for his categorical analysis.

These selections are taken from two diverse sources. The first comes from an article in a popular magazine, The Saturday Evening Post; *the second is from Tillich's massive life work,* Systematic Theology. *In the* Post *article entitled "The Lost Dimension in Religion," Tillich analyzes the current religious revival, locating it historically, philosophically, and theologically. He defines religion as "the state of being grasped by an infinite concern" and points out that although contemporary man is grasped by solid and even intense concerns, the concerns are no longer infinite. Because man has not ceased to be man, even in a social landscape that today has changed completely from biblical and traditional landscapes, his need for an infinite concern—what Tillich here calls "the dimension of depth"—remains.*

Tillich is content in the first piece to present the problem analytically; he offers no systematic solution. A brief portion of Systematic Theology *is therefore included to suggest his solution. No one selection can, of course, do justice to the scope of his thought and learning. Yet in this passage on faith, Tillich recapitulates rigorously his arguments on the experience of faith, an experience which seems to most modern men only a subjective and personal matter, but which for Tillich is the human being's ground of being.*

Faith, argues Tillich, has nothing to do with belief in the unproved or the absurd. It is not, as he remarked elsewhere, "an act of knowledge that has a low degree of evidence." Instead, faith is the state of being ultimately concerned, of "being grasped by that toward which self-transcendence aspires." All men, then, necessarily have faith, for all men are ultimately concerned about something—money, love, power—even if what they are ultimately concerned with has no real worth, no ultimate ground of being.

Tillich recognizes that his definition bears little resemblance to customary ideas, since most men associate faith with some mental function—the intellect, the will, or feeling. He therefore takes pains to show that such association is erroneous. Faith does not make statements about external reality that can be verified scientifically or objectively, for it is a form of being beyond apprehension of any identifiable kind; in fact, it is the form of being that allows all modes of apprehension to exist and function.

Neither is faith an act of will—the "will to believe." Tillich remarks that "if one is asked to accept the Word of God in obedience . . . one is asked to do something which can be done only by one already in the state of faith who acknowledges the word heard to be the Word of God."

The last popular view is that faith is a matter of feeling, a view not merely vulgar or common but also held professionally by scientists and philos-

ophers. Tillich admits that faith, as an act of the whole person, necessarily includes emotional elements; but to confine faith to feeling is to miss its embracing nature, which "includes elements of the life processes under all dimensions."

Man, then, cannot grasp faith; faith grasps man. The most man can do is to open himself to receive the Spiritual Presence which will enable him to be a "new being." This passivity—rather like Wordsworth's "wise passiveness"— is the first step. The second step is to display courage—the famous "courage to be"—in the face of this overwhelming Spiritual Presence. And the last step is to hope that the "Presence" will accomplish the rebirth which the first two steps have prepared.

Once Tillich has given a formal definition of faith—a "state of being ultimately concerned"—regardless of the content of the faith, he has his reader trapped. After all, no word is more opposed to immediate *than* ultimate; *with profound cleverness Tillich has started from the psychic immediacy of Santayana and transferred the grounds of that immediacy to ultimacy, from here and now to everywhere and always. If the transcendently immediate concerns of the human psyche are really ultimate, "other-worldly," then the life of reasonable sensationalism advocated by Santayana becomes trivial and unreal. Therefore, the use of chemicals as stimulants to religious experience would be a denial of ultimate concern, a denial of a reasoning and doubting faith. And a philosophy based on the slogan "God is dead"—that there is no permanent "ground of being"—would be, for Tillich, as absurd as the meaninglessness which existentialists attribute to the word* meaning.

/ from "The Lost Dimension in Religion"

Every observer of our Western civilization is aware of the fact that something has happened to religion. It especially strikes the observer of the American scene. Everywhere he finds symptoms of what one has called religious revival, or more modestly, the revival of interest in religion. He finds them in the churches with their rapidly increasing membership. He finds them in the mushroomlike growth of sects. He finds them on college campuses and in the theological faculties of universities. Most conspicuously, he finds them in the tremendous success of men like Billy Graham and Norman Vincent Peale, who attract masses of people Sunday after Sunday, meeting after meeting. The facts cannot be denied, but how should they be interpreted? It is my intention to show that these facts must be seen as expressions of the predicament of Western man in the second half of the twentieth century. But I would even go a step further. I believe that the predicament of man in our period gives us also an important insight into the predicament of man generally—at all times and in all parts of the earth.

There are many analyses of man and society in our time. Most of them show important traits in the picture, but few of them succeed in giving a general key to our present situation. Although it is not easy to find such a key, I shall attempt it and, in so doing, will make an assertion which may be somewhat mystifying at first hearing. The decisive element in the predicament of Western man in our period is his loss of the dimension of depth. Of course, "dimension of depth" is a metaphor. It is taken from the spatial realm and applied to man's spiritual life. What does it mean?

It means that man has lost an answer to the question: What is the meaning of life? Where do we come from, where do we go to? What shall we do, what should we become in the short stretch between birth and death? Such questions are not answered or even asked if the "dimension of depth" is lost. And this is precisely what has happened to man in our period of history. He has lost the courage to ask such questions with an infinite seriousness— as former generations did—and he has lost the courage to receive answers to these questions, wherever they may come from.

I suggest that we call the dimension of depth the religious dimension in man's nature. Being religious means asking passionately the question of the meaning of our existence and being willing to receive answers, even if the answers hurt. Such an idea of religion makes religion universally human, but it certainly differs from what is usually called religion. It does not describe religion as the belief in the existence of gods or one God, and as a set of activities and institutions for the sake of relating oneself to these beings in thought, devotion and obedience. No one can deny that the religions which have appeared in history are religions in this sense. Nevertheless, religion in its innermost nature is more than religion in this narrower sense. It is the state of being concerned about one's own being and being universally.

There are many people who are ultimately concerned in this way who feel far removed, however, from religion in the narrower sense, and therefore from every historical religion. It often happens that such people take the question of the meaning of their life infinitely seriously and reject any historical religion just for this reason. They feel that the concrete religions fail to express their profound concern adequately. They are religious while rejecting the religions. It is this experience which forces us to distinguish the meaning of religion as living in the dimension of depth from particular expressions of one's ultimate concern in the symbols and institutions of a concrete religion. If we now turn to the concrete analysis of the religious situation of our time, it is obvious that our key must be the basic meaning of religion and not any particular religion, not even Christianity. What does this key disclose about the predicament of man in our period?

If we define religion as the state of being grasped by an infinite concern we must say: Man in our time has lost such infinite concern. And the resurgence of religion is nothing but a desperate and mostly futile attempt to regain what has been lost.

How did the dimension of depth become lost? Like any important event, it has many causes, but certainly not the one which one hears often mentioned from ministers' pulpits and evangelists' platforms, namely that a widespread impiety of modern man is responsible. Modern man is neither more pious nor more impious than man in any other period. The loss of the dimension of depth is caused by the relation of man to his world and to himself in our period, the period in which nature is being subjected scientifically and technically to the control of man. In this period, life in the dimension of depth is replaced by life in the horizontal dimension. The driving forces of the industrial society of which we are a part go ahead horizontally and not vertically. In popular terms this is expressed in phrases like "better and better," "bigger and bigger," "more and more." One should not disparage the feeling which lies behind such speech. Man is right in feeling that he is able to know and transform the world he encounters without a foreseeable limit. He can go ahead in all directions without a definite boundary.

A most expressive symbol of this attitude of going ahead in the horizontal dimension is the breaking through of the space which is controlled by the gravitational power of the earth into the world-space. It is interesting that one calls this world-space simply "space" and speaks, for instance, of space travel, as if every trip were not travel into space. Perhaps one feels that the true nature of space has been discovered only through our entering into indefinite world-space. In any case, the predominance of the horizontal dimension over the dimension of depth has been immensely increased by the opening up of the space beyond the space of the earth.

If we now ask what does man do and seek if he goes ahead in the horizontal dimension, the answer is difficult. Sometimes one is inclined to say that the mere movement ahead without an end, the intoxication with speeding forward without limits, is what satisfies him. But this answer is by no means sufficient. For on his way into space and time man changes the world he encounters. And the changes made by him change himself. He transforms everything he encounters into a tool; and in doing so he himself becomes a tool. But if he asks, a tool for what, there is no answer.

One does not need to look far beyond everyone's daily experience in order to find examples to describe this predicament. Indeed our daily life in office and home, in cars and airplanes, at parties and conferences, while reading magazines and watching television, while looking at advertisements and hearing radio, are in themselves continuous examples of a life which has lost the dimension of depth. It runs ahead, every moment is filled with something which must be done or seen or said or planned. But no one can experience depth without stopping and becoming aware of himself. Only if he has moments in which he does not care about what comes next can he experience the meaning of this moment here and now and ask himself about the meaning of his life. As long as the preliminary, transitory concerns are not silenced, no matter how interesting and valuable and important they may be, the voice of the ultimate concern cannot be heard. This is the deepest root of the loss of the dimension of depth in our period—the loss of religion in its basic and universal meaning.

If the dimension of depth is lost, the symbols in which life in this dimension has expressed itself must also disappear. I am speaking of the great symbols of the historical religions in our Western world, of Judaism and Christianity. The reason that the religious symbols became lost is not primarily scientific criticism, but it is a complete misunderstanding of their meaning; and only because of this misunderstanding was scientific critique able, and even justified, in attacking them. The first step toward the non-religion of the Western world was made by religion itself. When it defended its great symbols, not as symbols, but as literal stories, it had already lost the battle. In doing so the theologians (and today many religious laymen) helped to transfer the powerful expressions of the dimension of depth into objects or happenings on the horizontal plane. There the symbols lose their power and meaning and become an easy prey to physical, biological and historical attack.

If the symbol of creation which points to the divine ground of everything is transferred to the horizontal plane, it becomes a story of events in a removed past for which there is no evidence, but which contradicts every piece of scientific evidence. If the symbol of the Fall of Man, which points to the tragic estrangement of man and his world from their true being is transferred to the horizontal plane, it becomes a story of a human couple a few thousand years ago in what is now present-day Iraq. One of the most profound psychological descriptions of the general human predicament becomes an absurdity on the horizontal plane. If the symbols of the Saviour and the salvation through Him which point to the healing power in history and personal life are transferred to the horizontal plane, they become stories of a half-divine being coming from a heavenly place and returning to it. Obviously, in this form, they have no meaning whatsoever for people whose view of the universe is determined by scientific astronomy.

If the idea of God (and the symbols applied to Him) which expresses man's ultimate concern is transferred to the horizontal plane, God becomes a being among others whose existence or nonexistence is a matter of inquiry. Nothing, perhaps, is more symptomatic of the loss of the dimension of depth than the permanent discussion about the existence or nonexistence of God—a discussion in which both sides are equally wrong, because the discussion itself is wrong and possible only after the loss of the dimension of depth.

When in this way man has deprived himself of the dimension of depth and the symbols expressing it, he then becomes a part of the horizontal plane. He loses his self and becomes a thing among things. He becomes an element in the process of manipulated production and manipulated consumption. This is now a matter of public knowledge. We have become aware of the degree to which everyone in our social structure is managed, even if one knows it and even if one belongs himself to the managing group. The influence of the gang mentality on adolescents, of the corporation's demands on the executives, of the conditioning of everyone by public communication, by propaganda and advertising under the guidance of motivation research, et cetera, have all been described in many books and articles.

Under these pressures, man can hardly escape the fate of becoming a thing among the things he produces, a bundle of conditioned reflexes without a free, deciding and responsible self. The immense mechanism, set up by man to produce objects for his use, transforms man himself into an object used by the same mechanism of production and consumption.

But man has not ceased to be man. He resists this fate anxiously, desperately, courageously. He asks the question, for what? And he realizes that there is no answer. He becomes aware of the emptiness which is covered by the continuous movement ahead and the production of means for ends which become means again without an ultimate end. Without knowing what has happened to him, he feels that he has lost the meaning of life, the dimension of depth.

Out of this awareness the religious question arises and religious answers are received or rejected. Therefore, in order to describe the contemporary attitude toward religion, we must first point to the places where the awareness of the predicament of Western man in our period is most sharply expressed. These places are the great art, literature and, partly at least, the philosophy of our time. It is both the subject matter and the style of these creations which show the passionate and often tragic struggle about the meaning of life in a period in which man has lost the dimension of depth. This art, literature, philosophy is not religious in the narrower sense of the word; but it asks the religious question more radically and more profoundly than most directly religious expressions of our time.

It is the religious question which is asked when the novelist describes a man who tries in vain to reach the only place which could solve the problem of his life, or a man who disintegrates under the memory of a guilt which persecutes him, or a man who never had a real self and is pushed by his fate without resistance to death, or a man who experiences a profound disgust of everything he encounters.

It is the religious question which is asked when the poet opens up the horror and the fascination of the demonic regions of his soul, or if he leads us into the deserts and empty places of our being, or if he shows the physical and moral mud under the surface of life, or if he sings the song of transitoriness, giving words to the ever-present anxiety of our hearts.

It is the religious question which is asked when the playwright shows the illusion of a life in a ridiculous symbol, or if he lets the emptiness of a life's work end in self-destruction, or if he confronts us with the inescapable bondage to mutual hate and guilt, or if he leads us into the dark cellar of lost hopes and slow disintegration.

It is the religious question which is asked when the painter breaks the visible surface into pieces, then reunites them into a great picture which has little similarity with the world at which we normally look, but which expresses our anxiety and our courage to face reality.

It is the religious question which is asked when the architect, in creating office buildings or churches, removes the trimmings taken over from past styles because they cannot be considered an honest expression of our own period. He prefers the seeming poverty of a purpose-determined style to the deceptive richness of imitated styles of the past. He knows that he gives no final answer, but he does give an honest answer.

/ from *Systematic Theology*

. . . There are few words in the language of religion which cry for as much semantic purging as the word "faith." It is continually being confused with belief in something for which there is no evidence, or in something intrinsically unbelievable, or in absurdities and nonsense. It is extremely difficult to remove these distorting connotations from the genuine meaning of faith. One of the reasons is that the Christian churches have often preached the message of the New Being in Christ as an "absurdity" which must be accepted on biblical or ecclesiastical authority whether the statements of the message are comprehensible or not. Another reason is the readiness of religion's many critics to concentrate their forces upon such a distorted image of faith as an easy object of attack.

Faith must be defined both formally and materially. The formal definition is valid for every kind of faith in all religions and cultures. Faith, formally or generally defined, is the state of being grasped by that toward which self-transcendence aspires, the ultimate in being and meaning. In a short formula, one can say that faith is the state of being grasped by an ultimate concern. The term "ultimate concern" unites a subjective and an objective meaning: somebody is concerned about something he considers of concern. In this formal sense of faith as ultimate concern, every human being has faith. Nobody can escape the essential relation of the conditional spirit to something unconditional in the direction of which it is self-transcendent in unity with all life. However unworthy the ultimate concern's concrete content may be, no one can stifle such concern completely. This formal concept of faith is basic and universal. It refutes the idea that world history is the battlefield between faith and un-faith (if it is permissible to coin this word in order to avoid the misleading term "unbelief"). There is no un-faith in the sense of something antithetical to faith, but throughout all history and, above all, in the history of religion, there have been faiths with unworthy contents. They invest something preliminary, finite, and conditioned with the dignity of the ultimate, infinite, and unconditional. The continuing struggle through all history is waged between a faith directed to ultimate reality and a faith directed toward preliminary realities claiming ultimacy.

This leads us to the material concept of faith as formulated before. Faith is the state of being grasped by the Spiritual Presence and opened to the transcendent unity of unambiguous life. In relation to the christological assertion, one could say that faith is the state of being grasped by the New Being as it is manifest in Jesus as the Christ. In this definition of faith, the formal and universal concept of faith has become material and particular; it is Christian. However, Christianity claims that this particular definition of faith expresses the fulfilment toward which all forms of faith are driven. Faith as the state of being opened by the Spiritual Presence to the transcendent unity of unambiguous life is a description which is universally valid despite its particular, Christian background.

Such a description, however, bears little resemblance to the traditional definitions in which the intellect, will, or feeling is identified with the act of faith. In spite of the psychological crudeness of these distinctions, they remained decisive in both scholarly and popular conceptions of faith. It is therefore necessary to make some statements about faith's relation to the mental functions.

Faith, as the Spiritual Presence's invasion of the conflicts and ambiguities of man's life under the dimension of the spirit, is not an act of cognitive affirmation within the subject-object structure of reality. Therefore it is not subject to verification by experiment or trained experience. Nor is faith the acceptance of factual statements or valuations taken on authority, even if the authority is divine, for then the question arises, On the basis of what authority do I call an authority divine? Such a statement as "a being, called God, does exist" is not an assertion of faith but a cognitive proposition without sufficient evidence. The affirmation and the negation of such statements are equally absurd. This judgment refers to all attempts that would give divine authority to statements of fact in history, mind, and nature. No such assertions have the character of faith, nor can they be made in the name of faith. Nothing is more undignified than to make faith do duty for evidence which is lacking.

An awareness of this situation has led to the establishment of a more intimate relationship between faith and moral decision. An endeavor is made to overcome the shortcomings of the cognitive-intellectual understanding of faith by a moral-voluntaristic understanding. In such an endeavor, "faith" is defined as the result of a "will to believe" or as the fruit of an act of obedience. But one asks: The will to believe what? Or, obedience to whom? If these questions are taken seriously, the cognitive interpretation of faith is re-established. Faith cannot be defined as "will to believe at large," and it cannot be defined as "obedience to order at large." But in the moment in which the contents of the will to believe or of the obedience to order are sought, the shortcomings of the cognitive interpretation of faith reappear. For instance, if one is asked to accept the Word of God in obedience—and if this acceptance is called "obedience of faith"—one is asked to do something which can be done only by one already in the state of faith who acknowledges the word heard to be the Word of God. The "obedience of faith" presupposes faith but does not create it.

The most popular identification is that of faith with feeling. Moreover, it is not only popular but also readily accepted by scientists and philosophers who reject the religious claim to truth but who cannot deny its tremendous psychological and sociological power. This they ascribe to the indefinite yet indisputable realm of "oceanic" or other feeling and oppose it only when it tries to surpass its limits and trespass upon the solid land of knowledge and action. Certainly, faith as an expression of the whole person includes emotional elements, but it does not consist solely of them. It draws every element of *theoria* and *praxis*[1] into itself and its ecstatic openness toward the Spiritual Presence; beyond these, it also includes elements of the life processes under all dimensions. . . .

Finally, there is an emotional element in the state of being grasped by the Spiritual Presence. This is not the feeling of a completely indefinite character referred to above. It is the oscillation between the anxiety of one's finitude and estrangement and the ecstatic courage which overcomes the anxiety by taking it into itself in the power of the transcendent unity of unambiguous life.

The preceding discussion of faith and the mental function has shown two things: first, that faith can neither be identified with nor derived from any of the mental functions. Faith cannot be created by the procedures of the intellect, or by endeavors of the will, or by emotional movements. But, second, faith comprehends all this within itself, uniting and subjecting it to the Spiritual Presence's transforming power. This implies and confirms the basic theological truth that in relation to God everything is by God. Man's spirit cannot reach the ultimate, that toward which it transcends itself,

---

[1]Tillich is referring to the classical concepts of the contemplative or theoretical life and the practical life. [Editors.]

through any of its functions. But the ultimate can grasp all of these functions and raise them beyond themselves by the creation of faith.

Although created by the Spiritual Presence, faith occurs within the structure, functions, and dynamics of man's spirit. Certainly, it is not *from* man, but it is *in* man. Therefore, in the interest of a radical transcendence of the divine activity, it is wrong to deny that man is aware of his being grasped by the divine Spirit, or as it has been said, "I only believe that I believe." Man is conscious of the Spiritual Presence's work in him. But that phrase does serve to provide us with a warning against self-assurance about the state of being in faith.

Considered as material concept, faith has three elements: first, the element of being opened up by the Spiritual Presence; second, the element of accepting it in spite of the infinite gap between the divine Spirit and the human spirit; and third, the element of expecting final participation in the transcendent unity of unambiguous life. These elements are within one another; they do not follow one after the other, but they are present wherever faith occurs. The first element is faith in its receptive character, its mere passivity in relation to the divine Spirit. The second element is faith in its paradoxical character, its courageous standing in the Spiritual Presence. The third element characterizes faith as anticipatory, its quality as hope for the fulfilling creativity of the divine Spirit. These three elements express the human situation and the situation of life in general in relation to the ultimate in being and meaning.

The Death of God

William Hamilton and Thomas J. J. Altizer / from *Radical Theology and the Death of God*

William Hamilton (1924-   ) is a prominent member of the group of younger American "God is dead" theologians. Other members of the group are Thomas J. J. Altizer, Paul van Buren, and Gabriel Vahanian. They take their roots in such Christian and anti-Christian thinkers as Dietrich Bonhoeffer, Kierkegaard, Nietzsche, Dostoyevski, Blake, and even Paul Tillich, to whose memory Hamilton and Altizer have dedicated their book Radical Theology and the Death of God. *It is from the preface to this book, signed by both Hamilton and Altizer, and from Hamilton's chapter entitled "The Death of God Theologies Today" that the selections printed below have been taken.*

Atheists, if they are profound enough, Santayana remarked (for these "God is dead" theologians partially reflect his ideas), are forerunners of a new orthodoxy. The "God is dead" theology seems to be following Santayana's observation. Philosophical theology has always tended to depersonalize God, and Christian theologians have substituted divinity and the divine for God as often as their pagan predecessors. Once the idea of a personal God is dead, it is no long step to saying that God himself is dead as well. Nietzsche, who trumpeted the announcement to the nineteenth century, has not heretofore been accounted a Christian, and his claim has usually been regarded as a sign of blasphemy coupled with madness. It has remained for the radical theologians to base a Christianity on His death-notice; the movement is often called "religionless Christianity."

Hamilton and Altizer, in their preface, are well aware of the philosophical growth of their movement; in a series of ten descriptive propositions, they define the spectrum of theological positions, "moving slowly from conventional atheism to theological orthodoxy." Quite conscious, and even self-conscious, of their position as advocates of a new and daring form of theology, they have sought, in numerous books and articles, to demarcate the tenets and implications of the movement. As Hamilton remarks, "My Protestant has no God, has no faith in God, and affirms both the death of God and the death of all forms of theism." Yet Hamilton wishes to avoid the charge of mere negation, "for if there is a movement away from God and religion, there is a more important movement into, for, toward the world, worldly life, and the neighbor as the bearer of worldly Jesus." He describes this state of godlessness as "waiting for God" and as a searching, while waiting in godlessness, for a style and language competent to describe the experience. He seeks to distinguish this state from mere atheistic humanism by claiming that the concentration on this-worldliness is Christological, Christ-centered.

Orthodox theologians have not, as yet, paid much serious attention to this new movement. Still, it is now apparent that the "God is dead" theologians are not simply making a shocking bid for attention. Recently there have appeared several sober articles analyzing the origin and problems of this movement— one which caught the public fancy before it engaged the concern of professional theologians.

Preface

Radical theology is a contemporary development within Protestantism
—with some Jewish, Roman Catholic and non-religious response and participation already forming—which is carrying the careful openness of the older
theologies toward atheism a step further. It is, in effect, an attempt to set
an atheist point of view within the spectrum of Christian possibilities. While
radical theology in this sense has not yet become a self-conscious "movement," it nevertheless has gained the interest and in part the commitment
of a large number of Christians in America, particularly from students of
all disciplines, and from the younger ranks of teachers and pastors. The aim
of the new theology is not simply to seek relevance or contemporaneity for
its own sake but to strive for a whole new way of theological understanding.
Thus it is a theological venture in the strict sense, but it is no less a pastoral
response hoping to give support to those who have chosen to live as Christian
atheists.

The phrase "death of God" has quite properly become a watchword,
a stumbling-block, and something of a test in radical theology, which itself
is a theological expression of a contemporary Christian affirmation of the
death of God. Radical theology thus best interprets itself when it begins to
say what it means by that phrase. The task of clarifying the possible meanings
of the phrase, "death of God," is scarcely begun in the essays of this volume,
but no student of Nietzsche will be surprised at this inconclusiveness, re-
calling the widely different interpretations Nietzsche's proclamation of the
death of God has received in the twentieth century. Nor should the phrase
"death of God" be linked to Nietzsche alone, for in one way or another
it lies at the foundation of a distinctly modern thought and experience.

Perhaps the category of "event" will prove to be the most useful answer
to the recurring question, "Just what does 'death of God' refer to?" But not
even this specification sufficiently narrows the meaning to make definition
possible, and if one wanted to, one could list a range of possible meanings
of the phrase along such lines as these, moving slowly from conventional
atheism to theological orthodoxy. It might mean:

1. That there is no God and that there never has been. This position
is traditional atheism of the old-fashioned kind, and it does seem hard
to see how it could be combined, except very unstably, with Christianity
or any of the Western Religions.

2. That there once was a God to whom adoration, praise and trust
were appropriate, possible, and even necessary, but that now there is
no such God. This is the position of the death of God or radical theology. It is an atheist position, but with a difference. If there was
a God, and if there now isn't, it should be possible to indicate why this
change took place, when it took place, and who was responsible for it.

3. That the idea of God and the word God itself are in need of radical reformulation. Perhaps totally new words are needed; perhaps
a decent silence about God should be observed; but ultimately, a new
treatment of the idea and the word can be expected, however unexpected and surprising it may turn out to be.

4. That our traditional liturgical and theological language needs

a thorough overhaul; the reality abides, but classical modes of thought and forms of language may well have had it.

5. That the Christian story is no longer a saving or a healing story. It may manage to stay on as merely illuminating or instructing or guiding, but it no longer performs its classical functions of salvation or redemption. In this new form, it might help us cope with the demons, but it cannot abolish them.

6. That certain concepts of God, often in the past confused with the classical Christian doctrine of God, must be destroyed: for example, God as problem solver, absolute power, necessary being, the object of ultimate concern.

7. That men do not today experience God except as hidden, absent, silent. We live, so to speak, in the time of the death of God, though that time will doubtless pass.

8. That the gods men make, in their thought and action (false gods or idols, in other words), must always die so that the true object of thought and action, the true God, might emerge, come to life, be born anew.

9. That of a mystical meaning: God must die in the world so that he can be born in us. In many forms of mysticism the death of Jesus on the cross is the time of that worldly death. This is a medieval idea that influenced Martin Luther, and it is probably this complex of ideas that lies behind the German chorale "God Himself is Dead" that may well be the historical source for our modern use of "death of God."

10. Finally, that our language about God is always inadequate and imperfect.

There are other pressing questions in addition to the one about the meaning of the phrase. If the death of God is an event of some kind, *when* did it happen and *why?* In response to this sort of self-query, radical theology is being more and more drawn into the disciplines of intellectual history and literary criticism to answer the "when" question, and into philosophy and the behavioral sciences to answer the "why" question. One of the major research tasks now facing the radical theologians is a thorough-going systematic interpretation of the meaning of the death of God in nineteenth-century European and American thought and literature, from, say, the French Revolution to Freud. This means finding a common principle of interpretation to handle such divergent strands as the new history and its consequent historicism, romantic poetry from Blake to Goethe, Darwin and evolutionism, Hegel and the Hegelian left, Marx and Marxism, psychoanalysis, the many varieties of more recent literature including such divergent figures as Dostoevsky, Strindberg and Baudelaire, and, of course, Nietzsche himself.

Of course the questions "why did it happen" and "when did it happen" cannot fully be answered in nineteenth-century terms. Nevertheless, it is increasingly true that the nineteenth century is to radical theology what the sixteenth century was to Protestant neo-orthodoxy. For only in the nineteenth century do we find the death of God lying at the very center of vision and experience. True, we can learn a great deal about the death of God in the history of religions, if only because gods have always been in the process of dying, from the time the sky gods fell into animism to the disappearance of a personal or individual deity in the highest expression of mysticism. Yet, it is in Christianity and Christianity alone that we find a radical or consistent doctrine of the Incarnation. Only the Christian can celebrate an Incarnation in which God has actually become flesh, and radical theology must finally understand the Incarnation itself as effecting the death of God. Although the death of God may not have been historically actualized or realized until the nineteenth century, the radical theologian cannot dissociate this event from Jesus and his original proclamation.

The radical theologian has a strange but compelling interest in the figure of Jesus. This must not be confused with the nineteenth-century liberal quest for the historical Jesus. The new theologian has died to the liberal tradition and is in quest of that Jesus who appears in conjunction with the death of God. Radical theology is peculiarly a product of the mid-twentieth century; it has been initiated by Barth and neo-orthodoxy into a form of theology which can exist in the midst of the collapse of Christendom and the advent of secular atheism. It has also learned from Paul Tillich and Rudolf Bultmann the necessity for theology to engage in a living dialogue with the actual world and history which theology confronts. Finally, we cannot fail to add that radical theology, as here conceived, has a distinctively American form. It reflects the situation of a Christian life in a seemingly neutral but almost totally secular culture and society. Hopefully it also reflects the choice of those Christians who have chosen to live in Christ in a world come of age. . . .

The death of God theologies today

. . . the death of God must be affirmed; the confidence with which we thought we could speak of God is gone, and our faith, belief, experience of him are very poor things indeed. Along with this goes a sharp attack on religion which we have defined as any system using God to meet a need or to solve a problem, even the problem of not having a God. Our waiting for God, our godlessness, is partly a search for a language and a style by which we might be enabled to stand before him once again, delighting in his presense. . . .

I must now attempt to draw some of these themes together, so that this death of God tradition may have as good a chance as possible of taking on a theological life of its own along with the other theological styles and visions that we are beginning to discern in this new post-existentialist, post-European period. (Professor Gilkey has listed five marks of the death of God tradition, and they should perhaps be set down: (1) the problematic character of God and of man's relation to him today, (2) the acceptance of the secular world as normative intellectually and ethically good, (3) the restriction of theological statements to what one can actually affirm oneself, and with this the rejection of certain traditional ideas of tradition and authority, (4) the centrality of Jesus as one who calls us into the world to serve him there, (5) uneasiness with mythological, super-historical, eschatological, supernatural entities or categories. Gilkey goes on to note how each of these five points is a direct attack on a certain portion of the neo-orthodox tradition.)

In a recent critical review of Julian Huxley's *Essays of a Humanist,* Philip Toynbee makes an attack on all psychologically inclined Christians, biologists who listen to Bach, mystical astronomers and humane Catholics. What can we put in their place, he asks.

> And the answer? Simply to wait—on God or whatever it may be, and in the meantime to leave the general alone and to concentrate all our natural energies and curiosities on the specific, the idiosyncratic, the personal.

This combination of waiting and attention on the concrete and personal is the theological point I have been trying to make. Waiting here refers to the whole experience I have called "the death of God," including the attack on religion and the search for a means by which God, not needed, may be enjoyed. We have insisted all along that "death of God" must not be taken as symbolic rhetoric for something else. There really is a sense of not-having, of not-believing, of having lost, not just the idols or the gods of religion, but God himself. And this is an experience that is not peculiar to a neurotic few, nor is it private or inward. Death of God is a public event in our history.

Thus we wait, we try out new words, we pray for God to return, and we seem to be willing to descend into the darkness of unfaith and doubt that something may emerge on the other side. In this way, we have tried to interpret and confirm the mystical images that are so central to the thought of Altizer.

But we do more than play the waiting game. We concentrate our energy and passion on the specific, the concrete, the personal. We turn from the problems of faith to the reality of love. We walk away from the inner anguish of a Hamlet or an Oedipus and take up our worldly responsibility with Prospero and Orestes. As Protestants, we push the movement from church to world as far as it can go and become frankly·worldly men. And in this world, as we have seen, there is no need for religion and no need for God. This means that we refuse to consent to that traditional interpretation of the world as a shadow-screen of unreality, masking or concealing the eternal which is the only true reality. This refusal is made inevitable by the scientific revolution of the seventeenth century, and it is this refusal that stands as a troublesome shadow between ourselves and the Reformation of the sixteenth. The world of experience is real, and it is necessary and right to be actively engaged in changing its patterns and structures.

This concentration on the concrete and the worldly says something about the expected context of theology in America today. It means that the theological work that is to be truly helpful—at least for a while—is more likely to come from worldly contexts than ecclesiastical ones, more likely to come from participation in the Negro revolution than from the work of faith and order. But this is no surprise, for ever since the Civil War, ever since the Second Inaugural of Lincoln, the really creative American theological expressions have been worldly rather than ecclesiastical: the work of Walter Rauschenbusch and the work of Reinhold Niebuhr are surely evidence for this. (It is not yet clear how the civil rights movement is going to take on its theological significance, but it has begun, as the radical, southern Negro student comes out of the movement to seminary. He brings a passionate interest in the New Testament doctrines of discipleship and following Jesus and very little interest in the doctrine of sin. One of the most pressing intellectual responsibilities of the Negro student and minister today is that of working out some of the ethical and theological clues that the Negro revolution is teaching him and us all.)

The death of God Protestant, it can be seen, has somewhat inverted the usual relation between faith and love, theology and ethics, God and the neighbor. We are not proceeding from God and faith to neighbor and love, loving in such and such a way because we are loved in such and such a way. We move to our neighbor, to the city and to the world out of a sense of the loss of God. We set aside this sense of loss or death, we note it and allow it to be, neither glad for it, nor insistent that it must be so for all, nor sorry for ourselves. And, for the time of our waiting we place ourselves with our neighbor and enemy in the world.

There is something more than our phrase "waiting for God" that keeps this from sheer atheist humanism. Not only our waiting but our worldly work is Christian too, for our way to our neighbor is not only mapped out by the secular social and psychological and literary disciplines, it is mapped out as well by Jesus Christ and his way to his neighbor. Our ethical existence is partly a time of waiting for God and partly an actual Christology. Our being in the world, in the city, is not only an obedience to the Reformation formula, from church to world, it is an obedience to Jesus himself. How is this so? How is Jesus being disclosed in the world, being found in the world in our concrete work?

First, Jesus may be concealed in the world, in the neighbor, in this struggle for justice, in that struggle for beauty, clarity, order. Jesus is in the world as masked, and the work of the Christian is to strip off the masks of the world to find him, and, finding him, to stay with him and to do his work. In this sense, the Christian life is not a longing and is not a waiting, it is a going out into the world. The self is discovered, but only incidentally, as one moves out into the world to tear off the masks. Life is a masked ball, a Halloween party, and the Christian life, ethics, love, is that disruptive task of tearing off the masks of the guests to discover the true princess.

In the parable of the last judgment (Matthew 25:34 ff.) the righteous did not know it was Jesus they were serving. The righteous today don't need to know it either, unless they are Christian, in which case they will say that what they are doing is not only service, work, justified for this and that structural reason; it is also an act of unmasking, a looking for, a finding and a staying with Jesus.

In this first sense, the Christian life, ethics, love, is public, outward, visible. It is finding Jesus in your neighbor: "as you did it to one of the least of these my brethren, you did it to me" (Matthew 25:40).

There is another form of the presence of Jesus Christ in the world. Here, we no longer talk about unmasking Jesus who is out there in the world somewhere, we talk about becoming Jesus in and to the world. Here, the Christian life, ethics, love, is first a decision about the self, and then a movement beyond the self into the world.

The form, if not the content, of the parable of the Good Samaritan should be recalled. Jesus is asked a question: which one, among all the many claimants out there, is my neighbor? Jesus answers the question with one of his characteristic non-answers: "Don't look for the neighbor, be one." Or, to put the form of his answer to work on our problem: "Don't look for Jesus out there, in scripture, tradition, sacraments, Ingmar Bergman movies, in the world behind a mask—become Jesus." Become a Christ to your neighbor, as Luther put it.

In this form, the Christian life is not a looking outwards to the world and its claims, it is first a look within in order to become Jesus. "For me to live," cried Paul in one of his most daring utterances, "is Christ." Ethics and love are first a dangerous descent into the self. And in this form, the Christian life, ethics, love, are not so active or worldly. At this point the Christian is the passive man, and doubtless tempted into all of the easily noted dangers of confusing the self with Jesus.

The Christian life as the discernment of Jesus beneath the worldly masks can be called work or interpretation or criticism; while the Christian life as becoming Jesus looks a little different. At this point the Christian is the sucker, the fall guy, the jester, the fool for Christ, the one who stands before Pilate and is silent, the one who stands before power and power-structures and laughs.

Whichever of the paths one takes to find or define Jesus in the world, and perhaps some of us are called to choose both ways, and some only one, the worldliness of the Protestant can never, because of this, have an utterly humanistic form. I may be proposing a too simple marriage between Christ-ology and ethics, a too narrowly ethical approach to Christological problems, but it should at least be noted that however acute the experience of the death of God may be for us, however much silence and loneliness are en-tailed during our time of waiting for the absent God, we are not particularly cast down or perplexed by this. A form of obedience remains to us in our time of deprivation. We dechristianize no one, we make no virtue of our defects, and we even dare to call men into the worldly arena where men are in need and where Jesus is to be found and served.

The Sovereign God

James Alvin Sanders / from "The Vitality of the Old Testament"

James Alvin Sanders (1927–   ) is professor of Hebrew and the Old Testa-ment at Union Theological Seminary. Before that, he was a colleague of William Hamilton at Colgate Rochester Divinity School. He is the author of several books and numerous articles on theology.

In his recent article entitled "The Vitality of the Old Testament," printed in the Union Seminary Quarterly Review, *Sanders argues that the "God is dead" movement is dependent on the vitality of the Old Testament. No move-ment, he says, has provided Christian theological circles with "headier thinking, frothier enthusiasm, or more sheer giddiness." To Sanders, "Altizer's Christ who is pure flesh, and Hamilton's Jesus who is the true Princess, make [their] world ... sound like a Hefner Bunny Club to which Christians can now belong with no feelings of guilt or shirking of Calvinist duty." It is clear that more orthodox theologians see, in the world-centered Christianity envisioned by the radical theologians, something dangerously emotive and unsystematic. Altizer's rhetoric reminds Sanders of "Snoopy in Peanuts," who "twirls around ... singing his Easter message, 'God is dead, God is dead'" in a "primitive choreographic joy."*

Despite these sarcastic forays, Sanders is soberly critical as well; he takes pains to list and explain what he finds good and bad in the movement. He admires the intellectual honesty of these younger theologians, who "are willing to express on their feet what we have all been pondering in our swivel chairs." He admires also their "affirmation of the world," and he acclaims their iconoclasm, for he sees in it hope that settled vocabularies and attitudes may be jostled into new vitality.

Having shown Christian patience in the face of what he clearly regards as a new blasphemy and idolatry, Sanders goes to work on his criticism. The admirable intellectual honesty has been made into a god, he says. "Kenotic Christology," or "Jesusology," is a sign not of radical thinking but rather of "ultra-orthodox" literalism. And Sanders sees the dichotomy of the sacred and profane as false; the God whom the radical theologians have buried as dead was never alive—he was only a "straw-god," who bore "no relation to the sovereign God of the Bible." Their movement has "run the course of the old Liberalism far beyond anything the Liberals ever imagined."

One of the values of Sanders' article is its bibliography on the "God is dead" movement; he lists numerous articles and books which analyze the new theology in historical terms and which either attack or defend it. The reader may find it useful to consult some of these, although there does not exist as yet any definitive work, since the movement is still developing and growing.

... My thesis is that "the Old Testament is vital to the current theological crisis heralded by the so-called death-of-God movement."

The death-of-God movement claims to be indigenous to our American shores. Certainly it is one of the most exhilarating modes of theological thinking to strike these shores in modern times. Never has there been, I think, in Christian theological circles, headier thinking, frothier enthusiasm, or more sheer giddiness. The most vigorous radical of them all, Thomas J. J. Altizer of Emory, at times, in his writing, seems to be executing a primitive choreographic joy, and, like Snoopy in Peanuts, twirls around and around singing his Easter message, "God is dead, God is dead." Thinkers like Altizer claim that they are the true Christians and that all who react against his kenotic Christology are the orthodox bad guys who are not Christian at all. Others among them, like Paul van Buren of Temple, and William Hamilton of Colgate Rochester, while no less clear in proclaiming the death of God, show considerably more hesitation and wonderment at what is happening to them. John B. Cobb, Jr., and Harvey Cox, as well as other so-called Christian relativists and secularists, are not to be confused with the genuine death-of-God group. The secularists claim that the theological vocabulary of orthodoxy is dead and must be completely altered, whereas the radicals claim that God is dead and Christianity must be completely altered. Altizer thinks that his kenotic Christology has never heretofore been expressed: "Until this day Christian theology has refused a consistently kenotic Christology. Yet an open confession of the death of God can be our path to the Christ who is fully Christ, the kenotic Christ who has finally emptied himself of Spirit in wholly becoming flesh." For William Hamilton God is man's idea of a problem-solver who has completely failed: he simply hasn't solved any problems and is therefore dead. But Jesus is not dead, for Hamilton. On the contrary, Jesus is playing hide and seek out in the world somewhere and the game is to go out into the world and tear off his mask. "Jesus is in the world as masked, and the work of the Christian is to strip off the masks of the world to find him, and finding him, to stay with him and to do his work. . . . Life is a masked ball, a Halloween party, and the Christian life, ethics, love, is that disruptive task of tearing off the masks of the guests to discover the true princess." Altizer's Christ who is pure flesh, and Hamilton's Jesus who is the true Princess, make the world which they cherish as truth, sound like a Hefner Bunny Club to which Christians can now belong with no feelings of guilt or shirking of Calvinist duty.

Fortunately, the death-of-God movement has an interpreter, sometimes called its scribe, who is not himself one of their number, Langdon Gilkey of Chicago. While the actual adherents are out there in their world "becoming Jesus," as Hamilton would say, Gilkey makes his acute observations on the side lines.[1] It is Gilkey who has shown most clearly how the death-of-God movement has grown out of Barthian neo-orthodoxy, a point which Hamilton agrees to and accepts. (Hamilton, my former colleague of eleven years, was until five years ago a thorough-going Barthian, a fact which even his *New Essence of Christianity* of .1961 did not dispel.) But Gilkey has also shown their indebtedness to Tillich and Bultmann as well.

The radicals have seemingly accepted the very points of thinking in Barth, Tillich and Bultmann which biblical scholars and careful biblical theologians have been reluctant to accept from those giants of the past generation. The Christocentrism of Barth's essentially dualistic cosmology, the non-theist ontology of Tillich, and the existentialist spiritualizing of biblical images in Bultmann are precisely those contributions of the past generation most puzzling and unacceptable to biblical students (that is, of course, students of the whole Bible).

The balancing positive elements in the thinking of these three greats, Gilkey goes on, "do not seem consciously to influence the new (theologians)." Those positive elements are precisely the lessons grasped and accepted by biblical theologians, namely, "the emphasis on God, revelation and the word in Barth; on an ontological analysis of existential 'depth', on revelation and on Being itself in Tillich; and on existential inwardness and self-understanding 'at the boundary' and 'before God' in Bultmann." But it appears

---

[1]Langdon B. Gilkey, "Is God Dead?" and "God is Not Dead," *The Voice* (Bulletin of Crozier Theological Seminary), lvii (1965), pp. 4-11.

that it has been their negative, the nether-side, contributions which have come to the fore in the radicals: Barth's Christocentric particularity as over against God's universal sovereignty and reign; and Tillich's and Bultmann's finding God only out at the frontier or edge of existence and not in ordinary living. Unwittingly each man seemed to deny God's immediate reign and sovereignty in the common stuff of life, the world into which the radicals now summon us to follow in exuberance.

Accepting this separation of holy and secular,[2] the radicals claim that truth is to be found not in the sacred special places of Word, Christ and Church, but in the ordinary places of the profane world where Jesus actually is and has been all along. All the non-verifiable and non-propositional truth of theology, eschatology and mythology are completely rejected in favor of the verifiable, provable world.

I should like to record both my positive reactions to and my serious criticisms of the New Theology. First and foremost, I admire and support their intellectual honesty. This is perhaps their strongest asset. They are saying out loud, in many ways, the honest reservations we are all harboring in the haven of faith. They are willing to express on their feet what we have all been pondering in our swivel chairs. Armed with such honesty they might just happen to be, for today, God's special people, his elite guard of madmen, his prophets of our day with the tongues of sword, his cherished iconoclasts of established thinking. In the face of such a force of intellectual honesty what they say cannot be ignored, no matter how outlandish it may seem. Those twins of falsehood which forever crouch at the door of faith, credulity and hypocrisy, cannot long remain lodged among us when prophets are on the loose. Is it not at the heart of the Old Testament to hear the prophets say, your view of God is not God—he isn't here, he's there; he's way ahead of you; nothing you think about him touches him; your thoughts are not his thoughts? For God is mobile not static; he is itinerant not stable; he is forever active, not immutable. (He told Moses of the children of Israel, "Go tell them I'll be there." And the women at the tomb were informed, "He is not here.") God is forever outside our beliefs about him. The orthodox belief we may pretend to have is itself under the judgment of God. One can only thank God for the intellectual honesty of the death-of-God theologians.

Secondly, I appreciate their affirmation of the world, the whole world I hope—and not just Hamilton's "pro-bourgeois, urban and political" worldliness, nor only Cox's "technopolis," but the whole world in all its aspects, the whole of creation and all of human experience. Here especially is the Old Testament truth of the wholeness of life being restated by the radicals. The so-called ethical dualism of the hellenistic and New Testament writings needs periodically to come under the judgment of Old Testament thinking. Harvey Cox has, at least partially, understood that the faith of Israel was a secularization of ancient Near Eastern thinking, a desacralization of all creation myths, a proclamation that God and his world are all there is. The world is good because it is whole.

---

[2]The dichotomy of the sacred and the profane is basic to all the radicals but especially important to Altizer. The most succinct, and perhaps the most helpful, statement of Altizer's position is in his "Theology and the Death of God," *The Centennial Review*, viii (1964), pp. 129-146.

Thirdly, I acclaim the iconoclasm of the new theology. If their "Wait Without Idols"[3] can truly be a waiting on the Lord, without idolatry, then let us pray that he will indeed renew their strength. By iconoclasm I mean not so much the destruction of our conventional understanding of idols, apostasy and sin, though that is ever-present, I mean rather the comfortable in-group thinking into which we have cozied our minds so that we have somehow managed to convince ourselves that salvation comes by jargon and slogan. If the young Turks shall but cause us to reexamine our established vocabulary and the settled theology of the establishment, they shall have effected a blessing upon us all. But even more important a boon might issue from an honest reappraisal of the relationship and interaction between the God of the Bible and the God of Christian metaphysics. For all our much-touted "Return to the Bible" in the past forty years have we honestly subjected the God of Western speculation to the judgment of the biblical God? There are a number of us stubborn students of the Bible who think not. If with Barth what we have managed to do is somehow to separate God from his world; and if with Tillich we have managed somehow to discount biblical personal theism; and if with Bultmann we have managed somehow to separate God from the biblical modes of speaking about him and of praising him —all this, mind you, with the purpose of replacing biblical thinking with modern understandable and acceptable thinking—then is not the resultant "God" of recent theology already very nearly remade in our image? Could we not have foreseen that a Christian theology which centered itself in an ontologically and existentially acceptable Christ would find its goal in losing its God? Has not Christian theology itself in its excessive Christocentrism perhaps indeed veiled God? Can we really blame Altizer for coming up with his so-called kenotic Christology? "God so loved the world that he died for it." The great hope I see in the new Jesusology is that when, in Hamilton's masked ball, we have found him, we may see something in him, not, pray God, of our kenotic and empty selves, but of the inexhaustible grace of God which, like the Syrian widow's cruse of oil, is always full, and that we finally may see in him the biblical Jesus who claimed nothing for himself. Then may we develop a truly theocentric Christology and set aside all vain attempts at a Christocentric theology.

But while I am very excited by the possibilities for Truth, in the sense of the Greek word for Truth, *aletheia,* which etymologically means unveiling or unmasking, as in Hamilton's Halloween party, I must take issue with three of their most basic tenets.

First, while I admire their honesty and feel that it will be an offense to our false faces and masks, I greatly fear that they have made of their honesty a god. The biblical God is not subject to the judgments of man's honesty; man's honesty is the subject of God's judgments. Have we not yet learned that the honesty we cherish today will tomorrow be seen as dishonesty? The next generation will look upon our soul-searching honesty of today with the same disdain by which we look back upon our Barthian or even our liberal-Victorian honesty. Bertrand Russell, of all people, made

---

[3]The title of a book by Gabriel Vahanian, *Wait Without Idols* (1964). Waiting on "God" is an important aspect of the New Theology, especially for Altizer and Hamilton.

my point in his essay, "On Being Modern-Minded": "Our age," said Russell, "is the most parochial since Homer. . . . New catchwords hide from us the thoughts and feeling of our ancestors, even when they differed little from our own. We imagine ourselves at the apex of intelligence. . . . There must be something which is felt to be of more importance than the admiration of the contemporary crowd."[4] The death-of-God movement bears the ear-marks of being perhaps the most parochial school of thought in all modern theological searching. By their own insistence they are peculiarly an Ameri-can movement. They claim to want to free American theology from the domi-nation of European attitudes. I find here a strange sort of theological isolationism. But by parochial I mean not only their desire to incubate their ideas in their own heat, I mean also their disdain of history. John B. Cobb pleads for a new breed of Christian theologian who will "reach out for a novelty that disdains all appeal to the authority of the past and dares to think creatively and constructively in the present." I hope that they shall do so, for experimentation can only help in giving birth to new thoughts. But certainly man's honesty cannot lead to a denial of God. Man's honesty can lead only to a recognition of the limitations of man's honesty. Man's honesty, to be honest, is judged by God. I have doubts aplenty; but I, for one, doubt man's omniscience considerably more than I doubt God's.

My second stricture on the New Theology is directed at their kenotic Christology, or Jesusology. God, like a good friend, has laid down his life for us. One must remember that these Christian radicals are not athe-ists, nor are they agnostics. They have more beliefs than most of us; what they believe is not that there is no god but that God has died for us. They might be called ultra-orthodox literalists. They believe in the Incarnation without a stopper. In the foreword to his novel *A Death in the Family,* James Agee described a summer evening in his boyhood neighborhood when all the fathers on the block, in their suspenders, quietly watered their lawns with the garden hoses, which, when turned off, were "left empty, like God, by the sparrow's fall." The radicals do not bother with the ontological question of the existence of God. God lived, right enough, but now he is dead. Not like El and the other gods of ancient Near Eastern pantheons, because of old age or battles among the gods, the way Marduk slew Tiamat or Yahweh slew Rahab. But rather, God gave himself, emptied himself, killed himself for man's sake, so that man might mature and come of age. God weaned us. Since man has now come of age, say the radicals, it is finally time to shout the Easter message, "God is dead." And that leaves us with man alone. They accept a basic dualism or radical distinction between the sacred and the profane, between God and the world, in order to be rid of the sacred and to proclaim the death of God. Man and the world are left without God or the gods: man and the world are completely secularized. God as a problem-solver is finished, they say. But the providence of God in biblical terms is not God in the guise of man's trouble-shooter. The provi-dence of God in biblical terms cuts across man's self-understood wants and needs: his wonders are alien; his gifts are strange (Isa. 28:21). Could we not have foreseen radical theology by our over-emphasis on the Lutheran

---

[4]Russell, *Unpopular Essays* (1950), pp. 88-94.

rediscovery of God in Bethlehem's cradle? Have we failed sufficiently to emphasize the *Deus Absconditus* and the judgments of God? God cannot die if he never existed; for according to classical Christian theology God does not exist, he gives existence.

My third stricture is directed against the false dichotomy of sacred and profane whereby the biblical transcendence of God is in effect ridiculed and man displaces a useless, impotent god, a straw-god, bearing no relation to the sovereign God of the Bible. There is a sense in which the central proclamation of the death-of-God movement fits a classic biblical definition of sin. In the Bible it is God alone who lives; it is man who dies.[5] "He lives" is the central message of Habakkuk in the sixth-century B.C. Exile, and it is the central message of the evangelists in the first-century A.D. Gospel.[6] No matter what valiant efforts may be exerted to avoid setting man up as his own god, or better as three billion gods, I fear that that is precisely what the death-of-God group are likely to do. Paul Tillich has recently said, "The temptation not to accept finitude, but rather to lift one's self to the level of the Unconditioned, the Divine, runs through all history."[7] Only he who fancies man to be god can call his God dead, that is, has convinced himself that there is no truth which transcends man. Only he who thinks that our current honesty is the final honesty can truly believe that God is dead. Does "man come of age" not mean man fancying himself to be God? But he who knows that tomorrow's honesty will stand in judgment over today's honesty, and that the work of Truth or unveiling and unmasking is never done, can truly believe that God is God. "What is truth?" asked Pilate of our Lord. And he did not answer, for Truth is judgment, divine judgment; it is the judgment of the condemned on the accuser, of the oppressed on the oppressor, of tomorrow's discovery on today's ignorance. It is the saving judgment of the Ultimate on all our penultima: it is the silence of God's Christ in the presence of our Pilate.

"Man utterly without God," writes Schubert Ogden, "is man utterly without the dignity and freedom by which he both can and should be (in Camus' phrase) something more than a dog." To believe that Jesus, without God, is out in the world today doing his work, which we should seek out to share, is simply to remythologize the New Testament message in a way vaguely acceptable today. *Christology without theology is anthropology.* To those in Israel who are confident that God is dead and Jesus is his son, Elijah issues his challenge on Mt. Carmel, "How long will you go limping with two different opinions? If the Lord is God, follow him; but if Baal, then follow Baal" (I Kings 18:21).

To opt for the world (Baal) as over against God is to set up a false dichotomy and then run the course of old Liberalism far beyond anything the Liberals ever imagined. To demand immediate relevance and meaning and significance, free of the judgments of seeming irrelevance and apparent insignificance, is to make the world, as we understand it, that is, to make of empiricism the canon of truth. Are we reduced to accepting as

---

[5]Sanders, "God is God," *Foundations,* vi (1963), pp. 343-361.
[6]Sanders, "Thy God Reigneth," *Motive,* xvi (February 1956), pp. 28-31.
[7]Paul Tillich, "Frontiers," *Journal of Bible and Religion,* xxxiii (1965), pp. 17-23; see p. 22.

Truth things simply as they appear? Gordon Allport has recently cautioned against over-belief in Itsy-Bitsy Empiricism, accepting the immediate results of verifiable studies as truth. Luther was right to say *"Entweder Gott oder Abgott"*: we do worship either the one, true God, or idols.[8]

The God who entered the huts and hovels of Pharaoh's slaves in Egypt is not dead, but is probably today in the huts and hovels of Vietnamese peasants. The God who spoke from a Burning Bush might be speaking from a jungle aflame. The God who served as Israel's guide in her desert of new-found freedom may be serving as our guide in our desert of new-found freedoms. And we may find, as those freed slaves found, that he is not dead, but has gone on three days' journey ahead of us. And we may also find, when our post-modern freedoms from the past have lost their lustre, that God has not weaned or abandoned us after all. The God who directed Nebuchadnezzer to take Israel into Exile and then joined them in Babylon's dungeons and jails might be with us yet *(Immanuel)* in the refugee camps of the world. The God who got down into the cradle of a baby Jew threatened by Herod's sword is still known in a world threatening its own destruction. And the God who got onto the cross of a man trapped in the justice of the combination of the two best legal systems of antiquity (the Hebraic and the Roman) surely is yet to be known in our justice, in Hayneville and Harlem. The Bible says when you get to prison, just remember he's already been there. Father John J. Hill, a parish priest in the Archdiocese of Chicago, tells of how after he had been arrested in Chicago and convicted, jailed and fined for sitting-in, an ancient Negro woman met him in front of his church on the Sunday after the trial. She shook his hand and said, "Thank you, Father, for being convicted." God's humility, in biblical terms, is not his impotence, but his sovereignty and his judgment upon us. So great is his majesty that it expresses itself in divine humility. To know the judgment upon us of God's humility is, in Thanksgiving, to pray, "Thank you, Father, for being convicted."

---

[8]Contrast Hamilton in the *Christian Scholar* [xlviii (1965) p. 40]. This point is tellingly made in one of the most trenchant critiques of the new Jesusology to date, by Harmon R. Holcomb, "Christology Without God," *Foundations,* viii (1965), pp. 49-61.

The Chemical Door in the Wall

Aldous Huxley / from *The Doors of Perception*

Aldous Huxley (1894–1966) belonged by blood and training to the great intellectual aristocracy of the Huxleys and the Arnolds. His brother, Sir Julian Huxley, is an eminent biologist, very active in UNESCO and in the movement called "atheistic humanism." Aldous Huxley achieved early fame as a novelist with such works as Brave New World *and* Point Counter Point; *after 1945 he virtually abandoned the novel and turned to criticism and philosophy, writing an occasional movie script from his new home in Hollywood. His book* The Perennial Philosophy *was an attempt to find unity in an eclectic study of the world's great religions.*

In 1953 Huxley, perpetually interested in psychic and religious phenomena, experimented with mescalin, one of the hallucinatory chemicals which have attracted widespread attention and have caused heated debate in recent years. He published an account of his experiences in 1954, under the title The Doors of Perception *which he took from William Blake. The essay from which the following selections are taken is a sensitive and inquiring summary of the phenomena induced by the chemical and of Huxley's speculations on its use as a stimulant to genuine religious experiences. Huxley's long career as a writer, especially one interested in both science and philosophy, makes his observations of special interest and competence. It is for this reason that his essay was included rather than one by such a recent figure as Timothy Leary or Alan Watts, both of whom are far more active and flamboyant proselytizers for LSD and similar hallucinogens than is Huxley.*

Fundamental to Huxley's experience was the diminution in significance of space and time, the two perceptual categories most susceptible to measurement. The sensations of immediate experience, no matter how trivial—an ordinary chair, a flower, a texture—became so overwhelming that the psyche was contentedly rapt in a vision of unity. The psyche saw and sensed what it either did not perceive before or what, if it perceived, it did not appreciate or value. This "expanded consciousness," as it is now called, seems to the user of the chemical co-extensive with the universe—he achieves a sense of oneness and peace which many claim is mystical. Huxley seems to be advocating such a sort of instant mysticism, a chemical formula to replace that long and detached discipline of philosophy, that Epicurean enjoyment, which Santayana strove for by reason rather than by stimulants.

Huxley, at the end of the essay, argues for widespread use of mescalin (peyote) and its derivatives as a means to authentic religious experience; he cites the Native American Church, an Indian sect "whose principal rite is a kind of early Christian agape, or love feast, where slices of peyote take the place of the sacramental bread and wine." He concludes by asserting that he who has experienced this transcendent "is-ness" and "who comes back through the Door in the Wall will never be quite the same as the man who went out. He will be . . . humbler in acknowledging his ignorance yet better equipped to understand the relationship of words to things, of systematic reasoning to the unfathomable Mystery which it tries, forever vainly, to comprehend."

It was in 1886 that the German pharmacologist, Ludwig Lewin, published the first- systematic study of the cactus, to which his own name was subsequently given. *Anhalonium Lewinii* was new to science. To primitive religion and the Indians of Mexico and the American Southwest it was a friend of immemorially long standing. Indeed, it was much more than a friend. In the words of one of the early Spanish visitors to the New World, "they eat a root which they call peyote, and which they venerate as though it were a deity."

Why they should have venerated it as a deity became apparent when such eminent psychologists as Jaensch, Havelock Ellis and Weir Mitchell began their experiments with mescalin, the active principle of peyote. True, they stopped short at a point well this side of idolatry; but all concurred in assigning to mescalin a position among drugs of unique distinction. Administered in suitable doses, it changes the quality of consciousness more profoundly and yet is less toxic than any other substance in the pharmacologist's repertory.

Mescalin research has been going on sporadically ever since the days of Lewin and Havelock Ellis. Chemists have not merely isolated the alkaloid; they have learned how to synthesize it, so that the supply no longer depends on the sparse and intermittent crop of a desert cactus. Alienists have dosed themselves with mescalin in the hope thereby of coming to a better, a first-hand, understanding of their patients' mental processes. Working unfortunately upon too few subjects within too narrow a range of circumstances, psychologists have observed and catalogued some of the drug's more striking effects. Neurologists and physiologists have found out something about the mechanism of its action upon the central nervous system. And at least one professional philosopher has taken mescalin for the light it may throw on such ancient, unsolved riddles as the place of mind in nature and the relationship between brain and consciousness. . . .

By a series of, for me, extremely fortunate circumstances I found myself, in the spring of 1953, squarely athwart that trail. One of the sleuths had come on business to California. In spite of seventy years of mescalin research, the psychological material at his disposal was still absurdly inadequate, and he was anxious to add to it. I was on the spot and willing, indeed eager, to be a guinea pig. Thus it came about that, one bright May morning, I swallowed four-tenths of a gram of mescalin dissolved in half a glass of water and sat down to wait for the results.

We live together, we act on, and react to, one another; but always and in all circumstances we are by ourselves. The martyrs go hand in hand into the arena; they are crucified alone. Embraced, the lovers desperately try to fuse their insulated ecstasies into a single self-transcendence; in vain. By its very nature every embodied spirit is doomed to suffer and enjoy in solitude. Sensations, feelings, insights, fancies—all these are private and, except through symbols and at second hand, incommunicable. We can pool information about experiences, but never the experiences themselves. From family to nation, every human group is a society of island universes.

Most island universes are sufficiently like one another to permit of inferential understanding or even of mutual empathy or "feeling into." Thus, remembering our own bereavements and humiliations, we can condole with others in analogous circumstances, can put ourselves (always, of course, in a slightly Pickwickian sense) in their places. But in certain cases communication between universes is incomplete or even nonexistent. The mind is its own place, and the places inhabited by the insane and the exceptionally gifted are so different from the places where ordinary men and women live, that there is little or no common ground of memory to serve as a basis for understanding or fellow feeling. Words are uttered, but fail to enlighten. The things and events to which the symbols refer belong to mutually exclusive realms of experience.

To see ourselves as others see us is a most salutary gift. Hardly less important is the capacity to see others as they see themselves. But what if these others belong to a different species and inhabit a radically alien universe? For example, how can the sane get to know what it actually feels like to be mad? Or, short of being born again as a visionary, a medium, or a musical genius, how can we ever visit the worlds which, to Blake, to Swedenborg, to Johann Sebastian Bach, were home? And how can a man at the extreme limits of ectomorphy and cerebrotonia ever put himself in the place of one at the limits of endomorphy and viscerotonia, or, except within certain circumscribed areas, share the feelings of one who stands at the limits of mesomorphy and somatotonia? To the unmitigated behaviorist such questions, I suppose, are meaningless. But for those who theoretically believe what in practice they know to be true—namely, that there is an inside to experience as well as an outside—the problems posed are real problems, all the more grave for being, some completely insoluble, some soluble only in exceptional circumstances and by methods not available to everyone. Thus, it seems virtually certain that I shall never know what it feels like to be Sir John Falstaff or Joe Louis. On the other hand, it had always seemed to me possible that, through hypnosis, for example, or autohypnosis, by means of systematic meditation, or else by taking the appropriate drug, I might so change my ordinary mode of consciousness as to be able to know, from the inside, what the visionary, the medium, even the mystic were talking about.

From what I had read of the mescalin experience I was convinced in advance that the drug would admit me, at least for a few hours, into the kind of inner world described by Blake and Æ. But what I had expected did not happen. I had expected to lie with my eyes shut, looking at visions of many-colored geometries, of animated architectures, rich with gems and fabulously lovely, of landscapes with heroic figures, of symbolic dramas trembling perpetually on the verge of the ultimate revelation. But I had not reckoned, it was evident, with the idiosyncrasies of my mental make-up, the facts of my temperament, training and habits. . . .

I took my pill at eleven. An hour and a half later, I was sitting in my study, looking intently at a small glass vase. The vase contained only three flowers—a full-blown Belle of Portugal rose, shell pink with a hint at every petal's base of a hotter, flamier hue; a large magenta and cream-colored carnation; and, pale purple at the end of its broken stalk, the bold heraldic blossom of an iris. Fortuitous and provisional, the little nosegay broke all the rules of traditional good taste. At breakfast that morning I had been struck by the lively dissonance of its colors. But that was no longer the point. I was not looking now at an unusual flower arrangement. I was seeing what

Adam had seen on the morning of his creation—the miracle, moment by moment, of naked existence.

"Is it agreeable?" somebody asked. (During this part of the experiment, all conversations were recorded on a dictating machine, and it has been possible for me to refresh my memory of what was said.)

"Neither agreeable nor disagreeable," I answered. "It just *is*."

Istigkeit—wasn't that the word Meister Eckhart liked to use? "Is-ness." The Being of Platonic philosophy—except that Plato seems to have made the enormous, the grotesque mistake of separating Being from becoming and identifying it with the mathematical abstraction of the Idea. He could never, poor fellow, have seen a bunch of flowers shining with their own inner light and all but quivering under the pressure of the significance with which they were charged; could never have perceived that what rose and iris and carnation so intensely signified was nothing more, and nothing less, than what they were—a transience that was yet eternal life, a perpetual perishing that was at the same time pure Being, a bundle of minute, unique particulars in which, by some unspeakable and yet self-evident paradox, was to be seen the divine source of all existence.

I continued to look at the flowers, and in their living light I seemed to detect the qualitative equivalent of breathing—but of a breathing without returns to a starting point, with no recurrent ebbs but only a repeated flow from beauty to heightened beauty, from deeper to ever deeper meaning. Words like "grace" and "transfiguration" came to my mind, and this, of course, was what, among other things, they stood for. My eyes traveled from the rose to the carnation, and from that feathery incandescence to the smooth scrolls of sentient amethyst which were the iris. The Beatific Vision, *Sat Chit Ananda*, Being-Awareness-Bliss—for the first time I understood, not on the verbal level, not by inchoate hints or at a distance, but precisely and completely what those prodigious syllables referred to. And then I remembered a passage I had read in one of Suzuki's essays. "What is the Dharma-Body of the Buddha?" ("The Dharma-Body of the Buddha" is another way of saying Mind, Suchness, the Void, the Godhead.) The question is asked in a Zen monastery by an earnest and bewildered novice. And with the prompt irrelevance of one of the Marx Brothers, the Master answers, "The hedge at the bottom of the garden." "And the man who realizes this truth," the novice dubiously inquires, "what, may I ask, is he?" Groucho gives him a whack over the shoulders with his staff and answers, "A golden-haired lion."

It had been, when I read it, only a vaguely pregnant piece of nonsense. Now it was all as clear as day, as evident as Euclid. Of course the Dharma-Body of the Buddha was the hedge at the bottom of the garden. At the same time, and no less obviously, it was these flowers, it was anything that I—or rather the blessed Not-I, released for a moment from my throttling embrace —cared to look at. The books, for example, with which my study walls were lined. Like the flowers, they glowed, when I looked at them, with brighter colors, a profounder significance. Red books, like rubies; emerald books; books bound in white jade; books of agate; of aquamarine, of yellow topaz; lapis lazuli books whose color was so intense, so intrinsically meaningful, that they seemed to be on the point of leaving the shelves to thrust themselves more insistently on my attention.

"What about spatial relationships?" the investigator inquired, as I was looking at the books.

It was difficult to answer. True, the perspective looked rather odd, and the walls of the room no longer seemed to meet in right angles. But these were not the really important facts. The really important facts were that spatial relationships had ceased to matter very much and that my mind was perceiving the world in terms of other than spatial categories. At ordinary times the eye concerns itself with such problems as *Where?—How far?—How situated in relation to what?* In the mescalin experience the implied questions to which the eye responds are of another order. Place and distance cease to be of much interest. The mind does its perceiving in terms of intensity of existence, profundity of significance, relationships within a pattern. I saw the books, but was not at all concerned with their positions in space. What I noticed, what impressed itself upon my mind was the fact that all of them glowed with living light and that in some the glory was more manifest than in others. In this context position and the three dimensions were beside the point. Not, of course, that the category of space had been abolished. When I got up and walked about, I could do so quite normally, without misjudging the whereabouts of objects. Space was still there; but it had lost its predominance. The mind was primarily concerned, not with measures and locations, but with being and meaning.

And along with indifference to space there went an even more complete indifference to time.

"There seems to be plenty of it," was all I would answer, when the investigator asked me to say what I felt about time.

Plenty of it, but exactly how much was entirely irrelevant. I could, of course, have looked at my watch; but my watch, I knew, was in another universe. My actual experience had been, was still, of an indefinite duration or alternatively of a perpetual present made up of one continually changing apocalypse. . . .

. . . The investigator suggested a walk in the garden. I was willing; and though my body seemed to have dissociated itself almost completely from my mind—or, to be more accurate, though my awareness of the transfigured outer world was no longer accompanied by an awareness of my physical organism—I found myself able to get up, open the French window and walk out with only a minimum of hesitation. It was odd, of course, to feel that "I" was not the same as these arms and legs "out there," as this wholly objective trunk and neck and even head. It was odd; but one soon got used to it. And anyhow the body seemed perfectly well able to look after itself. In reality, of course, it always does look after itself. All that the conscious ego can do is to formulate wishes, which are then carried out by forces which it controls very little and understands not at all. When it does anything more—when it tries too hard, for example, when it worries, when it becomes apprehensive about the future—it lowers the effectiveness of those forces and may even cause the devitalized body to fall ill. In my present state, awareness was not referred to as ego; it was, so to speak, on its own.

This meant that the physiological intelligence controlling the body was also on its own. For the moment that interfering neurotic who, in waking hours, tries to run the show, was blessedly out of the way.

From the French window I walked out under a kind of pergola covered in part by a climbing rose tree, in part by laths, one inch wide with half an inch of space between them. The sun was shining and the shadows of the laths made a zebra-like pattern on the ground and across the seat and back of a garden chair, which was standing at this end of the pergola. That chair—shall I ever forget it? Where the shadows fell on the canvas upholstery, stripes of a deep but glowing indigo alternated with stripes of an incandescence so intensely bright that it was hard to believe that they could be made of anything but blue fire. For what seemed an immensely long time I gazed without knowing, even without wishing to know, what it was that confronted me. At any other time I would have seen a chair barred with alternate light and shade. Today the percept had swallowed up the concept. I was so completely absorbed in looking, so thunderstruck by what I actually saw, that I could not be aware of anything else. Garden furniture, laths, sunlight, shadow— these were no more than names and notions, mere verbalizations, for utilitarian or scientific purposes, after the event. The event was this succession of azure furnace doors separated by gulfs of unfathomable gentian. It was inexpressibly wonderful, wonderful to the point, almost, of being terrifying. And suddenly I had an inkling of what it must feel like to be mad. Schizophrenia has its heavens as well as its hells and purgatories. I remember what an old friend, dead these many years, told me about his mad wife. One day in the early stages of the disease, when she still had her lucid intervals he had gone to talk to her about their children. She listened for a time, then cut him short. How could he bear to waste his time on a couple of absent children, when all that really mattered, here and now, was the unspeakable beauty of the patterns he made, in this brown tweed jacket, every time he moved his arms? Alas, this paradise of cleansed perception, of pure one-sided contemplation, was not to endure. The blissful intermissions became rarer, became briefer, until finally there were no more of them; there was only horror.

Most takers of mescalin experience only the heavenly part of schizophrenia. The drug brings hell and purgatory only to those who have had a recent case of jaundice, or who suffer from periodical depressions or a chronic anxiety. If, like the other drugs of remotely comparable power, mescalin were notoriously toxic, the taking of it would be enough, of itself, to cause anxiety. But the reasonably healthy person knows in advance that, so far as he is concerned, mescalin is completely innocuous, that its effects will pass off after eight or ten hours, leaving no hangover and consequently no craving for a renewal of the dose. Fortified by this knowledge, he embarks upon the experiment without fear—in other words, without any disposition to convert an unprecedently strange and other than human experience into something appalling, something actually diabolical.

Confronted by a chair which looked like the Last Judgment—or, to be more accurate, by a Last Judgment which, after a long time and with considerable difficulty, I recognized as a chair—I found myself all at once on the brink of panic. This, I suddenly felt, was going too far. Too far, even though the going was into intenser beauty, deeper significance. The fear, as I analyze it in retrospect, was of being overwhelmed, of disintegrating under a pressure of reality greater than a mind, accustomed to living most of the time in a cosy world of symbols, could possibly bear. The literature of religious experience abounds in references to the pains and terrors overwhelming those who have come, too suddenly, face to face with some manifestation of the *Mysterium tremendum.* In theological language, this fear is due to the incompatibility between man's egotism and the divine purity, between man's self-aggravated separateness and the infinity of God. Following Boehme and William Law, we may say that, by unregenerate souls, the divine Light at its full blaze can be apprehended only as a burning, purgatorial fire. An almost identical doctrine is to be found in *The Tibetan Book of the Dead,* where the departed soul is described as shrinking in agony from the Pure Light of the Void, and even from the lesser, tempered Lights, in order to rush headlong into the comforting darkness of selfhood as a reborn human being, or even as a beast, an unhappy ghost, a denizen of hell. Anything rather than the burning brightness of unmitigated Reality—anything!

The schizophrenic is a soul not merely unregenerate, but desperately sick into the bargain. His sickness consists in the inability to take refuge from inner and outer reality (as the sane person habitually does) in the homemade universe of common sense—the strictly human world of useful notions, shared symbols and socially acceptable conventions. The schizophrenic is like a man permanently under the influence of mescalin, and therefore unable to shut off the experience of a reality which he is not holy enough to live with, which he cannot explain away because it is the most stubborn of primary facts, and which, because it never permits him to look at the world with merely human eyes, scares him into interpreting its unremitting strangeness, its burning intensity of significance, as the manifestations of human or even cosmic malevolence, calling for the most desperate countermeasures, from murderous violence at one end of the scale to catatonia, or psychological suicide, at the other. And once embarked upon the downward, the infernal road, one would never be able to stop. That, now, was only too obvious. . . .

That humanity at large will ever be able to dispense with Artificial Paradises seems very unlikely. Most men and women lead lives at the worst so painful, at the best so monotonous, poor and limited that the urge to escape, the longing to transcend themselves if only for a few moments, is and has always been one of the principal appetites of the soul. Art and religion, carnivals and saturnalia, dancing and listening to oratory—all these have served, in H. G. Wells's phrase, as Doors in the Wall. And for private, for everyday use there have always been chemical intoxicants. All the vegetable sedatives and narcotics, all the euphorics that grow on trees, the hallucinogens that ripen in berries or can be squeezed from roots—all, without exception, have been known and systematically used by human beings from time immemorial. And to these natural modifiers of consciousness modern science has added its quota of synthetics—chloral, for example, and benzedrine, the bromides and the barbiturates.

Most of these modifiers of consciousness cannot now be taken except under doctor's orders, or else illegally and at considerable risk. For unrestricted use the West has permitted only alcohol and tobacco. All the other chemical Doors in the Wall are labeled Dope, and their unauthorized takers are Fiends.

We now spend a good deal more on drink and smoke than we spend on education. This, of course, is not surprising. The urge to escape from selfhood and the environment is in almost everyone almost all the time. The urge to do something for the young is strong only in parents, and in them only for the few years during which their children go to school. Equally unsurprising is the current attitude towards drink and smoke. In spite of the growing army of hopeless alcoholics, in spite of the hundreds of thousands of persons annually maimed or killed by drunken drivers, popular comedians still crack jokes about alcohol and its addicts. And in spite of the evidence linking cigarettes with lung cancer, practically everybody regards tobacco smoking as being hardly less normal and natural than eating. From the point of view of the rationalist utilitarian this may seem odd. For the historian, it is exactly what you would expect. A firm conviction of the material reality of Hell never prevented medieval Christians from doing what their ambition, lust or covetousness suggested. Lung cancer, traffic accidents and the millions of miserable and misery-creating alcoholics are facts even more certain than was, in Dante's day, the fact of the Inferno. But all such facts are remote and unsubstantial compared with the near, felt fact of a craving, here and now, for release or sedation, for a drink or a smoke.

Ours is the age, among other things, of the automobile and of rocketing population. Alcohol is incompatible with safety on the roads, and its production, like that of tobacco, condemns to virtual sterility many millions of acres of the most fertile soil. The problems raised by alcohol and tobacco cannot, it goes without saying, be solved by prohibition. The universal and ever-present urge to self-transcendence is not to be abolished by slamming the currently popular Doors in the Wall. The only reasonable policy is to open other, better doors in the hope of inducing men and women to exchange their old bad habits for new and less harmful ones. Some of these other, better doors will be social and technological in nature, others religious or psychological, others dietetic, educational, athletic. But the need for frequent chemical vacations from intolerable selfhood and repulsive surroundings will undoubtedly remain. What is needed is a new drug which will relieve and console our suffering species without doing more harm in the long run than it does good in the short. Such a drug must be potent in minute doses and synthesizable. If it does not possess these qualities, its production, like that of wine, beer, spirits and tobacco will interfere with the raising of indispensable food and fibers. It must be less toxic than opium or cocaine, less likely to produce undesirable social consequences than alcohol or the barbiturates, less inimical to heart and lungs than the tars and nicotine of cigarettes. And, on the positive side, it should produce changes in consciousness more interesting, more intrinsically valuable than mere sedation or dreaminess, delusions of omnipotence or release from inhibition.

To most people, mescalin is almost completely innocuous. Unlike alcohol, it does not drive the taker into the kind of uninhibited action which results in brawls, crimes of violence and traffic accidents. A man under the influence of mescalin quietly minds his own business. Moreover, the business he minds is an experience of the most enlightening kind, which does not have to be paid for (and this is surely important) by a compensatory hangover. Of the long-range consequences of regular mescalin taking we know very little. The Indians who consume peyote buttons do not seem to be physically or morally degraded by the habit. However, the available evidence is still scarce and sketchy.[1]

Although obviously superior to cocaine, opium, alcohol and tobacco, mescalin is not yet the ideal drug. Along with the happily transfigured majority of mescalin takers there is a minority that finds in the drug only hell or purgatory. Moreover, for a drug that is to be used, like alcohol, for general consumption, its effects last for an inconveniently long time. But chemistry and physiology are capable nowadays of practically anything. If the psychologists and sociologists will define the ideal, the neurologists and pharmacologists can be relied upon to discover the means whereby that ideal can be realized or at least (for perhaps this kind of ideal can never, in the very nature of things, be fully realized) more nearly approached than in the wine-bibbing past, the whisky-drinking, marijuana-smoking and barbiturate-swallowing present.

The urge to transcend self-conscious selfhood is, as I have said, a principal appetite of the soul. When, for whatever reason, men and women fail to transcend themselves by means of worship, good works, and spiritual exercises, they are apt to resort to religion's chemical surrogates—alcohol and "goof pills" in the modern West, alcohol and opium in the East, hashish in the Mohammedan world, alcohol and marijuana in Central America, alcohol and coca in the Andes, alcohol and the barbiturates in the more up-to-date regions of South America. In *Poisons Sacrés, Ivresses Divines* Philippe de Félice has written at length and with a wealth of documentation on the immemorial connection between religion and the taking of drugs. Here, in summary or in direct quotation, are his conclusions. The employment for religious purposes of toxic substances is "extraordinarily widespread. . . . The practices studied in this volume can be observed in every region of the earth, among primitives no less than among those who have reached a high pitch of civilization. We are therefore dealing not with exceptional facts,

---

[1] In his monograph, *Menomini Peyotism,* published (December, 1952) in the Transactions of the American Philosophical Society, Professor J. S. Slotkin has written that "the habitual use of Peyote does not seem to produce any increased tolerance or dependence. I know many people who have been Peyotists for forty to fifty years. The amount of Peyote they use depends upon the solemnity of the occasion; in general they do not take any more Peyote now than they did years ago. Also, there is sometimes an interval of a month or more between rites, and they go without Peyote during this period without feeling any craving for it. Personally, even after a series of rites occurring on four successive weekends, I neither increased the amount of Peyote consumed nor felt any continued need for it." It is evidently with good reason that "Peyote has never been legally declared a narcotic, or its use prohibited by the federal government." However, "during the long history of Indian-white contact, white officials have usually tried to suppress the use of Peyote, because it has been conceived to violate their own mores. But these attempts have always failed." In a footnote Dr. Slotkin adds that "it is amazing to hear the fantastic stories about the effects of Peyote and the nature of the ritual, which are told by the white and Catholic Indian officials in the Menomini Reservation. None of them have had the slightest first-hand experience with the plant or with the religion, yet some fancy themselves to be authorities and write official reports on the subject."

which might justifiably be overlooked, but with a general and, in the widest sense of the word, a human phenomenon, the kind of phenomenon which cannot be disregarded by anyone who is trying to discover what religion is, and what are the deep needs which it must satisfy."

Ideally, everyone should be able to find self-transcendence in some form of pure or applied religion. In practice it seems very unlikely that this hoped for consummation will ever be realized. There are, and doubtless there always will be, good churchmen and good churchwomen for whom, unfortunately, piety is not enough. The late G. K. Chesterton, who wrote at least as lyrically of drink as of devotion, may serve as their eloquent spokesman.

The modern churches, with some exceptions among the Protestant denominations, tolerate alcohol; but even the most tolerant have made no attempt to convert the drug to Christianity, or to sacramentalize its use. The pious drinker is forced to take his religion in one compartment, his religion-surrogate in another. And perhaps this is inevitable. Drinking cannot be sacramentalized except in religions which set no store on decorum. The worship of Dionysos or the Celtic god of beer was a loud and disorderly affair. The rites of Christianity are incompatible with even religious drunkenness. This does no harm to the distillers, but is very bad for Christianity. Countless persons desire self-transcendence and would be glad to find it in church. But, alas, "the hungry sheep look up and are not fed." They take part in rites, they listen to sermons, they repeat prayers; but their thirst remains unassuaged. Disappointed, they turn to the bottle. For a time at least and in a kind of way, it works. Church may still be attended; but it is no more than the Musical Bank of Butler's *Erewhon*. God may still be acknowledged; but He is God only on the verbal level, only in a strictly Pickwickian sense. The effective object of worship is the bottle and the sole religious experience is that state of uninhibited and belligerent euphoria which follows the ingestion of the third cocktail.

We see, then, that Christianity and alcohol do not and cannot mix. Christianity and mescalin seem to be much more compatible. This has been demonstrated by many tribes of Indians, from Texas to as far north as Wisconsin. Among these tribes are to be found groups affiliated with the Native American Church, a sect whose principal rite is a kind of Early Christian agape, or love feast, where slices of peyote take the place of the sacramental bread and wine. These Native Americans regard the cactus as God's special gift to the Indians, and equate its effects with the workings of the divine Spirit.

Professor J. S. Slotkin, one of the very few white men ever to have participated in the rites of a Peyotist congregation, says of his fellow worshipers that they are "certainly not stupefied or drunk. . . . They never get out of rhythm or fumble their words, as a drunken or stupefied man would do. . . . They are all quiet, courteous and considerate of one another. I have never been in any white man's house of worship where there is either so much religious feeling or decorum." And what, we may ask, are these devout and well-behaved Peyotists experiencing? Not the mild sense of virtue which sustains the average Sunday churchgoer through ninety minutes of boredom. Not even those high feelings, inspired by thoughts of the Creator and the

Redeemer, the Judge and the Comforter, which animate the pious. For these Native Americans, religious experience is something more direct and illuminating, more spontaneous, less the homemade product of the superficial, self-conscious mind. Sometimes (according to the reports collected by Dr. Slotkin) they see visions, which may be of Christ Himself. Sometimes they hear the voice of the Great Spirit. Sometimes they become aware of the presence of God and of those personal shortcomings which must be corrected if they are to do His will. The practical consequences of these chemical openings of doors into the Other World seem to be wholly good. Dr. Slotkin reports that habitual Peyotists are on the whole more industrious, more temperate (many of them abstain altogether from alcohol), more peaceable than non-Peyotists. A tree with such satisfactory fruits cannot be condemned out of hand as evil.

In sacramentalizing the use of peyote, the Indians of the Native American Church have done something which is at once psychologically sound and historically respectable. In the early centuries of Christianity many pagan rites and festivals were baptized, so to say, and made to serve the purposes of the Church. These jollifications were not particularly edifying; but they assuaged a certain psychological hunger and, instead of trying to suppress them, the earlier missionaries had the sense to accept them for what they were, soul-satisfying expressions of fundamental urges, and to incorporate them into the fabric of the new religion. What the Native Americans have done is essentially similar. They have taken a pagan custom (a custom, incidentally, far more elevating and enlightening than most of the rather brutish carousals and mummeries adopted from European paganism) and given it a Christian significance.

Though but recently introduced into the northern United States, peyote-eating and the religion based upon it have become important symbols of the red man's right to spiritual independence. Some Indians have reacted to white supremacy by becoming Americanized, others by retreating into traditional Indianism. But some have tried to make the best of both worlds, indeed of all the worlds—the best of Indianism, the best of Christianity, and the best of those Other Worlds of transcendental experience, where the soul knows itself as unconditioned and of like nature with the divine. Hence the Native American Church. In it two great appetites of the soul— the urge to independence and self-determination and the urge to self-transcendence—were fused with, and interpreted in the light of, a third— the urge to worship, to justify the ways of God to man, to explain the universe by means of a coherent theology.

Lo, the poor Indian, whose untutored mind
Clothes him in front, but leaves him bare behind.

But actually it is we, the rich and highly educated whites, who have left ourselves bare behind. We cover our anterior nakedness with some philosophy—Christian, Marxian, Freudo-Physicalist—but abaft we remain uncovered, at the mercy of all the winds of circumstance. The poor Indian, on the other hand, has had the wit to protect his rear by supplementing the fig leaf of a theology with the breechclout of transcendental experience.

I am not so foolish as to equate what happens under the influence of mescalin or of any other drug, prepared or in the future preparable, with the realization of the end and ultimate purpose of human life: Enlightenment, the Beatific Vision. All I am suggesting is that the mescalin experience is what Catholic theologians call a "gratuitous grace," not necessary to salvation but potentially helpful and to be accepted thankfully, if made available. To be shaken out of the ruts of ordinary perception, to be shown for a few timeless hours the outer and the inner world, not as they appear to an animal obsessed with survival or to a human being obsessed with words and notions, but as they are apprehended, directly and unconditionally, by Mind at Large—this is an experience of inestimable value to everyone and especially to the intellectual. For the intellectual is by definition the man for whom, in Goethe's phrase, "the word is essentially fruitful." He is the man who feels that "what we perceive by the eye is foreign to us as such and need not impress us deeply." And yet, though himself an intellectual and one of the supreme masters of language, Goethe did not always agree with his own evaluation of the word. "We talk," he wrote in middle life, "far too much. We should talk less and draw more. I personally should like to renounce speech altogether and, like organic Nature, communicate everything I have to say in sketches. That fig tree, this little snake, the cocoon on my window sill quietly awaiting its future—all these are momentous signatures. A person able to decipher their meaning properly would soon be able to dispense with the written or the spoken word altogether. The more I think of it, there is something futile, mediocre, even (I am tempted to say) foppish about speech. By contrast, how the gravity of Nature and her silence startle you, when you stand face to face with her, undistracted, before a barren ridge or in the desolation of the ancient hills." We can never dispense with language and the other symbol systems; for it is by means of them, and only by their means, that we have raised ourselves above the brutes, to the level of human beings. But we can easily become the victims as well as the beneficiaries of these systems. We must learn how to handle words effectively; but at the same time we must preserve and, if necessary, intensify our ability to look at the world directly and not through that half opaque medium of concepts, which distorts every given fact into the all too familiar likeness of some generic label or explanatory abstraction. . . .

Systematic reasoning is something we could not, as a species or as individuals, possibly do without. But neither, if we are to remain sane, can we possibly do without direct perception, the more unsystematic the better, of the inner and outer worlds into which we have been born. This given reality is an infinite which passes all understanding and yet admits of being directly and in some sort totally apprehended. It is a transcendence belonging to another order than the human, and yet it may be present to us as a felt immanence, an experienced participation. To be enlightened is to be aware, always, of total reality in its immanent otherness—to be aware of it and yet to remain in a condition to survive as an animal, to think and feel as a human being, to resort whenever expedient to systematic reasoning. Our goal is to discover that we have always been where we ought to be. Unhappily we make the task exceedingly difficult for ourselves. Meanwhile, however, there are gratuitous graces in the form of partial and fleeting realizations. Under a more realistic, a less exclusively verbal system of education than ours, every Angel (in Blake's sense of that word) would be permitted as a sabbatical treat, would be urged and even, if necessary, compelled to take an occasional trip through some chemical Door in the Wall into the world of transcendental experience. If it terrified him, it would be unfortunate but probably salutary. If it brought him a brief but timeless illumination, so much the better. In either case the Angel might lose a little of the confident insolence sprouting from systematic reasoning and the consciousness of having read all the books.

Near the end of his life Aquinas experienced Infused Contemplation. Thereafter he refused to go back to work on his unfinished book. Compared with *this,* everything he had read and argued about and written—Aristotle and the Sentences, the Questions, the Propositions, the majestic Summas— was no better than chaff or straw. For most intellectuals such a sit-down strike would be inadvisable, even morally wrong. But the Angelic Doctor had done more systematic reasoning than any twelve ordinary Angels, and was already ripe for death. He had earned the right, in those last months of his mortality, to turn away from merely symbolic straw and chaff to the bread of actual and substantial Fact. For Angels of a lower order and with better prospects of longevity, there must be a return to the straw. But the man who comes back through the Door in the Wall will never be quite the same as the man who went out. He will be wiser but less cocksure, happier but less self-satisfied, humbler in acknowledging his ignorance yet better equipped to understand the relationship of words to things, of systematic reasoning to the unfathomable Mystery which it tries, forever vainly, to comprehend.

Profane Mysticism

R. C. Zaehner / from *Mysticism Sacred and Profane*

R. C. Zaehner (1913–) is Spalding Professor of Eastern Relgions and Ethics at Oxford. He is editor of the Encyclopedia of Living Religions *and has written many books dealing with Zoroastrianism, Hinduism, and other oriental religions.*

About the time Huxley was engaged in publishing his work on "the perennial philosophy," Zaehner was converting to Roman Catholicism. In 1957, Zaehner published a book entitled Mysticism Sacred and Profane. *As he admits on the opening page, the entire book was designed as an answer to Huxley's* The Doors of Perception. *To Zaehner, Huxley's claim that chemically induced states are equivalent to authentic moments of mysticism approaches blasphemy. Hence Zaehner set out to analyze Huxley's argument, to duplicate his experiences, and to show, by assessing the nature of non-chemical mysticism, that Huxley did not really know what mysticism was. One of the most curious parts of the book is Appendix B, in which Zaehner records his own experiences with mescalin. The chemical seems to have done nothing for Zaehner. Except for the rose window in Christ Church Cathedral, the rest of the phenomena he courted, a la Huxley, continued to look the way they always had. He did experience certain physiological differences—especially a feeling of cold—and he laughed immoderately during the interview. But nothing in his account would lead one to suspect that the experience was even so powerful as taking ether from an old-time dentist. Zaehner summarizes the effect of the mescalin by saying that it plunged him into "a universe of farce."*

Zaehner claims to have had a mystical experience, similar to Huxley's experience but not induced by any external means, when he was a young man. Furthermore, although his specialty has been Zoroastrianism, a religion which has no mysticism, he is clearly familiar with and sympathetic to the mystical experience. Like a good professor—and a good Roman Catholic—he is dubious about claims to such experiences and wishes to test them against the records of such figures as Henry Suso, a pupil of Meister Eckhart. But his doubts are not a sign of hostility. Our selections are taken from the introduction and second chapter of Mysticism Sacred and Profane. *As Zaehner makes abundantly clear, he regards Huxley's book as a "challenge" in the knightly sense of that word; he takes up the challenge and goes forth to do battle with the potions and drugs of "Puff the Magic Dragon."*

His principal objection to Huxley's praise of mescalin is that it comes from an urge to escape, which is characteristic of such heresies as Gnosticism and Manichaeanism. Huxley has failed to distinguish, says Zaehner, between "escape from selfhood" and "escape from the environment." The first is a sign of what William James calls the "sick soul"; the second, of what one of his authorities, Commaraswamy, terms the "spiritual proletariat." As the debased industrial worker escapes his drab surroundings by liquor, so Huxley seems to be counselling the spiritual proletariat to use chemicals to escape the drabness of its world: opium is the religion of the people. All such escapism is, however, unrealistic and perhaps even profane. For Zaehner, the sacred way is the right way, and the bulk of his book is devoted to distinguishing the sacred from the profane.

Introduction

It should be said at the outset that this book owes its genesis to Mr. Aldous Huxley. Had *The Doors of Perception* never been published, it is extremely doubtful whether the present author would have been rash enough to enter the field of comparative mysticism. Mr. Huxley left us no choice. For however much we may be disposed to make allowances for enthusiastic exaggeration in Mr. Huxley's account of his experiences when under the influence of mescalin, we cannot escape the fact that there underlies Mr. Huxley's attitude to praeternatural experiences a conviction that they must all be basically the same and that what he experienced under mescalin can therefore be related to the highest concepts of religion which the mystic claims to realize at least in part. The Beatific Vision, *Sac-cid-ānanda*, the Dharma-Body of the Buddha, these tremendous words all became "as evident as Euclid" to Mr. Huxley when under the influence of the drug.

In *The Doors of Perception* Mr. Huxley seemed to assume that praeter-natural experiences, conveniently described by the all-embracing term "mysticism," must all be the same in essence, no matter whether they be the result of intensive ascetic training, of a prolonged course of Yoga techniques, or simply of the taking of drugs. In making these assumptions, of course, Mr. Huxley was doing nothing new. We have been told *ad nauseam* that mysticism is the highest expression of religion and that it appears in all ages and in all places in a more or less identical form, often in a religious milieu that would seem to be the reverse of propitious. This view has recently been reaffirmed by Professor A. J. Arberry who writes: "It has become a platitude to observe that mysticism is essentially one and the same, whatever may be the religion professed by the individual mystic: a constant and un-varying phenomenon of the universal yearning of the human spirit for personal communion with God." Similarly Dr. Enid Starkie, in discussing Rimbaud's ecstasies, writes: "In his experience of God Rimbaud reached, without orthodox beliefs, the stage which mystics seek to attain, where there is no longer possibility for belief or disbelief, for doubt or for reflection, but only pure sensation, ecstasy and union with the Almighty." And again we are told: "In *Les Illuminations* is found expressed, as nowhere else—except perhaps in the poems of Saint John of the Cross—man's eternal longing for spiritual satisfaction and beauty." In actual fact there would appear to be nothing in Rimbaud to show that the poet ever considered that he had at-tained to union with God or that his ecstasies had any direct connexion with Him: nor does Dr. Starkie see fit to develop the interesting comparison with St. John of the Cross, nor is any attempt made to establish its validity. This is only too typical of the great majority of writers on mysticism. It will suffice to quote only one more example, for, as Professor Arberry has rightly re-marked, "it has become a platitude."

The platitude was earlier enunciated by Professor Arberry's eminent predecessor in the Chair of Arabic at the University of Cambridge, E. G. Browne, the great Orientalist who did so much to familiarize the English-speaking world with Persian civilization. On the subject of mysticism he wrote: "There is hardly any soil, be it ever so barren, where it [mysticism] will not strike root; hardly any creed, however stern, however formal, round which it will not twine itself. It is, indeed, the eternal cry of the human soul for rest; the insatiable longing of a being wherein infinite ideals are fettered and cramped by a miserable actuality; and so long as man is less than an angel and more than a beast, this cry will not for a moment fail to make itself heard. Wonderfully uniform, too, is its tenor: in all ages, in all countries, in all creeds, whether it come from the Brahmin sage, the Greek philosopher, the Persian poet, or the Christian quietist, it is in essence an enunciation more or less clear, more or less eloquent, of the aspiration of the soul to cease altogether from self, and to be at one with God."

Always it is *assumed* that mysticism is "essentially one and the same": rarely is any attempt made to substantiate the assumption, and rarely are the equally significant differences analysed. We are greatly indebted to Mr. Huxley in that, in *The Doors of Perception,* he has carried the popular view to its logical conclusion: for since he has proved that praeternatural experi-ence of the most vivid kind can be acquired by the taking of drugs and since the state of the drug-taker's consciousness bears at least a superficial resemblance to that of the religious mystic in that time and space appear to be transcended, must it not follow that this experience is "one and the same" as that of the generally accredited mystics?

Huxley could, and should, have gone farther. Mescalin is clinically used to produce artificially a state akin to schizophrenia, more specifically the manic phase of the manic-depressive psychosis. It must therefore follow, if we accept the fatal "platitude," that not only can "mystical" experience be obtained artificially by the taking of drugs, it is also naturally present in the manic.[1] It must then follow that the vision of God of the mystical saint is "one and the same" as the hallucination of the lunatic. There would appear to be no way out, unless the original "platitudinous" premiss is unsound; and it is into the validity of this premiss that this book will enquire. The book, however, makes no claim to be anything more than a preliminary investigation into what is believed to be a fairly typical cross-section of mystical writing selected from both European and Asiatic sources. In dealing with a category of experience where words have little meaning, it would be hopeless to expect to make out a watertight case to which we could affix that most satisfying of all formulae, "Q.E.D." We can, however, compare the various mystical traditions and show, without allowing ourselves to draw unwarrantable conclusions from seemingly similar phenomena in parallel traditions, what is the distinctive characteristic of each. Further we should be able to decide how far these different experiences are classifiable into types. Since *The Doors of Perception* is the occasion of this book, we must also draw on the experience of people who have taken drugs, of manic-depressives, and of those people,—not so rare as is sometimes thought,—who have been visited by similar experience without any outside stimulus being applied and independently of any religious belief. In the present work we shall have occasion to consider the "mystical" experiences of Richard Jefferies, Proust, and Rimbaud, all of whom help to throw light upon this vexatious problem. In addition we shall have to consider the all-important mystical tradition developed in India, as well as that of the Christians and of the Muslim mystics of Sūfīs. Relying on what the mystics say themselves we will try to ascertain what each different "school" of mysticism considered to be its goal and to see whether they do, in fact, agree either with each other or with the "free-lance" mystics of the type of Jefferies and Rimbaud.

I am aware that it may not be considered legitimate to compare the experiences or the theories of specifically religious mystics with the experiences of Mr. Huxley while under the influence of mescalin on the ground that Mr. Huxley's experiences do not tally with those of other mescalin-takers. It will be pointed out that while the incredible heightening and deepening of the sense of colour seems to be experienced by a large majority of those who take the drug, the sense of rising superior to the "ego" and of what Huxley calls being a "not-self," is not typical. To avoid the impression that I suppose Huxley's experience to be typical of what occurs to all who have taken mescalin, it has seemed worthwhile to attach as an appendix two separate accounts written by independent "patients," both of which have

---

[1] For some details of an actual case of mania see Chapter V [Zaehner's note].

appeared in the British press; and for the sake of further comparison I have also appended an account of my own experiences with the drug.

My interest, however, has been not so much in the drug itself, for, as a producer of what is usually called a "natural mystical experience" it seems to be less effective than nitrous oxide or even hashish; it has been rather in what Mr. Huxley experienced himself and in his assumption that his experience had religious significance. Baudelaire, of course, made similar experiments with hashish and has recorded them, with very different conclusions, in his *Le Poème du Haschisch*. William James, too, took nitrous oxide and, like Huxley, was so shattered by his experience that he found that, in his assessment of reality, he could not possibly disregard the profound transformation of consciousness which it produced. Thus, though Huxley's experiences may not be typical of the effects of mescalin, they are sufficiently similar to those of James with nitrous oxide and Baudelaire's with hashish to be of considerable interest. Moreover, they are so strikingly similar to the experience of nature mystics as to be of value in any general discussion of the subject.

It may seem surprising that the present author who has hitherto specialized on Zoroastrianism, the one major religion that never developed mysticism of any kind, should think fit to enter the field of comparative mysticism, —a field into which angels might well fear to tread. There are three reasons which have decided the present writer to take this step. First it seemed to him that in *The Doors of Perception* Mr. Huxley had thrown down a challenge which no one with any religious convictions at all could afford to neglect, for Huxley did not seem to be merely advocating yet another variety of religious "indifferentism"; he was, simply by equating his own drug-induced experiences with the experiences of those who approach their goal by more conventional means, striking at the roots of all religion that makes any claim to be taken seriously. Such a challenge, when thrown down by an author of Mr. Huxley's standing and popularity, could not, with decency, be allowed to remain unanswered.

Thanks to the good offices of mescalin Mr. Huxley claims to have known "contemplation at its height" though, he is modest enough to add, "not yet in its fullness." On reading these prodigious syllables it occurred to me that I too must have known "contemplation at its height" and that I was, on these grounds alone, qualified to offer some mild criticism of Mr. Huxley's more extravagant conclusions. At the impressionable age of twenty I was in fact the subject of a "mystical" experience which combined all the principal traits described in *The Doors of Perception*. When Mr. Huxley speaks of being a "Not-self in the Not-self which was a chair," I know that, as far as the normal, rational consciousness is concerned, he is talking horrid gibberish, but I equally know that I have myself experienced precisely this and the joy experienced as a result of this uncontrollable and inexplicable expansion of the personality is not to be brushed aside as mere illusion. On the contrary: beside it the ordinary world of sense experience seems pathetically unreal. This occurred to me when I was still an undergraduate and *before* I became interested in Oriental languages: it came wholly unheralded and no stimulants of any kind were involved. I know now that it was a case of what is usually called a "natural mystical experience" which may occur to anyone, whatever his religious faith or lack of it and whatever moral, immoral, or amoral life he may be leading at the time. It is perhaps not without relevance to mention that at the time of this unsolicited experience, apart from a profound dislike of conventional Christianity, I had no religious beliefs of any kind, nor did it occur to me that the experience was in any sense religious. The experience was there in its own right, and I had no desire to explain it.

The wheel has now turned full circle, and I find myself once again a Christian, having entered the Roman Catholic Church in 1946. This is a fact that the reader should know since it would be disingenuous to pretend that, however painstakingly an author may strive after complete objectivity, he will actually achieve it if he has any views of his own at all. It is then only fair to the reader to inform him in advance what the author's religious views actually are although, in at least nine cases out of ten, the intelligent reader should be able to detect the bias (for bias there is bound to be) at an early stage. . . .

Mescalin interpreted

In our last chapter we did little more than summarize Mr. Huxley's experiences under the influence of mescalin. It now remains for us to summarize the conclusions he draws from his experiences.

One thing is certain; and that is that Huxley was taken off his guard by his experiment and almost overwhelmed by it: and the reason for this appears to be that it was the first time he had had an experience of this kind. This is somewhat surprising: for it seemed natural to suppose that an author who has gone through all the outward manifestations of a religious conversion and who, ever since he published *Time Must Have a Stop*, has written about little except his new philosophy of life, must have gone through some supremely meaningful experience which occasioned his conversion and which led him to adopt the esoteric philosophy he has since favoured. This philosophy, which he calls the *philosophia perennis*, claims to be based on the experience of religious mystics of all nations and all faiths. It seemed, then, fair to assume that Huxley had had some praeternatural experience which, by enabling him to discern in all mystics an absolute unity of idea behind a considerable diversity of expression, had convinced him that what the mystics were trying to describe was essentially the same experience, however different the expression of it might be. It came, then, as something of a shock to the present author at least when he read that "until this morning I had known contemplation only in its humbler, its more ordinary forms—as discursive thinking; as a rapt absorption in poetry or painting or music; as a patient waiting upon those inspirations, without which even the prosiest writer cannot hope to accomplish anything; as occasional glimpses, in nature, of Wordsworth's 'something far more deeply interfused'; as systematic silence leading, sometimes, to hints of an 'obscure knowledge.' "

Huxley's concept of "contemplation" seems to have been extremely wide, extending indeed to all the activities of normally educated and cultivated persons. It would never have occurred to the great majority of these to refer to their appreciation, rapt or otherwise, of poetry, painting, or music as "contemplation," a term which has come to have religious overtones. Nor does the word naturally occur to one in connexion with discursive thinking, —a process which is generally regarded as being the reverse of contemplation. It seems, then, fairly clear that, before taking mescalin, Huxley had only the haziest notion of what "contemplation," used in a religious sense, meant. On taking mescalin, he was pitchforked into a realm of experience about which he had written volumes, but which he appears never to have lived. He would, then, appear to have been converted to the *philosophia perennis* on purely intellectual grounds. Because there were certain common characteristics between the mystics of all religions, Huxley came to the conclusion that these common characteristics must represent one metaphysical truth. He does not seem to have realized that even in the writings of the mystics there are divergences not only of approach, which can be attributed to the different religious backgrounds on which they are grafted, but of substance; and that any arbitrary selection from their writings can demonstrate nothing except the subjective views of an individual. What attracted him in the mystics,—using this word in a wide sense for the moment,—was that one and all they claimed to have transcended the empirical "self" and broken into a new and larger sphere of perception. Mysticism, so interpreted, could include not only the classical monistic mysticism of India, but the strictly pantheistic and "pamphysistic" outpourings of, for instance, Walt Whitman: it could include not only those solipsistic Muslim mystics who identified themselves with God, but also pure visionaries who did no such thing, but lived in a different private universe of their own in the manner of William Blake. The only common factor between these different types of mysticism is that, one and all, they provide release from the everyday, humdrum existence of subject-object relationship and of what, for lack of a better word, we must continue to call the individual "ego." That it was precisely such release from the "ego" that Huxley was in search of, emerges clearly from the epilogue of *The Doors of Perception*. . . .

Before proceeding to the discussion of Huxley's experiences after taking mescalin and before seeking to explain it by similar experiences which others have had, and before we attempt to fit it into a general pattern, it would be as well to summarize the conclusions that Huxley has himself drawn from his excursion into the extra-temporal world and to study his recommendations for the greater use of drugs in the furtherance of the happiness of the human race. These recommendations and conclusions will be found in the epilogue to *The Doors of Perception*. They are remarkable. But nowhere does Huxley seem to face up to the main problem: what is the relationship between the ecstasies of persons of heroic sanctity and those of the mescalin-taker?

In the concluding section of his book Huxley implies that the taking of drugs is, or should be, part and parcel of all religion; and on this basis he criticizes Christianity for not "baptizing" mescalin or similar drugs and incorporating them into Christian worship. This sounds outrageous: but it is not really so if we continue to bear in mind his major premiss that "the urge to escape from selfhood and the environment is in almost everyone almost all the time." The premiss seems false, for it does not correspond to observed fact; and it would be only side-stepping the issue to say that this "urge" is more often than not unconscious, since until the urge has been brought up into consciousness, it cannot be stated that it is there at all. The premiss should be emended to some such formula as this: "the urge to escape selfhood and the environment (which are two very different things) is in almost every introspective introvert who is naturally retiring, over-cerebral, and over-sensitive, and who has been brought up in a materialist and industrialized environment, almost all the time." If we are prepared to "emend" the premiss in this way, Huxley's panacea for society becomes intelligible,—except, of course, that we can no longer speak of society as such, but only of a limited number of hyper-civilized persons in search of their soul. In lumping together "the urge to escape from selfhood" and "the urge to escape from the environment" Huxley is confusing two quite separate things. It is what William James calls the "sick soul" which longs to escape from itself, and it is what Coomaraswamy calls the "spiritual proletariat" that aspires to escape from its environment. This "proletariat" now forms a large part of any industrial society. Its members are occupied in doing intrinsically boring jobs, and if they seek relief in the cinema, television, and the "comics," they do so not in order to escape from themselves, but in order to project themselves into what seems to them a more meaningful existence. Their plight is the exact opposite of that of the neurotic intellectual; for the latter lives by and on introspection and is bound, sooner or later, to long to escape from a subject that has become a monomania, whereas the former has not yet got as far as finding a "self" from which he could wish to escape. He feels no urge to escape from himself, only an urge to escape from the dullness of everyday life in which no "self" of any sort has any chance to develop.

On the subject of how mescalin could be utilized for the good of humanity, Huxley's ideas appear to be extraordinarily confused. He oscillates in the most alarming manner between identifying the mescalin experience with the Beatific Vision on the one hand and regarding it as a safe substitute for alcohol on the other. The baffled reader finds himself wondering whether he regards the highest states of the mystics as being not only comparable to, but identical with, the effects of alcohol and drugs, or not. . . .

Huxley is admittedly both incoherent and self-contradictory. Nevertheless, if I understand him correctly, what he seems to be arguing is this. Religion means principally escape from the ego. What have all the great mystics of all time done? They have shaken off their egos, they have become gods, Not-selfs, or what you will. What do alcohol and mescalin do for you? They do precisely this: they enable you to shake off the ego and give you a glorious feeling of release. Therefore they must be of the same nature as religion: therefore they are good. St. Paul, if we interpret the passage at all correctly, took a different view. For what was he trying to say to those ever back-sliding Corinthians?

We are at liberty to imagine him addressing them somewhat as follows: "You Corinthians have come over to Christ because the story of the life, death, and resurrection of Jesus of Nazareth which has taken place in Judaea in our own times, seems so striking a confirmation and actualization in history and in time of what your mystery religions have always taught. In your Bacchic orgies you thought that, by devouring the quivering flesh of beasts, you were entering into direct contact with the divine. This you did in a state of frenzy, even madness. You may have thought that this was what I offered you in the sacrificial meal we call the *agape*. If you did, you were wrong: for whereas your own sacrificial meals may well have pre-figured the Christian sacrament, they were essentially different in kind. They provided you certainly with a temporary release from your egos; and that is why they satisfied you, and will probably satisfy others like you till the end of time. Strong drink, you found, contributed to the attainment of ecstasy, and for that reason you used it in your ceremonies. This is not, however, what I preach. I preach to you redemption through Christ. When you come to take part in the sacrificial meal, I would prefer that you came without having taken any stimulants. Christ came to make you whole: he did not come to make you ecstatics. He came to make you sane: he did not come to make you mad. Therefore it is wrong to approach his table when you are half-drunk, because, if you do so, you are confusing this new mystery with your own more ancient ones. By the Christian mystery you enter into the life of Christ which is the life of God transmitted by grace to this im-perfect world. In your ancient mysteries you sought to escape out of your-selves: you wanted ecstasy. The Christian mystery is not primarily designed for this purpose. Its purpose is that Christ should live in you, and you should live in Christ. Our Lord said that each and all of us should make full use of the talents that are his; each person must complete and fulfil his natural self. Only then will he be ripe for the life of grace which elevates him above nature on to a supernatural plane. During this process it may be that you will have praeternatural experiences: you may have ecstasies; you may see visions and dream dreams. All this means nothing, for the same effects can be produced by the use of wine or drugs. Do not be led astray into thinking that what happens in the Eucharist is the same as, or even comparable to, what happens to you in a Bacchic orgy. In the Christian Eucharist you will probably have no sensible impression at all. It is not exciting: you will feel nothing; you will *experience* nothing. But something is in fact going on in your soul which in the fullness of time will become apparent in your life. Above all do not mistake elation for grace. Elation or exaltation is a state that is common to saints and sinners alike: it can be produced by alcohol or drugs, but do not confuse that with the grace that is infused into you at our *agape*. For in this *agape* which we call a 'rational oblation,' there is no room for ecstasy. It is a receiving of Christ quietly into the inmost essence of your soul. You must realize that there is a total difference between the two."

I probably have no right to put such words into the mouth of St. Paul personally; but I do think that the sentiments expressed in these words are in harmony with what the Church at large thinks and has always thought on these matters. It would, however, be a grave mistake to underrate the challenge thrown down by Mr. Huxley and by many who think like him. What, then, is this challenge? It is this: that religion is a matter of experi-ence, almost of sensation; that religious experience means "mystical" experi-ence; and that mystical experiences are everywhere and always the same. Acting on this assumption Huxley first became interested in the Vedānta philosophy of the Hindus since only in that philosophy is praeternatural experience, deduced from the contents of the Upanisads, made the basis of all speculation. This teaching, in its extreme form, is the philosophy, not so much of the oneness of all things, but of the actual identity of the individual soul with the *Brahman* which can best be translated as "the Absolute." All mystical experience, according to this school of thought, ultimately leads to this identity,—a conclusion that Westerners may find surprising. By a mystical experience Huxley seems to understand not only the experiences of all the recognized mystics, but experiences such as his own under the influence of mescalin; and, since he is honest, he would be forced to add, the experiences of madness. In Chapter V we will be dealing with the experiences of a manic-depressive; and these show the clearest possible resemblance to Huxley's own experiences. It is not for nothing that Huxley said that he thought he knew what it felt like to be mad. . . .

LAW

James Gould Cozzens chose as a motto for his novel *The Just and the Unjust* this dictum from Lord Hardwicke: "Certainty is the Mother of Repose; therefore the Law aims at Certainty." Yet many lawyers today, especially those whose conception of the law is sociological, deny that certainty is the aim of law. In this section, the late Judge Jerome Frank expresses the relativistic view of law. Opposing him is the late John Courtney Murray, S. J., who argues for an unchanging natural law on which to base human law.

Suspicion of the law and lawyers is both old and prevalent, and for every magnificent and eloquent expression of the law's majestic perfection, such as we find in Richard Hooker, there are satiric mockeries of its rapacious inefficiency, like the picture of Chancery in Dickens' novel *Bleak House*.

In his poem entitled "Law Like Love," W. H. Auden presents a catalogue of legal conceptions held by the various classes of society. For the gardener and the farmer, law is the sun or nature. For grandparents, it is the wisdom of the old; for grandchildren, it is the "senses of the young." For the priest, it is "the words in my priestly book." For the judge, "Law is the Law." For "law-abiding scholars," it is "only crimes/Punished by places and by times." For some it is "fate," for others it is the "state," and for still others it is dead and gone. The "loud and angry crowd" says "Law is We"; the "soft idiot" says it is "Me." The crowd represents mobocracy, the tyrannous majority; the idiot—whether his privacy be taken as pathological or willful— represents egocentric anarchism. To mediate between the claims of the individual and of the group is one of law's principal goals. At this point two major views of jurisprudence contend: the liberal faith that law must, in order to subserve immediate human needs, be capable of flexible adjustment to changing social circumstances and the conservative conviction that the law is superior to the flux of particular interests and claims.

The two legal issues chosen, desegregation and obscenity, clearly and sharply reflect the tension between legal relativism and legal absolutism. The problem of desegregation is rooted in the early history of this country—the first slaves arrived in the same year that representative government began in Virginia. As the Negro population has grown, spreading from agricultural slavery to urban "ghettos," slavery's diseased consequences have infected the cultural, moral, and economic life of the nation. In dealing with them, traditional ideas of law and order have been subjected to intense and even violent strains.

More specifically cultural, the problems arising from obscene literature test fundamental Western commitments to reason and decency. Society inevitably seeks to protect itself from insidious ethical influence and disruptive social change. To what extent society may exercise public criticism—for censorship is a form of criticism—is still unsettled by the courts and the laws of the land. At the heart of the matter lies the problem of whether "ideas have consequences"—in Richard Weaver's phrase—for to abandon all forms of public criticism is to deny literature its power either to corrupt or to edify.

Arguments about desegregation and censorship, therefore, aptly exemplify the attempts by men of good will to define the proper ratio of permanence to change in the good society. All such attempts necessitate the examination of legal principles.

The Myth of Legal Certainty
Jerome Frank/from *Law and the Modern Mind*

Judge Jerome Frank (1889–1957), a professional lawyer, was one of those legalists who found scope for their sociological commitments in governmental service. Active in the New Deal under Franklin Roosevelt, he participated in the work of the Agricultural Adjustment Administration and the Reconstruction Finance Corporation and was for years on the board of the Securities and Exchange Commission. Such interests and experience are the natural outgrowth of Frank's views, set forth with caustic clarity in his book Law and the Modern Mind *(1930). Portions of the first two chapters of this book are reprinted here. Frank reveals his position in the opening heading: "The Basic Legal Myth, and Some of Its Consequences." Extending the thought of jurists like Maitland, Holmes, Pound, Cardozo, and Radin, Frank asserts that "the law always has been, is now, and will ever continue to be, largely vague and variable." How, then, Frank asks, can the public fondly insist on exactness and predictability in law? His answer—foreshadowed by his pejorative use of the word* myth—*is that the demand for what he calls "excessive legal stability" originates "not in reality but in a yearning for something unreal."*

For a partial explanation of this phenomenon, Frank turns, in heavily psychological language, to human nature, particularly the nature of the child. In appealing to human nature, Frank meets on common yet disputed ground with John Courtney Murray, S. J., who is presented as polar spokesman; there are for Frank basic laws of human nature, but they are not such that a legal system can be built on them. Instead, we can only use them to demolish legal systems that are inflexible. It is in the child's craving for an authority figure, a father figure, that the adult's craving for an absolute and eternal law takes its obscure mythic roots. Father Murray's conception of human nature is far different. It is clear that Frank's theories convert Father Murray's notion of a divinely based natural law into an infantile fantasy; in Frank we find a sharp example of rationalistic religious skepticism, one of the liberal's principal attitudes.

This mixture of psychology and sociology is, of course, fertile soil for such issues as desegregation and obscenity, the two selected here for exposition and analysis. Liberal spokesmen on these two issues couch their arguments in terms that are either specifically psychological and sociological or that presuppose the concepts of these two fields. In general, the liberals avoid strict legal terminology and appeal to cultural norms. The conservative spokesmen, in contrast, lean heavily on the letter of the law and seek to avoid the reproach of being narrow-minded and pharisaical by appealing to the authority of principles that underlie human laws. In Frank's view, this authority reduces to childish and Freudian needs; it is merely biological.

The basic myth
The lay attitude towards lawyers is a compound of contradictions, a mingling of respect and derision. Although lawyers occupy leading positions in government and industry, although the public looks to them for guidance in

meeting its most vital problems, yet concurrently it sneers at them as tricksters and quibblers.

Respect for the bar is not difficult to explain. Justice, the protection of life, the sanctity of property, the direction of social control—these fundamentals are the business of the law and of its ministers, the lawyers. Inevitably the importance of such functions invests the legal profession with dignity.

But coupled with a deference towards their function there is cynical disdain of the lawyers themselves. . . .

Diatribes against lawyers contain such words and phrases as "duplicity," "equivocation," "evasions," "a vast system of deception," "juggling," "sleight of hand," "craft and circumvention," "the art of puzzling and confounding," "darken by elucidation," "the pettifoging, hypocritical, brigandage rampant under forms of law." Kipling expresses the feeling of many in his fling at the "tribe who describe with a gibe the perversions of Justice.". . .

What lies back of this popular criticism? It appears to be founded on a belief that the lawyers complicate the law, and complicate it wantonly and unnecessarily, that, if the legal profession did not interpose its craftiness and guile, the law could be clear, exact and certain. The layman thinks that it would be possible so to revise the law books that they would become something like logarithm tables, that the lawyers could, if only they would, contrive some kind of legal slide rule for finding exact legal answers. Public opinion agrees with Napoleon who was sure that "it would be possible to reduce laws to simple geometrical demonstrations, so that whoever could read and tie two ideas together would be capable of pronouncing on them."

But the law as we have it is uncertain, indefinite, subject to incalculable changes. This condition the public ascribes to the men of law; the average person considers either that lawyers are grossly negligent or that they are guilty of malpractice, venally obscuring simple legal truths in order to foment needless litigation, engaging in a guild conspiracy of distortion and obfuscation in the interest of larger fees.

Now it must be conceded that, if the law can be made certain and invariable, the lawyers are grievously at fault. For the layman is justified in his opinion that the coefficient of legal uncertainty is unquestionably large, that to predict the decisions of the courts on many a point is impossible. Any competent lawyer, during any rainy Sunday afternoon, could prepare a list of hundreds of comparatively simple legal questions to which any other equally competent lawyer would scarcely venture to give unequivocal answers.

Yet the layman errs in his belief that this lack of precision and finality is to be ascribed to the lawyers. The truth of the matter is that the popular notion of the possibilities of legal exactness is based upon a misconception. The law always has been, is now, and will ever continue to be, largely vague and variable. And how could this well be otherwise? The law deals with human relations in their most complicated aspects. The whole confused, shifting helter-skelter of life parades before it—more confused than ever, in our kaleidoscopic age.

Even in a relatively static society, men have never been able to construct a comprehensive, eternized set of rules anticipating all possible legal disputes and settling them in advance. Even in such a social order no one can foresee all the future permutations and combinations of events; situations are bound to occur which were never contemplated when the original rules were made. How much less is such a frozen legal system possible in modern times. New instruments of production, new modes of travel and of dwelling, new credit and ownership devices, new concentrations of capital, new social customs, habits, aims and ideals—all these factors of innovation make vain the hope that definitive legal rules can be drafted that will forever after solve all legal problems. When human relationships are transforming daily, legal relationships cannot be expressed in enduring form. The constant development of unprecedented problems requires a legal system capable of fluidity and pliancy.[1] Our society would be strait-jacketed were not the courts, with the able assistance of the lawyers, constantly overhauling the law and adapting it to the realities of ever-changing social, industrial and political conditions; although changes cannot be made lightly, yet law must be more or less impermanent, experimental and therefore not nicely calculable. *Much of the uncertainty of law is not an unfortunate accident: it is of immense social value.*

In fields other than the law there is today a willingness to accept probabilities and to forego the hope of finding the absolutely certain. Even in physics and chemistry, where a high degree of quantitative exactness is possible, modern leaders of thought are recognizing that finality and ultimate precision are not to be attained. The physicists, indeed, have just announced the Principle of Uncertainty or Indeterminacy. If there can be nothing like complete definiteness in the natural sciences, it is surely absurd to expect to realize even approximate certainty and predictability in law, dealing as it does with the vagaries of complicated human adjustments. . . .

It would seem, then, that the legal practitioners must be aware of the unsettled condition of the law. Yet observe the arguments of counsel in addressing the courts, or the very opinions of the courts themselves: they are worded as if correct decisions were arrived at by logical deduction from a precise and pre-existing body of legal rules. Seldom do judges disclose any contingent elements in their reasoning, any doubts or lack of wholehearted conviction. . . .

Here we arrive at a curious problem: Why do men crave an undesirable and indeed unrealizable permanence and fixity in law? Why in a modern world does the ancient dream persist of a comprehensive and unchanging body of law? Why do the generality of lawyers insist that law should and can be clearly knowable and precisely predictable although, by doing

---

[1]Unheeded by most members of the Bar, a minority group of brilliant critics of our legal system have demonstrated that anything like complete legal certainty cannot be realized. They have made clear that, in the very nature of things, not nearly as much rigidity in law exists or can be procured as laymen or most lawyers suppose. The law, they point out, can make only relative and temporary compromises between stability and indispensable adjustment to the constantly shifting factors of social life. "All thinking about law has struggled to reconcile the conflicting demands of the need of stability and the need of change." And this struggle has been incessant. Law, in attempting a harmony of these conflicting demands, is at best governed by "the logic of probabilities." This point the reader will find expounded by such writers as Maine, Holmes, Pound, Cohen, Cardozo, Cook, Demogue, Geny, Gmelin, Gray, Green, Coudert, Bingham, Yntema, Hutcheson, Radin, Llewellyn, and Lehman.

Evidence of the uncertain character of the law will appear in the following chapters.

so, they justify a popular belief in an absurd standard of legal exactness? Why do lawyers, indeed, themselves recognize such an absurd standard, which makes their admirable and socially valuable achievement—keeping the law supple and flexible—seem bungling and harmful? Why do men of our time repeat the complaint made by Francis Bacon several hundred years since, that "our laws, as they now stand, are subject to great incertainties" and adhere to his conviction that such "incertainties" are pernicious and altogether avoidable?

Why this unceasing quest of what is unobtainable and would often be undesirable? . . .

A partial explanation

We are on the trail of a stubborn illusion. Where better, then, to look for clues than in the direction of childhood? For in children's problems, and in children's modes of meeting their problems, are to be found the sources of most of the confirmed illusions of later years. . . .

The child at birth is literally forced from a small world of almost complete and effortless security into a new environment which at once sets up a series of demands. Strange sensations of light, sound, touch and smell attack him. The nearly perfect pre-birth harmony and serenity are over. The infant now must breathe and eat. His struggle for existence has begun. But his wants, at first, are few and are satisfied with a minimum of strain on his own part. The parents do their best to meet, almost instantly, the infant's desires. In this sense, he approximates omnipotence, because, relative to his askings, he achieves nearly complete obedience. His hand-wavings and cries magically command responses on the part of the environment.

As infancy recedes his direct omnipotence diminishes. But that there is omnipotence somewhere the child does not doubt. Chance does not yet exist for him. Everything is explainable. All events can be accounted for. There is, he believes, no happening without a knowable reason. The contingent and the accidental are unthinkable. There must always be whys and wherefores. Chaos is beyond belief. Order and rule govern all.

As early childhood passes and consciousness grows keener, now and again the child becomes sharply aware of his incapacity for controlling the crushing, heedless, reluctant and uncertain facts of the outer world. Recurrently confusion descends upon him. Sudden experiences surprise him, crash in on his childish scheme of things, and temporarily overwhelm him. Fears beset him—fear of the vague things that stalk the darkness, fear of the unruly, the unseen, the horrible bogies of the unknown.

Then he rushes to his parents for help. They stand between him and the multitudinous cruelties and vagaries of life. They are all-powerful, all-knowing. If the child can no longer believe himself capable of controlling the universe, he can still believe that his parents do so—and for him. They hold sway over the outer world, they run things, they are rulers and protectors. They know everything. They understand the strange ways of life which are at times oppressively baffling to him. Father and mother are unabashed by complications. They know what is right and what is wrong. They bring order out of what seems to be chaos.

The child still possesses omnipotence—but now, vicariously. Through his dependence upon his parents' omnipotence he finds relief from unbearable uncertainty. His overestimation of the parental powers is an essential of his development.

It must not be overlooked that a significant division of parental functions takes place early in the life of the child. In all communities where the father is head of the family, the mother comes to "represent the nearer and more familiar influence, domestic tenderness, the help, the rest and the solace to which the child can always turn," writes Malinowski in a recent anthropological study. But "the father has to adopt the position of the final arbiter in force and authority. He has gradually to cast off the rôle of tender and protective friend, and to adopt the position of strict judge, and hard executor of law." And so, in the childish appraisal of the parents, the mother tends to become the embodiment of all that is protectively tender while the father personifies all that is certain, secure, infallible, and embodies exact law-making, law-pronouncing and law-enforcing. The child, in his struggle for existence, makes vital use of his belief in an omniscient and omnipotent father, a father who lays down infallible and precise rules of conduct.

Then, slowly, repeated experiences erode this fictional overestimate. "Adam," said Mark Twain's Eve, "knows ever so many things, but, poor dear, most of them aren't so." To the child, parental wisdom now comes to seem like Adam's. There are many things father doesn't know, things he can't do. Other humans successfully oppose him. And there are forces loose in the world beyond his control. One's own father is at times helpless, deficient; he is all-too-human. The child's lofty conception of fatherly dignity and infallibility crumbles before the cumulative evidence of disappointing paternal weakness and ignorance.

But the average child cannot completely accept this disillusionment. He has formed an irresistible need for an omniscient and omnipotent father who shall stand between him and life's uncertainties. The child's own sense of power and control vanished in early infancy. Now life seems to demand that he shall take a next step and abandon his reliance on the conviction that someone close to him possesses consummate wisdom. His attitudes and adaptations had been built upon his relations to his idealized, his incomparable father. The child is disoriented. Again panic fear attacks him. He is unwilling and largely unable to accept as realities the ungovernable, the unorderable aspects of life. Surely, he feels, somewhere there must be Someone who can control events, make the dark spots light, make the uncertain clear. Chance and contingency he will not submit to as finalities; the apparently fortuitous must be susceptible of subjection to the rule of some person—a person, too, like his father, whom the child can propitiate.

Many are the persons who become substitutes for the deposed father: the priest or pastor, the rulers and leaders of the group. They, too, turn out to be disappointing. But the demand for fatherly authority does not die. To be sure, as the child grows into manhood, this demand grows less and less vocal, more and more unconscious. The father-substitutes become less definite in form, more vague and impersonal. But the relation to the father has become a paradigm, a prototype of later relations. Concealed and submerged, there persists a longing to reproduce the father-child pattern, to escape uncertainty and confusion through the rediscovery of a father.

For although as we grow older we are compelled to some extent to acknowledge the existence of reasonless, limitless and indeterminate aspects of life, yet most of us strive to blind our eyes to them. And then, at moments when chaos becomes too evident to be denied, we rush, fear-ridden, as if we were children, to some protective father-like authority. Most men, child-ishly dreading the unknown, strive to find behind everyday experiences a Something resembling paternal control, a Something that can be relied upon to insure, somehow, against the apparent reality of the chanciness and disorder of events. Few are the persons able to relinquish the props of child-hood and bravely admit that life is full of unavoidable hazards beyond the control, direct or indirect, of finite humans. . . .

That religion shows the effects of the childish desire to recapture a father-controlled world has been often observed. But the effect on the law of this childish desire has escaped attention. And yet it is obvious enough: To the child the father is the Infallible Judge, the Maker of definite rules of conduct. He knows precisely what is right and what is wrong and, as head of the family, sits in judgment and punishes misdeeds. The Law—a body of rules apparently devised for infallibly determining what is right and what is wrong and for deciding who should be punished for misdeeds—inevitably becomes a partial substitute for the Father-as-Infallible-Judge. That is, the desire persists in grown men to recapture, through a rediscovery of a father, a childish, completely controllable universe, and that desire seeks satisfaction in a partial, unconscious, anthropomorphizing of Law, in ascribing to the Law some of the characteristics of the child's Father-Judge. That childish longing is an important element in the explanation of the absurdly unrealistic notion that law is, or can be made, entirely certain and definitely predictable.

Immutable Natural Law
John Courtney Murray, S.J./from "Natural Law and Public Consensus"

John Courtney Murray, S.J., (1904–1967) for a long time a professor of theology at Woodstock College, belonged to that class of Roman Catholics who baptized their orthodoxy in the mainstream of American secularism. The result has been an urbane and penetrating refreshening of both traditions. Father Murray's intellectual roots are in the Middle Ages—as his frequent citations from St. Thomas Aquinas show—and thus he is allied to the great conservative tradition reaching directly back to Aristotle. Psychology—the science of the psyche—for him is not only biological but also spiritual. Father Murray is often credited with having laid the groundwork for the liberal decree of the Vatican II Council in 1965 dealing with religious liberty. He was posthumously given the second annual Adlai E. Stevenson Award by the Catholic Adult Education Center of Chicago. He participated in the work of the Center for the Study of Democratic Institutions, the principal activity of the Fund for the Republic, Inc., which Robert Maynard Hutchins heads. The alliance with the neo-Thomistic Hutchins was natural.

The selection chosen is taken from Father Murray's contribution to a series of papers delivered at the Center, entitled Natural Law and Modern Society (1962), to which Hutchins also contributed. The title of that collection is clearly polar to Jerome Frank's book, Law and the Modern Mind. Both titles contain the words law and modern; the significant changes in the Center's collection are the words natural, modifying law, and society, substituted for mind. Father Murray goes right to the heart of the matter in the title of his chapter: "Natural Law and the Public Consensus."

Consensus is not, as Father Murray says, a synonym for majority opinion, although most people take it that way today; instead, its validity transcends opinion, either of the majority or the minority. As he points out, the Declaration of Independence—a supreme example of pure consensus—begins with the words: "We hold these truths . . . ." (Father Murray has written a book with these words as the title.) Father Murray argues that these words cannot mean: "This is the convergent trend of opinion among us."

Having rejected this vulgar formulation, he asks where these truths, this public consensus, find their justification. Confronted with facts, especially economic facts, what can Americans do to attain economic democracy with justice? The answer, Father Murray says, cannot be stated merely in economic terms. Instead, one must turn to political terms, and these necessarily involve us in moral terms. Hence, he begins the part of his essay excerpted here with this statement: "My proposition is that only the theory of natural law is able to give an account of the public moral experience that is the public consensus." Only by an appeal to natural law can men justify and explain alterations in their mode of government. Consequently, any such alterations will have to be in accordance with this natural law. Awareness of natural law will thus prevent mere sociological change. The implications of this argument for the two issues discussed here—desegregation and obscenity—will become apparent in the conservative spokesmen selected.

My proposition is that only the theory of natural law is able to give an account of the public moral experience that is the public consensus. This consensus is the tradition of reason as emergent in developing form in the special circumstances of American political-economic life.

. . . In order to understand this proposition it is necessary first to rid the doctrine of natural law from the accretion of misunderstandings that have conspired to obscure it. Some of the misunderstandings are naive; others are learned. Some are the product of sheer ignorance; others are the result of polemic preoccupations. It is sometimes said, for instance, that one cannot accept the doctrine of natural law unless one has antecedently accepted "its Roman Catholic presuppositions." This, of course, is silly. So far as I know, and my knowledge goes far enough, the doctrine of natural law has no Roman Catholic presuppositions. Its only presupposition is threefold: that man is intelligent; that reality is intelligible; and that reality, as grasped by

intelligence, imposes on the will the obligation that it be obeyed in its demands for action or abstention. Even these statements are not properly
"presuppositions"; they are susceptible of verification.

The permeability of reality, especially moral reality, to intelligence is
limited, as human intelligence itself is limited. But the limitations do not
destroy the capacity of intelligence to do three things, in an order of diminishing ease and certainty.

First, intelligence can grasp the ethical *a priori*, the original and common
principles of the moral consciousness, which do not originate in experience,
as reason itself does not so originate, but which dawn, as it were, as reason
itself emerges from the darkness of infant animalism. Human reason that is
conscious of itself is also conscious of the primary truths both of the intellectual and of the moral consciousness—that what is true cannot at the same
time and in the same respect be false, and that what is good is to be done
and what is evil avoided. Second, after some elementary experience of the
basic situations of human life, and upon some little reflection on the meaning
of terms, intelligence can grasp the meaning of "good" and "evil" in these
situations and therefore know what is to be done or avoided in them. For
instance, to know the meaning of "parent" and of "disrespect" is to know
a primary principle of the natural law, that disrespect to parents is evil,
intrinsically and antecedent to any human prohibition. Third, as the experience of reality unfolds in the unfolding of the relationships and situations that are the reality of human life, intelligence, with the aid of simple
reasoning, can know, and know to be obligatory, a set of natural law principles that are derivative. These, in general, are the precepts of the Deca-
logue (excepting the third, which is positive divine law).

These three achievements—requiring, as they do, only common human
experience and only a modicum of reflection and reasoning—are accessible
to the human intelligence as such, at least *ut in pluribus* [for the most part],
in St. Thomas' repeated qualification. The qualification means that rational
human nature works competently in most men, but in particular instances
it may fail. In other words, man is not an animal, ruled by unerring instinct.
His guide to action is practical judgment; and this act of reason may go astray,
for discernible causes, here and there, now and then.

There is a fourth area of achievement open to the moral reason of man.
It concerns particular principles which represent the requirements of rational
human nature in more complex human relationships and amid the institutional developments that accompany the progress of civilization. This area
is reserved for those whom St. Thomas called "the wise" *(sapientes)*. The
reason for the reservation is clear. The farther the human mind advances
toward apprehending the particulars of morals, the greater is the part that
knowledge, experience, reflection, and dispassionateness of judgment must
play. To grasp the bearing of fundamental moral truth on particular human
relations and on concrete social institutions requires a prior understanding
of these relations and these institutions. They are, in the case, the "reality"
in whose dense depths the demands of reason must be discerned and then
obeyed. No reflection on experience is needed to know the principle of
justice, *suum cuique* ("to each what is his"). But a scientific analysis of the

functioning of economic co-operation is needed to know what a just settlement of a wage dispute might be.

The elaboration of these particular and detailed—or, in traditional language, "remote"—principles of natural law falls therefore to the wise. One might even better say, in George Washington's famous phrase, "the wise and honest." Not just knowledgeability but rectitude of judgment is required. In farthest antiquity the wise were the lawgivers, who declared the law—that is, the customs—to the community and thus brought to consciousness the moral principles of community life which otherwise would not or perhaps could not be grasped by the individual. This is still the function of civil legislation, which has not lost its character as a moral discipline, even though much legislation is now technical. In the course of human evolution the wise came to include the philosophers as well as the jurists. And in the growing complexity of the full human reality that is the characteristic of advanced civilization, these wise men have come to depend more and more on other scientific disciplines for aid in that analysis of reality which is the condition of all moral judgment. The dynamism behind the whole process was stated by St. Thomas: "Since a rational soul is the proper form of man, there is in every man a natural inclination to act according to reason; and this is to act according to virtue."[1] To act against reason is to act against nature, that is, to sin.

St. Thomas, of course, also had quite clearly in mind that "man" is not an abstract essence but a historical existent, who does not act in a vacuum of time and space, at the same time that he must always act as a man, and not as an animal or an angel. The fundamental structure of man's nature is, of course, permanent and unchanging; and correlatively constant are the elementary human experiences. Every man, simply because he is a man, has to "meet" himself, others, and God, and in these relationships to avoid the evil and do the good that must come home to him as evidently evil or good, if he at all understands the situation, as he must—*ut in pluribus.* These are truths that even the ethical relativists go to great trouble to avoid in their theories, however little trouble they have in recognizing them in their own practical lives. Normally they are men who keep to moderation and avoid extremes; who render to others their due; who fulfill their contracts; who love their wives and cherish their children; who flee ignorance and seek truth; who honor their God, or at least their idols; and who otherwise conduct themselves as well-behaved natural law jurists, even though they would be horrified to be thought of as such. History does not alter the basic structure of human nature, nor affect the substance of the elementary human experiences, nor open before man wholly new destinies. Therefore history cannot alter the natural law, insofar as a natural law is constituted by the ethical *a priori,* by the primary principles of the moral reason, and by their immediate derivatives. History has not, for instance, abolished the Ten Commandments.

But history, as any history book shows, does change what I have called the human reality. It evokes situations that never happened before. It calls into being relationships that had not existed. It involves human life in an

---

[1] *Summa theologiae, Prima secundae,* q. 94, art. 3 (ed. Marietti, Taurini-Romae, 1952, II, 427).

increasing multitude of institutions of all kinds, which proliferate in response to new human needs and desires, as well as in consequence of the creative possibilities that are inexhaustibly resident in human freedom. History has spread mankind over all the earth in a variety of climates and conditions that call for some adaptation of the human reality. History has here halted, and there hastened, the progress of civilization. It has done the fateful thing of dividing men into nations, thus creating areas of collective self-interest whose harmony is by no means automatic. History, too, has set afoot the great enterprise of science, which has altered the relationship of man to the forces of cosmic nature and imparted to the whole concept of power a qualitatively new dimension. In a word, it has been abundantly proved in history that the nature of man is a historical nature. "The nature of man is susceptible of change," St. Thomas repeatedly states. History continually changes the community of mankind and alters the modes of communication between man and man, as these take form "through external acts." In this sense, the nature of man changes in history, for better or for worse, at the same time that the fundamental structure of human nature, and the essential destinies of the human person, remain untouched and intact.

As all this happens, continually new problems are being put to the wisdom of the wise, at the same time that the same old problems are being put to every man, wise or not. The issue is always the same: What is man or society to do, here and now, in order that personal or social action may fulfill the human inclination to act according to reason? The same old problems get the same old answers, in terms of the same old primary principles of the natural law which, as primary, follow on the permanent structure of the nature of man and furnish the norms whereby man must always act in the constant recurrent basic human situations. In the case of the new problems, however, which are created by the changing structure of human social living, and which concern the particulars of morals, the answers may contain new specifications of old principles: "Things that are just and good may be considered in two ways. There is the formal consideration; and in this sense they are always and everywhere the same, because the principles of right, which are in the natural reason, do not change. There is also the material consideration; and in this sense the same things are not always and everywhere good and just. They have to be determined by the law [he means by custom, or by the declaration of the wise]. This happens on account of the mutability of human nature, and the diverse conditions of men and affairs according to the diversity of times and places."[2]

Even this brief account of the mode and style of natural law thought, and of the various areas in which it operates, should suffice to show the fallacy of certain misunderstandings.

The theory is accused of abstractionism, as if it disregarded experience and undertook to pull all its precepts like so many rabbits out of the metaphysical hat of an abstract human "essence." The theory is also interpreted as an intuitionism, as if it maintained that all natural law precepts were somehow "self-evident." It is also derided as a legalism, as if it proclaimed a

---

[2]*Quaestiones disputatae de malo*, q. 2, art. 4, ad 13m. (ed. Marietti, II, 476).

detailed code of particularized do's and don'ts, nicely drawn up with the aid of logic alone, absolutely normative in all possible circumstances, ready for automatic application, whatever the factual situation may be. The theory is also rejected for its presumed immobilism, as if its concept of an immutable human nature and an unchanging structure of human ends required it to deny the historicity of human existence and forbade it to recognize the virtualities of human freedom.

There is also the biologist interpretation, which imputes to natural law theory a confusion of the "primordial," in a biological sense, with the "natural." This is a particularly gratuitous misinterpretation, since nothing is clearer in natural law theory than its identification of the "natural" with the "rational," or, perhaps better, the "human." Its whole effort is to incorporate the biological values in man, notably his sexual tendencies, into the order of reason, and to deny them the status of the primordial. The primordial in a man—that which is first in order—is his rational soul, the form of humanity, which informs all that is biological in him. There is also the objectivist-rationalist interpretation, which is the premise from which to criticize natural law theory for its supposed neglect of the values of the human person and its deafness to the resonances of intersubjectivity. In point of fact, the theory never forgets that the "nature" with which it deals has no existence except in the person, who is a unique realization of the nature, situated in an order of other unique realizations, whose uniqueness, nevertheless, does not make them atomistic monads, since it is in each instance a form of participation and communication in the one common nature.

Finally, there is the charge that natural law theory is not "Christian," that is, not Protestant. If it be a question of the articulated theory, this is true. The theory is alien to the general Protestant moral system, insofar as there is such a thing. It would not, of course, be difficult to show that the theory is, in germinal fashion, scriptural. But this whole question lies outside the scope of this essay. I shall say only four things.

First, natural law theory does not pretend to do more than it can, which is to give a philosophical account of the moral experience of humanity and to lay down a charter of humanism. It does not show the way to sainthood but only to manhood. It does not promise to transform society into the City of God on earth, but only to prescribe, for the purposes of law and social custom, that minimum of morality which must be observed by the members of a society, if the social environment is to be human and habitable. At that, for a man to be reasonably human, and for a society to be truly civil— these are no mean achievements. They carry man and society to the limits of the obligatory. This moral horizon lies at sufficient distance from the inertness and perversity which are part of the human stuff; it sets for man a goal that is not ignoble.

Second, beyond the fulfillment of the ideal of the reasonable man there lies the perennial question of youth, whatever its age. It is asked in the Gospel: "What do I still lack?" (Matthew 19:20). And there remains the Gospel's austere answer, put in the form of an invitation, but not cast in the categories of ethics, which are good and evil and the obligation to choose between them. It opens the perspectives of a higher choice, to "be a follower of mine." For the making of this choice there is no other motive, no other inner impulse, than the free desire to respond to the prior choice of Him whom one chooses because one has been first chosen.

Third, the mistake would be to imagine that the invitation, "Come, follow me," is a summons somehow to forsake the universe of human nature, somehow to vault above it, somehow to leave law and obligation behind, somehow to enter the half world of an individualist subjectivist "freedom" which pretends to know no other norm save "love." In other words, the Gospel invitation, insofar as it is a summons to the moral life, is not a call to construct a "situation ethics" that knows no general principles of moral living but only particular instances of moral judgment, each one valid only for the instance; and that recognizes no order of moral law that is binding on freedom, but only a freedom that is free and moral only insofar as it is a lawless spontaneity.

Fourth, the law of nature, which prescribes humanity, still exists at the interior of the Gospel invitation, which summons to perfection. What the follower of Christ chooses to perfect is, and can only be, humanity. And the lines of human perfection are already laid down in the structure of man's nature. Where else could they be found? The Christian call is to transcend nature, notably to transcend what is noblest in nature, the faculty of reason. But it is not a call to escape from nature, or to dismantle nature's own structure, and least of all to deny that man is intelligent, that nature is intelligible, and that nature's intelligibilities are laws for the mind that grasps them. Insofar as they touch the moral life, the energies of grace, which are the action of the Holy Spirit, quicken to new and fuller life the dynamisms of nature, which are resident in reason. Were it otherwise, grace would not be supernatural but only miraculous. . . .

Democracy and Desegregation

Sidney Hook / from *Political Power and Personal Freedom*

Sidney Hook (1902–) has had a long and distinguished career as a professor of philosophy, notably at the College of the City of New York. He is the author of many books and articles dealing with social questions in a no-nonsense manner; characteristic titles include Common Sense and the Fifth Amendment; Heresy, Yes—Conspiracy, No; *and* The Paradoxes of Freedom. *The selection excerpted below comes from his book* Political Power and Personal Freedom: Critical Studies in Democracy, Communism, and Civil Rights.

Controversy about desegregation reached a new level of intensity and analysis with the famous decision made by the Supreme Court in 1954, Brown v. Board of Education of Topeka. *As with all decisions made by the Supreme Court on this burning social question, argument has concentrated on the problem of whether the Court is interpreting the Constitution or rewriting and amending it. Conservatives maintain that the Court has disregarded precedent and admitted dubious sociological evidence; liberals claim that the Court showed wisdom in ignoring or reëvaluating previous decisions in the light of new social circumstances. Hook, who strongly supports the Court's decision, does not wish to defend it on legal grounds, for such a defense, in his eyes, "evades the basic moral issues that in the last analysis underlie every fundamental conflict of values and social policy." Hook's use of the word* moral *should not be misinterpreted; for Hook,* moral *does not imply some appeal to a human law based on natural or divine law. Instead, he defines* moral *as "simple ethical principles which are implicit in the Declaration of Independence," principles which, he admits, are "expressed in the language of natural rights" but which "are* best defended in terms of their empirical consequences" *(emphasis ours).*

Hook distinguishes sharply between prejudice and discrimination; prejudice is involuntary, discrimination is a matter of choice. Hence the psychological and sociological evidence is that, whatever one's personal prejudices may be and however much one may be entitled to personal feelings, these prejudices ought not to be enacted in the form of discriminatory behavior which violates the socially justifiable equality of all men. Hook attacks William Faulkner's dictum that "enforced integration is no better than enforced segregation" on the grounds that "the human freedoms we safeguard by legal action against segregation and unfair discrimination are more important than those we restrict." One sees behind this argument the appeal to empirically based social norms, to a humanitarian and liberal relativism. One should, Hook argues, distinguish carefully between "discriminating against" and "discriminating between." He concludes by asserting that "the lawful spread of integrated education in South and North . . . measures the authentic growth of the democratic idea."

Democracy and desegregation

It is commonly agreed that the United States Supreme Court's decision on integration in education is one of the most important rulings in its long

and controversial history. Since its promulgation the decision has been subjected to a steadily mounting barrage of criticism on all sorts of grounds and
from almost all points of the ideological compass. What has been most surprising is the absence of a principled defense of desegregation and the
program of school integration from the point of view of the ethics of democracy. Most defenses of the decision, particularly since Little Rock, have
consisted in shifting the issue by insisting that the supreme law of the land,
whatever we may think of its wisdom, should be obeyed. Although this is
a justifiable position with respect to the laws of a democracy, which, if
unwise and unjust, are modifiable and reversible, it evades the basic moral
issues that in the last analysis underlie every fundamental conflict of values
and social policy.

The opposition to desegregation comes from various groups. The old-
line Southerners, who represent the majority of the opposition, hardly
deign to offer reasons for their opposition except that laws against desegregation destroy their traditional "way of life." They are more convinced of the validity of their way of life than of the abstract rights of man
and of citizens in whose name such ways of life may be condemned. That
their way of life has a history; that it involves the use and abuse of other
human beings who are bitterly opposed to this way of life; and that, unless
they have some other justification for the *status quo* than that it is a *status quo*,
a new *status quo* may be imposed upon them with the same warrant—all this
they are content to ignore. For they hope to reverse the decision or transform
it into a dead letter not by argument or reason but by delaying tactics and
sporadic outbursts of recalcitrance.

A second group opposes desegregation on constitutional grounds.
Some regard this area of human relations as one in which the Supreme
Court is really legislating and therefore usurping the functions of Congress
and state legislatures. Others believe that education is exclusively a matter
for state jurisdiction and no concern of the Federal Government. A third
group protests against the clear violation of previous controlling precedents
—especially *Plessy vs. Ferguson*—which established the "separate but equal"
doctrine. These constitutional questions are not really germane to the basic
argument. It is true that the Supreme Court "legislates." It always has. The
ultimate question is the character, grounds·and wisdom of its legislation.
Education may be exclusively a matter for state jurisdiction. Yet the effects
of some state actions may have consequences affecting the rights and privileges of citizens. Aside from this, the moral issue of segregation in education
still remains, whether it is a question for the states or the Federal Government. That the Supreme Court decision overturns earlier precedents is
true. This is not unusual. The real question is: Should the precedents be
retained or overturned? I shall, therefore, avoid the strictly legalistic aspects
of the question.

Finally, I come to the criticism made by some conservative liberals
and liberal conservatives who see in the legal prohibition of segregation
in educational facilities (as in employment and in housing) a violation of
one's personal freedom or private right to choose one's associations, compan-
ions, neighbors and fellow workers. There is some written criticism of de-

segregation along these lines, but the volume of spoken criticism is much greater. Even before the Supreme Court decision, some exponents of discrimination as a personal right related it to the defense of free enterprise. Natural law as well as Judeo-Christian ideals have been invoked to prove that man is essentially a discriminatory creature because he is capable of choice. The greater his knowledge, the greater his range of discrimination. According to this argument, many of our difficulties arise from attempts to curb by law the exercise of a discrimination which is ours by natural right and which is justified in addition by the greater power it gives us to advance the arts of civilization. . . .

Since the desegregation decision, this note has been struck with increasing frequency by critics who believe that discrimination in education lies in the field of private morals and is thus beyond the reach of law. They are prepared to defend the human rights, they tell us, of all minorities, but they insist that the right to discriminate in education, even if this results in segregated schools, is one of the basic human rights. The more liberal among these critics make a distinction between the public and private domain according to which it would be wrong to *permit* segregation on buses and railroads because these lie in the public domain but wrong to *prevent* segregation, on the ground of personal freedom, in private life. Education, they say, is one of those areas of personal life that are by their very nature outside the purview of law in a democratic society.

The case against Negro segregation in any area of public life, whether enforced by law or by custom, rests upon simple ethical principles which are implicit in the Declaration of Independence and which later guided the adoption of the Thirteenth and Fourteenth Amendments. These principles of equality and freedom are expressed in the language of natural rights, but they are best defended in terms of their empirical consequences: The Negroes are part of the human race and as such should enjoy the same human rights of freedom and the same protection of our laws as any other group of human beings in the United States. The Thirteenth Amendment abolished their slavery and involuntary servitude generally. In so doing, we sought to redress a crime—one perhaps even greater than those committed in some settlements against the Indians. If slavery is abolished, then all the institutional restraints and indignities which constituted servitude must be abolished too. There can be no justification for first- and second-class citizens derivative from a previous condition of servitude. Morally, Negroes are entitled to life, liberty, property, and equal protection of laws on the same terms as the rest of us. This is independent of vicissitudes in the Supreme Court's interpretations of these rights we enjoy as citizens of our individual states or as citizens of the Federal Republic.

Atoning in part for the long history of moral evasion by previous Courts, the Supreme Court in *Brown vs. Board of Education of Topeka* declared that segregated public educational facilities are "inherently unequal." Despite the obscurity of the Court's language, this was not based on a discovery of a new fact or on recovery of an old law, but on the reaffirmation of a moral principle that led to a new law in the land. The moral principle is the same one which justified the abolition of slavery. In the light of the *historical* situation which has developed since the abolition of slavery, segregated educational facilities are "inherently unequal," not because of the actual differences in facilities, great as they are, but because they are inherently cruel, unjust and degrading to the group discriminated against. They are degrading in the same way that the yellow patch or badge of inferiority, the mark of the pariah, the stigma of the outcast, are degrading. Even if the physical facilities of Negro schools (or buses) were physically better than those set aside for the whites, segregation would still be degrading for the same reason that we regard a well-fed slave as still a slave.

Prejudice is sometimes distinguished by psychologists and sociologists from discrimination. Prejudice is an antipathetic feeling or attitude against some person or group not rationally justified by objective evidence. Discrimination is a pattern of behavior in which one acts against others by excluding them from opportunities commonly enjoyed. At the moment it is experienced, one can't help feeling prejudiced. But one *can* help discriminating unless under some compulsion. No one chooses to be prejudiced. But one chooses to discriminate. And because one does, one's choice can be inhibited or influenced by many things besides his prejudice. In a sense, everyone has a right to his thoughts or feelings. But not everyone has a right to discriminate. Neither the state by law nor society by custom has a moral right to discriminate prejudicially against individuals and groups in public life. Such a pattern of discrimination is segregation. . . .

Opponents of integration do not contest the right of every child, Negro or white, to receive an education in the public schools. They know that the public schools are supported by tax money levied directly or indirectly upon all citizens irrespective of race. They contend, however, that it is wrong to force parents to send their children to an integrated school. For this deprives them of rights which clearly belong to them in all free societies—the private right over their children and the social right to free association. At most, these spokesmen hold, the state may prescribe some of the content of education but not the context of association and social life which invariably develops out of attendance at school. . . .

Actually, parents are *not* forced to send their children to an integrated school. Parents may choose to send their children to private schools which are not integrated. Or, in most states, they may provide education at home. This the law permits (*Pierce vs. Society of Sisters*). To be sure, they have to pay a certain economic price for it, even though in its tradition of tolerance the community subsidizes these private schools by giving them remission from taxes and allowing those who contribute to their support to deduct contributions from their income tax. One would think that this was a generous, even over-generous attitude toward individuals whose prejudice against permitting their children to associate with Negroes was so overwhelming. But—the objection runs—it will not do to tell parents they can educate their children at home or send them to private schools. This involves another kind of discrimination. Since private education requires the possession of means, it would make the safeguarding of certain private rights dependent upon economic status and consequently underprivilege those who are forced to send their children to public school.

In other words, unless we can guarantee the equal economic status of the prejudiced, segregation would be a privilege of the rich! But why should we be concerned with economic equality here? Why not make the segregationists pay the costs of their prejudices? If the cost is sufficiently high, they may give up their opposition to integration if not their prejudices. In time even their prejudices may wither. . . .

One of the main premises of the segregationist's position is contained in the explicit acceptance of William Faulkner's declaration that "enforced integration is no better than enforced segregation." This is a very curious statement. Leaving aside the strictly legal questions created by the most recent interpretations of Section I of the Fourteenth Amendment, particularly the provision extending the equal protection of laws to all citizens, this equation in condemnation seems to me completely inadmissible morally. It assumes either that integration and segregation are, morally, on all fours, or that the evils of enforcement *always* outweigh any alternative good to be derived therefrom. This is not necessarily true and in the case in hand—the historical situation of the Negro in the United States—patently false. To deny children equal public educational opportunities and possibilities of proper vocational fulfilment merely because of the color of their skin or their religion or national origin, whether enforced by law or by social custom, is manifestly unjust. On the other hand, to require students, if they wish a public school education supported by tax monies levied upon all alike, to attend unsegregated schools is not unjust.

There are situations in which legally to compel certain practices is as bad as legally to prohibit them. This is so when the practices in question are equally evil, or when they are morally indifferent. Legally to compel us to consume bananas is as bad as legally to prohibit us from doing so. But what is true for bananas would not be true for habit-forming drugs, or for smoking in a powder plant. To enforce vaccination or the medical segregation of children with contagious diseases is certainly not as bad as preventing it even if we admit it is always deplorable to compel parents to comply with school and health laws.

Some anti-integrationists make a distinction between segregation as a "social custom" and segregation as "discrimination enforced by law." They oppose the latter—but then, just as resolutely, oppose the legal prohibition of such discrimination as a social custom. They do so on the ground that this violates the personal freedom of those who discriminate to act as they please "within the four walls" of their own home.

There are social customs and social customs. A social custom which violates human rights, and imposes unfair and cruel penalties upon individuals, hurts no less even if it is not enforced by law. It is enough that it is enforced by habit, custom, use and wont. Suttee was a social custom, too— as was child marriage, infanticide, dueling, and quite a number of other quaint practices described in anthropological texts. If there is any relation between morality and law, the existence of certain evil social practices *may* (not must) justify us in taking legal action to prevent them. And if this is of necessity an abridgment of some human freedom, as is true of every law, it is taken in behalf of other human freedoms. The human freedoms we safeguard by legal action against segregation and unfair discrimination are more important than those we restrict. Some Southern moderates see this in the case of certain public facilities, such as transportation. But surely the social discrimination which prevents a Negro student from attending a medical or engineering school, which bars him from certain vocations even after he has spent years of his adult life in preparing himself for it, which denies him housing in restricted communities without even providing him with the separate and equal facilities of the segregated bus, is a much crasser violation of his rights as a human being. The classification which puts transportation in the field of the political, and education and employment in the field of the personal, is completely arbitrary as well as irrelevant. For the moral question is primary and it cuts across all categories.

It is on moral grounds that we are justified in adopting a Fair Education Practices Act prohibiting certain discriminatory practices not only in public schools but sometimes even in private schools which are dependent upon the public largesse in various ways. It is on moral grounds that we are justified in adopting a Fair Employment Practices Act. If it is morally wrong for a trade union to exclude from membership individuals of certain racial or religious groups, when such membership is essential to continued employment, it is just as morally wrong for an employer, except in some highly special circumstances of personal service, to deny people work on the same grounds. Finally, it is on moral grounds that we are justified in adopting a Fair Housing Law the exact provisions of which we need not specify here. I believe I am as much concerned with preserving the rights of privacy as any segregationist, but I cannot see how the right of every person to do as he pleases within the four walls of his own house is undermined by legislation designed to make it possible for our colored neighbor to live within *his* four walls. For make no mistake about it: Social discrimination in housing in effect confines Negroes and other minority groups to ghettos where they must share their four walls with multiple families and are in consequence denied their own sacred rights of privacy. Actually there are both moral and legal limits to what a person can do in the privacy of his own home; but, even if the right of privacy were absolute, it would not carry with it the right to push out one's walls until they encompassed the public neighborhood, school and factory.

Many inconsistencies and confusions in this position flow from vague distinctions between the political, the public, the social, and the personal or private. According to this view, only the political sphere is the sphere of equality. Focal to it is the right to vote. The social sphere is the sphere in which discrimination is legitimate even if unwise. The public sphere includes both. The private sphere is one of exclusion. But to what sphere, then, belong the inalienable human rights "to life, liberty, and the pursuit of happiness"?

A moment's reflection will show that they have mixed everything up. Equality "exists" *first* in the field of human rights. It is the premise from which we derive the most powerful argument against slavery. Political equality, especially equality in voting, is only one form of equality. Negroes desire political equality in order to enforce recognition of their human rights, which they believe they have even when they lack political equality. They were liberated and admitted to citizenship even before the Fifteenth

Amendment specifically forbade abridgment of the right to vote on account of race, color or previous condition of servitude. Under certain historical conditions, restrictions on the right to vote—age, literacy, residence—provided they are *equitably* applied to all, may actually lead to inequality in the exercise of the vote. It is manifestly improper to confuse the political realm with one very special form of political life—a democracy of universal suffrage. It is clear that sometimes we may wonder whether a people is ready for universal suffrage but never whether they have human or social rights, no matter how primitive they are.

The social realm, the locus of most of our associations with other human beings, is the sphere in which the questions of justice arise in their most complex as well as most acute form. The social realm is emphatically not in the first instance the realm of discrimination and inequality, although they are found there. That would automatically and necessarily make it one of injustice. It is precisely here that, as moral creatures, reflecting upon the consequences of our actions on others, we are called upon to apply appropriate rules of equality and, where differences are relevant, rules of equitable inequality in the light of some shared ideal, even if it be no more than the ideal of peace or mutual sufferance. The nub of many an error here is the confusion, where social relationships and membership in social groups are involved, between "discriminating *against*" and "discriminating *between*" and treating them as synonymous expressions. In identifying the social world with discriminating *against,* one is describing it as it appears to the eyes of the snob with vestigial cultural longings for feudal hierarchy. . . .

It is a hateful thing to enforce laws in education, where ideally there should be no coercion except the inescapable cogencies encountered in the quest for truth and beauty. But ideal societies exist only in heaven. It is commonly acknowledged that the state may not only enforce compulsory attendance but prescribe the content or subject matter of instruction in order to insure an education appropriate for the exercise of citizenship. The content of education has some fixed elements, but its variables depend on the *kind* of society in which instruction is given and on its history. The mode of association within a school may have a definite bearing on the content and values of the education it gives. This has always been true of the American public school, which has played a great and unique role in the creation of the modern American nation. It not only provided a ladder of opportunity on which millions climbed out of poverty, but by virtue of its integrated classrooms, in which students studied and played in common, unified the most diverse ethnic groups that elsewhere lived together in snarling hostility. It never even tried to do this in the South, because the pattern of segregation prevailed from the beginning in the schools, which were late in getting founded. The requirements of citizenship in a *democratic* community require the integration of the public classrooms even more than integration in the armed services. Unassailable evidence shows that Negro students, especially in high schools, smart under the restrictions of the segregated school. The more willingly they accept the promised heritage of American ideals, the more they resent their educational conditions. A typical study among Negro high school students in Dade County, Florida, shows that, when asked to state the changes they most desired in their way of life, they named most frequently changes in the area of education. Can the democratic state be indifferent to this? . . .

Although gradualness and patience are a *sine qua non* of peaceful enforcement, once the law is openly flouted it must be enforced. Worse in such situations than the risks of a firm and rapid enforcement would be the abandonment of the legal position already won or the indefinite postponement of further integration until such time as God softens the hearts of the hard-core segregationists. Beyond a certain point, the longer the delay, the more costly in tears and suffering will be the process of desegregation for everyone concerned, but especially for those who have so far endured the greatest indignities. For a basic human right is violated wherever segregation is practiced, no less in public education, than in public transportation, and the denial of this right to Negroes in education seriously affects the expression of their basic political rights as well.

I conclude as I began. The same argument which opposes slavery opposes the perpetuation of the discrimination that continues in another form some of the practices of slavery. If slavery was a crime, segregation is the still open and unhealed wound it left on the body of the Negro. It bleeds afresh every time the pattern is imposed upon him. Freedom opened the doors not only to citizenship for Negroes but to personhood and brought them into the kingdom of moral ends. In a way, those who oppose legal desegregation in the name of personal freedom were answered a long time ago by Mr. Justice Harlan, grandfather of the present Justice, in his famous dissent in the Civil Rights Cases, with which the present Court is only now catching up [109 U.S. 26]. Their argument, were it accepted widely, would help pin the badge of servitude upon our Negro fellow citizens in their vocations, their education, their housing, and even their use of public accommodations. Generalized, it is an argument against razing by legal measures the walls of the ghettos by which a local majority arbitrarily and unfairly keeps any minority—racial, religious or ethnic—fenced in and deprived of the benefits of their rights as American citizens and as members of a democratic community.

The history of America has been not only a history of promises made but of promises redeemed. For a long time, American Negroes were excluded from even the promise of American life. After the Civil War, they were cruelly denied the fulfilment of the promise implied in their liberation. For the greater part of the near-century since the Emancipation Proclamation, progress was slow, uncertain and gained through bitter struggle. Since the war against Nazism and its racial ideology, however, enormous gains have been made in integrating Negro citizens into the pattern of democratic life. Little Rock is a severe defeat in a long war which the American people are winning—a war which must be won if we are to survive as a free culture the assaults of Communist totalitarianism. The processes of education work gradually but effectively in eroding the bigotry of fanaticism. That is why the lawful spread of integrated education in South and North is our best hope for making promises of American life come true. The tide of its advance measures the authentic growth of the democratic idea.

The Shattered Precedents

Eugene Cook and William I. Potter / "Opposing the Opinion of the Supreme Court"

Eugene Cook and William I. Potter are both southern lawyers; Cook has been Attorney General of Georgia since 1945 and Potter practices law in Kansas City, Missouri. It was their unenviable choice to oppose the Supreme Court decisions in the school segregation cases of 1954 and 1955, a task which they undertook, in strictly legal terms, in the American Bar Association Journal, *vol. 42, 1956. In the same issue, the purely legal counter-arguments appear in an article by George W. Stumberg, professor of Law at the University of Texas.*

In essence, their position is that "the Supreme Court rejected the tra-ditional rule of constitutional construction and substituted the intent of the Court for the intent of the people." The authors appeal to the cumulative consistency of Supreme Court decisions over the course of nearly a century to buttress their legal position, and they appeal to the Court's 1954 admission that past decisions were not wrong but had become outmoded. The old doctrine of "separate but equal" facilities was not bad law, the Court argued; it was, however, bad sociology. Instead of relying on previous decisions, on precedent, and on the intent of the framers of the Constitution, the Court chose to base its decision on more recent findings in "psychological knowledge." Cook and Potter point out that such psychological evidence is not admissible by rules of law, especially since it was not introduced in the actual proceedings. They quote Justice Felix Frankfurter, who in 1952 argued that "the Supreme Court was not competent to take judicial notice of opinions in the relatively new fields of sociology and psychology." And they cap their anti-sociological case with a telling quotation from Judge Jerome Frank, an advocate of the legal use of sociology: "Inferences derived therefrom are almost certain to be im-portantly false. For the consequences of the operation of certain customs or group attitudes are often cancelled out by the consequences of other conflicting customs and attitudes."

The particular sociological evidence used by the Court comes under the authors' critical purview, and they are—perhaps less dispassionately than they claim—indignant at the extra-legal evidence provided by the Swedish writer Gunnar Myrdal, on whom the Court seems to have relied heavily. Myrdal's attack on the Constitution as "impractical and unsuited to modern conditions" renders his position, in their eyes, highly suspect; by implication, any Court decision based on his work is equally suspect.

The mass of legal citations which Cook and Potter employ in their case against the Supreme Court's decision does not lend itself to ready summary; these citations should be read carefully in order to determine their relevance and competence. A far more rhetorical criticism of the decision is "The Supreme Court Must Be Curbed," by James J. Byrnes, former Justice of the Supreme Court, a powerful figure under Roosevelt, and former Governor of South Carolina. It appeared in the May 18, 1956, issue of U.S. News & World Report.

The purpose of this article is to discuss without heat and, it is hoped, with some light, from a strictly legal, and not emotional, viewpoint the precedent-shattering decisions of the Supreme Court in the school segregation cases of 1954 and 1955.[1]

The decisions of the United States Supreme Court of May 17, 1954, and May 31, 1955, in the school segregation cases, *Brown* v. *Board of Education*, reported in 347 U. S. 483 and 349 U. S. 294, constitute a crisis in American constitutional law, for these reasons:

1. They are a radical departure from the doctrine of *stare decisis* firmly established in American and English jurisprudence. Moreover, the Court, as hereinafter pointed out, sustains its conclusion by a reasoning process which was heretofore unknown to jurisprudence, which conflicts with prior opinions of the same Court less than five years old, and which is sharply deprecated even by those who otherwise approve the result of the decision. If the reasoning by which the Court arrives at its conclusion is fatally defective, is not the result itself fatally defective?

2. The Court has, without any implementing act of the Congress such as is required under the terms of the Fourteenth Amendment, and by an order unprecedented in judicial history, assumed the power under that Amendment to enforce commingling of the white and colored races in state-supported schools, thus rendering a nullity state laws providing for separate but equal educational facilities—an anomalous assumption of power that constitutes further encroachment by the central Government upon the rights reserved to the states and to the people by the Federal Constitution.

3. In construing segregated schools as unconstitutional and discriminatory against the Negro by reason of the equal protection clause of the Fourteenth Amendment, the Court reached the conclusion that the Negro was deprived of equal protection because the segregated school generated in him a feeling of inferiority that *may* (italics supplied) affect his heart and mind in a way *unlikely* (italics supplied) ever to be undone. To support this thesis it cited as authority college professors, psychologists and sociologists. Absent from the opinion was reference to the effect on the hearts and minds of white children and their parents because of enforced commingling with Negro children. The state, in providing segregated schools, gave heed to this preference of white parents and their children, and, desiring that state-maintained free public schools should exist to educate the children of both races, solved this basic human problem by enacting laws and providing for equal educational facilities in separate schools. Reason supports the soundness and fairness of the state program, and reason supports prior decisions of the United States Supreme Court since the adoption of the Fourteenth Amendment in 1868, upholding the constitutionality of state-maintained separate-but-equal educational facilities.

The first point the Court had to resolve in the *Brown* case was whether the framers and ratifiers of the Fourteenth Amendment intended the equal

---

[1] A brilliant and highly critical legal argument dissecting the Court's opinion in the segregation cases was made by United States Senator James Eastland, of Mississippi, in the Senate on May 26, 1955. See CONGRESSIONAL RECORD, pages 6068 *et seq.* The writers recommend it.

protection clause to abolish segregation in the public schools. To this question the Supreme Court pleaded ignorance by saying that the intent of the framers and ratifiers "cannot be determined with any degree of certainty."

The Court said this, even though the briefs show that the same 39th Congress that promulgated the Fourteenth Amendment passed two bills dealing with separate schools for white and colored children in the District of Columbia. In addition, the briefs show that of the thirty-seven states in existence at that time, only five abolished segregation contemporaneously with ratification of the Fourteenth Amendment, and three of these restored segregation after the removal of federal troops.

The overwhelming majority either established or continued segregation in their public schools contemporaneously with ratification of the Fourteenth Amendment. Georgia's first public school segregation laws were enacted at the same session at which the Fourteenth Amendment was ratified. They were enacted by a Republican legislature which had thirty-three Negro members and were signed by a Republican governor.

In a recent article, Alexander M. Bikel, who was one of two law clerks to Mr. Justice Frankfurter during the segregation arguments, had this to say:

> (1) The legislative history of the 14th Amendment makes clear that it was not intended to abolish segregation immediately,
>
> (2) But it did not foreclose to a court the authority to find a different application under different circumstances years later.

We agree with his first proposition, but the latter, if correct, rules out precedent entirely and leaves the Constitution as unstable as the wind. It suggests that all constitutional amendments should include express provisions as to what they mean at different periods of time and under different circumstances. To attempt any such constitutional mechanism would be an absurdity. Why have a written constitution if the Court will not be bound by the intent of the framers and ratifiers?

In rendering its decision, the Supreme Court rejected the traditional rule of constitutional construction and substituted the intent of the Court for the intent of the people.

In its article entitled "The Supreme Court 1953 Term" the *Harvard Law Review* (68 *Harv. L. Rev.* 96) said:

> In dealing with prior cases, especially *Plessy* v. *Ferguson*, the Chief Justice did not seek to demonstrate that the court had once blundered. His point, rather, was that these prior decisions were simply outmoded in present day society.

Thus, it is seen that a new rule of testing the constitutionality of a state's public policy as expressed in its statutes and as authorized by the Tenth Amendment has been formulated. No longer is there a question of whether there exists a conflict with precedent or whether precedent is wrong but rather whether the intent of the framers as recognized in previous decisions, is, in the opinion of the Judges, "outmoded."

The purpose of all sincere investigations is the discovery of truth. Basic truth is discoverable in the midst of external realities. It may not be manufactured by the mind. It is a tangible reality and is never new. Once found, we may seize and hold fast to it. Now let us seek and follow the truth wherever it may lead, as applied to the *Brown* case.

In its decision, the Supreme Court did not hold that the old "separate but equal" doctrine, laid down in *Plessy* v. *Ferguson,* 163 U. S. 537, was bad law. It held that it was bad sociology. It did not hold that the facts (or truths) disclosed by the records in the cases before the Court justified a departure from the "separate but equal" doctrine. It held that "psychological knowledge," apart from these records, was of more validity than factual truths.

Without doubt there is no precedent in any recorded decision of any court, and it is hoped there will be none hereafter, reading as follows: "Whatever may have been the extent of psychological knowledge at the time of *Plessy* v. *Ferguson,* this finding is amply supported by modern authority." (Citing as authority six lay textbooks, not introduced in evidence in any of the pending cases, clearly inadmissible if offered, and written, for the most part, by authors to whose affiliations and convictions the Court cannot have given the slightest investigation or attention, but which will hereafter be discussed in this article).

The Court conceded that the records in the cases before it demonstrated equality of white and colored schools in respect to all "tangible factors." The decision could not "turn on" such "tangible factors," said the Court:

> We must look instead [not also] to the effect of segregation itself on public education.

The Court then asked:

> Does segregation . . . [alone] . . . deprive the children of the minority group of equal educational opportunities?

The answer was: "We believe that it does."
Why? Because, the Court said:

> Whatever may have been the psychological knowledge at the time of *Plessy* v. *Ferguson,* this finding is amply supported by modern authority. Any language in *Plessy* v. *Ferguson* contrary to this finding is rejected.

A judicial "finding" is, of course, supposed to be based on admissible evidence or on commonly accepted facts of which a court can take judicial notice, including congressional or state legislative declarations. In these cases the applicable congressional and state legislative declarations were to the contrary. Indeed, in 1946, Congress, in the national grants-in-aid legislation for school lunches, still in force, recognized the existence of separate school systems and merely required equal treatment, in the following language (42 U.S.C.A. 1760):

If a state maintains separate schools for minority and for majority races, no funds made available pursuant to this chapter shall be paid or disbursed to it unless a just and equitable distribution is made within the state for the benefit of such minority races, of funds paid to it under this chapter.

Congress deliberately chose to recognize "separate but equal treatment" instead of requiring desegregation.

How did such "intangibles" become "findings" in these cases? They were not authenticated as "authority" by any method known to Anglo-Saxon jurisprudence or rules of evidence. If not in evidence, the universal rule is that it was harmful error, prejudicial to the parties defendant, for them to be considered by the Court.

We have scanned legal literature since May, 1954, in an effort to find a respectable vindication of the Supreme Court's conduct, but have found none that appeals to reason.

Under elementary and elemental law, a court may not consider treatises in a field other than law, unless the treatises themselves are the very subject of inquiry. The doctrine of judicial notice extends only to those things of common knowledge that lie without the realm of science, or to that one science in which judges are presumed to be learned or experts themselves —the science of law.

As late as 1952, Mr. Justice Frankfurter said that the Supreme Court was not competent to take judicial notice of opinions in the relatively new fields of sociology and psychology. *Beauharnais* v. *Illinois*, 343 U.S. 250, 263.

Speaking for a majority of the court, he wrote:

It is not within our competence to confirm or deny claims of social scientists as to the dependence of the individual on the position of his racial or religious group in the community. . . .

That rule vanished as the Court founded its judgment on pseudo-socioscience, not made a part of the record either as evidence or as law.

The findings of social science are sometimes regarded as elaborate statements of what everybody knows in language that nobody can understand.

While little harm can come from such an undertaking, great harm will result when a social scientist takes his deductions and generalizations into the field of judicial interpretation and treats them as the equivalent of "law."

United States Circuit Judge Jerome Frank recently wrote that these generalizations and the "inferences derived therefrom are almost certain to be importantly false. For the consequences of the operation of certain customs or group attitudes are often cancelled out by the consequences of other conflicting customs and attitudes."

Even the latest book cited by the Court itself in footnote 11 of the *Brown* case (Witmer and Kotinsky) states:

Unfortunately for scientific accuracy and adequacy, thoroughly satisfactory methods of determining the effects of prejudice and discrimination on health or personality have not yet been devised, nor has a sufficient number of studies dealing with the various minority groups been made.

But the Court blandly and extra-judicially accepts as "psychological *knowledge*" what the lay experts themselves are as yet completely unsure of!

Indeed, even stronger views have been expressed of the present wholly inadequate and unscientific state of sociological knowledge of majority-minority problems.[2]

A recent writer, Edmond Cahn, who agrees with the result of the *Brown* case nevertheless sharply criticizes the use of sociological authority and shows its danger by saying:

The word "danger" is used advisedly, because I would not have the constitutional rights of Negroes—or of other Americans—rest on such flimsy foundations as some of the scientific demonstrations in these records.

Since these behavioral sciences are so very young, imprecise and changeable, their findings have an uncertain expectancy of life. Today's observation may be cancelled by tomorrow's new revelation—or new technical fad.

Should our fundamental rights rise, fall or change along with the latest fashions of psychological literature? How are we to know that in the future social scientists may not present us with a collection of notions similar to those of Adolf Hitler and label them as modern science? If Mr. Justice Holmes was correct when he insisted that the Constitution should not be tied to the wheels of any economic system whatsoever, shouldn't it be similarly uncommitted in relation to other social sciences?

What of this modern authority upon which the Court based its decision?

The first one cited of the six—K. B. Clark—was, at the time of the arguments before the Court, on the payroll of the National Association for the Advancement of Colored People as a so-called "social-science expert," a questionable procedure in view of the fact that the NAACP was the real party in interest waging the litigation in these cases.

The book *An American Dilemma*, written by Swedish socialist Gunnar Myrdal on a grant from the Carnegie Foundation, was cited in its entirety by the Supreme Court as an authority for its ruling.

A contributor to this work was Negro educator W. E. B. DuBois, who sent a message of condolence upon the death of Joseph Stalin.

It was *in this book* that Myrdal declared the United States Constitution to be "impractical and unsuited to modern conditions" and its adoption to be "nearly a plot against the common people." Furthermore, he openly

---

[2]"The Survival of the Moralistic-Legalistic Orientation in Sociology," a paper delivered to the Sociological Research Association, September 2, 1952, by Dr. George A. Lundberg, University of Washington, Seattle, Washington, and printed in *The Sociologist* published at the University of Colorado, Boulder, Colorado.

avowed that liberty must be forsaken for the benefit of what he called "social equality."

Has the present Supreme Court now adopted Myrdal's view of the Constitution? In all fairness have not we Southerners good reason to be deeply disturbed over the Court's attitude toward the Constitution? Has not every citizen good reason to be deeply disturbed?

What has become of the accepted tests of the constitutionality of statutes? . . .

It is our firm opinion that the United States Supreme Court in *Brown* v. *Topeka* not only usurped the prerogatives of the people by amending the Federal Constitution in violation of Article V relating to amendment, but it pursued its pseudo-socio-psychological pattern by usurping the prerogatives of the United States Congress. It handed down an implementation decision on May 31, 1955, in spite of the fact that the Fourteenth Amendment itself vests in Congress the power of implementation.

The fifth section of the Fourteenth Amendment itself declares that "Congress shall have the power to enforce by appropriate legislation the provisions of this article."

The first construction of the Fourteenth Amendment by the United States Supreme Court was in the *Slaughter House* Cases, 16 Wall. 36, where it was held that the main purpose of the Fourteenth Amendment was to establish the citizenship of the Negro, to give definitions of citizenship of the United States and of the states, and to protect from hostile legislation by the states the privileges and immunities of citizens of the United States as distinguished from those of citizens of the states.

In the *Civil Rights* Cases, 109 U.S. 4,3 S. Ct. 18, decided by the Supreme Court in October, 1883, that Court held:

> [The Fourteenth Amendment] nullifies and makes void all state legislation, and state action of every kind, which impairs the privileges and immunities of citizens of the United States, or which injures them in life, liberty, or property without due process of law, or which denies to any of them the equal protection of the laws. It not only does this, but, in order that the *national will, thus declared* [italics supplied], may not be a mere *brutem fulmen* [an empty threat], the last section [5] of the amendment invests congress with power to enforce it by appropriate legislation. To enforce what? To enforce the prohibition . . . [by] appropriate legislation for correcting the effects of such prohibited state law and state acts, and thus to render them effectually null, void and innocuous. . . . Positive rights and privileges are undoubtedly secured by the fourteenth amendment; but they are secured by way of prohibition against state laws and state proceedings affecting those rights and privileges, and by power given to congress to legislate for the purpose of carrying such prohibition into effect. . . .
>
> If those [state] laws are adverse to his rights and do not protect him, his remedy will be found in the corrective legislation which congress has adopted, or may adopt, for counteracting the effect of state laws, or state action, prohibited by the fourteenth Amendment. . . . If the [state] laws themselves make any unjust discrimination,

amenable to the prohibition of the fourteenth amendment, congress has full power to afford a remedy under that amendment and in accordance with it.

To protect the Negro's rights under the Fourteenth Amendment against hostile state laws and acts Congress has enacted:

Title 28, Section 1863 U.S.C.A., which prohibits exclusion from service as grand or petit juror in any court of the United States on account of race or color.

Title 42, Section 1981 U.S.C.A., which provides that all persons within the jurisdiction of the United States shall have the same right to make and enforce contracts, sue, be parties, give evidence and to full and equal benefit of all laws for the security of persons and property as is enjoyed by white citizens, and shall be subject to like punishment, pains, penalties, taxes, licenses and exactions of every kind, and to no other.

Title 42, Section 1982 U.S.C.A., which provides that all citizens of the United States shall have the same right as is enjoyed by white citizens to inherit, purchase, lease, sell, hold and convey real and personal property.

Title 42, Section 1983 U.S.C.A., which authorizes civil action for deprivation of any right, privileges and immunities secured by the Constitution and laws of the United States.

Title 42, Section 1971 U.S.C.A., which provides that all citizens of the United States regardless of race, color or previous condition of servitude, who are otherwise qualified to vote in any state, may vote at any election regardless of the constitution or laws of any state.

Title 42, Sections 1751-60 U.S.C.A., which, providing for a school lunch program by the Department of Agriculture for public and non-profit schools, provides: "If a state maintains separate schools for minority and majority races, no funds made available pursuant to this chapter shall be paid or disbursed to it unless a just and equitable distribution is made within the state, for the benefit of such minority races, of funds paid to it under this chapter."

Since the Congress has not, pursuant to its power under Section 5 of the Fourteenth Amendment, attempted to prohibit the maintenance by the states of segregated schools, but has impliedly by the enactment of said Sections 1751-60, Title 42 U.S.C.A., aforementioned, approved them, it is apparent that the present Supreme Court has overruled both the Congress and the will of the people as expressed in state constitutions and laws. It is also apparent that the Congress has not been remiss in enacting legislation to protect the legal and political rights of the Negro under the Fourteenth Amendment, but has refused to interpret that amendment as compelling the commingling of the races in mixed schools against the wishes of the people. Moreover, the acts of Congress, Title 8, Section 1151 U.S.C.A., setting up the quota system of immigration which practically excludes immigration to the United States from geographical areas containing Negroes and Mongolians, were justified by reason of the fact that such races are not readily assimilated into the predominantly white, Caucasian race here. Such is a sound and necessary public policy to preserve the essentially Western civilization in the Continental United States. Clearly, therefore, that long-established public policy of the Congress and of the states is sought to be overturned, without their consent by a strained construction of the equal protection clause of the Fourteenth Amendment and by an apparent disregard of Article I, Section 8, Subparagraph 18, of the Constitution, which provides: "The Congress shall have power to make all laws which shall be necessary and proper for carrying into execution the foregoing powers, and all other powers vested by this Constitution in the Government of the United States or in any department or officer thereof."

In *Plessy* v. *Ferguson*, 163 U.S. 537, 16 S. Ct. 1138, decided by the United States Supreme Court in May, 1896, that Court said:

> The object of the [Fourteenth] amendment was undoubtedly to enforce the absolute equality of the two races before the law, but in the nature of things, it could not have been intended to abolish distinctions based upon color, or to enforce social, as distinguished from political equality, or a commingling of the two races upon terms unsatisfactory to either. Laws permitting, and even requiring, their separation, in places where they are liable to be brought into contact, do not necessarily imply the inferiority of either race to the other, and have been generally, if not universally, recognized as within the competency of the state legislatures in the exercise of their police power. The most common instance of this is connected with the establishment of separate schools for white and colored children, which have been held to be a valid exercise of the legislative power even by courts of states where the political rights of the colored race have been longest and most earnestly enforced. . . .
>
> [We cannot accept the proposition that] the enforced separation of the two races stamps the colored race with a badge of inferiority . . . that social prejudices may be overcome by legislation, and that equal rights cannot be secured to the Negro except by an enforced commingling of the two races. . . . If the two races are to meet upon terms of social equality, it must be the result of natural affinities, a mutual appreciation of each other's merits, and a voluntary consent of individuals. . . .
>
> "This end can neither be accomplished nor promoted by laws which conflict with the general sentiment of the community upon whom they are designed to operate. When the government, therefore, has secured to each of its citizens equal rights before the law, and equal opportunities for improvement and progress, it has accomplished the end for which it was organized, and performed all the functions respecting social advantages with which it is endowed." [Quoting from *People* v. *Gallagher*, 93 N.Y. 438]. Legislation is powerless to eradicate racial instincts, or to abolish distinctions based upon physical differences, and the attempt to do so can only result in accentuating the difficulties of the present situation. If the civil and political rights of both races be equal, one cannot be inferior to the other civilly or politically. If one race be inferior to the other socially, the constitution of the United States cannot put them on the same plane.

Until the recent decision of the present Supreme Court, that Court has adhered to the position that substantially equal educational facilities furnished by the state for white and colored was not a violation of the equal protection clause of the Fourteenth Amendment. See *Sweatt* v. *Painter*, 339 U.S. 629, decided in 1950; *State of Missouri* ex rel. *Gaines* v. *Canada*, 305 U.S. 337, decided in 1938.

In its singlemindedness and preoccupation in seeking to justify a radically new construction of the equal protection clause of the Fourteenth Amendment so as to outlaw state-segregated schools, it by-passed and overrode the much greater constitutional principles that the people are sovereign, that the national Government has only specific powers delegated to it by the Constitution, and that all other powers reside in the states and the people. The Court has thus dealt a vital blow to the very heart and framework of our constitutional republic, which fits in with the pattern set in recent years of encroachment by the executive and judicial departments upon the rights reserved to the states and to the people by the Constitution. When, by this process, the Constitution is finally completely whittled away without a vote of the people or consent of the states, the dreams envisioned by some of the authors cited by the Court are ready for attainment, and then comes death to liberty in America.

The Cultural Cost of Prudery
Eric Larrabee/from "The Cultural Context of Sex Censorship"

Eric Larrabee (1922–) has been an editor of Harper's Magazine, *Amer-ican* Heritage, *and* Horizon, *an editorial consultant for Doubleday, and has recently accepted the post of provost of the faculty of Arts and Letters of the State University of New York at Buffalo. He is also the author of several books on what is sometimes called "the American scene." The title of his essay, re-printed in part here—"The Cultural Context of Sex Censorship"—reveals the moral latitude of his liberal position.*

Larrabee's objections to laws against obscenity are as various as the most recent findings in anthropology, psychology, and sociology. He hits hard at the lack of a precise legal definition of the word obscenity *and points out that proponents of censorship are guilty of using the same "speculative social psychology" which they claim to abhor and which they attribute to the relativ-istic liberals. After all, the central argument of those who defend censorship rests ultimately on whether or not tendencies to corrupt can be socially verified. Pornography, he observes, is the "most helpless of quarries," since almost no one will openly defend it any more than sympathizers will speak in behalf of communism or homosexuality. Larrabee speaks of the "smut-hunters"—a phrase in sharp contrast to "smut peddlers," the phrase used by James Kil-patrick, his opponent on this issue. In the triumphant decency of the smut-hunters, Larrabee sees a great danger: the careless and sloppy identification of liberal with libertine, of pornographer with Communist, and the attendant encroachment of censorship on civil liberties.*

In attempting to place the entire problem of obscenity in a larger cultural context, Larrabee remarks that all legal efforts to censor obscenity operate on "some kind of theory of the American sex life—of what it is, or ought to be." He suggests that America may be displaying those "symptoms of sexual neurosis" in which we may find "a moral perspective that diminishes the healthy and accentuates the sick." The cult of the so-called "great American love goddess" represents "the commercial exploitation of the assumption that the American public is composed largely of Peeping Toms." Such flagrant titillation of sexual impulses infects even the advertisements for women's underwear—and all the while the public allows and even hankers after the more perverse titillation based on the well-exploited "theme of homosexuality and violence." Larrabee cites Gershon Legman's thesis that, in America, love is legal in fact but not on paper, while murder is legal on paper but not in fact.

Larrabee's conclusion is that we ought not to sneer at efforts to treat "the subject matter of sex . . . tastefully—or even beautifully . . . if we have never tried to treat it so." Failure to make such an attempt is made worse by our concomitant "public consumption of human suffering, in virtually every form and every media." This, he says, is the true obscenity of American life.

The cultural context of sex censorship

In the United States today, no less than in other times and places, the subject of sex is charged with anxiety. In merely raising it, the writer must court suspicion—and consciously, for taboos surround him; immoderate interest would alert, though for different reasons, both the popular and professional mind. Sexual restrictions, moreover, have this logic on their side: while customs vary, the maintenance of emotional tension between male and female—hence, of society's biological vigor—is characteristically associated with some form of social "censorship." The "natural" state of freedom from sexual inhibition is far more likely to be a fantasy of the sophisticated. Indeed, the rational background of restraint may be better understood by the primitive than by the modern mind. A young West African writer, for example, has explained with awareness and regret why his tribesmen surround with mystery the initiation ceremony of pre-adolescent males:

> Not only do they keep women and children in a state of uncertainty and terror, they also warn them to keep the doors of the huts firmly barred. . . . It is obvious that if the secret were to be given away, the ceremony would lose much of its power . . . [N]othing would remain of the trial by fear, that occasion when every boy has the opportunity to overcome his . . . own baser nature. . . . But, at the moment of writing this, does any part of the rite still survive? The secret. . . . Do we still have secrets?

Where sex is concerned, the imposition of partial curbs serves a double purpose: to stimulate and to hold back—never too much of either. A counterpoise to individual desires may also measure their intensity, in such an interlocked fashion as to become virtually a condition of their being. This is partly what the would-be censor means when he says that there has always been "censorship," or that the social structure depends on preserving it. In that sense, we all "censor," internally, our own actions and those of others whom we influence. We define in our heads, as a matter of course, the range between what our contemporaries will and will not tolerate. We play between these definitions, stretching them now one way, now another. We live in a state of permanent conflict between our daring and our decency; and, though few go out of their way to say as much, few would have it otherwise.

Yet, censorship, as we commonly know it, differs sharply from this internalized mechanism for enforcing communal assumptions. Of all forms of sex censorship, that of the individual psyche—which sees to it that some things simply cannot be said, even to oneself—is undoubtedly the most effective. It is truly effective, however, only for those tradition-bound societies in which sexual inhibitions are more or less uniformly shared. The modern world, where more than one set of assumptions exist about what is and is not to be allowed, can make sex censorship of literature and the arts a subject of heated dispute. Censorship as an issue, in other words, is almost by definition a by-product of class rivalry. It arises along the shared boundaries between two or more antagonistic schools of thought; and in societies like our own, where law has replaced the rule of universally accepted custom, it is inevitably (though not always successfully) dealt with by law.

Some forms of sexual behavior the law forbids outright: rape, "statutory" rape, incest, sodomy, prostitution, lewd acts with children, adultery, fornication, abduction, and miscegenation—all of which may be defined in terms of a concrete act. Sex censorship arises, however, not from what is done—at least, not hitherto—but from what is said, written, seen, heard, thought, or felt. The prohibited area in word or image is conveniently characterized by the terms "obscene" or "obscenity," and it falls under the "law" of obscenity—that is to say, an accumulation of statutes and precedent which reflect, but do not necessarily reveal, prevailing definitions of the sexually forbidden. The law underlines the vague sanctions of community disapproval with a tangible threat. It establishes certain minima of censorship, and maxima of license, and, therefore, the limits of acceptable variation in erotic tone. But it suffers severe criticism, even as law, both from its lack of grounding in the material or exact and from its exposed position between rival conceptions of the sexual and social—not to mention the esthetic—good.

Difficulties begin with the idea of "obscenity" itself. Not all that is obscene has to do with sex (*e.g.,* scatology), nor is everything sexually prohibited (*e.g.,* contraception) necessarily obscene. Typically, the word carries one or more of at least three distinct meanings: as (1) something which contravenes accepted standards of propriety, (2) something which tends to corrupt, and (3) something which provokes erotic thoughts or desires. The second and third are often thought to subsume the first, though not the other way around (as one Hemingway character might say to another, "I obscenity in the milk of thy mother's obscenity," without passion of any kind). The first is a common, if ill-defined, phenomenon, including the venerable four-letter Anglo-Saxon monosyllables as well as most of the improper anecdotes that are at any time considered proper to tell. The second and third have sometimes been regarded as identical, not only by censors, but by courts, as though the fact of sex were in fact obscene. Even when examined from a purely legal view, the law of obscenity is so hazy and illogical that it tends to disintegrate—to lead inevitably to a conclusion that "[n]o one seems to know what obscenity is."

In the forty-seven states where statutes relating to obscenity exist, all but six define it "by adding one or more of the following words: disgusting, filthy, indecent, immoral, improper, impure, lascivious, lewd, licentious, and vulgar." These words have no objective meaning. Dictionaries often define them circularly (as the young and curious are frustrated to discover), in terms of one another. They partake of reality only through shared judgments and largely through assumed standards of sexual behavior or assumed theories of social cause-and-effect. Even in the rare instances where a modern court has held obscenity to be a fact, determinable on examination by a judge or jury, the "true test" of this determination has been found in speculative social psychology—"whether the tendency of the matter charged as obscenity is to deprave and corrupt those whose minds are open to such immoral influences . . ."—the notorious *Hicklin* rule.

To the extent that the law of obscenity is the sum of the cases tried under it, the law deals with only a limited part of the relationship between sex censorship and the arts. Censorship may be highly effective, through coercion or consent, and yet be extralegal if not illegal. The study of the law, case by case, tends to reduce the "problem" of obscenity to the problems posed in a series of court proceedings of a rather specialized character,

largely concerned with books and most often with books of a special kind—
those that fall somewhere between the categories of obvious trash and of
invulnerable classic—whose publishers are sufficiently tenacious or self-
confident to sustain litigation. Since the law offers apparently endless
possibilities for reinterpretation, both parties to an obscenity dispute tend
to regard it as a critical test—a step, in whichever direction, along the linear
scale between total censorship and total liberality. Thus, a lawyer may see in
the *Ulysses* decision "a great stride forward, possibly a greater stride than in
any previous single case," while a congressional committee can see it as
"the basis for excuse to print and circulate the filthiest most obscene literature without concurrent literary value to support it, ever known in history."
Both share the flattering illusion (for lawyers) that society takes its erotic
cues from the bench; but the *Ulysses* decision, after all, followed a decade of
sustained onslaught on social prudery of all kinds, and it was not, in its
consequences, the mortal blow to the *Hicklin* rule that it seemed at the time
to be.

The legal defense of literature against legal censorship, concurrently,
has had a somewhat confusing effect on debates over obscenity. It has
focussed attention on near-irrelevancies, such as the question of artistic
merit or the number of equally objectionable elements in Shakespeare and
the Bible, and distracted it from the conflicts more importantly at issue—
"the fight between the literati and the philistines," as two scholars have put
it, for jurisdiction over sexual manners and customs. Both adversaries have
frequently found it advantageous, for their respective reasons, to conduct
this battle in the courtroom: the censorious, because they see the shock value
of bringing before the public selected passages of books that might privately
be inoffensive to most literate adults; the defenders of such books, because
they see that common sense and most of the law is on their side. The outcome
is then in the lap of extremely whimsical deities, and both parties—in defeat
—tend to be victimized by the eloquence of their briefs. The literati despair-
ingly conclude that the victories of reason are seldom permanent; the
philistines, that "the blackest mud"—the words are Anthony Comstock's—
"is to be found behind the trees on which the sun shines brightest. In that
shadow the slime lies thick."

II

Comstockery, as Shaw named the disease, is ever with us. No generation
lacks for frightened witnesses to the power of obscenity to corrupt, even
where such testimony must necessarily cast a curious light on the individual
who offers it. The cause-and-effect relationship between obscenity and
lowered morals, perversion, or crime is simply—for many—an article of
faith which no evidence could disturb. Such evidence as there is, regrettably,
would not disturb them anyhow since it is likely to be negative and prove
mainly that no relationship can be proved—scholarly but superfluous support
for Mayor Walker's dictum that no girl was ever ruined by a book. The
very idea of literature having a tendency to corrupt can be amply shown
to depend on assumptions about the affecting agent, the nature of the
effect, the audience affected, and the arbiter of that effect which "are often

inconsistent with each other, unprecise and confusing." But the censor marches serenely on.

To those concerned with the inadequacies of the obscenity laws, it has inevitably occurred that a reasonable way out would be to make the demonstration of obscenity contingent on the demonstration of a corrupting effect. One commentator has semiseriously suggested that "[i]t might be an interesting innovation if censorship laws operated only when a plaintiff could prove that he himself had been depraved for lack of proper public safeguards." Short of this, it might still be possible to require the prosecution of allegedly obscene works to produce at least one witness who would admit to being corrupted by it. Typically, such testimony is offered by the committed proponents of censorship or by law officers. The cases in which any objective effect of the work can be adduced are rare, however, and there would be grave obstacles, I should think, to requiring that individuals demean themselves in order to incriminate an object. If censorship is wrong in principle, as so many of its opponents believe, then they do ill to grapple with it in terms of tactical trivialities that may win them the engagement but lose the campaign.

Moreover, the so-called "advances" within the law can very quickly be cancelled by retrogressions outside it—a point less appreciated by the literati than by the philistines, who are not so bedazzled by legality. The past few years, in particular, have witnessed an extraordinary comeback among the believers in sex censorship—not simply among its traditional friends, but what can only be called their new intellectual allies. Even without the latter's help, however, the former have learned to mask their objectives and to seek them without putting the matter of methods to a legal test. In this they have been encouraged (and considerably instructed) by a committee of the Eighty-second Congress, the Select Committee of the House of Representatives on Current Pornographic Materials, known for short as the Gathings Committee, which tried to discover ways of achieving sex censorship without having to endorse it. . . .

The nature of any censorship, in other words, is often a function of the anxieties generated by the medium or inherent in the milieu which the medium seeks to serve. At twenty-five to fifty cents, the pocket-size paperbacks are available not only to many adults who had not thought of themselves as book-buyers before, but to adolescents. Despite the overpowering incoherence and banality of its report, the Gathings Committee manages to make perfectly clear its desire to establish a connection between the corruption of the young, pornography, and the mass market enjoyed by the seven major paperback publishers then in operation. It denies to soft-cover books a degree of freedom it must allow to hard-cover ones, on the presumptive grounds that the increasing dissemination of the former constitutes a "menace to the moral structure of the Nation, particularly in the juvenile segment." The implication is that an adult who can afford to pay three dollars and fifty cents for obscenity can take care of himself. It is where the paperback book represents a penetration of "mature" attitudes from the minority bookstore class through to the majority newsstand class that the Committee is alarmed; it would like this process to be either halted or reversed. It sees its real enemies, as Comstock did, among the respectable, the partisans of the liberal enlightenment who insist upon unloosing evil—in the name of mere principle—on susceptible and unprotected youths.

Censorship and obscenity, as such, are not the real issues here—they are only camouflage for issues so embittered they cannot be openly posed. Nor are these, as they are often said to be, merely religious; one of the least sensible crochets of the anti-censorship school lies in attributing to Catholicism attitudes which are equally often, and often more vigorously, espoused by Protestants. In this respect, the Gathings Committee Report is especially instructive; it can representatively be described—like so much of the contemporary support for censorship—as a counterattack on an assumption of aristocratic invulnerability made by the forces that have been called the "discontented classes," vocal and dissident blocs formed by the intellectually dispossessed in the aftermath of the Roosevelt era. The Committee comes out against "modern" literature and "liberal" interpretations of the law in virtually the same breath, as though both had equally undermined the Republic. Often, views of this kind are called anti-intellectual, though they are, in many respects, not so much anti-intellectual as anti-chronological—part of a massive, integrated gripe against the passage of time. Clearly their holders are less antagonized by the work of the mind for its own sake than by the dominant literary and artistic style which has made them feel, for more than two decades, that they were esthetically out of fashion. Now that the wheel has turned, turned so far that the excesses of "liberalism" and "modernism" are deplored by those who once committed them, the day has come for revenge. A crusade against pornography, that most helpless of quarries, is made to order.

Thus it is that literature and its advocates find themselves so continually on the defensive, unprotected by the juridical triumphs of the past generation from the smut-hunters of the present one. The open competition among ideas cannot be relied on, where pornography is concerned, as long as no one will openly defend it. Like Communism or homosexuality, it can be attacked in the secure knowledge that no one will dare occupy its position. It then becomes the focal point for resentments less safe to assert, and everything suspect tends to be lumped together (not surprisingly, numerous citizens, loud in the pursuit of the dirty book, believe it to be somehow connected with the Communists). Often the "liberal" argument, as a way of touching base with respectability, has allowed that "smut for smut's sake" must be rigorously dealt with—forgetting that this is the only concession the would-be censor has ever needed to ask. As long as an exception is made for the indefensible or even the detestable—"Freedom for everybody, except Communists and pornographers"—then there will be people perfectly prepared to state that you or I are Communists and pornographers, or their dupes, until we prove to the contrary. It is at such times that one remembers why freedom has been said to be indivisible.

III

An equally serious objection to the treatment of obscenity as a largely legal problem arises from the distorting effect this has on any discussion of sexual morality. Concentration on what is forbidden, according to such arbitrary and variable rules, distracts attention from what is permitted— and from any perspective that might put the two in balance. It would surely seem desirable, where a subject is, by its nature, so delicate, to take into account the extraordinarily wide range of "normal" behavior, the fact that prudes are not the only ones entitled to reticence, and the universal human inability to draw a sharp line between lust and love. An adversary situation over obscenity reduces these factors to their ultimate fragility; it is the native environment of the neurotic, and Comstockery is its natural corol- lary. It renders the total effects of American sexuality even more ridiculous than they might naturally appear.

Yet, one cannot deal fairly with questions of obscenity without de- scribing the context out of which they emerge—the muddle of preoccupa- tions and prohibitions which define, at any given time, the standards each individual must reckon with long before the law does. On these, sex cen- sorship by law has pronounced effects, but they must be regarded as pre- existing—as the raw material of experience in which the law works—rather than as exterior accidents or consequences. Otherwise, consideration in the courtroom of the social effects of obscenity is absurd. If the law cannot recognize the effects which would be found in the absence of a given work of putative obscenity, then it cannot very well determine the effect of that work. However haltingly, in a rough-and-ready fashion, it must operate on some kind of theory of the American sex life—of what it is, or ought to be. . . .

American attitudes toward sex illustrate the inter-relationship between censorship and provocation in almost clinically pure form; to foreign critics, we offer the most striking example available of a society in which excitation and restraint have the continuous function of intensifying one another. Every censorship breeds evasion; it is in our highly developed techniques for evading our own censorship that the American culture fascinates the visitor—or the few local observers sufficiently alert to notice them. To the European eye, we give the impression of mak[ing] an unwholesome fetish of the female breast, of overwhelming our adolescents with erotic stimuli, and of hiding behind a "puritan façade" the reality of "un des pays sexuelle- ment les plus libres du monde." Confronted with the contrast between our preaching and our practice, we are hard put to refute the thesis propounded a decade ago by Philip Wylie: that the United States is "technically insane in the matter of sex."

The point need scarcely be labored that the American popular culture is saturated with sexual images, references, symbols, and exhortations; this is a conclusion that both literati and philistines might well agree on, and they might further agree that it reflects a condition of pervasive psychological disease. The difference would be in diagnosis. The censor sees a justification for intensified effort; his opponent sees the result of the censorship now in effect and a warning of disasters to come if more is applied. My own inclina- tion is toward the latter view; and, though I appreciate the obligation to con- vince those who think differently, I can only fill it by inviting them to examine their own experience from this vantage-point before abandoning it entirely. It is my contention that the symptoms of the American sexual neurosis, if there is such a thing, are the reflected distortions of a moral perspective that diminishes the healthy and accentuates the sick. . . .

Expecting much of sex, but feeling as individuals that much is denied them, Americans, as a mass, create in the substance of suppressed desire the remarkable symbolic figures that are found here as in no other culture. The existence of "the great American love goddess" is more often noted than explained. It is apparent that she enjoys high status, that she is attended by elaborate ceremonials, and that the titular embodiment of the divinity (at this writing: Marilyn Monroe) is only the reigning head of a hierarchy of sub-divinities, all of whom possess similar attributes. She is most often a movie star, though her talents as an actress and the merits of the films in which she appears are plainly immaterial. Her primary function is widely understood but rarely mentioned—that is, to serve as the object of autoerotic reverie. She represents, in brief, the commercial exploitation of the assumption that the American public is composed largely of Peeping Toms.

The assumption would appear to be well founded. It draws sustenance from the approach to sex on similar principles institutionalized by the advertising business. Diverted from literature and the arts, the forces that underlie obscenity or pornography expend themselves in this characteristic American medium. Here sex may be treated as powerful motivation, but only by expressing it in warped and perverted forms—*e.g.,* the women's underwear that is advertised far beyond its proportion of the market, so that we are daily surrounded with pictures of the feminine bosom, leg, and abdomen tightly constrained by clothing (the difference in effect between these and the "bondage photos" confiscated by the police seems to me one of degree only). To serve the hunger for the unattainable, we have brought into existence an entire class of women whose profession is catering to voyeurs, not even in the flesh, but through photographs—namely, the models. At its top are found the handful who pose for the fashion magazines and set the pace in cosmetics, posture, style, and aura at the outer reaches of unreal sophistication, where their taut, nerveless langour stands unchallenged— for lack of more fullblooded substitutes—as an ideal of the sensual.

Then, there is the theme of homosexuality, which runs through American popular culture (as well as literature) like a thread of not-so-innocent deceit. What is deceitful about it is not the conspiratorial existence forced on, accepted by, or darkly attributed to homosexuals. It is the connivance of the public in something it wishes to be titillated by, but not name—in its approval of novelists whose major theme of hatred for women is rarely mentioned; of comedians whose stock-in-trade is the exhibitionism of spastic, semi-hysterical effeminacy; of Western and detective-story heroes who rigorously spurn their heroines in the search for sadomasochistic purification. All these are not only permitted, but profuse. Not a word of complaint about them comes from the self-appointed custodians of morality, who are far too busily occupied protecting teen-agers from de Maupassant. Censorship, official and unofficial, lets pass into the social mainstream countless images and innuendoes that could only be identified—if they were to be identified— as perverse. Of the normal, the lustful thoughts and desires of one sex for the other, it faithfully removes whatever trace it can.

This paradox has been the subject of a book, the most important study of Anglo-Saxon censorship yet to appear—Gershon Legman's *Love and Death*. Mr. Legman's subject is the literary sadism which is intensified by the censorship of sex; his motif is the shameful anomaly of American mores which make love, which is legal in fact, illegal on paper, while murder, which is illegal in fact, is not only legal on paper, but the basis of the greatest publishing successes of all time. To be sure, affection and hatred are opposite poles of human experience, and art necessarily concerns itself with each— the act in which life begins and that in which it ends. The highest skill need not morbidly exaggerate the physical details of either, but neither will be denied it. Deny one only, and the other takes its place. Mr. Legman overpoweringly documents his case that in contemporary America, this is what has substantially occurred.

Though we often speak of sex and sadism together—as two equally regrettable qualities in the novels of Mickey Spillane, for example—in actual practice, we tolerate blood and guts in a quantity and concreteness wholly denied to sexual love. The time-tested formula for the "sexed-up" cover of a paperback book is a near-naked girl with a revolver, and it is curious that critics should comment so often on the nudity and ignore the imminence of death. Within the letter of the law, as in the popular culture, sex and violence tend to be entangled—we label an atomic bomb with the title of a Rita Hayworth movie and call an abbreviated bathing suit a "Bikini"—but in the courts, it is exceptional that the two are prosecuted with equal emphasis. The typical law against obscenity prohibits it in company with other incitements to crime as well as lust, but we all take for granted the state of general acceptance for printed murdering, whipping, gouging, and wholesale blood-letting which makes half the law unenforceable.

And this is only part of the price we pay for prudery. Is it not too high?

IV

Needless to say, despite these distractions, society survives. The vanity of lawyers in assuming that the law has a significant effect on sexual habits is matched by the vanity of writers in assuming that literature has a comparable effect. Fortunately, there are other forces at work determining conduct. Almost by definition, such enjoyment of life as there is by the vast majority escapes observation and reporting. Young people, determined to explore the mysteries for themselves, continue to grow up without having been successfully convinced that sex is unclean; nor are they always unwilling to scandalize their elders. Throughout this society that resolutely pretends to the contrary, there remains a streak of amiable lewdness and bawdry that has nothing to do with literature and breaks through censorship of any kind at the most unexpected times and places. There is a shudder of outraged horror in each community where a "non-virgin club" is uncovered, but as far as I am aware, these remarkable institutions neither take their inspiration from books nor are in any way discouraged by censorship. They testify to the extent to which sex can be self-induced, self-sustaining, and ultimately self-justified.

But even the sophisticated objectors to pornography, who define it as "calculated to stimulate sex feelings independent of another loved and chosen human being," suppress or distort any suggestion that Eros has, in its own right, a civilizing and illuminating potential. They seem to regard its exclusive function as the continuation of the race, and they are somewhat arbitrarily cruel in their strictures on those whose desires fail to be co-ordinated with the propagative process. Mrs. Banning imagines the ads in "sexy magazines" to be directed at "frustrated men, who were too short or too fat or too friendless or too far from home to have a successful sex rela-tionship"; while Margaret Mead defines the difference between bawdry and pornography as that between the music hall and the "strip tease, where lonely men, driven and haunted, go alone. . . ." Such views impress me as inadequately informed by an appreciation of sex, not simply as a genetic mechanism, but as one of the avenues through which reality is exposed to us. This blessing has been conferred on mankind impartially and is luckily not within anyone's province to allocate.

There is a sense in which every nation gets the pornography it deserves. If we forbid the writing of erotica to all but those who are willing to break the law, we have no fair complaint if the results are trivial, mean, and in-artistic. We are little entitled to the conclusion that the subject matter of sex cannot be tastefully—or even beautifully—treated if we have never tried to treat it so. Least of all can we pride ourselves on our moral stature as a people until we have further progressed beyond the outhouse phase, mani-fested by the Gathings Committee and its numerous facsimiles, in which a sniggering shame is our characteristic approach to sex. The true obsceni-ties of American life lie in our vicious public consumption of human suf-fering, in virtually every form and every media. By comparison, the literature of sexual love would seem to me vastly preferable, but in offering a personal opinion, I hasten to take counsel—while the chance remains—from the words of a distinguished jurist [Judge Curtis Bok].

> There will always be battle in the arena of free opinion; there always has been since Plato thought that Homer should be expurgated and said so. I believe in the constant working of these laws of natural censorship and am willing to work my own as a part of the process. . . . I know of no more important time for courageous good taste than when there is not much of it about. Liberty is easier to win than to deserve, and if it is treated as either a license or a vacuum, the police will come or the walls will fall.

The Social Cost of Obscenity
James Jackson Kilpatrick/from *The Smut Peddlers*

James Jackson Kilpatrick (1920–   ), a newspaperman, has been editor of the Richmond News Leader *since 1961 and, more recently, has also been associated with the* National Review. *He has written and edited several books, among them a judicious study entitled* The Southern Case for Segre-gation. *An ardent defender of free speech, he has made a careful study of commercial obscenity and of the legal problems involved in its suppression. The results of that study are embodied in a book entitled* The Smut Peddlers, *from which portions of the chapter "The Case of Censorship" have been selected. It is Kilpatrick's virtue to be able to defend censorship without incurring Larrabee's epithet "smut-hunter." Where Larrabee is urbane and discursive, Kilpatrick is blunt—yet both men cover the same range of topics. Kilpatrick takes pains first to show, by reference to repeated decisions of the courts of the land, that obscenity has never been considered a form of free speech: "The strong rock of the First Amendment was intended to be a bulwark of liberty; it was never conceived as a shield for the merchant of filth."*

The term obscenity, *argues Kilpatrick, is not so obscure and elusive as the liberals maintain, and it is certainly no more obscure than such terms as* justifiable homicide *or* consent *in a case of rape. He then meets directly the objection that no causal connection can be made between obscene literature and vicious conduct. Of course, no immediate causal connection can be established, he admits,—but a corruptive tendency is attested to by many psychiatrists, sociologists, and police officers. Furthermore, there is an ancillary form of corruption—affecting those debauched by the trade of producing such materials. The profitableness of the trade leads, inevitably, to control by racketeers and gangsters.*

Kilpatrick has no illusions that obscenity can be prevented; he does, however, argue that it can be controlled and checked. In general, throughout his article, he is dealing not with high-priced and exotic erotica but with what he calls "hard-core" pornography, the sort of "vicious slickness" that is aimed at young people and is sold over, or under, counters throughout the nation. He concludes by agreeing that education, at home and in the school, is the ultimate answer; but, in the light of the evidence he has accumulated, he sees an immediate need for measures which will start checking the corrupting flood at once. Generally, he remarks, the initial experience of other vices, like drunkenness, does not leave an indelible mark upon the psyche; but a sudden and brutal exposure to sexual perversion, even in the vicarious medium of a book or movie, can distort a youth's capacity for normal sexual expectations and experiences.

The case for censorship

Very well. Let one or two things be said at the outset of a statement in behalf of the case *for* censorship. The proponents here, taking the affirmative side in this debate, are aggrieved at the abuse they have been receiving from the liberal team. They are weary of being depicted in the grim garb of the late Mr. Volstead; the hat doesn't fit. They are becoming increasingly resentful of the role in which the disciples of free expression would cast them, as prudes, bluenoses, Comstocks, crackpots, fuzzy threads on the lunatic fringe. They have had the contemptuous question thrown at them often enough: "What right do *you* have to judge of the literature to be read in a community?" Speaking as a legion of decent, normal, unashamed citizens and parents, they throw back a blunt reply: "Our right as free men to speak freely."

They are angry, these decent and normal people. The publisher or editor who mistakes this anger deceives only himself. They are angry at the obscene filth that, all unwanted, floods into their homes with the stench of a stopped-up toilet; they are angry at what they conceive to be the corrupting effects of pornographic literature; they are angry at the imputation that they are somehow poorer Americans than, say, the ex-pimp author of some paperback book or the cynical publisher of a nudie magazine. Of course, they agree, an author has rights. But what of the community? Does the community have no rights? Does freedom of speech exist only for the writer, publisher, and peddler of salacious books? Or do those who object to filth have some freedom of expression also?

The proponents of obscenity statutes have not the slightest hesitation in responding to the principal arguments of their opponents.

Then Wayne came back. "I've done all the work so far," I said. "You take off my panties." And he did, and let me tell you that felt like nothing in the world, having Wayne Whitney take off my panties. I mean it was a lovely feeling. . . .

This is what is meant by the great American ideal of freedom of the press? Freedom for this?

"Perhaps the most widespread and popular form of perversion," Cardinal Spellman once remarked, "is the perversion of 'freedom.' When hypocrites apply this sacred term to contemptible schemes in order to prey upon the weaknesses of unformed characters under the banner of 'freedom of speech' or 'freedom of the press,' they are not only victimizing our children, but endangering our nation's treasured heritage. . . ."

Those who imagine that, in drafting the First Amendment, the founding fathers intended to protect obscene and profane writings mistake both the law and the mores of that day. Judge Desmond has pointed out that for more than sixty years prior to ratification of the First Amendment the publication of an obscene book, picture, or article was a common-law offense in England. And far from repudiating the English common law, such states as Virginia made it the cornerstone of their own law. The strong rock of the First Amendment was intended to be a bulwark of liberty; it never was conceived as a shield for the merchant of filth. . . .

Mr. Justice Frankfurter, to cite one . . . authority, has no doubt of the constitutional validity of state laws in this field. His concurring opinion in *Smith* v. *People*, the California case decided in December of 1959, sounds a recurring theme:

The Court accepts the settled principle of constitutional law that traffic in obscene literature may be outlawed as crime. . . . It ought at least to be made clear that the Court's decision in its practical effect is not intended to nullify the conceded power of the state to prohibit booksellers from trafficking in obscene literature. . . . The constitutional protection of nonobscene speech cannot absorb the constitutional power of the states to deal with obscenity. . . . [The Court's requirements as to *scienter*] cannot be of a nature to nullify for all practical purposes the power of the state to deal with obscenity. . . . As a practical matter therefore the exercise of the constitutional right of a state to regulate obscenity will carry with it some hazard. . . .

True enough, no adjudications by the Supreme Court as to the constitutionality of anything may be viewed as permanent. The Southern states, in their maintenance of racially separate schools, were unanimously within the Constitution at noon on that May 17, and unanimously outside the Constitution at one o'clock, the Constitution not having been altered by a comma during the lunch hour. Are motion pictures entitled to the guaranties of free speech? In 1915, when McKenna wrote *Mutual,* a unanimous court said no. In 1959, when Harlan wrote the decision on *Lady Chatterley,* a unanimous court said yes. Same Constitution. It is sometimes hard to adjust to these things. But this phenomenon aside, the constitutionality of obscenity laws must be viewed, as this book is written, as certain, definite, and unshakable. The courts demand only that obscenity statutes meet the same general requirements laid down for other criminal laws.

The term "obscenity" is no more vague or elusive than many another concept of law; objections on this score are captious.

It is often said, generally with some solemn wagging of judicial heads, that obscenity law is a very delicate and difficult field of jurisprudence. Sometimes this is expressed in the superlative: it is the "most delicate" or "most difficult" field of them all. The standards are "vagrant breezes to which the mariner must ever trim his sails." Nothing is fixed; nothing is definite. That which was obscene yesterday is not obscene today, and so on.

To these arguments the defenders of obscenity statutes answer simply, bosh! In their view truly precise criminal statutes are the exception, not the rule. For every sharp and cleanly delineated law, such as the law on honest weight, or the laws on speeding, or the laws that divide petit from grand larceny at the fifty-dollar mark, they cite a dozen statutes in which a jury's judgment, discretion, and flexible interpretation spell the difference between guilt and innocence. What constitutes justifiable homicide? What constitutes non-negligent manslaughter? How is "consent" proved in a rape case? These are all questions of judgment. And on the civil side of the law a thousand discretionary questions depend entirely upon the opinion of the twelve good men and true. What is simple negligence? What is gross negligence? Due care? The prudent man? Reasonable doubt? The chancery and appellate courts daily must feel their way into questions of testamentary intent, tax avoidance in anticipation of death, the four corners of an inconsistent will. What of the ten thousand individual and particular issues of due process? What constitutes a fair trial? How long may a prisoner be questioned prior to arraignment? It would be wonderfully convenient if appellate courts had some convenient thermometer, measured in degrees of inflammatory oratory, by which the reversible passions of a summation speech could be read.

The law of obscenity is not different. The word "obscene" is a word of common usage. Jurors know what it means, precisely as they know what other elusive terms of the law mean—*to them*. And if an obscenity law cannot be drafted as neatly as a speed-limit law, one ought not to complain excessively.

"I confess I see nothing absurd or benighted about leaving the law in such a state," Judge Desmond commented tartly. "No book has a brother, and it is, I think, beyond human ingenuity to devise a legal text for obscenity so precise that it can be laid alongside a book for comparison with an automatic mathematical result made instantly available. The law does not claim to be an exact science. It is a set of behavioral rules applied by human judges to human acts. Even theologians differ." . . .

> *A causal relationship between obscene materials and antisocial behavior may not be susceptible to statistical proof—by its very nature, the relationship is unprovable—but the common sense of mankind, supported by the opinions of experts, holds strongly that such a relationship exists.*

The proponents of obscenity statutes are entirely willing to meet Judge Bok, Judge Frank, and the philosophers of the Civil Liberties Union on this crucial question of causal relationship. Bok's proposed requirement of "clear and present danger" seems to them as unfair as it is unrealistic; many other fields of the law recognize the evils of a gradual or continuing social ill. The smog laws, for example, do not rest upon the theory that one belch of smoke, from one chimney, causes grave damage to the public welfare; it is the smoke of many chimneys, mixed together, that adversely affects the public welfare. Neither does the law, in other fields, insist upon a chain of cause and effect that runs from A to B only; the law recognizes that C and D may be gravely, if indirectly, affected also.

The first contention of proponents is that the precise relationship between pornography and antisocial behavior is simply unknowable. No one ever has contended that obscene materials are the *entire* cause of juvenile delinquency, or the *entire* cause of adult perversion either; the most that is contended is that obscene materials are a contributory factor toward inciting behavior that society has every right to suppress. To demand, as Judge Bok demanded, that one demonstrate evidence of immediate and direct incitement to overt acts—evidence of readers who lay down their dirty books and rush to the streets for a night of satyriasis—is to lay upon the proponents of obscenity statutes a burden not required elsewhere in the law. Obscenity does not operate with the immediacy of a cyanide pellet, but with the imperceptible slowness of leukemia. Father Terence J. Murphy, speaking before a Loyola University Law School symposium, remarked that in demanding empirical-statistical evidence of such a causal relationship the followers of Judge Bok and Judge Frank demand the impossible.

> They call for evidence produced by experiments which would require thousands of persons to be isolated from all erotic visual material over a number of years. And then their behavior pattern would have to be compared to that of a group of similar psychological make-up, influenced by the same environmental factors, but subjected to controlled exposure to obscenity. This demand by the men who know

only of one method is completely unrealistic. The practical difficulties of carrying out such experiments in our society are readily evident.

The best one can do, in attempting soberly and realistically to appraise the dangers of the obscenity racket, is to apply common sense to known social ills and to weigh the testimony of experts. One such social ill, by general acceptance, is the appalling increase in juvenile delinquency. Between 1948 and 1957 juvenile court cases increased by 136 per cent while the under-seventeen population was increasing by only 27 per cent. FBI reports show a shocking increase in juvenile prostitution. The divorce rate has more than tripled since 1900. Plainly enough, something is wrong with national patterns of moral behavior, especially among adolescents and young adults, and doubtless a hundred factors have contributed in one degree or another to this disturbing picture. But our inquiry here goes to the effect of one factor only.

Said Monsignor George H. Guilfoyle, of New York, before the Granahan Committee of the House: "Without exception, it is the experience of the directors and staffs in [youth] programs, that the damage caused to children by obscene publications and pornography is readily noticeable, affects the entire personality and values of the person, and is extremely difficult and at times practically impossible to correct."

Dr. George W. Henry, professor of clinical psychiatry at the Cornell University College of Medicine, appeared before the Kefauver Committee of the Senate in 1955. He examined a book of sadomasochistic drawings offered as an exhibit in the hearings. This colloquy ensued:

> MR. GAUGHAN: I ask you, Doctor, specifically, can you see any purpose for this publication other than the one purpose to cause erotic stimuli by showing acts of sexual perversion?
>
> DR. HENRY: No, the sole purpose is to stimulate people erotically in an abnormal way.
>
> MR. GAUGHAN: Doctor, I ask you, could children be sexually perverted by looking at, by studying, and by dwelling upon photos of this nature and the contents of this book?
>
> DR. HENRY: Yes.
>
> CHAIRMAN KEFAUVER: Doctor, is it a very unwholesome influence, this sort of thing?
>
> DR. HENRY: It is.
>
> CHAIRMAN KEFAUVER: In your opinion the increase in sex crimes, deviations, that we are having—does that increase result in part at least from the reading and looking at magazines and pictures of this kind by children?
>
> DR. HENRY: I would think that was an important factor in the increase.

The Kefauver Committee also heard from William Deerson, dean of discipline at Haaren High School in New York. He was asked about pornographic material he had confiscated among the two thousand male students. Did such material in any way affect the juvenile delinquency rate of the students? He replied: "There is definitely a connection between the juvenile delinquency rate and the reading of this material. I feel that the material when read excites the young man; it stimulates him and may lead to some overt act."

Dr. Benjamin Karpman, chief psychotherapist of St. Elizabeth's Hospital in Washington, D.C., testified that pornographic literature draws a boy "into all sorts of gang life, which later discharges itself as juvenile delinquency." He found a "very direct relationship between juvenile delinquency, sex life, and pornographic literature."

Such testimony could be extended at length. Both the Kefauver Committee and the Granahan Committee also developed examples of specific crimes apparently directly attributable to the influence of pornographic or sado-masochistic magazines. One such case occurred in Florida, where a seventeen-year-old boy, nude, was found fatally suspended from a bondage device copied from a fetish publication.

The evil effects of the obscenity traffic are not confined to the customer's end of the commerce. If a causal relationship is being sought between the sale of a filthy magazine and some antisocial consequence, one may well ponder the supplier's end of the business also. As the racket grows, a steady stream of teen-age girls must be attracted into nude modeling, perversion, and prostitution. Boys must be tempted into the sordid business of serving as sex partners, photographers, film processors, and salesmen. And inexorably, as the racket swells toward new records of annual take, it attracts those overlords of crime and corruption who do not hesitate to work upon police and legislative bodies.

Nor are adolescents and young people the only ones harmed by steady subjection to obscene materials. In a Delaware trial in 1952 Dr. M. A. Tarumianz, state psychiatrist, was asked about the effect of obscene movies on others. He testified: "I have found that such films are not only detrimental to the youth, but detrimental to any human being who has normal endowments and is not peculiarly psychopathically inclined. It creates various deviations of thinking and emotional instability in regard to sex problems. A happily married individual who is considered a mature adult individual, seeing such films, becomes seriously concerned with whether he is obtaining the necessary gratification of his sex desires from his normally endowed and inclined wife. It may deviate him in accepting that there is something which arouses him to become interested in an abnormal type of sex satisfaction which he has had perhaps from this picture. So it is unquestionably detrimental to adults."

But it is hardly necessary for one to be a psychiatrist, a psychologist, a police officer, or a priest to form an opinion on the consequences of prolonged exposure to obscenity. The common experience of mankind provides eloquent examples of the manner in which anti-social patterns develop from perhaps harmless beginnings. Such patterns may not be plotted exactly; expert evidence in the form of tidy statistical charts, tabulated to the second decimal point, never can be compiled. The question of cause and effect may be debated endlessly.

"I say that we can no longer afford to wait for an answer," J. Edgar Hoover said in 1959. "What we do know is that in an overwhelmingly large number of cases sex crime is associated with pornography. We know that sex criminals read it, are clearly influenced by it. I believe pornography is a major cause of sex violence. I believe that if we can eliminate the distribution of such items among impressionable school-age children, we shall greatly reduce our frightening crime rate."

It is no more futile to combat obscenity than it is to combat other social evils that may gain allurement from the fact of their suppression.

Police officials and decent-literature committees are well aware that existing statutes have not wiped out the obscenity racket. Postal authorities are convinced, indeed, that the racket is growing vastly larger. But they do not see these trends as evidence of the futility of their efforts. If this complaint were valid most criminal statutes would be equally subject to repeal. The drunk driver is still on the road; the narcotics peddler still goes about his evil trade; embezzlers daily find the temptation of easy money more than they can resist. No laws ever have been wholly successful in curbing man's predilection for sin. The churches are still doing business; so are the jailers.

The proponents do contend this: where obscenity statutes have been effectively enforced, the volume of seriously offensive material has been greatly reduced. They contend also that the familiar analogy between bootleg liquor and bootleg smut is more apparent than real. The man who is determined to have booze will find it. His craving is immediate and urgent, and it can be easily satisfied by the illicit sale of an otherwise licit item; bellhops do not customarily deal in moonshine put up in Mason jars, but in legal whisky legally bought. The ordinary male in search of a sexy magazine, however, is not so aggressive; he will settle for whatever reading matter is at hand, and ordinarily his wants can be sidetracked. In smaller towns and cities the number of newsstands, terminals, and drugstores is limited, and the number of such retail outlets deliberately dealing in prurient stuff is more limited still. Obscenity statutes, it is contended, indeed can be effective in reducing the total volume of obscene material in such communities and in making it harder to find.

There is this argument also, that even where such laws may not be relentlessly enforced, their very existence on the statute books accomplishes two desirable ends: the statutes reflect community censure upon a social evil, and they do provide a deterrent to dealers in hard-core items who otherwise could engage freely in their ugly traffic. And if one effect of an obscenity statute is to make forbidden fruit seem sweeter, and to run up the price on dirty pictures, that is too bad, but it would be a strange sort of morality that would sanction immorality at bargain prices.

Postmaster General Summerfield responded to Morris Ernst's proposal for an open market in pornographic items in a strong address before a women's conference in Washington in the spring of 1959:

What is likely to happen if we do not rid ourselves of this social cancer? First, we may as well concede that the obscenity business, with its vast revenue, will be taken over by organized crime to a far greater extent. It will become a gigantic organized racket, with millions more of our children its principal victims. The undermining of the moral fiber of the nation's children will spread; with the poisoning of increasing millions of minds. Sex crimes will be a spreading blight on our society, and will become far more prevalent than they are today. And overall, we could expect an ultimate breakdown of order and decency in this country.

Judge Desmond wraps up the proponents' case on this point in two sentences:

> Obscenity, real, serious, not imagined or puritanically exaggerated, is today as in all past centuries, a public evil, a public nuisance, a public pollution. When its effective control requires censorship, I see no reason why democratic government should not use democratic processes on a high administrative level, under the control of the courts, to suppress such obscenity.

Yes, education is of course the ultimate answer to the obscenity racket, but ultimate solutions need to be supplemented by more immediate remedies.

On the fifth point of disagreement one finds no disagreement. In all of its publications the National Office for Decent Literature emphasizes affirmative and constructive reading, even as it censures the magazines and paperbacks that seem to its readers obscene. Americans for Moral Decency advances a nine-point program "on the positive side," in which the organization urges parents to cultivate in their children a love of good books, to support public libraries, and to foster the development of home libraries. The Citizens for Decent Literature, perhaps the most militant of the clean-up associations, hopes in time to launch a positive program, but attorney Charles H. Keating, Jr., founder of the CDL, is a realist. He says:

> In some families good, solid training may offset the lure of these publications, but I'm afraid they are in the minority. The plain fact is that this pornography, contrived by photographers and writers who know all the tricks of their trade, is deliberately designed to appeal to youths for whom a great curiosity about the human body is a normal thing. There is a vicious slickness about these publications. It is absurd for us to expect youths to resist these enticements, and then call them delinquents when they do not.

In the view of proponents the vice of obscenity, especially as young people may be caught in it, is not one that yields readily to education or home instruction. It is a secret sort of thing, operating upon the mind, not readily detectible. The young man who experiments with alcohol or narcotics soon enough evidences some physical reaction; his excesses can be detected early, and no lasting consequences may develop. The sex thing is another matter. In testimony before congressional committees, psychiatrists have emphasized the terrible lifelong effects that obscene materials—especially materials that emphasize perversion and homosexuality—can have on boys and girls in the impressionable years of puberty. Sex attitudes can be fixed at this age, so deeply that no parental affection or discipline can ever alter them, and if an attitude is built up of casualness, coarseness, brutality, and sheer carnal satisfaction, damage is done that cannot be undone later on. The high-school student who takes too much to drink will be all right the next day, but the seventeen-year-old who witnesses a stag movie in which men and women engage like animals in wanton copulation will find the image burned upon his subconscious. "The mind that becomes soiled in youth," Mark Twain once remarked, "can never again be washed clean." And when a youth accepts the idea of sex without love he is stained inside.

That is the viciousness of this racket, that it stains. The worst of the obscene magazines and books are engaged in a perverted educative process of their own. Keating speaks from a prolonged study of the field when he says:

> The magazines are not just amoral. They are openly and avowedly anti-Christian. It is not a question of depicting sin as virtue. Believe me, our problem would not be so complicated if these magazines merely contained too much unadorned flesh and indecent language.
>
> These magazines attack morality by ridiculing virtue, chastity, fidelity or restraint. Anyone who lives by a code of virtue is laughed at as a victim of outmoded hypocritical prudery. To have any scruples about free sexual indulgence is to be neurotically repressed.
>
> Instead of the Christian concept of love and marriage, the magazines advocate a pagan, libertine life.

Thus the case for the proponents. They conceive their war upon obscenity as a duty they owe society and as a responsibility they hold as parents and good citizens. They are deeply alarmed by what seem to them the manifest evil consequences of the traffic in pornography, and they are determined to put down these consequences as best they can. And on two main fronts they propose to carry their battle to the enemy. They are proceeding, that is to say, through private action and through public law.

The problem of education began when the first child was born, a problem which may be summed up in the apparently simple question, "What is man?" All educational theories and practices are attempts to answer this question and efforts to rear the child to correspond with the answer.

The ancient Greeks were the first to be fully conscious of both the problem of education and the range of solutions. Since progress cannot be made within fundamentals, but only from them, the Greek definitions of the problem are the ones we still work with. First, either all men are basically alike, in which case their education should be the same, or else they have differences sufficiently radical to justify corresponding differences in education. Second, if their educations are different, the question arises whether practices will differ in degree or in kind. Both formulations are radically political, social, and economic; it is no wonder that ever since the ancient Greeks, education has been a fundamental concern of Western society.

Ancient education was designed primarily for what we today call an "elite"; neither the lowest class, the slaves, nor those just above them had the leisure requisite for literature—the Greek word for *school* (*scholê*) means "leisure." In modern times, industry and technology have increasingly emancipated society's economic slaves, and there has been a proportionate increase in the number of those educated. Gone are the days when such diverse kinds of humanists as Erasmus, Montaigne, and Machiavelli directed their efforts toward the education of princes; today even the most aristocratic temperaments must deal with the problem of educating the multitude.

Increased economic freedom has enabled men to center their attention on their children, first as persons, second as future citizens—sometimes the order of importance has been reversed. Perhaps ideally the two roles should coalesce, but in fact they tend to become poles around which conflicting theories of education crystallize. John Dewey and Robert M. Hutchins are spokesmen for these polar views. Dewey's influences on American education in the primary and secondary schools has been enormous—so enormous that many crimes have been committed in his name. It is refreshing to return to his own words and to find there an intelligent analysis of the twentieth-century educational needs of America. Hutchins has made his influence felt mostly in the colleges; a remarkable number of American college presidents have come from the University of Chicago, where he was president and chancellor. Where Dewey is experimental and pragmatic, Hutchins is theoretical and dogmatic—yet Dewey was a philosopher of education, not an educator, and Hutchins was a practical administrator of a great university. That paradox should help avoid stock responses to the pejorative adjectives that often are applied to each.

Progressive Education
John Dewey/"The Need for a Philosophy of Education"

John Dewey (1859–1952) was one of America's most important philosophers of education; the most violent of his critics—of whom there are many—testify to his importance by their virulence. As often happens with seminal thinkers, Dewey has been the victim of many misguided disciples. Readers are often told not to judge Dewey by the notions and practices of his followers, but such admonitions seldom are effective until his works have been read. The essay presented here, "The Need for a Philosophy of Education," will cause many anti-Deweyites to revise their opinions. Under its modest misnomer lies no mere exhortation but rather the principles of that philosophy of education which Dewey is calling for. In this respect, it is like Emerson's famous essay on the American Scholar.

Dewey's essay is written with such insight and cogency—and uncharacteristic clarity—that one finds it difficult to disagree with its implications. Education, says Dewey, is a process of development, of growth—"and it is the process *and not merely the result that is important." Since education is part of life, it should, he argues, be treated not just as a means but as an end in itself. Dewey clearly sees the purpose of education as social, but for him a society is good to the extent that it develops to the fullest the potentialities of its citizens. And he means* all *its citizens. No elite, he writes, however small or large, can reach its potential if a part of the same society is denied the opportunity to develop. He is never tired of censuring the great cultures of the past for resting on a basis of slavery.*

By placing emphasis on the individual process and not on uniform subject matter, Dewey opened the doors of schoolhouses to every kind of subject in order to cater to the varying abilities and interests of the students. The relationship of Dewey's theories to our two issues is clear: the almost sacred importance of the individual's "process" and growth requires that there be equality of opportunity in education for all; hence there can be no intellectual segregation, no cultural elite with its own schools and programs, no "aristocracy of the intellect" such as John Adams looked for.

Furthermore, the very process of progressive "democratization" will require that students participate in organizing their own education, in what is now called "the decision-making process." According to Dewey, the child's natural potentialities must control the form of education and not the other way around. The recent outbreaks of riotous clamor for "student power" are a natural outgrowth of Dewey's theory that the child should not be on the receiving end of education but should be an active participant in the process. It may be doubtful that Dewey would have sanctioned the violence which characterizes the cry for power, but it is likely that he would have pointed to the riots as symptoms of education's failure to embrace and embody his theories.

The phrase "progressive education" is one, if not of protest, at least of contrast, of contrast with an education which was predominantly static in subject-matter, authoritarian in methods, and mainly passive and receptive from the side of the young. But the philosophy of education must go beyond any idea of education that is formed by way of contrast, reaction and protest. For it is an attempt to discover what education *is* and how it takes place. Only when we identify education with schooling does it seem to be a simple thing to tell what education actually is, and yet a clear idea of what it *is* gives us our only criterion for judging and directing what goes on in schools.

It is sometimes supposed that it is the business of the philosophy of education to tell what education *should* be. But the only way of deciding what education should be, at least, the only way which does not lead us into the clouds, is discovery of what actually takes place when education really occurs. And before we can formulate a philosophy of education we must know how human nature is constituted in the concrete; we must know about the working of actual social forces; we must know about the operations through which basic raw materials are modified into something of greater value. The need for a philosophy of education is thus fundamentally the need for finding out what education really *is*. We have to take those cases in which we find there is a real development of desirable powers, and then find out how this development took place. Then we can project what has taken place in these instances as a guide for directing our other efforts. The need for this discovery and this projection is the need for a philosophy of education.

What then is education when we find actual satisfactory specimens of it in existence? In the first place, it is a process of development, of growth. And it is the *process* and not merely the result that is important. A truly healthy person is not something fixed and completed. He is a person whose processes and activities go on in such a way that he will continue to be healthy. Similarly, an educated person is the person who has the power to go on and get more education. Just what do we mean by growth, by development? Some of the early educational philosophers, like Rousseau and his followers, made much use of the analogy of the development of a seed into the full-grown plant. They used this analogy to draw the conclusion that in human beings there are latent capacities which, if they are only left to themselves, will ultimately flower and bear fruit. So they framed the notion of *natural* development as opposed to a directed growth which they regarded as artificial.

But in the first place the growth of a seed is limited as compared with that of a human being; its future is largely prescribed by its antecedent nature. It has not got the capacities for growth in different directions toward different outcomes that are characteristic of the more flexible and richly endowed human young. The latter is also, if you please, a seed, a collection of germinal powers, but he may become a sturdy oak, a willow that bends with every wind, a thorny cactus or a poisonous weed.

This fact suggests a second fallacy. Even the seed of a plant does not grow simply of itself. It must have light, air and moisture in order to grow. Its development is after all controlled by conditions and forces that are outside of it. Native inherent forces must interact with those of its surroundings if there is to be life and development. In fact, development, even with a plant, is a matter of the *kind of interaction* that goes on between itself and the conditions and forces that form its environment. A stunned oak, a stalk of maize that bears few ears with only a few scattered grains, exhibit so-called natural development as truly as does the noble tree with expanding branches or the ear of maize that wins the prize at an exhibition. The difference in result may in part be due to native stock, but it is also due in part to what the environment has provided. And even the finest native stock would come to an untimely end or result in a miserable product if its own energies could not interact with favorable conditions of light, moisture, air, etc.

Since there are two factors involved in the existence of any interaction, the idea and ideal of education must take account of both. Traditional school methods and subject-matter failed to take into account the *diversity* of capacities and needs that exists in different human beings. It virtually assumed that, for purposes of education at least, all human beings are as much alike as peas in a pod, and it therefore provided a uniform curriculum for all.

In the second place, it failed to recognize that the *initiative* in growth comes from the needs and powers of the pupil. The *first* step in the interaction that results in growth comes from the reaching out of the tentacles of the individual, from an effort, at first blind, to procure the materials that his potentialities demand in order that they may come into action and find satisfaction. As with the body, hunger and power of taking and assimilating nourishment are the first necessities. Without them, the food that is theoretically most nutritious is offered in vain. Nothing would be more extraordinary if we had a proper system of education than the assumption, now so commonly made, that the mind of the individual is naturally averse to learning, and has to be either browbeaten or coaxed into action. Every mind, even of the youngest, is naturally or inherently seeking for those modes of active operation that are within the limits of its capacities—precisely as the body of the baby is constantly active as long as the infant is awake. The problem, a difficult and delicate one, is to discover what tendencies are especially seeking expression at a particular time and just what materials and methods will serve to evoke and direct a truly educative development.

The practical counterpart of the failure of traditional education to see that the initiative in learning and growth is with the individual learner lay in the method of imposition from the side of the teacher and reception, absorption, from the side of the pupil. Unwillingness to learn naturally follows when there is failure to take into account tendencies that are urgent in the existing make-up of an individual. All sorts of external devices then have to be resorted to in order to achieve absorption and retention of imposed subject-matter and skills. This method of teaching may be compared to inscribing records upon a passive phonographic disc to result in giving back what has been inscribed when the proper button is pressed in recitation or examination.

It is impossible, of course, for any teacher not to observe that there *are* real differences among pupils. But because these differences are not carried back to concrete differences in individuality, to differences in needs, in desires, in direction of native interest, they are too often generalized by being summed up under two main heads. Some pupils are just naturally bright while others are dull and stupid! Some are docile and obedient and others are unruly and troublesome! Conformity then becomes the criterion by which the pupil is judged in spite of the fact that initiative, originality and independence are precious qualities in life.

While the raw material and the starting-point of growth are found in native capacities, the environing conditions which it is the duty of the educator to furnish are the indispensable means by which intrinsic possibilities are developed. Native capacities are the beginning, the starting-point. They are not the end and they do not of themselves decide the end. A gardener, a worker of metals, will not get far in his work if he does not observe and pay attention to the properties of the material he deals with. But if he permits these properties to dictate what he does, he will not get *anywhere*. Development will be arrested, not promoted. He must bring to his consideration of what he finds an ideal of possibilities not realized. This idea and ideal must be in line with the constitution of the raw material; it must not do violence to them; it must express *their* possibilities. But, nevertheless, it cannot be extracted from any study of them as they now exist. It must come from seeing them imaginatively, reflectively; and hence it must come from a source other than what is already at hand.

In the case of the educator the demand for imaginative insight into possibilities is greater. The gardener and worker in metals may take as their measure of the end to be accomplished the things that have already been done with plants and ores, although if they are original or inventive they will introduce some variation. But human individuals vary in their structure and possibilities as plants and metals do not. While the educator must use results that have already been accomplished he cannot, if he is truly an educator, make them his final and complete standard. Like the artist he has the problem of creating something that is not the exact duplicate of anything that has been wrought and achieved previously.

In any case, development, growth, involve change, modification, and modification in definite directions. It is quite possible for a teacher, under the supposed sanction of the idea of cultivating individuality, to fixate a pupil more or less at his existing level. Respect for individuality is primarily *intellectual*. It signifies studying the individual to see what is there to work with. Having this sympathetic understanding, the *practical* work then begins, for the practical work is one of modification, of changing, of reconstruction continued without end. The change must at least be towards more effective techniques, towards greater self-reliance, towards a more thoughtful and inquiring disposition, one more capable of persistent effort in meeting obstacles.

The weakness of some schools and teachers that would like to claim the name of progressive is that in reaction from the traditional method of external and authoritative imposition, they stop short with the recognition of the importance of giving free scope to native capacities and interests. They do not, in the first place, examine closely enough and long enough to find out what these actually may be. In the second place, they are inclined to take the individual traits that are showing themselves as finalities, instead of possibilities which by suitable direction can be transformed into something of greater significance, value and effectiveness. There is still current in many quarters the idea that evolution and development are simply matters of unfolding from within and that the unfolding will take place almost automatically if hands are kept off.

This point of view is natural as a reaction from the manifest evils of external imposition. But there is an alternative; and this alternative is not just a middle course or compromise between the two procedures. It is something radically different from either. Existing likes and powers are to be treated as possibilities, as starting-points, that are absolutely necessary for any healthy development. But development involves a point *towards* which as well as one *from* which; it involves constant movement in a given direction. Then when the point that is for the time being the goal and end is reached, it is in its turn but the starting-point of further reconstruction. The great problems of the adult who has to deal with the young is to see, and to feel deeply as well as merely to see intellectually, the forces that are moving in the young; but it is to see them as possibilities, as signs and promises; to interpret them, in short, in the light of what they may come to be. Nor does the task end there. It is bound up with the further problem of judging and devising the conditions, the materials, both physical, such as tools of work, and moral and social, which will, once more, so *interact* with existing powers and preferences as to bring about transformation in the desired direction.

The essential weakness of the old and traditional education was not just that it emphasized the necessity for provision of definite subject-matter and activities. These things *are* necessities for anything that can rightly be called education. The weakness and evil was that the imagination of educators did not go beyond provision of a fixed and rigid environment of subject-matter, one drawn moreover from sources altogether too remote from the experiences of the pupil. What is needed in the new education is more attention, not less, to subject-matter and to progress in technique. But when I say more, I do not mean more in quantity of the same old kind. I mean an imaginative vision which sees that no prescribed and ready-made scheme can possibly determine the exact subject-matter that will best promote the educative growth of every individual young person; that every new individual sets a new problem; that he calls for at least a somewhat different emphasis in subject-matter presented. There is nothing more blindly obtuse than the convention which supposes that the matter actually contained in textbooks of arithmetic, history, geography, etc., is just what will further the educational development of all children.

But withdrawal from the hard and fast and narrow contents of the old curriculum is only the negative side of the matter. If we do not go on and go far in the positive direction of providing a body of subject-matter much richer, more varied and flexible, and also in truth more definite, judged in terms of the experience of those being educated, than traditional education supplied, we shall tend to leave an educational vacuum in which anything may happen. Complete isolation is impossible in nature. The young live in some environment whether we intend it or not, and this environment is constantly interacting with what children and youth bring to it, and the result is the shaping of their interests, minds and character—either educatively or mis-educatively. If the professed educator abdicates his responsibility for judging and selecting the kind of environment that his best understanding leads him to think will be conducive to growth, then the young are left at the mercy of all the unorganized and casual forces of the modern social environment that inevitably play upon them as long as they live. In the educative environment the knowledge, judgment and experience of the teacher is a greater, not a smaller factor, than it is in the traditional school. The difference is that the teacher operates not as a magistrate set on high and marked by arbitrary authority but as a friendly co-partner and guide in a common enterprise.

Development, however, is a *continuous* process, and continuity signifies consecutiveness of action. Here was the strong point of the traditional education at its best. The subject-matter of the classics and mathematics involved of necessity, for those who mastered it, a consecutive and orderly development along definite lines. Here lies perhaps the greatest problem of the newer efforts in education. It is comparatively easy to improvise, to try a little of this today and this week and then something else tomorrow and next week. Things are done on the basis of some immediate interest and stimulation but without sufficient regard to what it leads to, as to whether or not something more difficult, setting new demands for information, need for acquisition of greater adequacy in technique and for new modes of skill, is led up to and grows naturally out of what is started. The need for taking account of spontaneous and uncoerced interest and activity is a genuine need; but without care and thought it results, all too readily, in a detached multiplicity of isolated short-time activities or projects, and the continuity necessary for growth is lost. Indeed, the new education processes require much more planning ahead on the part of teachers than did the old—for there the planning was all done in advance by the fixed curriculum.

I have spoken of the importance of environment, but a sound philosophy of education requires that the general term environment be specified. It must be seen to be dominantly human and its values as social. Through the influence of the social environment each person becomes saturated with the customs, the beliefs, the purposes, skills, hopes and fears of the cultural group to which he belongs. The features of even his physical surroundings come to him through the eyes and ears of the community. Hills and plains, plants and animals, climate and change of seasons, are clothed with the memories and traditions, and characteristic occupations and interests, of the society of which he is part. In the earlier years of education, it is particularly important that subject-matter be presented in its human context and setting. Here is one of the commonest failures of the school. We are told that instruction must proceed from the concrete to the abstract, but it is forgotten that in the experience of the child only that which has a human value and function is concrete. In his nature study and geography, physical things are presented to him as if they were independent and complete in themselves. But in the actual experience of a child, these things have a meaning for him only as they enter into human life. Even those distinctively human products, reading and writing, which have developed for the purposes of furthering human association, of making human contacts closer and richer, are treated as if they were subjects in themselves. They are not used as friendly speech is used in ordinary life, and so for the child they become abstract, a kind of mystery that belongs to the school but not to life outside the school.

As the material of genuine development is that of human contacts and associations, so the end, the value that is the criterion and directing guide of educational work, is social. The acquisition of skills is not an end in itself. They are things to be put to use, and that use is their contribution to a common and shared life. They are intended, indeed, to make an individual more capable of self-support and of self-respecting independence. But unless this end is placed in the context of services rendered to others, skills gained will be put to an egoistic and selfish use, and may be employed as means of a trained shrewdness in which one person gets the better of others. Too often, indeed, the schools, through reliance upon the spur of competition and the bestowing of special honors and prizes, only build up and strengthen the disposition that makes an individual when he leaves school employ his special talents and superior skill to outwit his fellows without respect for the welfare of others.

What is true of the skills acquired in school, is true also of the knowledge gained there. The educational end and the ultimate test of the value of what is learned is its use and application in carrying on and improving the common life of all. It should never be forgotten that the background of the traditional educational system is a class society and that opportunity for instruction in certain subjects, especially literary ones and in mathematics beyond the rudiments of simple arithmetical subjects, was reserved for the wellborn and the well-to-do. Because of this fact, knowledge of these subjects became a badge of cultural superiority and social status. For many persons the possession of knowledge was a means of display, almost of showing off. Useful knowledge, on the other hand, was necessary only for those who were compelled by their class status to work for a living. A class stigma attached to it, and the uselessness of knowledge for all purposes save purely personal culture was proof of its higher quality.

Even after education in many countries was made universal, these standards of value persisted. There is no greater egoism than that of learning when it is treated simply as a mark of personal distinction to be held and cherished for its own sake. Yet the only way of eliminating this quality of exclusiveness is that all conditions of the school environment should tend in actual practice to develop in individuals the realization that knowledge is a possession held in trust for the furthering of the well-being of all.

Perhaps the greatest need of and for a philosophy of education at the present time is the urgent need that exists for making clear in idea and effective in practice that its end is social, and that the criterion to be applied in estimating the value of the practices that exist in schools is also social. It is true that the aim of education is development of individuals to the utmost of their potentialities. But this statement in isolation leaves unanswered the question as to what is the measure of the development. A society of free individuals in which all, through their own work, contribute to the liberation and enrichment of the lives of others, is the only environment in which any individual can really grow normally to his full stature. An environment in which some are practically enslaved, degraded, limited, will always react to create conditions that prevent the full development even of those who fancy they enjoy complete freedom for unhindered growth.

There are two outstanding reasons why in the conditions of the world at present a philosophy of education must make the social aim of education the central article in its creed. The world is rapidly industrialized. Individual groups, tribes and races, once living completely untouched by the economic regime of modern capitalistic industry, now find almost every phase of their lives affected for better or worse—and often for worse—by the expansion of that system. What the Geneva Commission reported after a study of natives in the mining districts of South Africa, holds of peoples all over the world, with proper change of some of the terms used: "The investment of Western capital in African industries has made the Native dependent upon the demand of the world markets for the products of his labor and the resources of his continent." In a world that has so largely engaged in a mad and often brutally harsh race for material gain by means of ruthless competition, it behooves the school to make ceaseless and intelligently organized effort to develop above all else the will for co-operation and the spirit which sees in every other individual one who has an equal right to share in the cultural and material fruits of collective human invention, industry, skill and knowledge. The supremacy of this aim in mind and character is necessary for other reasons than as an offset to the spirit of inhumanity bred by economic competition and exploitation. It is necessary to prepare the coming generation for a new and more just and humane society which is sure to come, and which, unless hearts and minds are prepared by education, is likely to come attended with all the evils that result from social changes effected by violence.

The other need especially urgent at the present time is connected with the unprecedented wave of nationalistic sentiment, of racial and national prejudice, of readiness to resort to the ordeal of arms to settle questions, that animates the world at the present time. The schools of the world must have somehow failed grievously or the rise of this evil spirit on so vast a scale would not have been possible. The best excuse, probably, that can be made is that schools and educators were caught unawares. Who could have dreamed that the demon of fear, suspicion, prejudice and hatred, would take possession of men's minds in the way it has done? But that excuse is no longer available. We now know the enemy; it is out in the open. Unless the schools of the world can engage in a common effort to rebuild the spirit of common understanding, of mutual sympathy and goodwill among all peoples and races, to ex[o]rcise the demon of prejudice, isolation and hatred, the schools themselves are likely to be submerged by the general return to barbarism, which is the sure outcome of present tendencies if they go on unchecked by the forces which education alone can evoke and fortify.

The Permanent Studies
Robert Maynard Hutchins/from *The Higher Learning in America*

Robert Maynard Hutchins (1899–   ) is currently described in Who's Who
*as a "fund executive." That mysterious classification—a new thing in American
civic and educational life—is appropriate to the man, for his career in American education has been unorthodoxly orthodox. Hutchins taught at the Yale
Law School; later, as president and chancellor of the University of Chicago,
he demonstrated his powerful abilities as both an administrator and a philosopher of education. Under him Chicago became a radical center of conservative
—neo-Aristotelian and neo-Thomist—theory and practice. Hutchins then
moved to the Ford Foundation, and since 1954 has been head of the Fund
for the Republic, Inc., a highly select "brain trust" for studying the philosophic
bases of American society. Outside of education, Hutchins has an independent
eclecticism of thought that makes the label* conservative *inadequate.*

*From the outset Hutchins has advocated a liberal education for all. He
means by* liberal education, *which he calls "the civilization of the Logos,"
an ability to read and discuss the literature and history of the Greco-Hebraic
Western world. To be able to do so is to participate in the "Great Conversation"
of the West, a civilized and civilizing activity that is, in general, superior to
that of any other culture. As he remarks in "General Education," the essay from*
The Higher Learning in America *reprinted here:*

> Education implies teaching. Teaching implies knowledge.
> Knowledge is truth. The truth is everywhere the same. Hence
> education should be everywhere the same.

*The bald, bluntly syllogistic sentences express a position from which he has
never varied, though in later years he has voiced it with more grace and tact.*

*Hutchins knows that his chief opponents are Dewey and Dewey's some-
times misguided followers. Hutchins therefore attacks them on their fundamental
thesis, that education should be concerned with fulfilling the diverse potentialities of each individual:*

> It will be argued that a program of liberal education for all
> ignores the most important thing about men, and that is that they
> are different. I do not ignore it; I deny it. I do not deny the
> fact of individual differences; I deny that it is the most important
> fact about men or the one on which an educational system should
> be erected.

*Dewey's insistence that education serve the individual often led him to isolate
the contemporary from the past. Conversely, Hutchins' emphasis on historical
continuity leads him to sanction control of contemporary education by the
great minds of the past. Underlying the opposition are different conceptions of
what man is. Hutchins' grim conclusion is that unless we can give men a*

uniform liberal education, we shall have to abandon universal suffrage, for only liberally educated men can participate adequately in a good society.

According to Hutchins, however, this general and liberal education is terminal; beyond its limits—ranging from the junior year in high school to the sophomore year in college—lies for a few the education of scholars and professional men. The elitist implications of this view are clear. It is equally clear that a thoroughgoing adoption of Hutchins' schematic theories would have prevented the kind of uprisings and clamors for "student power" which shook Berkeley and other American campuses. Outcries against the impersonality of the multiversity would have been forestalled since the potential agitators and "youth leaders" would have found themselves, at the end of two years of college, identified with professional elites. As a result, their voices would have been heard in ways more orthodox than riots and sit-ins.

General education

My excuse for devoting one chapter to general education in a series on the higher learning is the relation between the two. We can never get a university without general education. Unless students and professors (and particularly professors) have a common intellectual training, a university must remain a series of disparate schools and departments, united by nothing except the fact that they have the same president and board of trustees. Professors cannot talk to one another, not at least about anything important. They cannot hope to understand one another.

We may take it for granted that we shall always have specialists; yet neither the world nor knowledge of it is arbitrarily divided up as universities are. Everybody cannot be a specialist in every field. He must therefore be cut off from every field but his own unless he has the same basic education that other specialists have. This means more than having the same language and the same general interest in advancing knowledge. It means having a common stock of fundamental ideas. This becomes more important as empirical science advances and accumulates more and more data. The specialist in a narrow field has all he can do to keep up with the latest discoveries in it. Other men, even in his own department, struggling to stay abreast of what is happening in their own segments of the subject, cannot hope to keep up with what is happening in his. They may now expect to have some general understanding of what he is doing because they all have something in common; they are in the same department. But the day will shortly be upon us when even this degree of comprehension will be impossible, because of the infinite splitting of subject matters and the progressive submergence of any ideas by our insistence on information as the content of education.

Efforts to correct this tendency by administrative devices are mere palliatives. Roving professorships at Harvard, the divisional organization at Chicago, the Institute of Human Relations at Yale, noble and praiseworthy as they are, serve to mitigate and not to remove the disunity, discord, and disorder that have overtaken our educational system. If professors and students had a common stock of fundamental ideas, it might be possible for those in physiology to communicate with those in physics, and even law and divinity might begin to find it worthwhile to associate with one another.

In this chapter I should like to talk about content, not about method. I concede the great difficulty of communicating the kind of education I favor to those who are unable or unwilling to get their education from books. I insist, however, that the education I shall outline is the kind that everybody should have, that the answer to it is not that some people should not have it, but that we should find out how to give it to those whom we do not know how to teach at present. You cannot say my content is wrong because you do not know the method of transmitting it. Let us agree upon content if we can and have faith that the technological genius of America will solve the problem of communication.

Economic conditions require us to provide some kind of education for the young, and for all the young, up to about their twentieth year. Probably one-third of them cannot learn from books. This is no reason why we should not try to work out a better course of study for the other two-thirds. At the same time we should continue our efforts and experiments to find out how to give a general education to the hand-minded and the functionally illiterate. Even these attempts may be somewhat simplified if we know what a general education is.

Please do not tell me that the general education I propose should not be adopted because the great majority of those who pass through it will not go on to the university. The scheme that I advance is based on the notion that general education is education for everybody, whether he goes on to the university or not. It will be useful to him in the university; it will be equally useful if he never goes there. I will admit that it will not be useful to him outside the university in the popular sense of utility. It may not assist him to make money or to get ahead. It may not in any obvious fashion adjust him to his environment or fit him for the contemporary scene. It will, however, have a deeper, wider utility: it will cultivate the intellectual virtues.

The trouble with the popular notion of utility is that it confuses immediate and final ends. Material prosperity and adjustment to the environment are good more or less, but they are not good in themselves and there are other goods beyond them. The intellectual virtues, however, are good in themselves and good as means to happiness. By the intellectual virtues I mean good intellectual habits. The ancients distinguish five intellectual virtues: the three speculative virtues of intuitive knowledge, which is the habit of induction; of scientific knowledge, which is the habit of demonstration; and of philosophical wisdom, which is scientific knowledge, combined with intuitive reason, of things highest by nature, first principles and first causes. To these they add the two virtues of the practical intellect: art, the capacity to make according to a true course of reasoning, and prudence, which is right reason with respect to action.[1]

In short, the intellectual virtues are habits resulting from the training of the intellectual powers. An intellect properly disciplined, an intellect

---

[1]Cf. Aquinas, St. Thomas, *Summa Theologica*, Part II, Q. 57, Art. 2-4.

properly habituated, is an intellect able to operate well in all fields. An education that consists of the cultivation of the intellectual virtues, therefore, is the most useful education, whether the student is destined for a life of contemplation or a life of action. I would remind you of the words of Newman:

> If then the intellect is so excellent a portion of us, and its cultivation so excellent, it is not only beautiful, perfect, admirable, and noble in itself, but in a true and high sense it must be useful to the possessor and to all around him; not useful in any low, mechanical, mercantile sense, but as diffusing good, or as a blessing, or a gift, or power, or a treasure, first to the owner, then through him to the world.[2]

I shall not be attentive when you tell me that the plan of general education I am about to present is remote from real life, that real life is in constant flux and change, and that education must be in constant flux and change as well. I do not deny that all things are in change. They have a beginning, and a middle, and an end. Nor will I deny that the history of the race reveals tremendous technological advances and great increases in our scientific knowledge. But we are so impressed with scientific and technological progress that we assume similar progress in every field. We renounce our intellectual heritage, read only the most recent books, discuss only current events, try to keep the schools abreast or even ahead of the times, and write elaborate addresses on Education and Social Change.

Paul Shorey said:

> If literature and history are a Heraclitean flux of facts, if one unit is as significant as another, one book, one idea, the equivalent of another, . . . we may for a time bravely tread the mill of scholastic routine, but in the end the soul will succumb to an immense lassitude and bafflement. But if . . . the flux is not all, if the good, the true, and the beautiful are something real and ascertainable, if these eternal ideals re-embody themselves from age to age essentially the same in the imaginative visions of supreme genius and in the persistent rationality and sanity of the world's best books, then our reading and study are redeemed, both from the obsessions of the hour, and the tyranny of quantitative measures and mechanical methods.

Our erroneous notion of progress has thrown the classics and the liberal arts out of the curriculum, overemphasized the empirical sciences, and made education the servant of any contemporary movements in society, no matter how superficial. In recent years this attitude has been accentuated by the world-wide depression and the highly advertised political, social, and economic changes resulting from it. We have been very much upset by all these things. We have felt that it was our duty to educate the young so that they would be prepared for further political, social, and economic changes. Some

---

[2]Cf. Aristotle, *Politics*, VIII, 3: "To be always seeking after the useful does not become free and exalted souls."

of us have thought we should try to figure out what the impending changes would be and frame a curriculum that embodied them. Others have even thought that we should decide what changes are desirable and then educate our students not merely to anticipate them, but also to take part in bringing them about.

One purpose of education is to draw out the elements of our common human nature. These elements are the same in any time or place. The notion of educating a man to live in any particular time or place, to adjust him to any particular environment, is therefore foreign to a true conception of education.

Education implies teaching. Teaching implies knowledge. Knowledge is truth. The truth is everywhere the same.[3] Hence education should be everywhere the same. I do not overlook the possibilities of differences in organization, in administration, in local habits and customs. These are details. I suggest that the heart of any course of study designed for the whole people will be, if education is rightly understood, the same at any time, in any place, under any political, social, or economic conditions. Even the administrative details are likely to be similar because all societies have generic similarity.

If education is rightly understood, it will be understood as the cultivation of the intellect. The cultivation of the intellect is the same good for all men in all societies. It is, moreover, the good for which all other goods are only means. Material prosperity, peace and civil order, justice and the moral virtues are means to the cultivation of the intellect. So Aristotle says in the *Politics:* "Now, in men reason and mind are the end towards which nature strives, so that the generation and moral discipline of the citizens ought to be ordered with a view to them." An education which served the means rather than their end would be misguided.

I agree, of course, that any plan of general education must be such as to educate the student for intelligent action. It must, therefore, start him on the road toward practical wisdom. But the question is what is the best way for education to start him and how far can it carry him. Prudence or practical wisdom selects the means toward the ends that we desire. It is acquired partly from intellectual operations and partly from experience. But the chief requirement for it is correctness in thinking. Since education cannot duplicate the experiences which the student will have when he graduates, it should devote itself to developing correctness in thinking as a means to practical wisdom, that is, to intelligent action.

As Aristotle put it in the *Ethics*, ". . . while young men become geometricians and mathematicians and wise in matters like these, it is thought that a young man of practical wisdom cannot be found. The cause is that such wisdom is concerned not only with universals, but with particulars, but a young man has no experience, for it is length of time that gives experience." Since practical wisdom is "a true and reasoned capacity to act with regard to the things that are good or bad for man," it would seem that education

---

[3]*Summa Theologica*, Part II, Q. 94, Art. 4: "It is therefore evident that, as regards the general principles whether of speculative or practical reason, truth or rectitude is the same for all, and is equally known by all."

can make its best contribution to the development of practical wisdom by concentrating on the reasoning essential to it.

A modern heresy is that all education is formal education and that formal education must assume the total responsibility for the full development of the individual. The Greek notion that the city educates the man has been forgotten. Everything that educated the man in the city has to be imported into our schools, colleges, and universities. We are beginning to behave as though the home, the church, the state, the newspaper, the radio, the movies, the neighborhood club, and the boy next door did not exist. All the experience that is daily and hourly acquired from these sources is overlooked, and we set out to supply imitations of it in educational institutions. The experience once provided by some of these agencies may be attenuated now; but it would be a bold man who would assert that the young person today lived a life less full of experience than the youth of yesterday. Today as yesterday we may leave experience to other institutions and influences and emphasize in education the contribution that it is supremely fitted to make, the intellectual training of the young. The life they lead when they are out of our hands will give them experience enough. We cannot try to give it to them and at the same time perform the task that is ours and ours alone.

Young people do not spend all their time in school. Their elders commonly spend none of it there. Yet their elders are, we hope, constantly growing in practical wisdom. They are, at least, having experience. If we can teach them while they are being educated how to reason, they may be able to comprehend and assimilate their experience. It is a good principle of educational administration that a college or university should do nothing that another agency can do as well. This is a good principle because a college or university has a vast and complicated job if it does what only it can do. In general education, therefore, we may wisely leave experience to life and set about our job of intellectual training.

If there are permanent studies which every person who wishes to call himself educated should master; if those studies constitute our intellectual inheritance, then those studies should be the center of a general education. They cannot be ignored because they are difficult, or unpleasant, or because they are almost totally missing from our curriculum today. The child-centered school may be attractive to the child, and no doubt is useful as a place in which the little ones may release their inhibitions and hence behave better at home. But educators cannot permit the students to dictate the course of study unless they are prepared to confess that they are nothing but chaperons, supervising an aimless, trial-and-error process which is chiefly valuable because it keeps young people from doing something worse. The free elective system as Mr. Eliot introduced it at Harvard and as Progressive Education adapted it to lower age levels amounted to a denial that there was content to education. Since there was no content to education, we might as well let students follow their own bent. They would at least be interested and pleased and would be as well educated as if they had pursued a prescribed course of study. This overlooks the fact that the aim of education is to connect man with man, to connect the present with the past, and to advance the thinking of the race. If this is the aim of education, it cannot be left to the sporadic, spontaneous interests of children or even of under-graduates.[4]

Mr. Gladstone once remarked that it is difficult to discern the true dimensions of objects in that mirage which covers the studies of one's youth. Even at stages beyond general education, when the student because he has had a general education and because he is more mature might be given wider latitude in selecting the subjects interesting to him, this can be permitted only to a limited degree. If there are an intellectual tradition and an intellectual inheritance in the law, for example, law schools must see to it that they are transmitted to law students even if law students are more interested in the latest devices for evading the Sherman Antitrust Act.

It cannot be assumed that students at any age will always select the subjects that constitute education. If we permit them to avoid them, we cannot confer upon them insignia which certify to the public that they are in our opinion educated. In any field the permanent studies on which the whole development of the subject rests must be mastered if the student is to be educated.

The variations that should be encouraged fall not in the realm of content but in that of method. Allowances for individual differences should be provided for by abolishing all requirements except the examinations and permitting the student to take them whenever in his opinion he is ready to do so. The cultivation of independent thought and study, now almost wholly missing from our program, may thus be somewhat advanced. And this may be done without sacrificing the content of education to the obsessions of the hour or the caprices of the young.

If we are educators we must have a subject matter, and a rational, defensible one. If that subject matter is education, we cannot alter it to suit the whims of parents, students, or the public. Whewell, Master of Trinity College, Cambridge, one hundred years ago, said:

> Young persons may be so employed and so treated, that their caprice, their self-will, their individual tastes and propensities, are educed and developed; but this is not Education. It is not the Education of a Man; for what is educed is not what belongs to man as man, and connects man with man. It is not the Education of a man's Humanity, but the Indulgence of his Individuality.

In general education we are interested in drawing out the elements of our common human nature; we are interested in the attributes of the race, not the accidents of individuals.

If our course of study reflects today an interest in the accidents of individuals; if the permanent studies are conspicuous by their absence from it, I can only say that these are the reasons why our course of study is bad. We know that our course of study leads to the most unfortunate results in

---

[4]Plato, *Republic*, Book IX: "'And it is plain,' I said, 'that this is the purpose of the law, which is the ally of all classes in the state, and this is the aim of our control of children, our not leaving them free before we have established, so to speak, a constitutional government within them and, by fostering the best element in them with the aid of the like in ourselves, have set up in its place a similar guardian and ruler in the child, and then, and then only we leave it free.'"

the organization of education, in the qualities and activities of professors and students, and in the cultivation of our people. It is surely not a criticism of the permanent studies that they have had no share in producing these results.

By insisting on the permanent studies as the heart of a general education I do not mean to insist that they are the whole of it. We do not know enough to know whether certain technological work, for example, may not have a certain subsidiary value in general education for some students. Nor do I overlook the fact that since by hypothesis general education may be terminal for most students, it must connect them with the present and future as well as with the past. It is as important for them to know that thinking is still going on as it is for them to know what has been thought before.

The question whether certain technical work shall be allowed to be a part of general education is rather a question of method than of content, a question how to teach rather than what. Technology as such has no place in general education. If it can be justified at all, it can only be because we discover that certain principles can best be communicated through technical work. The question of present thought is largely answered by saying that it is impossible to think of a teacher who contented himself with elucidating the thought of the past without intimating that these ideas have a history running to the present day.

The proponents of current events as the subject matter of education gain little by insisting on the importance of present thought; for they are not much interested in thought of any kind. They would be only less horrified if contemporary thought were made the heart of general education than they would be if St. Augustine or Spinoza were central in it. They would get little consolation from the remarks of Whewell about what he called the progressive studies, which were to make their first appearance at a much later stage of education than the one we are here considering. He said:

> It is not enough that we take for this purpose any expression of the present activities of men's minds. Progressive studies, too, must be a part of the development of humanity in its general form. They must express an activity which belongs to man as man. They must be, though not permanent in their form, universal in their principles. They must be the results, not of individual caprice, or fancy, but of human Reason. They must aim, not at mere change or novelty, but at Truth. And since the progress of the human mind is from Truth to Truth, the new Truths must be founded upon the old ones. The progressive studies which education embraces must rest upon the permanent studies which it necessarily includes. The former must be its super-structure, the latter, its foundation.

Again he says:

> A man who really participates in the progress of the sciences, must do so by following their course when the time of education is past. . . . Modern Science and Philosophy ought to be introduced into education

so far as to show their nature and principles; but they do not necessarily make any considerable or definite part of it. The intellectual culture, though it will be incomplete if these are excluded, may still be a culture which connects him with the past, and prepares him for the present; but an education from which classical literature or mathematical reasoning is omitted, however familiar it may make a man with the terms of modern literature and philosophy, must leave him unprepared to understand the real purport of literature and philosophy, because he has not the intellectual culture which the greatest authors in literature and philosophy have always had.[5]

Let us avoid all questions of administration and method. Let us assume that we have an intelligible organization of education under which there is a four-year unit, beginning at about the beginning of the junior year in high school and ending at about the end of the sophomore year in college. Let us assume that we are going to try to teach in that unit everybody who can learn from books. Let us assume further that the conclusion of their work in this unit will mark the end of formal instruction for most students. They will not go on to the university. Nevertheless we must have a curriculum which will, in the main, do as well for those who are going on as those who are not. What shall this curriculum be?

We have excluded body building and character building. We have excluded the social graces and the tricks of trades. We have suggested that the curriculum should be composed principally of the permanent studies. We propose the permanent studies because these studies draw out the elements of our common human nature, because they connect man with man, because they connect us with the best that man has thought, because they are basic to any further study and to any understanding of the world. What are the permanent studies?

They are in the first place those books which have through the centuries attained to the dimensions of classics. Many such books, I am afraid, are in the ancient and medieval period. But even these are contemporary. A classic is a book that is contemporary in every age. That is why it is a classic. The conversations of Socrates raise questions that are as urgent today as they were when Plato wrote. In fact they are more so, because the society in which Plato lived did not need to have them raised as much as we do. We have forgotten how important they are.

Such books are then a part, and a large part, of the permanent studies. They are so in the first place because they are the best books we know. How can we call a man educated who has never read any of the great books in the western world? Yet today it is entirely possible for a student to graduate from the finest American colleges without having read any of them, except possibly Shakespeare. Of course, the student may have heard of these books, or at least of their authors. But this knowledge is gained in general through textbooks, and textbooks have probably done as much to degrade the Ameri-

---

[5]Consider the importance to English law of Aristotle's distinctions of misadventure, mistake, an act of injustice, and the unjust act of an unjust man. *Ethics*, 1135b. Consider also the influence on Anglo-Saxon jurisprudence of Locke's *Second Essay of Civil Government*.

can intelligence as any single force. If the student should know about Cicero, Milton, Galileo, or Adam Smith, why should he not read what they wrote? Ordinarily what he knows about them he learns from texts which must be at best second-hand versions of their thought.

In the second place these books are an essential part of general education because it is impossible to understand any subject or to comprehend the contemporary world without them. If we read Newton's *Principia,* we see a great genius in action; we make the acquaintance of a work of unexampled simplicity and elegance. We understand, too, the basis of modern science. The false starts, the backing and filling, the wildness, the hysteria, the confusion of modern thought and the modern world result from the loss of what has been thought and done by earlier ages. The Industrial Revolution begins our study of history and the social sciences. Philosophy begins with Descartes and Locke and psychology with Wundt and William James. Natural science originates with the great experimenters of the nineteenth century. If anything prior is mentioned, it is only as a reminder that our recent great achievements in these fields must, of course, have had some primitive beginnings in the dark earlier centuries. The classics, if presented at all, are offered in excerpts out of context, and for the most part for the sake of showing the student how far we have progressed beyond our primitive beginnings.

Yet we may with profit remember the words of Nicholas Murray Butler:

> Only the scholar can realize how little that is being said and thought in the modern world is in any sense new. It was the colossal triumph of the Greeks and Romans and of the great thinkers of the Middle Ages to sound the depths of almost every problem which human nature has to offer, and to interpret human thought and human aspiration with astounding profundity and insight. Unhappily, these deeplying facts which should be controlling in the life of a civilized people with a historical background, are known only to a few, while the many grasp, now at an ancient and well-demonstrated falsehood and now at an old and well-proved truth, as if each had all the attractions of novelty.

You will note that Mr. Butler says that only a scholar can realize these things. Why should this insight be confined to scholars? Every educated person should know the colossal triumph of the Greeks and Romans and the great thinkers of the Middle Ages. If every man were educated—and why should he not be?—our people would not fall so easily a prey to the latest nostrums in economics, in politics, and, I may add, in education. . . .

Education for Social Equality
George Z. F. Bereday/"Selective Education Versus Education for All"

George Z. F. Bereday (1920–   ) was born in Poland and became a citizen of the United States in 1955. After receiving a Ph.D. from Harvard, he taught history at Boston College before turning to the field of education. He is an expert on Soviet education and was on the first United States Cultural Mission to the U.S.S.R. He has written two books dealing with Soviet methods of education. Currently teaching comparative education at Teachers College, Columbia University, Bereday is a follower of John Dewey in both locale and philosophy. He has, however, by a full awareness of the complexities involved in "education for all," tempered some of the more simplistic conclusions often drawn from Dewey's work. Just as no contemporary "elitist" in America envisions a feudal dichotomy between the lettered and the vulgar, so no contemporary Deweyite advocates one kind of education for all regardless of native intelligence. But after all the qualifications have been made, the positions are discernibly and even dramatically different. Bereday, in a series of articles on the problems of dealing fairly with intellect and inequality in American education, has elsewhere singled out Douglas Bush as an opponent. He counters Bush's proposition that "education for all is education for none" by appealing to "the unprecedented advancement of the American people as a whole *in the last twenty-five years."*

Bereday's essay entitled "Selective Education Versus Education for All" illustrates the liberal position. Here Bereday argues that education for all is a "public service, a privilege and a duty"; it is "not a triangle, narrow at the apex, in which the less well suited are thinned out, but a rectangle in which all partake." The United States, a "pioneer in one-stream education," is now engaged in the radical experiment of universal college education. If, as Bereday suggests, America's unprecedented and miraculous prosperity is attributable to the belief that education is for all, then the belief is important not just because it enables any student to improve his position in life, but also because it is the source of "this country's pride and strength."

To meet the argument that we cannot give equal education to persons who are naturally unequal—a fact which no one denies—Bereday distinguishes sharply between "equality" and "equalization." Equality, he maintains, is a static concept; equalization, on the other hand, is a working proposition, a dynamic principle, which functions in two ways: "The schools have been promoters of social mobility, and they have been agents of reduction of social distance." As long as education for social equalization continues to function, "it does not matter much who makes more of a career if all succeed according to their merit, and if the social positions reached are after all not so very far apart" *(emphasis ours). For Bereday, the spectacle of garbage men raised in rank and title to "sanitary engineers" is not something to provide snobbish jokes for the intellectual upper classes. The experience of education, even in a janitorial course, "will rub off on the student," and the memory of the school will encourage him, and his children, to change their lives through a continuous process of "uplifting." Bereday does not wish to call this conception the American "myth" or "dream"; for him it is the American "ideal"—and a working one.*

Some months ago there appeared in better magazines an advertisment of a life insurance company. It presented two pictures of a teenage boy in contrasting life situations. The first picture carried the caption "Will he be the *kid who left school* . . . to whom *doors are closed* even before he begins?" and showed the boy trudging along dejectedly, presumably on his way to work. Wearing a leather jacket and clutching toolboxes, badges of his working-class status, he marched on sadly, the target of laughing comments by some young bystanders. The second picture bore the caption ". . .or a boy who's sure of getting off to a good start in life, whatever happens?" and depicted the same youngster, now seated in the classroom, smiling happily, wearing a white collar, a tie, and a tweed jacket (now the badges of his status), doing presumably what youngsters crave most in life, copying material into a notebook. The message to fathers, of course, was clear.

The two themes

This advertisement is a symbol of one important and basic theme in America—education for a career. Here, as in many other countries, education is expected to give status. Through education one seeks position and social advancement. Through education one hopes to become the boy or girl "most likely to succeed." Education is an economic investment. It enables people to get ahead and "make good." High grades as against indifferent ones, sixteen years of schooling as against twelve—these are items immediately rewarded by good or bad placement opportunities. Education is thus a channel of social mobility. It establishes expectations. It earns one material and social rewards. In the words of that oracle of homely wisdom, the New York cab driver, "Nowadays, if you haven't got eddication, you've got to live by your wits."

Side by side with the theme of striving for a career, however, American education embodies another major theme. It is a public service, a privilege and duty of all. Every day millions of youngsters leave their parents, the traditional and natural agents of education, and under penalty of the law appear in public buildings, to be instructed by public servants in subjects which the public deems appropriate. Education is for all; not a triangle, narrow at the apex, in which the less well suited are thinned out, but a rectangle in which all partake. It is a free public institution. It does not wage a battle of social justice, like the selective systems of other countries, to change the nineteenth century principle of selection by ability to pay into the now postulated principle of selection by talent. The United States is a pioneer in one-stream education for all. While countries like Liberia strive for simple achievement of fundamental education for all, or like Turkey attempt to enforce primary education for all, or like England battle for secondary education for all, the United States long ago accepted the principle of a high-school diploma for all and is moving into the era of universal college education.

In practice much remains to be done in American secondary education, as long as the compulsory laws in many states do not apply beyond the age of sixteen, and as long as only some 65 per cent of all adolescents do, in fact, graduate from high school. But the ideological problems of education for all have now been shifted beyond high school. With thirty out of every one hundred Americans attending college and with the prospect of this number doubling within twenty years, the problems of whom to admit or what policy to follow in hitherto small private universities occupy an increasing share of public attention. Education for all from childhood to adulthood is becoming a universal postulate which the United States is already implementing and to which the rest of the world is beginning to lend an increasingly attentive ear. For it may well be that education for all is responsible for the miracle that "with only 6 per cent of the world's land and 7 per cent of its population the United States publishes 27 per cent of the world's newspapers, owns 31 per cent of all radio and television sets, produces 40 per cent of all electrical power, uses 58 per cent of the world's telephones, and drives 76 per cent of its automobiles." It may well be that maximization of individual opportunity has released tremendous dynamic forces and that the sum total of free individual efforts has mobilized productive energies striven for in vain by totalitarian planners. Education for all, more than education for a career, has been this country's pride and strength.

The problem

But how can these two profiles exist side by side? If on one side education is to supply careers, and on the other it is to encompass all, how is one to reconcile the two? Are *all* going to make a career? Are all going to become school superintendents, college presidents, professionals?

There is profound and tragic incongruity between the two themes. One remembers what happened in Weimar Germany, when the vast numbers of school and college graduates were unable to find jobs commensurate with their expectations. One can see what happens in Japan or India, where the United States and Britain introduced their respective systems of education only to confront those who graduate with prospects of jobs as street-sweepers. And one is daily witnessing what happens in the Soviet Union, where over and above the much-publicized reports about the large output of professionals, the regime never ceases to appeal to its young to enter industrial or agricultural work instead of continuing to press for admission to already overcrowded universities and institutes. It is plain that disparities between the demand and supply of educated men only serve to create a class of dissatisfied intellectuals, and history contains much evidence that dissatisfied intellectuals are notorious leaders of unrest and revolution.

Fortunately, on the manpower level of analysis the United States has not been troubled by the contradiction between its two dominant educational profiles. It is one of the very few countries which could reconcile education for all with education for status. It could do that for two reasons. First, owing to the growth of its population and economy, the "room at the top" has been steadily expanding. More children must mean more schools, more teachers, and more superintendents. Larger demand for refrigerators has meant more producing plants, more plant managers, more vice presidents of manufacturing companies. But the mere fact of the expanding room at the top can be greatly overrated. What matters is clearly not mere expansion, but expansion in keeping with the output of qualified graduates. Sufficient expansion could never be maintained to satisfy the volume of output of education for all. Reliance on the expansion of room at the top alone could soon produce most formidable bottlenecks.

The second reason seems much more relevant. While the room at the top expanded, the bottom level of occupations has at the same time steadily risen. Elbridge Sibley has pointed out that much of the apparent social mobility in the United States has been due to the general upping of the character of technological occupations. The immigrant who became a push-cart fruit peddler, sent his son through public grade school to become a truck driver delivering fruit to a supermarket. His grandson, having finished high school, appears as a skilled mechanic servicing fruit automats. The character of the occupation, distribution of fruit, changed little. But, thanks to education and technology, the social status of the occupation has been notably upgraded. A third-generation American looking at the increasing educational opportunity for all and at his own success within it can congratu-late himself on the apparent harmony with which these two seemingly contradictory principles have operated to his advantage.

But on the social level of analysis the United States is not immune to the cleavage between education for status and education for all. Striving for careers creates emotional attitudes and psychological drives that cannot be left out of consideration in planning a system of education for all. In particular they can seriously obstruct the operation of one of the basic goals of education for all—the proposition that education serves as a tool of social equality.

Equality and education

Social equality, through its unfortunate connection with early Soviet Communism, has recently come in for a lot of abuse. Arguments that it cannot be achieved, that it leads to standardization and loss of freedom, are now common occurrence. But what was meant by social equality in American education was in reality quite a working proposition. For equality is a static concept, while American schools have operated instead on a dynamic prin-ciple of not equality but equalization. The persistent neutralization by the schools of social distinctions which naturally arise over a period of genera-tions has proved a worthy ideal. This equalization through education has been accomplished in two ways: the schools have been promoters of social mobility, and they have been agents of reduction of social distance.

The first function, that schools should be agents of social mobility, is well known as equality of opportunity. If the school is a channel through which youngsters flow, the equality of their opportunity implies the openness of the channel. An open school system serving an open society means that irrespective of other considerations such as religion, race, ethnic origin, economic well-being, or social status, youngsters with aptitude for high-status occupations should be able to find their way to these occupations. "Schools free men to rise to the level of their natural abilities. . . . By pro-viding a channel for ambition, they have taken the place of the frontier, and in a highly technical era have preserved the independent spirit of a pioneer nation. The schools stand as the chief expression of the American tradition of fair play for everyone, and a fresh start for each generation." The many familiar facets of American education now in force are an explicit instrument to prevent the creation of barriers to mobility. Merit and achievement (albeit somewhat nebulously defined and identified even more poorly) are supposed to be the only admissible criteria of appointment and promotion. Education is to keep the flow of talent unhindered. This has been its first equalizing function. A high degree of circulation of social newcomers among the older elite groups was bound to create an atmosphere of equality and fluidity that has since become a matter of national pride. Whereas in Europe it is one of the major concerns of self-made men to conceal their origin, in the United States, boasting of humble background is an honorable habit which few captains of industry can resist.

The second equalitarian function of schools has been even more significant. It has to do with bridging social gaps between people. Most old-type social structures could be drawn in the form of a triangle: a few very well-to-do or otherwise privileged people at the top, a more numerous middle class, and the majority at the bottom—an industrial or agricultural proletariat. This is a familiar Marxian profile. But the American social structure can no longer be drawn in this way. Rather it is a diamond shaped structure with the majority not at the bottom but in the middle. The task of the schools has been to place an increasing number of people in the middle, sometimes by an overt catering to the average (much criticized, especially by the people at the top), more often by lifting and incorporating the people from the bottom into the middle class. American schools, like the American economy through its anti-trust laws, income and inheritance taxes, welfare policies, and price controls, are supposed to be continuously pounding the top and the bottom of the diamond in order to flatten it out. . . . Nowhere else does one catch a glimpse of a plumber entering a forty-room house of a millionaire, looking around, shrugging his shoulders and commenting, "Nice place you've got here." And nowhere else can one find a letter such as appeared in *Time Magazine* after it featured an article on American intellectuals:

> Sir,
>
>   Why the fuss over the intellectuals? Most of them are laggards who think the world owes them a living. I am just a die-caster who owns a $14,000 home with a swimming pool in the backyard and a new Buick. Who's smartest—me or them?

• • •

This is America's heritage. One may not wish to perpetuate it. One may feel that our schools were inherited from European prototypes and that they have wandered too far away from these prototypes. One may call the equalitarian tradition, as some sociologists now call it, the American "myth" or the American "dream." Or one may prefer to believe, as this writer does, that it is the American ideal. Be that as it may, the equalitarian role of the schools is a fact of history, a source of America's strength in the past and an inseparable part of American culture.

This historic function of education can also be a theme of the future. Technology and education are more capable than ever of effecting a wholesale revolution of the occupational prestige patterns. A waitress, for instance, occupies a low-status position. Hers is a poorly paid, transitory occupation with low admission standards and little prestige. But require this same girl to have a high-school diploma, put her through "charm school," give her a smart uniform, and add the romance of flight, and you have an air-stewardess; essentially a waitress, yet a semiprofessional, with a function far transcending the simple labor of waiting. The same principle can be demonstrated with garbage men. In some American cities garbage is still collected in open trucks. In those cities the job of garbage collecting recruits many marginal people, mental and psychological misfits. But take a garbage man in New York, have him operate from a white incinerator truck, dress him in a uniform and a cap such as distinguishes policemen, and call him a sanitary engineer and you have an entirely different occupation.

Education can give the charwoman the status of cleaning lady, a janitor the status of building superintendent. The girl who took home economics courses using most modern equipment will not be content with the potbellied stove. The boy who has lived in an ultramodern college dormitory will not settle for an unpainted shack and outdoor plumbing. Education for all has tremendous potentialities. Something, somewhere will rub off on the student. The memory of the school will trigger his efforts. It will enable him and, through his influence, his children to remake their lives in terms of completely new and better criteria. The equalitarianism inherent in this process of uplifting leaves less and less room for the belief that one's gifts, one's achievements, or the mental rather than the manual character of one's occupation, set one above and apart from one's fellow men. As R. H. Tawney used to say, superior brain, like superior beauty, is an accident of birth and imposes obligations rather than conferring privileges.

Inequalitarian trends

And here lies the problem. For it is at this point that education for status clashes with education for all. If the latter theme implies equality, the former implies inequality. Deep down, in spite of tradition, in spite of professed ideals, people are not equalitarian. In their public and private roles people act differently and in contradiction. And when put to a final test their private motives always seem to win. One is reminded of George Orwell's telling phrase: "All animals are equal, but some are more equal than others." People like distinctions and enjoy feeling superior. Not only wives, and not only the psychologically insecure search for status symbols; everybody looks for them. If no criteria of distinction are available, people will invent them. . . . People like inequalitarian symbols. They really care more for admission tickets to exclusive social groups than for an equalitarian system where no such tickets are required. Nobody seems to mind social discrimination and exclusivity, provided that he himself is neither excluded nor discriminated against. To paraphrase Evelyn Waugh, everybody believes himself to be a gentleman, but everybody draws the line of demarcation immediately below his own heels.

What matters, however, is not so much that people search for inequalitarian status symbols, but rather that they search for these symbols in education. As the equalitarian temper of our time abolishes the old criteria one by one, more and more pressure is exerted upon education to find within it new social compensations. For a growing number of occupations, the road to a superior career increasingly leads through schools. Without education fewer and fewer people can fulfill their ambitions by entering directly politics, business, or even the theater. Thus there is a constant search in education not for equality but for socially invidious symbols. Only selective, discriminating education can satisfy those craving social distinction. Academic degrees, culture and refinement, intellectual acumen, these are worth little if everyone can possess them. The more one succeeds, the less one is prone to accept the "cheapening" of one's achievements which universality seems to bring about. Thus the pattern of education for all is under constant attack. Simple diversification, natural and laudable in all educational activity, becomes ground for cultivating old and new patterns of snobbery. Intricate prestige hierarchies of schools and colleges, the pecking order among teachers according to rank and function, the run on the paperbacks, not for their intrinsic value but as social symbols for intellectual name droppers, or even "inverted snobbery," all these carry symptoms of persisting search for status. "The knowledge that one's parents ate and still eat in the kitchen," writes Margaret Mead, "can jeopardize the pleasure with which a university professor enjoys the rosy candlelight and the old linen at the college president's table, and can give an enormous relish to the discovery that the college president's wife's father kept a garage."

As American education comes of age, the evidence of these tensions increases. Equality and snobbery are now fighting a perpetual battle in the schools. The concern of the great depression for Proper Bostonians and Babbitts has been almost completely replaced by the contemplation of the High Brow, Low Brow, and Middle Brow, and of the Man in the Gray Flannel Suit. It is obviously not enough to assume that the abolition of elite education in the past has forever settled the question. The new education carries within it the seeds of new elitism. Even the popular pressure for education that has been the historic strength of the common school has been partly generated by motives inequalitarian in character. In an excellent passage the editors of the *Yearbook of Education* describe the operation of these motives in an area that comes perilously close to home for the readers of this journal.

> Within the American university one can detect signs of prestige hierarchy. There was a time when the theologian, philosopher, or historian looked with some misgiving upon those who worked in physical, chemical, and biological laboratories. Science seemed a smelly, manual, pragmatic sort of occupation. Now it is accepted, and the natural scientist in his turn has been somewhat sceptical of the economist, psychologist, sociologist, and anthropologist attempting to claim the mantle of academic respectability and scientific sanctity with their "social studies." One thing has tended to unite the old and the new: the appearance of an even less "academic" intruder, namely the professional educationist.
>
> The school of education, in spite of the fact that it trains for the largest single profession in the United States, is often looked upon as hardly more than a "trade school," offering pompous and verbose lectures on the most absurdly minute fractions of the teaching process. Variations of Shaw's famous quip that "he who can, does; and he

who can't, teaches [and he who can't teach, teaches teachers—my variation]" are quoted in disparagement of the mushrooming activities of such schools. Schools or departments of education are now at least two generations old and with this maturity has come a differentiation of the status-strata even within their highly specialized ranks. Thus the professor of philosophy, or history, or sociology, or psychology of education cannot quite believe that a professor of educational administration or curriculum or methodology is really as "academic" and hence as acceptable as he is. And all these probably secretly consider their studies to be intrinsically somewhat above those of professors of folk dancing, or swimming, or making a salad.

It is perhaps understandable that older elite groups resist the idea of education for all as a crackpot scheme. It cannot be pleasant to see oneself deprived by events of long-practiced modes of life and established expectations. The very intellectuality of the older groups has rendered them contemplative and thus unable to withstand the competition of determined, active, newer groups. But one must account also for these newer groups. The rising groups which once protested against the educational barriers set against them by superior social groups suddenly undergo a change of heart as soon as they themselves succeed in crossing these barriers. All at once they try to blend assiduously with the groups which were once their rivals and become staunch upholders of the very restrictions against which they once protested. There is a persistent temptation to those who have climbed the ladder of educational success to try to kick it over from above. People behave in education like a man who pushes his way violently into an overcrowded trolley car. Yet the minute he himself gains a foothold, he joins in shouting to those still struggling to get aboard, "Full up, no more room!"

That is why Lawrence Cremin half-jokingly named this the "trolley-car theory of education." There is a point at which education, formerly a channel of opportunity, becomes a block to opportunity. The agent of social mobility becomes an agent of social insurance. As the success of equalitarian education means that increasing numbers succeed in reaching superior social status, there is always the concomitant danger that those segments of public opinion hostile to equalitarianism in education will also be strengthened.

Can the pressures for intellectualization of American public schools and the accompanying criticism of progressive education be adequately understood without taking account of the social nature of these pressures? Can the cry for "education of leaders" and the many proposals for separation of "the gifted" be properly appraised without examining the possible social motives behind them? The demands for return to a two-stream educational system, the use of public money for private schools, ethnic and racial difficulties, reluctance of the colleges to enlarge admissions—these and many other crucial current problems ought to be examined in the light of the cleavage between education for equality and education for status. No reform of education, no decision of policy, can be successfully carried through if it does not take into account these persistent stratifying tendencies. It must be a constant concern of educational theorists committed to the preservation of the American heritage not to advocate viewpoints which consciously or otherwise serve as "fronts" for these motives. Sincere educational endeavors must not become prey to those forces which under the masquerade of concern for democratic education attempt to advance inequalitarian and elitist concepts to the detriment of the nation as a whole.

The Pressure of Numbers

Douglas Bush/"The Humanities"

Douglas Bush (1896–   ), recently retired to a life of continued active scholarship after many years as professor of English at Harvard University, has distinguished himself by producing works of impeccable scholarship written in a style of lucid and graceful precision. Author of such definitive works as Mythology and the Renaissance Tradition, *its companion volume* Mythology and the Romantic Tradition, *and one of the finest volumes in the* Oxford History of English Literature, *Bush has also displayed his tough-minded critical grace in essays dealing with the social problems of the scholarly life. These essays have been recently collected in a volume entitled* Engaged and Disengaged.

One of these essays called, with innocent accuracy, "The Humanities," is reprinted here. In it Bush presents the case for a democratically elitist education. It is important to note that neither Bush nor his opponent, George Z. F. Bereday, adopts an extreme position; American thinkers on the subject of education have tempered, to the realities of our times, any feudal or egalitarian passions they have. But tendencies are still apparent—as when Bush speaks of Dewey's "philosophy of barbarism" (a polemical phrase that receives scholarly elucidation).

The problem of education, as Bush phrases it, is to preserve "minority culture against . . . mass civilization." Only if society does so can we hope to extend that culture to the "rising flood of students" which is "very much like the barbarian invasions of the early Middle Ages." Bush's hierarchy of studies is much like that proposed by Hutchins, but Bush's humanism takes root in the Thomism of More, not in that of Aquinas.

To inculcate such a Thomism—an essentially humanistic and Erasmian culture—has become the work of teachers of humanities. It is in literature, read with the kind of patient and loving sensitivity now characteristic of modern critics, that students find whatever is still available to man of "the vision of human experience achieved by a great spirit." Bush acknowledges that one cannot, of course, measure with charts and graphs the progress of any student toward becoming a person "of richer moral and imaginative insight, of finer wisdom and discrimination and stability." Such experience is individual, "and nothing that is really important can be measured."

To do such work one must have able and willing students, small classes, and training in foreign languages. This last would itself serve as a means of distinguishing those who should go to college from those whose education

*is to be terminal. But only if America can make such distinctions will it be pos-
sible to preserve and transmit the very cultural values which we claim to admire
but which we are now vitiating in our massive attempts to educate all. The
question which Bush's essay poses is this: Are we raising the level of the student
or are we degrading the education which we give him?*

No one would ever speak of "the plight of the natural sciences," or of "the
plight of the social sciences," but it is always proper to speak of "the plight
of the humanities," and in the hushed, melancholy tone of one present at
a perpetual deathbed. For something like twenty-five hundred years the
humanities have been in more or less of a plight, not because they are themselves weak, but because their war is not merely with ignorance but with
original sin; and as civilization has advanced, the means of stultifying the
head and heart have multiplied in variety and power. As a sample of cultural
leadership, or of a common attitude, I should like to read a declaration of
faith delivered some years ago by the chairman of the department of humanities in a well-known technological institution. We will call him Professor X.
This is most of the report, from the *New York Times,* of his speech to a convention of engineers:

> Professor X . . . asserted last night that it would be "morally wrong"
> for him to advise the reading of the literary classics in this fast-moving
> age of television, radio and movies. . . .
>
> One should read for the purpose of doing something with what
> one reads, he asserted: not of polishing one's mind like a jewel, but of
> improving the world around.
>
> Take up a book because it will tell you something of the world . . . ;
> read what you want to read, not what you think you should read.
> "This is the frame of mind that makes reading worthwhile and often
> deeply rewarding.
>
> "For example, it would be morally wrong of me to urge you to take
> up a classic like 'David Copperfield' and to settle yourselves in easy
> chairs for winter evenings' reading. If you tried 'David Copperfield'
> you would grow restive; you would think of all the other things you
> might be doing more consistent with your daily environment—
> looking at television, listening to the radio, going to the movies.
>
> "Moreover, you would wonder why you should spend so much time
> laboriously reading 'David Copperfield' when you could see the book
> as a film, should it return some time to the neighborhood movie." . . .
>
> "The single prescription for adult reading," he added, "should
> be to read something different, something that will change your
> mind. Herein lies compensation for the loss of the purely reflective
> life."

Engineers are not, to be sure, in common repute the most cultivated
branch of mankind, but did even they deserve such counsel, and from
such a source? The humanities, as I said, have always had to contend with

the crude urges of the natural man, with his resistance to higher values than his own, but the speech I just quoted from reminds us of the many new ways there are of escaping from active thought and feeling into a state of lazy collapse, of passive surrender to unthinking action or external sensation. Many people would endorse our oracle's view that one should not read to polish one's mind like a jewel but for the sake of improving the world around. The humanistic tradition has always stood for improvement of the world, but it has always insisted that a man must make himself worthy of such an enterprise; one of our perennial troubles is that improvement of the world is undertaken by so many unpolished minds. Then our touching faith in machinery is illustrated by the quaint assumption that a movie is the same thing as a great book. And that Ersatz doctrine extends down through television to the comics, which have now joined the march of mind by reducing literary classics to capsule form. That sort of thing, by the way, was done, and done much better, a dozen centuries ago, and has been commonly labeled a symptom of the Dark Ages. But this is only a reminder; there is no need of enlarging upon such powerful elements in our popular civilization. The opposition to such elements comes from the humanities.

Negative terms, however, are not enough. The "humanities," in the original meaning of this and kindred words, embraced chiefly history, philosophy, and literature. These were the studies worthy of a free man, that ministered to *homo sapiens*, man the intellectual and moral being, and not to *homo faber*, the professional and technical expert. And these, with divinity, completed the central circle of human knowledge and understanding. Divinity went overboard long ago; history, which once was literature, is now a social science; and philosophy, though still grouped with the humanities, has become a branch of mathematics. Thus in common usage the humanities mean literature and the fine arts. That is an unfortunate narrowing but we may take things as we find them and concentrate on literature, which is central and representative.

One plain fact nowadays is that the study of literature, which in itself is comprehensive and complex, has had to take over the responsibilities that used to be discharged by philosophy and divinity. Most young people now get their only or their chief understanding of man's moral and religious quest through literature. Anyone who has been teaching literature for twenty-five years, as I have, can testify to the marked change there has been in the spiritual climate during that time. (A rigorously scientific colleague of mine, in psychology, will not permit the use of the word "spiritual," but I use it anyhow.) I am speaking mainly of the higher order of college students, but it would be hard to imagine even the better students of twenty-five or thirty years ago reading Dante and George Herbert and Milton and Hopkins and Eliot with the real sympathy that many now show. For the more intelligent and sensitive young people of today, and there are very many of that kind, are a serious and a conservative lot. They not only live in our unlovely world, they have no personal experience of any other. They are aware of hollowness and confusion all around them, and, what is still more real, of hollowness and confusion in themselves. They feel adrift in a cockboat on an uncharted sea, and they want a sense of direction, of order and integration. And in literature they find, as countless people have found before them, that their problems are not new, that earlier generations have been lost also. Most of the young people I see find in literature, literature of the remote past as well as of the present, what they cannot find in text-books of psychology and sociology, the vision of human experience achieved by a great spirit and bodied forth by a great artist.

I apologize for elaborating what may be called clichés, but those familiar lists of courses in catalogues make one forget that the frigid label "English 10" or "French 20" may represent an illumination and a rebirth for John or Betty Smith. Not that courses are the only or even the main road to enriched experience and sensitivity, but they are one road; and a teacher can help as a guide or catalyst. Josiah Royce is said to have complained that a philosopher was expected to spiritualize the community. The modern philosopher is expected only to semanticize the community; the other function, as I said, falls upon the teacher of literature. I do not of course mean inspirational gush. I mean that teachers, conducting a critical discussion of a piece of great literature, necessarily deal not only with the artistic use of words and materials but with the moral and spiritual experience that are its subject matter. That is why, as President Pusey has said, the humanities must be the cornerstone of a liberal education. Naturally teachers will have their methods under constant scrutiny, but their material, the world's great literature, can hardly be improved; all it needs is a chance to work upon responsive minds and characters.

While I cannot guess the temper of this gathering, and while all the administrators present may, for all I know, regard the humanities as a pearl of great price, that is not their general reputation. Administrators are commonly said to prize the solid and tangible virtues of the natural and social sciences and to look upon the humanities as a nice luxury for the carriage trade. How far that general reputation is true or false I wouldn't know, but, just in case it has a modicum of truth, I have been insisting that the humanities are not a luxury; they are the most practical of necessities if men and women are to become fully human. The humanities commonly suffer in esteem because they do not lend themselves to statistical reports of achievement. You cannot demonstrate with graphs and charts that John or Betty Smith, through reacting to a piece of literature, became a person of richer moral and imaginative insight, of finer wisdom and discrimination and stability. For the experience of literature is an individual experience, and nothing that is really important can be measured.

When we look at the American educational scene, the diversity of standards is so great that generalizations about this or that part of it may be violently contradictory. At any rate educational history of the past fifty years seems to furnish a pretty good forecast of the bad effects of the deluge to be expected in the next fifteen. In school, college, and university, the results of the huge increase in the student body suggest that the principle of education for all, however fine in theory, in practice leads ultimately to education for none. An editorial in the *New York Times* of September 13, 1954, takes the usual line of defense. The principle of education for all, it says, forces us "to accept the principle, also, that the function of education is primarily social and political rather than purely intellectual." "It cannot be denied," the *Times* proceeds, "that this means a down-grading of the learning process. We are adjusting to an 'average' that must be spread so widely that it comes down automatically. Education is no longer the intellectual privilege of the gifted few. It is held to be the democratic right of all." The *Times* does go a little beyond this orthodox assent to express uneasiness over the sacrifice, in elementary and secondary schools, of quality to quantity.

To mention one of many results, there has been an appalling growth of illiteracy at all levels, even in the graduate school. (Somehow stenographers are still literate, even if their college-bred employers are not.) At every orgy of Commencements one wonders how many of the hordes of new bachelors of arts can speak and write their own language with elementary decency, or read it with understanding. After all, the polished mind is suspect, whether in a student, a professor, or a Presidential candidate. And illiteracy, and contentment with illiteracy, are only symptoms of general shoddiness.

Obviously one main cause of this state of things has been the sheer pressure of numbers, along with a deplorable shrinkage in the number of qualified teachers. But the situation would not be so bad as it has been if the downward pressure of numbers had not been powerfully strengthened by misguided doctrine and practice. The training of teachers and the control of school curricula have been in the hands of colleges of education and their products, and these have operated on principles extracted from John Dewey's philosophy of barbarism. (If that phrase seems unduly harsh, I may say that I have in mind Dewey's hostility to what he regarded as leisure-class studies; his antihistorical attitude, his desire—intensified in his followers—to immerse students in the contemporary and immediate; and his denial of a hierarchy of studies, his doctrine that all kinds of experience are equally or uniquely valuable; and it would not be irrelevant to add his notoriously inept writing.) The lowest common denominator has been, not an evil, but an ideal. The substantial disciplines have been so denuded of content that multitudes of students, often taught by uneducated teachers, have been illiterate, uninformed, and thoroughly immature. There is no use in priding ourselves on the operation of the democratic principle if education loses much of its meaning in the process. When we think, for instance, of education for citizenship, which has been the cry of modern pedagogy, we may think also of the volume and violence of popular support given to the anti-intellectual demagoguery of the last few years. Mass education tends to reflect mass civilization, instead of opposing it. Even if education were everywhere working on the highest level, it would still face tremendous odds.

The great problem has been, and will be, first, the preservation of minority culture against the many and insidious pressures of mass civilization, and, secondly, the extension of that minority culture through wider and wider areas. The rising flood of students is very much like the barbarian invasions of the early Middle Ages, and then the process of education took a thousand years. We hope for something less overwhelming, and for a less protracted cure, but the principle is the same; Greco-Roman-Christian culture not only survived but triumphed, and with enrichment. If we think of our problem in the light of that one, we shall not be disheartened but recognize both as phases of man's perennial growing pains.

Throughout history it has been a more or less small minority that has created and preserved what culture and enlightenment we have, and, if adverse forces are always growing, that minority is always growing too. In spite of the low standards that have commonly prevailed in public education during the last fifty years, I think the top layer of college students now are proportionately more numerous than they were thirty years ago and are more generally serious and critical. There is a growing nucleus of fine minds, and teachers are concerned with the enlargement of that all-important group. At the same time, without retreating from that position, one wonders what it is in our educational process or in our culture at large that often causes a liberal education to end on Commencement Day.

I have no novel and dramatic remedy for the evils that have shown themselves so clearly already and will become more formidable still. But I might mention a few things of varying importance which do not seem utopian. Of course I represent no one but myself, and I cannot even say, like a member of the House of Lords, that I enjoy the full confidence of my constituents.

In the first place, I see no reason why the flood of students should be allowed to pour into college, why automatic graduation from school should qualify anyone for admission. We ought to recognize, and make people in general recognize, that a desire for economic or social advantage, or for merely four years of idle diversion, is not enough. Under such pressure as is coming, surely the state universities have the strength to set up bars and select their student body, instead of admitting all who choose to walk in the front door and then, with much trouble and expense, trying to get rid of some through the back door. Doubtless such procedure would require a campaign of enlightenment and persuasion, but legislators always have an alert ear for the cry of economy, and the public must be convinced that higher education, or what passes for that, is neither a birthright nor a badge of respectability, and that useful and happy lives can be led without a college degree. As things are, we have an army of misfits, who lower educational standards and increase expense, and no branch of a university staff has grown more rapidly of late years than the psychiatric squad.

Secondly, many people have grounds for the belief that the multiplying junior colleges can and will drain off a large number of the young who for various reasons are unfitted for a really strenuous four-year course. Junior colleges, however, should not be recreational centers for the subnormal.

Thirdly, I think the need for formal education beyond high school would be much lessened, and the quality of both secondary and higher education obviously improved, if the colleges and universities, getting the public behind them, make a concerted and effectual demand that the schools do their proper work and do it much better than a great many schools have been doing it.[1] Quite commonly, a distressing proportion of a college course now consists of high-school work. For instance, we have grown so accustomed to a battalion of instructors teaching elementary composition to freshmen

---

[1] Since 1955 there seems to have been a good deal of improvement, though the ideal is still some way ahead.

that we take it as a normal part of college education, whereas in fact it is a monstrosity. Imagine a European university teaching the rudiments of expression! If high-school graduates are illiterate, they have no business in college. For a long time, and for a variety of reasons, we have had slackness all along the line; somehow, sometime, strictness and discipline have got to begin.

Increased enrollments have almost inevitably led to increased reliance upon large lecture courses. There are administrators who assume that there is no limit to the effectiveness of a lecture course except the size of the auditorium, and there are also some teachers who see positive virtues in lectures and can themselves display them. Perhaps because I never remember anything I hear, I do not share that faith. I favor classes small enough to allow discussion, and they are expensive. But there are possible economies that would be highly desirable in themselves. We do not need to maintain the naive doctrine that there has to be a course in everything or anything in which anyone has ever been or might be interested, and that no one can look into a subject for himself. Further, a good many catalogues list courses that can only be called fantastic, and I do not think I am guilty of partisan prejudice if I say that these are rarely found among the humanities. At any rate, if we had fewer and less specialized courses, and if we did not have our armies of composition teachers, a considerable number of man-hours would be released for smaller classes.

One thing that has suffered grievously and conspicuously in this last generation has been the study of foreign languages. The usual reason given is again the pressure of numbers, the numbers who are not going beyond high school, but again a positive reason has been open or quiet hostility. Languages have been pretty well crowded out of the school curriculum, and of course there has been a corresponding decline in college study. Nothing has been commoner in recent decades than the applicant for admission to a graduate school who has had little or no acquaintance with any foreign language except possibly a year or two of Spanish. Serious study of a foreign language means work, and a first principle of modern pedagogy has been the elimination of work. Thus, during the years in which we have all become conscious of one small world, and in which this country has become the leader of that world, educational theory and practice have retreated into cultural parochialism. There is no need to argue how necessary for the ordinary citizen is some knowledge of a foreign language and a foreign people. In the last few years a good many parents have been aroused, and the Modern Language Association has been putting on a vigorous campaign, so that progress has been made; but there is a long way to go. It is encouraging that in some cities successful experiments have been made in the teaching of languages in elementary schools, where, for good psychological reasons, they ought to begin. I wish there were something encouraging to be said about the ancient languages, but we are concerned with actualities.

Finally, since I touched on the large number of young people who are in college and should not be, I might mention those who are not and should be, and who may be lost in the oncoming flood. Educators and others are more conscious than they once were of our failure to recognize and foster promising students who cannot afford college, and increasing efforts are being made in that direction; but we are still very far behind England, where bright students are picked out at the age of ten or eleven and brought along on scholarships. If we spent on exceptional students a fraction of the time and money we have spent on nursing lame ducks, there would be a considerable change in the quality of education.

One last word on a different matter. Like everything else, the Ph.D. has been cheapened by quantitative pressure, and it might be earnestly wished that it were not a union card for the teaching profession. There are plenty of young men and women who would be good teachers without such a degree, and the degree itself ought to mean something more than it does. Along with that may go another earnest wish, that both administrators and members of departments would abandon the principle of "Publish or perish." Socrates would never have had a chance at an assistant professorship.

Trainees for Obedience
Bradford Cleaveland/from "A Letter to Undergraduates"

Bradford Cleaveland was, at the time he wrote the open letter reprinted here, a former graduate student in the Department of Political Science at Berkeley. The letter appeared in the SLATE *Supplement Report (Vol. I, No. 4), a publication of one of the off-campus groups functioning at the University of California, Berkeley, in the fall of 1964. Its tone, like its rhetoric, reeks of dramatic, almost melodramatic, immediacy, but beneath the rhetoric lies a number of sharp arguments and observations. Cleaveland's open letter is a powerful contrast with the polar piece chosen—a speech made by Dr. Grayson Kirk, president of Columbia University. The transcontinental distance is irrelevant; what is important is an almost menacing confrontation between figures who have opposite designs for the control of educational power.*

Cleaveland makes clear at once his disdain for the basic "myth" of American education, that students are being trained for leadership. In reality, he tells his student audience, "you are training for obedience." The university, or multiversity, equips its students with a "basic suspicion of intellectuals" and with a "fear of the kinds of thought necessary for you to meet the 20th century world-in-revolution." All educators recognize the woeful gap that exists between promise and performance, but the gap has not hitherto seemed to be unbridgeable. According to Cleaveland, the intellectual life of colleges is controlled by the nexus of what he calls the "course/grade/unit system." No tampering with or revising of the system is possible, he claims; all that can be done is to "organize and split this campus wide open!" In Cleaveland's view, only by such violence can the nature of the multiversity and the college be changed and made educational. As things stand now, "the multiversity is not an education center but a highly efficient industry: it produces bombs, other war machines, a few token 'peaceful' machines, and enormous numbers of safe, highly skilled, and respectable automatons to meet the immediate needs of business and government." To underline his point (already capitalized in the original), Cleaveland lists the Regents of the University of California; the list itself is an informative and devastating piece of rhetoric.

Cleaveland concludes with an eight-point program of action; one point calls for the resignation of Clark Kerr, another for the reconstitution of the Board of Regents. Although Kerr has resigned, it is doubtful that the University of California or any other university is prepared to enact the other points on the list. Failure to do so, Cleaveland seems to argue, can only perpetuate what he calls an educational "sham." Although his remarks are directed primarily at Berkeley, it is clear that he intends them to apply to colleges and universities throughout America.

Dear Undergraduates,

On May 13, 1963, SLATE published the *Cal Reporter,* a newspaper which charged this university with a total failure to educate undergraduates. The paper said that the university pushed the myth that you, as undergraduates, are "training for leadership," when in reality you are training for obedience;

that you leave the university with a basic suspicion of intellectuals, and fear of the kinds of thought necessary for you to meet the 20th century world-in-revolution. The theme of a quote from Bertrand Russell ran through the paper:

> We are faced with the paradoxical fact that education has become one of the chief obstacles of intelligence and freedom of thought.

This is not a *minor* charge. The charges were clearly focused upon your situation as an undergraduate, and not the graduate schools. The response to the newspaper was astonishing. The *Daily Cal* made the coy comment that SLATE had again emerged like a "grouchy bear," but that it offered no "constructive solutions." This casual and inappropriate response represented the views of a great many of you and your professors and administrators. But those charges were not minor, they were *seriously radical,* and for the *Daily Cal* to suggest that we all sit around picking our noses while asking for "constructive solutions" is astonishing!! If the rising waters of a flood threaten to immerse you in death and suffocation, it would be more than ridiculous to reflect on "constructive solutions." Or:

There Is No Blueprint for an Educational Revolution!!!

It was like this: on the one hand there was substantial agreement that the university stamps out consciousness like a super-Madison-Avenue-machine; on the other, people saying, "So what?" or "Bring me a detailed and exhaustive plan." *But there is no plan for kicking twenty thousand people* IN THEIR ASSES! No plan will stop excessive greed, timidity, and selling out. At best the university is a pathway to the club of "tough-minded-liberal-realists" in America, who sit in comfortable armchairs talking radical while clutching hysterically at respectability in a world explosive with revolution. At worst the university destroys your desires to see reality and to suffer reality with optimism, at the time when you most need to learn that painful art. In between those two poles is mostly garbage: Bus. Ad. Ph.D. candidates "on the make"; departmental enclaves of "clever and brilliant" students who will become hack critics; and thousands of trainees for high-class trades which will become obsolete in ten years. . . .

Your Undergraduate Routine

The *Cal Reporter*'s charges were that the routine life of the university is *destructive* of anything we know of educational tradition: especially at the level where we might reasonably expect to see painstaking efforts to give mass education its highest expression—at your level as undergraduate. In the place of such efforts, your routine is comprised of a systematic psychological and spiritual brutality inflicted by a faculty of "well-meaning and nice" men who have decided that your situation is hopeless when it comes to actually participating in serious learning. As an undergraduate you receive a four-year-long series of sharp staccatos: eight semesters, forty courses, one hundred twenty or more units, fifteen hundred to two thousand impersonal lectures, and over three hundred oversized "discussion" meetings. Approaching what is normally associated with learning—reading, writing, and exams—

your situation becomes absurd. Over a period of four years you receive close to fifty bibliographies, ranging in length from one to eight pages, you are examined on more than one hundred occasions, and you are expected to write forty to seventy-five papers. As you well know, reading means "getting into" hundreds of books, many of which are secondary sources, in a superficial manner. You must cheat to keep up. If you don't cheat you are forced to perform without time to think in depth, and consequently you must hand in papers and exams which are almost as shameful as the ones you've cheated on. You repeat to yourselves over and over as an undergraduate that "It doesn't make any difference . . . it's the grade that counts," a threadbare and worn phrase (if you are lucky enough to make it to the third or fourth year) used as commonly as your word "regurgitation" in place of "exam." You know the measure of truth in those bits of slang: it *is* nauseous . . . you almost *do* "puke up your work" to professors. I personally have known students who have gotten physically sick by merely reflecting upon their routine. In the sciences and technical fields your courses are bluntly and destructively rigorous. . . . you become impatient with "that social sciences and humanities crap." How did you get to be such puppets? You *perform*. But when do you think? Dutifully and obediently you follow, as a herd of grade-worshiping sheep. If you are strong at all, you do this with some sense of shame, or if you are weak, you do it with a studied cynicism . . . as jaded youth with parched imaginations that go no further than oak-paneled rooms at the end of the line. . . . BUT WHETHER YOU ARE STRONG OR WEAK YOU PERFORM LIKE TRAINED SEALS, AND LIKE SHEEP YOU FOLLOW . . . WITH THE THOROUGHBRED PHI BETA KAPPA SHEEP LEADING YOU!! up the golden stairway to the omnipotent A, to the Happy Consciousness, to success and a very parochial mind. This is the core of your dutiful daily lives, and your homage to respectability. Reluctantly or otherwise, you permit it to be applied by administrators who use computers on you as much because they are afraid of personal contact with you as for the reason that they wish to keep the assembly line moving efficiently. You permit professors to extract your performance by the coercion of grades. Why do you permit this apostasy of learning . . . a process which prevents you from extending your thought beyond a shallow dilettantism?

IF THE FACTS OF YOUR UNDERGRADUATE EXISTENCE WERE SOLELY DETERMINED BY THE "COURSE/GRADE/UNIT SYSTEM," YOUR "INCIPIENT REVOLT," TO WHICH PRESIDENT KERR HIMSELF IRRESPONSIBLY ALLUDED IN THE GODKIN LECTURES, WOULD PROBABLY HAVE ALREADY OCCURRED.[1]

The reason why, dear undergraduates, you permit your minds to be abused, is because you are given a magnificent bread and circus. What a

---

[1]"There is an incipient revolt of undergraduate students against the faculty; the revolt that used to be against the faculty in loco parentis is now against the faculty in absentia," from page 103 of *The Uses of the University*, Harvard, 1963 (Godkin Lectures given in 1963 at Harvard). Kerr's comments throughout the book on higher education are made from the vantage point of a sort of disinterested observer, as though the president was not talking about his own "multiversity," or as though he was really nothing more than a bureaucrat-employee of the Regents. Or, as Kerr himself puts it, ". . . he is mostly a mediator," on p. 36.

pain reliever! . . . these "extra-curricular" activities. Coming to you from your ASUC student "government," other special bureaucracies such as the Committee on Arts and Lectures, and added to by more intellectual offerings from departmental and special-grants lecture series, is a semesterly tidal wave of exciting and highly intense stimuli which dazzles you away from the fact that you are obstructed from learning, or even questioning whether you should be learning while you are here. This bread and circus assures you that the world is really *not* in the midst of anything so serious as *revolution,* much less within your own sacred borders!! From the powerfully entertaining to the scholastically intellectual you get films, debates, art exhibits, athletics, drama, "spirit" groups, recreation, seductions of hundreds of social groups; this pyrotechnical explosion of *Kultur* is something terribly "other directed"; happily away from your puppetlike performance in the course/grade/unit procedural core. Your attention is diverted away from your treadmill to the candied goodness of the bread and circus. Hopefully, when you get your bachelor's degree, you will step up to higher plateaus, where many kinds of "success" await you. You are blinded to the fact that you are really getting something of terrible importance while you are here. . . .

Dear Undergraduates!!

I am no longer interested in cajoling you, arguing with you, or describing, to you something you already know. What I am about to say to you at this point concerns you more directly. I will entreat you to furiously throw your comforting feelings of duty and responsibility for this institution to the winds and act on your situation. This institution, affectionately called "Cal" by many of you, or, as the *Daily Cal* might put it, "the Big U," does not deserve a response of loyalty and allegiance from you. There is only one proper response to Berkeley from undergraduates: that you *organize and split this campus wide open!*

> FROM THIS POINT ON, DO NOT MISUNDERSTAND ME. MY INTENTION IS
> TO CONVINCE YOU THAT YOU DO NOTHING LESS THAN BEGIN AN OPEN,
> FIERCE, AND THOROUGHGOING REBELLION ON THIS CAMPUS.

I would like to briefly explain to you now why such a course of action is necessary, and how, if such a revolt were conducted with unrelenting toughness and courage, it could spread to other campuses across the country and cause a fundamental change in your own futures.

I have used the phrase "world-in-revolution" several times to this point. I would like to say to you now that most of you are incompetent to deal with that phrase. It is a phrase which betrays a distinct view of reality . . . a view of reality out of which might grow an effective "opposition" in the present American scene where the only opposition seems to be crystallizing along reactionary lines. "World-in-revolution" is a phrase . . . a view of reality which contains a large measure of truth, one which is certainly debatable. BUT IT IS NOT DEBATED BY YOU. The catastrophic gap between the incubator world of your multiversity and the world of reality is represented by your ignorance of what "world-in-revolution" means. The university teaches you to bury your heads in the sand, trembling in ignorance of the American black revolution for civil rights, the impending revolution in automation, and likewise in ignorance of political revolutions, which, like thunder-clapping salvos, explode the world over. The multiversity is the slickest appeal ever made for you to fortify your organization-man mentalities, for you to lead privatized lives in which it is a virtue for you to go greedily "on the make." In urging you to rebellion, I have action in mind, not further understanding. What more is there to understand when you can so easily discover that a Peace Corpsman who left Cal is now living in Nigeria in a separate small house with the conveniences of suburban America, plus two houseboys, and that a young girl civil-rights worker from the Bay Area who goes to Mississippi lives in abject poverty with a family of eleven black American citizens, in a shack with no running water, with lice, with rats, and in constant fear for her life?

In this multiversity, you will not learn so much as a cursory meaning of what a world-in-revolution means to you. You will not learn the utterly profound fact of what a revolution is:

THAT A REVOLUTION COMES ABOUT WHEN ENORMOUS NUMBERS OF FELLOW HUMAN BEINGS ARE OPPRESSED TO POINTS FAR BEYOND WHAT WE BLANDLY LABEL AN "INTOLERABLE SET OF CONDITIONS."

Nor will you learn that to be a counter-revolutionary is to go about the business of slaughtering enormous numbers of human beings whose in-flamed spirits and starved stomachs force them to cry out for the freedoms which you spit upon in your apathy. . . .

The only large group of students I personally respect, other than the Freedom Fighters, are the dropouts. Ignominious lot! What a fate . . . that one would be forced to give up that little registration card with respect-ability written all over it! This "Hidden Community" of unseemly hangers-on in Berkeley now numbers in the thousands. Those most bugged by this "element" are the ASUC types. They screech, "You can't even tell them from students sometimes (although some are very dirty) . . . and they're using *our* student union!" If they have flunked out (or dropped out) of the university how can they deserve respect? Well . . . if I thought it was a virtue to perform like sheep I wouldn't be urging revolt. The fact is that these students are the real ones. Many have had the guts to cut their social umbilical cords, become genuinely *free,* and to begin coughing up their own mistakes. They don't take the fatal step which the Cowell Psychiatric Clinic calls "regressive:" which means to go back to Mama, or, God forbid, to a junior college. They face life in its own terms, and many do something rather shocking around Berkeley: they learn to read a book. And I might add that many of them are also Freedom Fighters. (Incidentally, do you know the latest figures? According to Cowell, close to fifty per cent of those of you who are graced with the mantle of "freshman at Cal," are eliminated by the end of the third year.)

Are you aware that the most salient characteristic of the "multiversity" is massive production of specialized excellence? SPECIALIZED EXCELLENCE. It will be some time before machines will displace the super-trades; thus massive training centers are necessary. But why do we insist upon calling them educational centers rather than training centers?

THE MULTIVERSITY IS NOT AN EDUCATIONAL CENTER, BUT A HIGHLY EFFICIENT INDUSTRY: IT PRODUCES BOMBS, OTHER WAR MACHINES, A FEW TOKEN "PEACEFUL" MACHINES, AND ENORMOUS NUMBERS OF SAFE, HIGHLY SKILLED, AND RESPECTABLE AUTOMATONS TO MEET THE IMMEDIATE NEEDS OF BUSINESS AND GOVERNMENT.

.   .   .

WHEN THIS OCCURS IN PUBLIC UNIVERSITIES, THE RESULT IS ABANDONMENT OF THE AMERICAN DEMOCRATIC EXPERIMENT IN WHICH THE RADICAL PROPOSITION OF EDUCATION FOR ALL IS THE CENTRAL AXIOM.

Dear undergraduate, your "learning" has come to an impasse. Below the level of formal responsibility (the Regents, president, and chancellors), the Academic Senate (the faculty) itself is guilty of a massive and disastrous default. It is said that the Regents have given to the faculty the power and responsibility to deal with your learning. To put it mildly, the Academic Senate has turned that power and responsibility into a sham, an unused fiction. If this be true, then who is responsible for seeing to it that the faculty do something? We can cancel out President Kerr: he has already admitted publicly that he is incompetent to attend to the matter of undergraduate learning. That takes us back up the bureaucratic ladder again . . . do you know what the phrase "The Regents of the University of California" means? Following is the meaning of that phrase:

Edward CARTER: Chairman of the Board of Regents, Director, Broadway-Hale Retail Stores, Northrup Aircraft, Pacific Tel & Tel, and First Western Bank; Dorothy CHANDLER: Director, L.A. *Times,* and wife of Norman CHANDLER of the Southern California News Publishing empire; William COBLENTZ: corporation lawyer, San Francisco; Frederick DUTTON: U.S. Assistant Secretary of State; Mrs. William Randolph HEARST: ("housewife"), of the Hearst national newspaper empire; Mrs. Edward HELLER: ("housewife"), widow and heir to Edward HELLER, Director, Permanente Cement, Wells Fargo Bank, Schwabacher & Fry partner, and Pacific Intermountain Express; William E. FORBES: Southern California Music Company; Lawrence KENNEDY: attorney, Redding, California, (just prior to Mr. Kennedy's appointment as a Regent, it was strongly urged that it might be appropriate to appoint an *educator* to the Board of Regents); Donald H. MC LAUGHLIN: ("mining geologist"), Director, Homestake Mining Company, one of the largest gold-mining operations in the world, recent interests in uranium mining, Director, Western Airlines, American Trust, and a Peruvian copper-mining operation; Samuel MOSHER: Director, Signal Gas & Oil, and Long Beach Oil Development Company, which was accused publicly a few months ago, by Lieutenant Governor Glenn Anderson, of trying to wrest public control of a recently discovered state owned oil field off Long Beach with a projected worth of over 3 billion . . . enough to shake up the world market and give California Petroleum men a virtual monopoly; Edwin PAULEY: Director, Pauley Oil, Western Airlines; William Matson ROTH: U.S. Special Deputy for Trade Relations, Director, National Life Insurance, Matson Shipping, Honolulu Oil, Pacific Intermountain Express; Norton SIMON: Director, Hunt Foods, McCalls, Wesson Oil & Snowdrift, and also "land developer"; Phillip BOYD: former mayor of Palm Springs, Director, Deep Canyon Properties, Security National Bank; John CANADAY: Vice President, Lockheed Aircraft, Director, Corporate Public Relations, Lockheed Aircraft; and Regent number sixteen on our list is the one and only representative of organized labor (the most reactionary element in labor at that): Cornelius HAGGERTY: President, Construction and Building Trades Council, AFL-CIO.

In these men you find substantial ownership and control of the vital raw materials and service industries in the West: communications, the press, television, air and surface transportation, fuel, and finance; virtually enough power to make or break five governors and ten university presidents. The board members are appointed for terms of sixteen years by the governor. There are also ex-officio members, ONE OF WHOM IS AN EDUCATOR: Clark Kerr. I would like to ask you to think for a moment about the "public" character of these men. In the first place, who even knows them? . . . except a few of us who are aware that they are "famous" or "very wealthy men." What do they do? AND WHY? FOR WHOSE INTEREST? . . .

FROM TIME IMMEMORIAL, MEN OF POWER HAVE CONSIDERED IT WISE TO KEEP THEIR CONSTITUENTS AT A LEVEL OF IGNORANCE WHEREBY THE PROCESS OF RULING THEM IS MOST EASILY ACCOMPLISHED.

Or are we to entertain the possibility that the Regents have upset the applecart of history? Have they become revolutionaries? Is it true that they recently removed the ban on Communist speakers on campus. Of course, they resisted for fifteen years . . . since the McCarthy era. And during the McCarthy era they were able to force the Academic Senate into adopting a loyalty oath. If you can forgive the faculty of a university for *that,* you can forgive them for *anything.* Many professors did not forgive the Senate, however, and resigned. The spine of this faculty, close to forty professors, left in disgust, left scars behind which will never heal. Moreover, what the hell difference does it make whether you hear a Communist every year or so. Most of you would laugh at him . . . like laughing at a movement which involves the entire world! If any one of you wisely decided to study a Communist speaker's proposals, to think about them, to read about them seriously, you not only would find it *impossible from the standpoint of time,* but you would also be considered a heretic by your fellow "students." It is probably accurate to say that the removal of the speaker ban on Communists was a great contribution on the symbolic level . . . like a Charter Day ceremony. Politically, it was very wise.

Speaking of politics, what relation exists between the university and the U.S. Government? Aside from providing trained personnel for public corporations (agencies, bureaus, etc.) as in private ones, is there as direct a relation between the university and government as between the university and the Regents? Yes, it seems that the university, or shall we call a spade a spade —the Regents—it seems that the Regents are snuggled up pretty tightly to the seats of power in Washington (though it is difficult to tell who-hugs-whom the hardest in Washington):

> Item—from the *Cal Reporter,* May 13, 1963, "According to the Financial Report of the 1961–62, the U. S. Government spent about 227 millions on Special Projects. These included 150 millions for Lawrence Radiation Laboratory (U.C.), 76 millions for Los Alamos Radiation Lab (U.C.). The income for the entire University (eight campuses) excluding these special projects was 250 millions."

•　•　•

Have I sufficiently taken care of your objections? If not, chances are that what remains is *fear,* and that is *your* problem. If I have taken care of your objections, then you might be asking, HOW DO YOU START A REBELLION ON THE CAMPUS? That's a tough one—and you might have to get tough in order to be heard. You also know that you will need legitimate demands behind your slogans of FREEDOM NOW! THE FREEDOM TO KNOW AND TO LEARN!!

Demands?

1. Immediate commitment of the university to the total elimination of the course/grade/unit system of undergraduate learning in the social sciences and humanities.

2. Immediate disbanding of all university dorm and living group rules which prescribe hours and which provide for a system of student-imposed discipline, thereby dividing students against themselves.

3. Immediate negotiations on the establishment of a permanent student voice which is effective (that is, independent) in running university affairs.

4. Immediate efforts to begin recruitment of an undergraduate teaching faculty to handle undergraduate learning in social sciences and humanities.

5. Immediate negotiations regarding two methods of undergraduate learning which provide for the basic freedom required in learning:

> *a. A terminal examination system which will be voluntary and an option with "b."*
>
> *b. Immediate creation of undergraduate programs of a wide variety in which the student will be given careful, but minimal guidance, without courses, grades, and units.*

6. Immediate establishment of a university committee to deal with these demands on the Berkeley campus.

Go to the top. Make your demands to the Regents. If they refuse to give you an audience: start a program of agitation, petitioning, rallies, etc., in which the final resort will be CIVIL DISOBEDIENCE. In the long run there is the possibility that you will find it necessary to perform civil disobedience at a couple of major university public ceremonies. Depending on the resistance, you might consider adding the following two demands:

7. *Resignation of Clark Kerr. Resignation of top administrators who might employ slick diverting tactics.*

8. *Reconstitution of the Board of Regents, either through firing or expansion, perhaps both.*

• • •

If it is necessary to go this far beyond formal "channels," and if you have the guts to get there, you will begin to learn how tough it is to effect radical change. If the *Daily Cal* decides to support you at various times along the way (very unlikely), they will be duly chastised by the so-called "Publications Board," and then the students' editors might have the guts to walk out (doubly unlikely). If such a walkout occurs again, as it did a couple of years ago, it might be wise to consider an effective picket to try to keep out the same types of fraternity scabs who took over last time in an action which was traitorous to the undergraduates.

And if you get this far you will also have witnessed nation-wide publicity which will have exposed Berkeley for the undergraduate sham that it is. Not to say that the public in general will feel that way, what with the press "redbaiting" you, but that students all over the country will read between the lines. By this time you may also be able to call for a mass student strike . . . something which seems unthinkable at present. If a miracle occurs, or two, you might even get to say that you were the seeds of an educational revolution unlike anything which has ever occurred. Remember one thing:

> "The task of genius, and man is nothing if not genius, is to keep the miracle alive, to live always in the miracle, to make the miracle more and more miraculous, to swear allegiance to nothing, but live only miraculously, think miraculously, to die miraculously." *(Henry Miller)*

Student Responsibility
Grayson Kirk/"Youth on the College Campus"

Dr. Grayson Kirk (1905–   ), president of Columbia University, belongs, like his transcontinental peer, Clark Kerr, to that class of administrators who in the eyes of campus radicals are impersonal and "faceless." Their genteel competence seems to irritate the more flamboyant among the advocates of "student power." Kirk is unfortunately vulnerable perhaps to the charge of facelessness because he had to follow Dwight Eisenhower in the office of Columbia's presidency. The speech reprinted here is one Kirk delivered in November 1965 before the Greater Hartford Forum in Hartford, Connecticut. In it he deals directly with the problems raised by Bradford Cleaveland; his comments are of particular interest since Kirk is the kind of administrator whom Cleaveland wants to oust. Kirk speaks with a trenchancy not masked by the bland pomposity that sometimes positions such as his seem to confer. He is fully conscious of the social and intellectual powers of his foes and he meets them head on, even if from a loftier and superior position. He remarks that "education is a rigorous process at best; too many of our young people want it to be effortless and painless. Overlooking all that has been accomplished, they indulge themselves in a demeaning self-pity because the society into which they are being inducted is not ideal" (emphasis ours).

Kirk's views are hardnosed, for all their administrative gentility. For example, he is perfectly willing to sanction "any off-campus activities, including demonstrations and picketing," provided that those involved are willing to face the consequences of their own self-chosen acts—including possible legal penalties. He quotes, with quiet relish, Sidney Hook's observation: "When Thoreau refused to pay his tax, he didn't run for the hills or refuse to plead." On-campus activities are treated similarly; they are considered lawful provided that they do "not interfere with the carrying out of university activities in a normal manner." The use of violence by students on campus should be subject to proper disciplinary action, even, in some cases, immediate separation." In general, he notes, students should not become so involved in "activist movements" that they sacrifice their paramount activist movement—the training of their minds under the professional guidance of the university to which they have voluntarily submitted themselves: the university should be "something more than an opportunity to mount an ivy-festooned soap-box."

Kirk's argument does not end in a trite expression of good will. His bias in favor of law and order, of channels and negotiation more diplomatic than dramatic, is clear. In the long run, the bulk of the students, who are— as most agree—committed neither to Mario Savio nor Clark Kerr, will have to decide which kind of man they trust to lead them. Even in a student-powered community, power has to be delegated. What matters is the quality of the mind behind the face—or facelessness—of the leaders.

In the whole field of higher education no development of recent years has so caught the imagination and interest of the public as the new wave of student radicalism that has swept across the nation. Dramatized by the endlessly-analysed affair at Berkeley last year, this movement has touched many universities and colleges. It has evoked a spate of newspaper editorials, magazine articles, speeches, and television programs.

Some observers see in it merely another of those student fads which from time to time have amused or irritated the adult population of the country. Others have concluded that it is primarily the work of professional left-wing groups who have used the students as pawns in a program designed to spread confusion and disunity across the nation. Some analysts believe that it is essentially a transfer to the university campus of the techniques and experience which some students have acquired through participation in civil rights activities in the South. Still others ask if it is not perhaps a surface manifestation of some more complex problem, unfortunately placed under assault before we even know its dimensions. But whatever the conclusions may be, there is general agreement that the phenomenon is important, that it ought to have serious examination, and that it may have some lasting effect on our system of higher education.

Oddly enough, many of those who deplore these new developments are the same people who, a few short years ago, were then criticizing our students for their adolescent antics and their seeming apathy about important issues of public policy. They wondered—frequently in print—why it was that in this respect our students seemed to differ so greatly from their comrades in Europe, Latin America, and Asia. Now that their questions have been answered by an outburst of radical activism, their reaction is one of dismay rather than satisfaction, and they deluge university authorities with demands for repressive disciplinary action. They realize that goldfish-swallowing had its merits, after all.

Let me begin my own comments tonight by reminding you that, in some form or other, student unrest and activism have been a feature of higher education ever since its beginnings in Western Europe more than a thousand years ago. If you will read the history of the universities of Bologna, Paris, Oxford, and Cambridge, you will find a record of persistent friction among student groups, between the students and the administration, and, on many occasions, between the academic community and the officials of the secular government.

On occasion the students dominated the institution completely, even levying fines upon professors whom the students had employed and who appeared to be falling behind in their courses of lectures. At other times, all students, no matter their maturity, were treated merely like children and were subjected to corporal punishment if they violated institutional regulations. Over the centuries the students generally have been obliged to accept institutional regulations as a condition of their continued membership in the academic community, but they have seldom been docile or meek in their role.

Inevitably, much of this protest has been intra-mural in origin and focus. In those countries where universities have undertaken to regulate personal conduct of their students—and this, of course, is most characteristic of those institutions that provide housing for their students—the students generally have objected, sometimes violently, to all efforts to enforce common codes regulating their personal habits. They regard themselves as young adults, quite capable of managing their own personal lives, and they are quick to resent institutional interference or regulation.

Other student protests throughout history have centered upon the alleged short-comings of individual professors, curricular standards and requirements, and, in general, the quality of the education set before them. There is, for example, a direct relationship between the persistent student protests in Latin American universities and the fact that many Latin American professors are employed on a part-time basis, devoting all too often their principal attention to their outside professions and being little concerned with the students who flock to their hastily-prepared university lectures.

We should also note that in most countries, most universities are created by, financed by, and ultimately are responsible to, the national government. Therefore, student unhappiness over the quality of education offered them inevitably takes the form of active opposition to individual government officials, to governing political parties, or even to the whole governmental structure. This understandable politicalization of student protest movements is most obvious in Latin America and in Asia where traditions of academic freedom *vis-a-vis* the government are less well developed than in Europe. Predictably, many governments respond by discharging professors who side with the students, by quelling student riots with police or military force, or, ultimately, by closing down the entire university.

It would be quite wrong, however, to conclude that in these countries where such violent conflict exists, student movements are entirely motivated by dissatisfaction with their education. Many student groups are openly hostile, politically, to the governments in power, and they seek to use their strength as a mass political movement to try to bring down the whole governmental structure. They are using their position as students to effect general political leadership in the country and thereby to use the university structure as a mechanism to force drastic social and political change, usually revolutionary in technique and purposes. This, for example, is clearly the case with the strong Left-wing Japanese student organization, the *Zenqakuren*.

In our own country, student complaints about the quality of education usually center today upon the size of the university, its impersonality, and its reliance upon bureaucratic administrative procedures. Students proclaim that they are little more than units in an anonymous mass, numbers on a computer tape, and— to the professor—faceless beings in a large lecture hall. They insist that they have no opportunity to develop meaningful personal relationships with professors who are indifferent to their needs and problems, and who are eager to escape from the classroom to the laboratory or to the airport.

In these complaints there is, of course, some truth. But the degree of truth varies from institution to institution and from department to department within a single institution. A student in an introductory course in a large department in a large institution will not have the same amount of individual professorial attention as he will find in an advanced course in a department which is less popular.

It is significant that the chief protests about size, impersonality, and automation of education have come from our large, publicly-supported institutions that have been obliged in recent years to struggle valiantly, and with varying degrees of success, to cope educationally with the hordes of students that have descended upon them. Some of these institutions have become so large—and they have become so large so rapidly—that it has been humanly impossible for them to develop smooth and efficient administrative procedures, or to recruit the necessary quality and quantity of teaching staff, to assure their students a personalized educational experience of optimum quality.

In one sense, this is a price that must be paid for three recent developments in American higher education. First is the increasing use being made, in the world's most affluent society, of our long-standing democratic commitment to make provision for higher education for all young men and women who seek it and who show some minimal promise of being able to profit from it. When an institution receives tens of thousands of students on a single campus, it cannot undertake to offer a student a Mark Hopkins on the other end of a log, or a Mr. Chips serving tea to a few boys in his study. In time, our educators may be able to deal more effectively, in personal terms, with this horde of students. On the other hand our young people must realize that they have an educational opportunity such as no other society in history has ever undertaken to provide. I would be happier if they appeared to be grateful for the opportunity rather than to indulge themselves in petulant complaints because they are obliged to be more self-reliant than they like. Education is a rigorous process at best; too many of our young people want it to be effortless and painless. Overlooking all that has been accomplished, they indulge themselves in demeaning self-pity because the society into which they are being inducted is not ideal.

A second development which affects the teaching process is the new commitment of our universities, public and private, to research. Through the indispensable help of the Federal Government the growth of university research, particularly in scientific fields, has been spectacular. It has been of enormous benefit to our country. It has made possible a rate of national scientific and technological progress unprecedented in history. But this sudden expansion in human knowledge does have some educational costs. Some faculty members, understandably, are more excited about their research than about their teaching, particularly when the teaching is at the undergraduate level.

It is incumbent upon a university administration to hold a balance between these two functions. In my own university the obligation to carry on both teaching and research is a stated condition for all professorial appointments. But the time is past, and happily so, when a great university can be no more than an institution for teaching. If we are to lead the world in research, our faculty members are not likely ever again to have quite as much time for personal contact with students as they did when they were content to repeat what they believed to be the old truths and were unconcerned about any search for new truth.

The third development about which students often complain is the new degree of professorial involvement in off-campus activities. While this varies from department to department, it is much greater now than it was in the past. Some of the people who once complained about the university as an ivory tower remote from the practical concerns of life, now complain because professors are involved in governmental policy-making, and in offering advice to industrial, civic, and professional groups. Here, too, the problem is one of balance. It is good for all concerned that the ivory tower is no more.

It would be a disservice for education, as many countries have discovered, if the focus of professorial interest and commitment were to shift too greatly off campus. But it is a service to education and to society if the two can maintain a fruitful interchange. The problem rests squarely on the shoulders of academic administrators. The solution is partly in wise regulatory measures, but it consists chiefly in finding the money with which to train and support faculties of sufficient size to enable all these three functions—teaching, research, and off-campus activity—to be carried on in such a way that no one of the three will suffer.

Thus far I have been addressing myself to some of the more common student complaints about the educational process in colleges and universities. It is a field in which rights and responsibilities as such are blurred. Students frequently enter higher education with expectations that few institutions can meet. On the other hand, many courses in many institutions have not been upgraded to meet the new high standards of educational achievement in our better secondary schools; and college students who find, as at times they do, that they had better teaching in high school, have every right to complain about it. Such complaints are not always welcomed by academic administrators, but they should be.

Inept teaching is by no means absent from our colleges and universities. Widespread publicity recently was given a plan for attacking this problem in which undergraduate honor students and graduate recipients of terminal degrees would submit critical evaluations of their teachers for the consideration of departmental chairmen in matters of tenure. This plan, in variation, is not unknown on American campuses. In my own university we treat this problem more flexibly. A crowded classroom in an elective course taught by a man with a reputation for vigorous grading indicates good teaching to us. So do spontaneously uttered words of praise by bright students, just as unsolicited comments of a more caustic nature can point to poor teaching.

Another acute conflict in recent years relates to the permissible area of student freedom in personal conduct. Students often feel that they are in fact adults and that they should be treated as such. Academic administrators usually feel that they have an obligation to exercise reasonable controls over the lives of their students, particularly at the undergraduate level, and particularly over those who are housed in residence halls maintained by the institution. Parents of undergraduates usually support the college authorities in this effort.

This is a difficult and complicated problem, one that never will be easily or fully solved. The entering college student frequently is freed from all family restraints on conduct for the first time in his life. He is at a time of life when self-discipline and self-imposed responsibility are less obviously necessary than they will be later on. The institution, on the other hand, has the obligation to maintain order, to protect its property, and to insist upon those standards of conduct which society can reasonably expect.

Students have a right to be freed from archaic parietal rules and regulations. They do not have a right to be freed from all regulation. The degree of relaxation will, and should, depend entirely upon the responsibility with which students conduct themselves. If they insist upon being treated like adults, then they must act like adults. And the institution must remember that today's students are more travelled, more experienced in the ways of the world, more sophisticated, and in many ways more mature than the students of a generation ago.

Another area of contention, and occasionally of conflict, concerns what might be called the political rights of students on the campus. For example, should the college or university authorities exercise control over the issuance of invitations to outside speakers by student organizations?

This is a problem of current practical importance. Some of our large universities have regulations requiring official approval for all invitations to outside speakers, and in at least one state there is legislation forbidding the issuance of any such invitation to Communist speakers. In another state, regulations provide that the chancellor of the university, whenever he believes necessary, "in furtherance of educational objectives" may require that the meeting be chaired by a tenure faculty member, that the speaker be subject to questions from the audience, and that the speaker be appropriately balanced in debate with a person of contrary opinions.

The argument in favor of regulation is simple and obvious. Why should a university which society has established and supported as a carrier and transmitter of its traditions offer hospitality to speakers whose objectives may be its destruction? In particular, why should young and impressionable students be exposed to such dangerous influences?

In my own university any recognized student organization is free, without prior clearance, to invite any speaker of its choice. I do not believe that any of our students have had their morals corrupted or their patriotism endangered by the application of this policy. On the contrary, I recall with no little satisfaction the published statement of a former editor of the *Daily Worker* that he had been completely disheartened by the heckling and the antagonism to which he had been subjected when addressing a Columbia student audience. Our students are not naive, waiting to be brain-washed by a speaker. They have a right to hear all opinions, and if we fear to permit them to do so, we betray a deep insecurity about our own society and the principles upon which it is built. We must not fear the test of the market place for truth.

Similarly, I believe that students should have a right to hold meetings to discuss any subject, however controversial, provided these meetings do not in any way disrupt normal university activities and functions. I must admit that I have winced, at times, when I read accounts in the student newspaper of what some of our speakers have said and the subjects they have discussed, but I remain convinced, nonetheless, that attempts at regulation would open a Pandora's box from which would emerge far greater dangers than benefits.

Obviously students, as citizens, have a right to take part in any off-campus activities, including demonstrations and picketing, that they wish. In so doing, they expose themselves, like everyone else, to such legal penalties as they may encounter. If they do get into trouble with the law, they have no right to seek special treatment or consideration because they are students. As Sidney Hook recently observed, " . . . the ethics of civil disobedience require that they cheerfully accept the punishment they voluntarily invited instead of making loud lamentation or whining complaint about the enforcement of the law. When Thoreau refused to pay his tax, he didn't run for the hills or refuse to plead."

Next we come to the question of student protests on campus about university policies or activities. As the Berkeley affair has shown, this is something that can develop into a genuine threat to peace and order on the campus and can disrupt seriously the normal operations of the university. My own views are well known, and I can do no more than repeat them on this occasion. As I see it, students have every right to make known their disapproval of university policies or practices. This right should extend to peaceful picketing on campus in designated areas, provided it does not interfere with the carrying out of university activities in a normal manner.

Such a right should not include any resort to violence or incitement thereto. If violence should occur, the university must take all appropriate steps to restore peace and order and to take such disciplinary measures as will be calculated to prevent a recurrence of disorder. A student must have every opportunity for the peaceful and orderly expression of his views; he may not, in so doing, be permitted to interfere with a similar exercise of rights by those who differ with him. A flagrant violation of this principle of non-violence should be followed by a fair hearing and, upon a finding or admission of guilt, should lead to severe disciplinary action, including the immediate separation of the individuals concerned from the university.

To refer again to the university which I know most intimately, we are very much aware of the problems lurking in this area. In an effort toward their further solution, we are even now in process of setting up a committee of representatives from the student body, from the faculty, and from the administration, charged with the duty of mapping the boundary lines of student protests on campus, and with the task of defining for the clear understanding of all concerned the rights and responsibilities in these matters of everyone in the university community.

I have now talked at some length about student rights and some of the limitations that must be placed upon their exercise for the protection of the university as an operating institution. Student responsibilities flow from these rights and from membership in an academic community.

As I have just said, a responsible student will not resort to, or incite, violence. He must respect the fact that a college or university is a place where men may argue to their heart's content for or against anything, but it is also a place where the same privilege must be accorded to others who hold different or opposing views, and neither group may attempt to deny to others the freedom of expression it claims for itself.

This is not a position which will be acceptable to all activist student leaders. Some of them appear to seek action and violence because they wish to have action for its own sake and because of the emotional release which it gives to them. Others seek violence because of the resultant publicity and the consequent dramatization given to their cause. For them, the martyrdom of police action and arrest is to be sought, not avoided. But it is a position that is sure to be approved and followed by the great majority of our students. This includes most of those who, though committed with all the idealism of youth to a given cause, realize that a decent respect for the opinions of others must be a cherished part of any academic community.

Moreover, the responsible student knows that a university would suffer irremediable damage if it allowed itself to become embroiled institutionally in a partisan fashion in any subject of current controversy. This is not out of fear that financial or other losses might be sustained because of the stand taken. Such a charge, though frequently made by those who demand institutional alignment, is too ignoble to be considered. The point is that if any university becomes politicized in this fashion, it will have lost its soul. The essence of a university's being is in its tolerance for all the winds of doctrine, but that tolerance by definition prevents the institution from official partisan involvement.

Another student responsibility is that of awareness about those who would use student groups for ulterior motives. It would be a serious mistake to conclude that recent manifestations of student activism represent only the influences exerted by ideological groups centered outside the campus. It would be equally wrong to assume that no such outside influences or efforts exist. The close alignment of certain student groups with certain national organizations is well recognized. That such an outside effort should be made to enlist campus support is inevitable because of the public attention which noisy student response is certain to attract.

The responsible student may at times be restless over what he feels to be a not-quite-adult role in society, but he knows that later on, when his student days are over, he will have full opportunity for all the social action he desires. Meanwhile, if he is truly responsible, he will realize that he has a primary and over-riding obligation to himself, to his family, and to society to make the best possible use of his precious student years in order to prepare himself for the long years ahead, the years in which he will not have the opportunity for study, the years in which he will wish he had made better use of the priceless opportunity to lay down the foundations for his profession, and to widen his intellectual and cultural horizons.

The responsible student will realize that excessive involvement in activist movements may rob him of much of the intellectual opportunity which the university offers to him. If a student's commitment to political activism means more to him than his education, then in all good conscience he should yield his place to someone who regards the university as something more than an opportunity to mount an ivy-festooned soap box.

At this point, let me make it quite clear that these young activists represent numerically only an insignificant proportion of the student body in any institution of higher learning. The minority is noisy and some of its members are conspicuous by a studied eccentricity in dress and— one suspects—in personal hygiene. But, taken as a whole, students today are brighter, more hard-working, more intellectually mature, and clearer in their career goals than at any time in the history of American higher education.

They realize that they must work very hard at the business of education if they are to be able to cope successfully with a world of bewildering and growing complexity, a world that offers few rewards and many heartaches to the dilettante. They are deeply concerned over social problems because they are at a time of life when idealism is at flood tide. They are aware that mere affluence is not the best of a successful society, and they worry for fear our own society may not be making much progress toward that true greatness that affluence ought merely to underpin.

They tolerate with good humour their fellows who, allegedly from this same concern, either reject our society or demand its violent overturn, but the majority are not really impressed either by the antics or the semantics of the extremists. They are too much aware of the infinite richness and promise of the life about them and ahead of them to be diverted into these intellectual by-ways. They are responsible, not because they have been told to be, but because, instinctively, they are serious students and good citizens of the academic community. Their voices are less shrill today than those of the vocal minority of their activist fellows, but they are the ones who will speak with reason, knowledge, and authority tomorrow.

This does not mean that I am advocating social apathy on the part of our students, nor that I condemn all those who seethe with indignation over the failure of their fathers to provide them with a flawless world. A keen awareness of the problems, the shortcomings, and the complexities of our society and our world is indispensable for responsible adulthood. But such an awareness of the items still on our national agenda is incomplete and distorted if it fails to take into account the problems we have solved, the progress we have made, and the assurance, through a quickened conscience of mankind, that future progress will be still more rapid.

In such a time the role of the university is to avoid alike those extremes of permissiveness that sap its spiritual strength and those extremes of arbitrary and repressive action that betray its heritage. By so doing, the university will demonstrate that it, too, has its own rights even *vis-a-vis* the students and that through the safeguarding of these rights it will continue to be fully responsible to our society with which it enjoys a fruitful interdependence.

POLITICS

Although Aristotle thought that politics was the culmination of ethics, few today, given a Rorschach-like vocabulary test, would associate ethics and politics. Yet clearly such issues as the two chosen for this section— the United Nations and the Great Society—are fundamentally as much matters of ethics as they are of politics and political machinery. The spokesmen selected to express the liberal and conservative philosophies that underlie the more specific debates, J. William Fulbright and Barry Goldwater, are both men of extreme ethical convictions. In fact, their ethical convictions are so strong that opponents, although respecting the sincerity and integrity of each, often complain that their intellectual grasp is inadequate to their ethical commitment.

The goal of the United Nations is peace; the goal of the Great Society is prosperous happiness. Liberals and conservatives do not disagree about the value of the goals themselves, of course. The issue in dispute is the extent to which the means each advocates is preferable. In general, liberals support a United Nations enlarged both in membership and in power, and beyond the loose alliance of the UN they often envision a world government, a sort of secular ecumenical movement. Similarly, liberals support federal programs for housing, slum clearance and urban renewal, publicly owned utilities, the war on poverty, and all other activities which promise to redress social ills under governmental sponsorship. To achieve these reforms, liberals are willing to increase both taxes and federal power, even at the cost of transforming the traditional relationships allying the federal government, the states, and the people. Liberals have long despaired that local governments, even on the state level, can take quick and adequate action to remedy the social ills of the nation. Although liberals are, for the most part, anti-Communist, they are not systematically anti-Socialist, and they tend to regard private ownership of major economic institutions as a constant temptation to monopoly and excessive profits, just as they often regard national sovereignty as a temptation to chauvinistic nationalism. For liberals, programs in foreign aid are a moral extension of promoting the general welfare.

Conservatives, by contrast, regard an increase in the size and power of the United Nations as a threat to national sovereignty, and as a weakening of America's power to act competently in its own interests and in those of its allies. Although conservatives have come to regard particular alliances like NATO and SEATO as permissible—their old isolationism is now dead—they fear the UN. Visions of a world government are, to them, an extension of the perversion. Although conservatives agree that domestically the economy and the society have sore spots, they see these either as inherent in the condition of man or as remediable by private means. Even when they concede, as they sometimes do, that the federal government might possibly do the job more quickly, they tend to feel that the price for such efficiency, in both money and freedom, is too much to pay. They see a parallel between the growth of federal power and the growth of power in the UN. They commonly label such growth "creeping socialism," a term which, in their eyes, is not sharply distinguishable from "communism." They believe that foreign aid is justified only if it strengthens America's allies.

Among leading political figures in the United States, Fulbright and Goldwater represent radically distinct positions on the liberal–conservative spectrum. Paradoxes abound in the political life of each man. Fulbright, a Democratic senator from Arkansas, has repeatedly taken a moderate or weak stand on civil rights—a favorite cause among liberals. As chairman of the powerful Senate Foreign Relations Committee, he has taken an extreme "dove" stance. In opposing the "hawks" on the issue of Vietnam, Fulbright has come into constant conflict with President Johnson, the designer of the Great Society; yet Fulbright supports the President on virtually all domestic issues. Goldwater, the Republican nominee in the last Presidential election, is now out of public office completely, but it was his unique triumph as a Republican candidate to have found the overwhelming bulk of his support in the South. His defeat is generally attributed to his "hawk" stand on the war in Vietnam; yet, though resoundingly defeated, he has seen many of his policies adopted by his Democratic opponent.

The styles of these two men differ as greatly as their political philosophies: Fulbright's is learned, sophisticated, and elegant; Goldwater's is simple and blunt. Yet both men express adequately the ideas and positions of the two traditions—the liberal and the conservative.

The Myth of Nationalism

J. William Fulbright/from *Old Myths and New Realities*

J. William Fulbright (1905—) has pursued a career which has constantly oscillated between academia and governmental service. At one time a law professor at Georgetown University, he has also taught law at the University of Arkansas, where he later served as president. In addition to holding these academic positions, he has worked with the anti-trust division of the U.S. Department of Justice, has been a member of the House of Representatives, has acted as delegate to the UN, and has served as a Democratic senator from Arkansas since 1945. In recent years, he has been chairman of the Senate Foreign Relations Committee, a position from which he has consistently and articulately advocated, in speeches and books, that money spent on the Vietnamese War, and on defense in general, ought to be redirected toward furthering the Great Society. An intellectual admired by the academic world in general, he displays analytical powers which command the respect even of those who oppose him.

The selections reprinted here are from one of Senator Fulbright's several books, Old Myths and New Realities *(1964)—a title originally used for a speech which attracted international attention. In these excerpts Fulbright urges that we need to cut loose from our outdated and "mythic" conceptions of a changed reality, even if it means thinking hitherto "unthinkable thoughts." Some of these thoughts, like the "disease" of nationalism, are, of course, old liberal ideas; what has made them unthinkable so far—"unexpressed" might be a better word—is that in the present climate of the Cold War, public leaders of Fulbright's prominence and capacity seldom have voiced them. The selections presented here are taken from the chapters entitled "The Cold War in American Life" and "Conclusion."*

The Cold War has, according to Fulbright, dislocated the energies and resources of America, diverting them "from the creative pursuits of civilized society to the conduct of a costly and interminable struggle for world power." In addition to dislocating material energies, the Cold War has altered the fabric of the American psyche by introducing "a strand of apprehension and tension into a national style which has traditionally been one of buoyant optimism." By forcing us to postpone, both psychologically and materially, our goal of "public happiness," the Cold War has, in Fulbright's judgment, encroached upon our national sovereignty far more than has the UN. The highest priority on Fulbright's national liberal "agenda" is given to redirecting part of our resources, as a people and as a nation, away from the Cold War and "back in on America itself."

The implicit nationalism and isolationism of this view are, however, specifically denied in the chapter entitled "Conclusion." Here Fulbright attacks nationalism, which he regards as the "most powerful single force in the world politics of the twentieth century, more powerful than communism or democracy. . . . It is also the most dangerous." Because of the power of nationalism, "the fatal expectancy of war" has become the major function of statesmanship; to reshape this expectancy is the principal item of the world's liberal agenda.

One can see in Fulbright's attack on nationalism, modulated and sustained by delicate articulation, an implicit plea for world government beyond the UN. As Fulbright says in his last sentence, "We must broaden the frontiers of our loyalties, never forgetting as we do so that it is the human individual, and not the state or any other community, in whom ultimate sovereignty is vested."

The Cold War in American life

The Constitution of the United States, in the words of its preamble, was established, among other reasons, in order to "provide for the common defense, promote the general welfare, and secure the blessings of liberty. . . ." In the past generation the emphasis of our public policy has been heavily weighted on measures for the common defense to the considerable neglect of programs for promoting the liberty and welfare of our people. The reason for this, of course, has been the exacting demands of two World Wars and an intractable cold war, which have wrought vast changes in the character of American life.

Of all the changes in American life wrought by the cold war, the most important by far, in my opinion, has been the massive diversion of energy and resources from the creative pursuits of civilized society to the conduct of a costly and interminable struggle for world power. We have been compelled, or have felt ourselves compelled, to reverse the traditional order of our national priorities, relegating individual and community life to places on the scale below the enormously expensive military and space activities that constitute our program of national security. Thus, we work ourselves into a fearful state of alarm over every incident on the Berlin access routes while blandly ignoring the increase of crime and violence in our great cities; we regard ourselves as gravely threatened by the rantings of a Cuban demagogue while taking little notice of the social disintegration caused by chronic unemployment; we undertake a $20-billion crash program to be first on the moon in order to avoid a possible blow to our pride while refusing to spend even a fraction of that amount for urgently needed federal aid to public education.

These of course are not the only effects of the continued world crisis on American life. There have been many others, some most welcome and constructive. Directly or indirectly, the world struggle with communism has stimulated economic and industrial expansion, accelerated the pace of intellectual inquiry and scientific discovery, broken the shell of American isolation, and greatly increased public knowledge and awareness of the world outside the United States. At the same time, the continuing world conflict has cast a shadow on the tone of American life by introducing a strand of apprehension and tension into a national style which has traditionally been one of buoyant optimism. The continuing and inconclusive struggle, new in American experience, has, in Walt Rostow's words, "imposed a sense of limitation on the nation's old image of itself, a limitation which has been accepted with greater or less maturity and which has touched the nation's domestic life at many points with elements of escapism, with a tendency to search for scapegoats, with simple worry, and with much thoughtful, re-sponsive effort as well."[1]

Overriding all these changes, however, good and bad, has been the massive diversion of wealth and talent from individual and community life for the increasingly complex and costly effort of maintaining a minimum level of national security in a world in which no nation can be immune from the threat of sudden catastrophe. We have had to turn away from our hopes in order to concentrate on our fears, and the result has been accumulating neglect of those things which bring happiness and beauty and fulfillment into our lives. The "public happiness," in August Heckscher's term, has become a luxury to be postponed to some distant day when the dangers that now beset us will have disappeared.

This inversion of priorities, I think, is the real meaning of the cold war in American life. It has consumed money and time and talent that could otherwise have been used to build schools and homes and hospitals, to re-move the blight of ugliness that is spreading over the cities and highways of America, and to overcome the poverty and hopelessness that afflict the lives of one-fifth of the people in an otherwise affluent society. It has put a high premium on avoiding innovation at home, because new programs involve controversy as well as expense and it is felt that we cannot afford domestic divisions at a time when external challenges require us to maintain the high-est possible degree of national unity. Far more pervasively than the United Nations or the Atlantic community could ever do, the cold war has en-croached upon our sovereignty; it has given the Russians the major voice in determining what proportion of our federal budget must be allocated to the military and what proportion, therefore, cannot be made available for domestic social and economic projects. This is the price that we have been paying for the cold war, and it has been a high price indeed.

At least as striking as the inversion of priorities which the cold war has enforced upon American life is the apparent readiness with which the American people have consented to defer programs for their welfare and happiness in favor of costly military and space programs. Indeed, if the Congress accurately reflects the temper of the country, then the American people are not only willing, they are eager, to sacrifice education and urban renewal and public health programs—to say nothing of foreign aid—to the requirements of the armed forces and the space agency. There is indeed a most striking paradox in the fact that military budgets of more than $50 billion are adopted by the Congress after only perfunctory debate, while domestic education and welfare programs involving sums which are mere fractions of the military budget are painstakingly examined and then either considerably reduced or rejected outright. I sometimes suspect that in its zeal for armaments at the expense of education and welfare, the Congress tends to overrepresent those of our citizens who are extraor-dinarily agitated about national security and extraordinarily vigorous about making their agitation known.

---

[1]W. W. Rostow, *The United States in the World Arena* (New York: Harper & Row, Publishers, Inc., 1960), p. 451.

It may be that the people and their representatives are making a carefully reasoned sacrifice of welfare to security. It may be, but I doubt it. The sacrifice is made so eagerly as to cause one to suspect that it is fairly painless, that indeed the American people prefer military rockets to public schools, and flights to the moon to urban renewal. In a perverse way, we have grown rather attached to the cold war. It occupies us with a seemingly clear and simple challenge from outside and diverts us from problems here at home which many Americans would rather not try to solve, some because they are genuinely and deeply preoccupied with foreign affairs, others because they find domestic problems tedious and pedestrian, others because they genuinely believe these problems to be personal rather than public, others because they are unwilling to be drawn into an abrasive national debate as to whether poverty, unemployment, and inadequate education are in fact national rather than local or individual concerns.

We have been preoccupied with foreign affairs for twenty-five years, and while striking progress has nonetheless been made in certain areas of our domestic life, the overall agenda of neglect has grown steadily longer. We can no longer afford to defer problems of slums and crime and poverty and inadequate education. In the long run, the solution of these problems has as vital a bearing on the success of our foreign policies as on the public happiness at home. We must therefore reassess the priorities of our public policy, with a view to redressing the disproportion between our military and space efforts on the one hand, and our education and human welfare programs on the other. We must overcome the "cold war" mentality that has persuaded millions of sensible and intelligent citizens that the prosecution of the cold war is our only truly essential national responsibility, that missiles and nuclear armaments and space flights are so vital to the safety of the nation that it is almost unpatriotic to question their cost and their proliferation, and that in the face of these necessities the internal requirements of the country, with respect to its schools and cities and public services, must be left for action at some remote time in the future—as if these requirements were not themselves vital to the national security, and as if, indeed, our generation is likely to know more tranquil days.

In the 1830s Alexis de Tocqueville saw America as a nation with a passion for peace, one in which the "principle of equality," which made it possible for a man to improve his status rapidly in civilian life, made it most unlikely that many Americans would ever be drawn to form a professional military caste. In 1961, President Eisenhower warned the nation of the pervasive and growing power of a "military-industrial complex." Tocqueville was quite right in his judgment that the United States was unlikely to become a *militarist* society. We have, however, as a result of world-wide involvements and responsibilities, become a great *military* power, with a vast military establishment that absorbs over half of our federal budget, profoundly influences the nation's economy, and exercises a gradually expanding influence on public attitudes and policies.

Without becoming militarist in the sense of committing themselves to the military virtues as standards of personal behavior, the American people have nonetheless come to place great—and, in my opinion, excessive —faith in military solutions to political problems. Many Americans have come to regard our defense establishment as the heart and soul of our foreign policy, rather than as one of a number of instruments of foreign policy whose effectiveness depends, not only on its size and variety, but also on the skill, and restraint, with which it is used.

Our faith in the military is akin to our faith in technology. We are a people more comfortable with machines than with intellectual abstractions. The military establishment is a vast and enormously complex machine, a tribute to the technological genius of the American people; foreign policy is an abstract and esoteric art, widely regarded as a highly specialized occupation of "eastern intellectuals," but not truly an "American" occupation. Our easy reliance on the military establishment as the foundation of our foreign policy is not unlike the reliance which we place on automobiles, televisions, and refrigerators: they work in a predictable and controllable manner, and on the rare occasions when they break down, any good mechanic can put them back in working order.

The trouble with the American technological bias is that it can conceal but not eliminate the ultimate importance of human judgment. Like any other piece of machinery, our military establishment can be no better than the judgment of those who control it. In a democracy, control is intended to be exercised by the people and their elected representatives. To a very considerable extent the American people are not now exercising effective control over the armed forces; nor indeed is the Congress, despite its Constitutional responsibilities in this field. Partly because of anxieties about the cold war, partly because of our natural technological bias, which leads us to place extraordinary faith in the ability of "technicians" to deal with matters that we ourselves find incomprehensible, and partly because of the vested interests of the "military-industrial complex," we are permitting the vast military establishment largely to run itself, to determine its own needs, and to tell us what sacrifices are expected of us to sustain the national arsenal of weapons.

David Lloyd George once declared that "there is no greater fatuity than a political judgment dressed in a military uniform." To the extent that the American people and the Congress shrink from questioning the size and cost of our defense establishment, they are permitting military men, with their highly specialized viewpoints, to make political judgments of the greatest importance regarding the priorities of public policy and the allocation of public funds. . . .

The time for such an effort is long overdue. We have allowed these problems to fester and grow during the long years of our preoccupation with crises and challenges abroad. To neglect them further is not to accept conditions as they now exist, but to acquiesce in the slow but relentless disintegration of our free society. The cold war, as David Riesman has written, "is a distraction from serious thought about man's condition on the planet."[2] My own belief is that the prevailing conditions of our foreign relations are favorable to a refocusing of our efforts on problems here at home, but even if they are not, it would still be essential to revise our priorities, because the success of our foreign policy depends ultimately on the strength and

---

[2]David Riesman, *Abundance for What?* (Garden City, N.Y.: Doubleday, 1964), p. 98.

character of our society, which in turn depend on our success in resolving the great social and economic issues of American life.

Of all the requirements on our national agenda, none warrants higher priority than the need to turn some part of our thoughts and our creative energies away from the cold war back in on America itself. If we do, and if we sustain the effort, we may find that the most vital assets of our nation, for its public happiness and its security as well, remain locked within our own frontiers, in our cities and in our countryside, in our work and in our leisure, in the hearts and minds of our people.

Conclusion

Of all the myths that have troubled the lives of modern nations the most pervading have been those associated with the nation itself. Nationalism, which is pre-eminently a state of mind rather than a state of nature, has become a dominant and universal state of mind in the twentieth century. Designating the sovereign nation-state as the ultimate object of individual loyalty and obligation, the idea of nationalism prevails in every region of the world, in rich nations as well as poor nations, in democracies as well as dictatorships. Nationalism, I believe, is the most powerful single force in the world politics of the twentieth century, more powerful than communism or democracy or any other system of ideas about social organization.

It is also the most dangerous. Dividing communities against one another, it has become a universal force at precisely the time in history when technology has made the world a single unit in the physical sense—interdependent for economic, political, and cultural purposes and profoundly interdependent for survival in the nuclear age. Having for many centuries represented a broadening of human loyalties from their family and tribal origins—as indeed it does even today in certain African countries which are still emerging from tribalism—the nation has now become a barrier to the historical process by which men have associated themselves in ever larger political and economic communities. In the face of a compelling need for broader associations, nationalism sets both great and small nations against one another, to their vast peril and at an enormous price in the welfare and happiness of their people.

"How," asked a seventeenth-century French historian, "does it serve the people and add to their happiness if their ruler extend his empire by annexing the provinces of his enemies; . . . how does it help me or my countrymen that my sovereign be successful and covered with glory, that my country be powerful and dreaded, if, sad and worried, I live in oppression and poverty?"

The question, phrased somewhat differently, is how and why it happens that the groups into which men organize themselves come to be regarded as ends in themselves, as living organisms with needs and preferences of their own which are separate from and superior to those of individuals, warranting, when necessary, the sacrifice of the hopes and pleasures of individual men. One of the paradoxes of politics is that so great a part of our organized efforts as societies is directed toward abstract and mystic goals—toward spreading a faith or ideology, toward enhancing the pride and power and self-respect of the nation, as if the nation had a "self" and a "soul" apart from the individuals who compose it, and as if the wishes of individual men, for life and happiness and prosperity, were selfish and dishonorable and unworthy of our best creative efforts.

Throughout history men have contested causes that had little to do with their own needs and preferences, but until quite recently this tendency, though irrational, has been less than irreparably destructive. Since the invention of nuclear weapons, it has become possible that the great struggles of international politics will bring about the destruction not merely of cities and nations but of much or all of human civilization. This great change has made international politics dangerous as it has never been before, confronting us with the need to ask ourselves whether there are not other causes to be served than the struggle for prestige and power, causes which are closer to human needs and far less likely to lead to nuclear incineration.

Science has radically changed the conditions of human life on earth. It has expanded our knowledge and our power but not our capacity to use them with wisdom. Somehow, if we are to save ourselves, we must find this capacity. We must find in ourselves the judgment and the will to alter the focus of international politics in ways which are at once less dangerous to mankind and more beneficial to individual men. Without deceiving ourselves as to the difficulty of the task, we must try to develop a new capacity for creative political action.

"If to do were as easy as to know what were good to do," wrote Shakespeare, "chapels had been churches, and poor men's cottages princes' palaces." The task of altering the character of international politics is of course infinitely more difficult than acknowledging the need to do so, and that is difficult enough. But if we are very clear about the difficulties of change, about how change occurs in human affairs and how it does not occur, then perhaps we can begin to alter the passions and prejudices that lead nations into wars as well as the weapons with which they fight them. We must recognize, first of all, that the ultimate source of war and peace lies in human nature and that nothing is more difficult to change than the human mind. "Even given the freest scope by their institutions," wrote Ruth Benedict, "men are never inventive enough to make more than minute changes. From the point of view of an outsider the most radical innovations in any culture amount to no more than a minor revision."

To recognize the difficulty of change is to recognize its possibility as well. Those who are sanguine about the power of reason to reshape human attitudes are soon disillusioned and driven to a pessimism which is no less erroneous than the false optimism with which they began. The beginning of wisdom, I think, is to understand that, difficult as it is, it is yet possible to alter human attitudes, and that to do so, to however slight a degree, is to shape the course of human events.

Some years ago a group of eight distinguished psychologists and social scientists issued a statement on the causes of nationalistic aggression and the conditions necessary for international understanding. They stated in part:

"To the best of our knowledge, there is no evidence to indicate that wars are necessary and inevitable consequences of 'human nature' as such.

While men vary greatly in their capacities and temperaments, we believe there are vital needs common to all men which must be fulfilled in order to establish and maintain peace: men everywhere want to be free from hunger and disease, from insecurity and fear; men everywhere want fellowship and the respect of their fellow men; the chance for personal growth and development."

If conflict and war are not indigenous to our nature, why, we may ask, are they so prevalent? "The crux of the matter," writes social psychologist Gordon Allport, "lies in the fact that while most people deplore war, they nonetheless *expect* it to continue. *And what people expect determines their behavior.* . . . the indispensable condition of war," says Professor Allport, "is that people must *expect* war and must prepare for war, before, under war-minded leadership, they make war. It is in this sense that 'wars begin in the minds of men.'"

This being so, there can be no "moral equivalent of war"—that is to say, a harmless outlet for aggression—because men are not endowed with a fixed reservoir of aggression which can be released through some "safety valve" and thus expended. Aggression is rather a habit, which feeds upon itself by building the expectancy that, once tried successfully, it will solve other problems as well. "If wars were simply a relief from tension," writes Professor Allport, "they might conceivably have their justification. But experience shows that not only does one war engender another, but it brings fierce domestic postwar strain and conflict into the nation itself."

This is precisely what has happened in the twentieth century. Crisis has fed upon crisis and each conflict has generated the *expectancy* of another. Meanwhile, the development of nuclear weapons and rockets has created the technological means of destroying, or virtually destroying, civilization. It follows quite obviously that the alteration of deeply rooted human attitudes, that is to say, the reshaping of the fatal expectancy of war, is the foremost requirement of statesmanship in the twentieth century.

We must generate expectancies of peace as powerful and self-generating as the expectancy of war. We must learn to deal with our adversaries in terms of the *needs* and *hopes* of both sides rather than the demands of one side upon the other. We must remove stridency and bad manners from our diplomacy, because the language of the ultimatum is the language of conflict, because there is no way more certain to turn tension into open conflict than to strike at an adversary's pride and self-respect.

We must strive, in the face of unprecedented need, toward unprecedented acts of political creativity. In one direction, we must move toward broadening forms of association more nearly appropriate to the interdependence of the world than the sovereign nation-state—and as we progress toward a broader world community, we must be prepared to encounter more than a few "unthinkable thoughts." In the other direction, we must turn a substantially greater proportion of our collective energies to the welfare of individuals—to the education and employment of our citizens, to creating societies in which the individual is encouraged and assisted in his striving for personal fulfillment.

It is the nation, or more exactly the pervading force of nationalism, that now obstructs our progress in both of these directions. Posing barriers between communities and exacting heavy sacrifices from its citizens to pursue the quarrels which these barriers engender, the sovereign nation itself is the most pervasive of the old myths that blind us to the realities of our time. Only when we have broken out of the constraints of nationalist mythology will the way be open to the only possible security in the nuclear age—the security of an international community in which men will be free of the terror of the bomb and free at last to pursue the satisfactions of personal fulfillment in civilized societies. We must broaden the frontiers of our loyalties, never forgetting as we do so that it is the human individual, and not the state or any other community, in whom ultimate sovereignty is vested.

The Delusion of Collectivism
Barry Goldwater/from *The Conscience of a Conservative*

Barry Goldwater (1909–   ) has had a markedly different career from that of Senator Fulbright. A millionaire businessman having had no professional contact with the academic world, Goldwater is a Major General in the United States Air Force Reserve and from 1955 to 1964 was Republican senator from Arizona. In 1964 he was defeated as the Republican candidate for President in one of the most unusual elections of the twentieth century. Running as an avowed conservative, Goldwater succeeded for the first time in over three decades in giving right-wing Republicans direct control of their party, something which the late Senator Taft—commonly called "Mr. Republican" —was never able to do. It was Goldwater's only electoral success, for when the ballots were counted, he carried but five southern states and Arizona.

Like Fulbright, Goldwater has written several books, and their titles bespeak the simple and direct approach which he takes to political problems— Why Not Victory? *and* Let's Try Freedom. *His most popular book, however, is* The Conscience of a Conservative, *from which the following selections are taken. On the opening page, Goldwater declares that "the ancient and tested truths that guided our Republic through its early days will do equally well for us." As he sees it, "The challenge to Conservatives today is quite simply to demonstrate the bearing of a proven philosophy on the problems of our own time." Clearly, for him, the old "myths" speak the true reality.*

In the chapter "The Welfare State," Goldwater replaces an old Communist myth with a new collectivist reality: the main threat to capitalistic democracy is no longer the state-owned economy envisioned by Marxists; instead, it is "welfarism" that the collectivists now conceive of as a means "to subordinate the individual to the state." The reason for the shift in tactics is this: the collectivists have discovered that "welfarism is much more compatible with the political processes of democracy." Votes are bought, Goldwater asserts, with promises of "'free' hospitalization, 'free' retirement pay and so on." He points out that the second biggest item on the federal budget is the cost of such "welfarism." To combat "socialism-through-welfarism" is difficult because of the power operating in "the rhetoric of humanitarianism." As Goldwater admits, opposing such rhetorical generosity makes conservatives look callous and inhuman; he seeks to defend conservatism from the charge by pointing to the degradation of the human being that welfarism inevitably brings: "It transforms the individual from a dignified, industrious, self-reliant spiritual *being into a dependent animal without his knowing it."*

Such a transformation is in keeping with the internationalistic "welfarism" of the United Nations; and although Goldwater does not think that withdrawal from the UN is practical, he is concerned about three dangers which he sees in its present operations. First, it elevates Communist propaganda "to the level of serious international debate." Second, its cost to the American taxpayer is not representational. Third, it threatens "an unconstitutional surrender of American sovereignty." If the UN is to serve any function, it ought to be an extension of American foreign policy. Goldwater says that "victory over Communism must come before the achievement of a lasting peace."

The welfare state

> Washington—The President estimated that the expenditures of the Department of Health, Education and Welfare in the fiscal year 1961 (including Social Security payments) would exceed $15,000,000,000. Thus the current results of New Deal legislation are Federal disbursements for human welfare in this country second only to national defense.
>
> The *New York Times,* January 18, 1960, p. 1.

For many years it appeared that the principal domestic threat to our freedom was contained in the doctrines of Karl Marx. The collectivists—non-Communists as well as Communists—had adopted the Marxist objective of "socializing the means of production." And so it seemed that if collectivization were imposed, it would take the form of a State owned and operated economy. I doubt whether this is the main threat any longer.

The collectivists have found, both in this country and in other industrialized nations of the West, that free enterprise has removed the economic and social conditions that might have made a class struggle possible. Mammoth productivity, wide distribution of wealth, high standards of living, the trade union movement—these and other factors have eliminated whatever incentive there might have been for the "proletariat" to rise up, peaceably or otherwise, and assume direct ownership of productive property. Significantly, the bankruptcy of doctrinaire Marxism has been expressly acknowledged by the Socialist Party of West Germany, and by the dominant faction of the Socialist Party of Great Britain. In this country the abandonment of the Marxist approach (outside the Communist Party, of course) is attested to by the negligible strength of the Socialist Party, and more tellingly perhaps, by the content of left wing literature and by the pro-

grams of left wing political organizations such as the Americans for Democratic Action.

The currently favored instrument of collectivization is the Welfare
State. The collectivists have not abandoned their ultimate goal—to subordinate the individual to the State—but their strategy has changed. They have
learned that Socialism can be achieved through Welfarism quite as well
as through Nationalization. They understand that private property can be
confiscated as effectively by taxation as by expropriating it. They understand that the individual can be put at the mercy of the State—not only
by making the State his employer—but by divesting him of the means to
provide for his personal needs and by giving the State the responsibility
of caring for those needs from cradle to grave. Moreover, they have discovered—and here is the critical point—that *Welfarism is much more compatible with the political processes of a democratic society.* Nationalization ran
into popular opposition, but the collectivists feel sure the Welfare State can
be erected by the simple expedient of buying votes with promises of "free"
hospitalization, "free" retirement pay and so on. . . . The correctness of this
estimate can be seen from the portion of the federal budget that is now allocated to welfare, an amount second only to the cost of national defense.[1]

I do not welcome this shift of strategy. Socialism-through-Welfarism
poses a far greater danger to freedom than Socialism-through-National-
ization precisely because it *is* more difficult to combat. The evils of Nationalization are self-evident and immediate. Those of Welfarism are veiled and
tend to be postponed. People can understand the consequences of turning
over ownership of the steel industry, say, to the State; and they can be
counted on to oppose such a proposal. But let the government increase
its contribution to the "Public Assistance" program and we will, at most,
grumble about excessive government spending. The effect of Welfarism on
freedom will be felt later on—after its beneficiaries have become its victims,
after dependence on government has turned into bondage and it is too late
to unlock the jail.

But a far more important factor is Welfarism's strong emotional
appeal to many voters, and the consequent temptations it presents the
average politician. It is hard, as we have seen, to make out a case for State
ownership. It is very different with the rhetoric of humanitarianism. How
easy it is to reach the voters with earnest importunities for helping the
needy. And how difficult for Conservatives to resist these demands without
appearing to be callous and contemptuous of the plight of less fortunate
citizens. Here, perhaps, is the best illustration of the failure of the Conservative demonstration.

I know, for I have heard the questions often. Have you no sense of
social obligation? the Liberals ask. Have you no concern for people who are
out of work? for sick people who lack medical care? for children in overcrowded schools? Are you unmoved by the problems of the aged and
disabled? Are you *against* human welfare?

---

[1]The total figure is substantially higher than the $15,000,000,000 noted above if we take into
account welfare expenditures outside the Department of Health, Education and Welfare—for
federal housing projects, for example.

The answer to all of these questions is, of course, no. But a simple "no" is not enough. I feel certain that Conservatism is through unless Conservatives can demonstrate and communicate the difference between being concerned with these problems and believing that the federal government is the proper agent for their solution.

The long range political consequences of Welfarism are plain enough: as we have seen, the State that is able to deal with its citizens as wards and dependents has gathered unto itself unlimited political and economic power and is thus able to rule as absolutely as any oriental despot.

Let us, however, weigh the consequences of Welfarism on the individual citizen.

Consider, first, the effect of Welfarism on the donors of government welfare—not only those who pay for it but also the voters and their elected representatives who decide that the benefits shall be conferred. Does some credit redound on them for trying to care for the needs of their fellow citizens? Are they to be commended and rewarded, at some moment in eternity, for their "charity"? I think not. Suppose I should vote for a measure providing for free medical care: I am unaware of any moral virtue that is attached to my decision to confiscate the earnings of X and give them to Y.

Suppose, however, that X approves of the program—that he has voted for welfarist politicians with the idea of helping his fellow man. Surely the wholesomeness of his act is diluted by the fact that he is voting not only to have his own money taken but also that of his fellow citizens who may have different ideas about their social obligations. Why does not such a man, instead, contribute what he regards as his just share of human welfare to a private charity?

Consider the consequences to the recipient of welfarism. For one thing, he mortgages himself to the federal government. In return for benefits—which, in the majority of cases, he pays for—he concedes to the government the ultimate in political power—the power to grant or withhold from him the necessities of life as the government sees fit. Even more important, however, is the effect on him—the elimination of any feeling of responsibility for his own welfare and that of his family and neighbors. A man may not immediately, or ever, comprehend the harm thus done to his character. Indeed, this is one of the great evils of Welfarism—that it transforms the individual from a dignified, industrious, self-reliant *spiritual* being into a dependent animal creature without his knowing it. There is no avoiding this damage to character under the Welfare State. Welfare programs cannot help but promote the idea that the government *owes* the benefits it confers on the individual, and that the individual is entitled, by right, to receive them. Such programs are sold to the country precisely on the argument that government has an *obligation* to care for the needs of its citizens. Is it possible that the message will reach those who vote for the benefits, but those who receive them? How different it is with private charity where both the giver and the receiver understand that charity is the product of the humanitarian impulses of the giver, not the due of the receiver.

Let us, then, not blunt the noble impulses of mankind by reducing charity to a mechanical operation of the federal government. Let us, by all means, encourage those who are fortunate and able to care for the needs of those who are unfortunate and disabled. But let us do this in a way that is conducive to the spiritual as well as the material well-being of our citizens—and in a way that will preserve their freedom. Let welfare be a private concern. Let it be promoted by individuals and families, by churches, private hospitals, religious service organizations, community charities and other institutions that have been established for this purpose. If the objection is raised that private institutions lack sufficient funds, let us remember that every penny the federal government does *not* appropriate for welfare is potentially available for private use—and without the overhead charge for processing the money through the federal bureaucracy. Indeed, high taxes, for which government Welfarism is so largely responsible, is the biggest obstacle to fund raising by private charities.

Finally, if we deem public intervention necessary, let the job be done by local and state authorities that are incapable of accumulating the vast political power that is so inimical to our liberties.

The Welfare State is *not* inevitable, as its proponents are so fond of telling us. There is nothing inherent in an industrialized economy, or in democratic processes of government that *must* produce de Tocqueville's "guardian society." Our future, like our past, will be what we make it. And we can shatter the collectivists' designs on individual freedom if we will impress upon the men who conduct our affairs this one truth: that the material and spiritual sides of man are intertwined; that it is impossible for the State to assume responsibility for one without intruding on the essential nature of the other; that if we take from a man the personal responsibility for caring for his material needs, we take from him also the will and the opportunity to be free.

The Soviet menace

And still the awful truth remains: We can establish the domestic conditions for maximizing freedom, along the lines I have indicated, and yet become slaves. We can do this by losing the Cold War to the Soviet Union.

American freedom has always depended, to an extent, on what is happening beyond our shores. Even in Ben Franklin's day, Americans had to reckon with foreign threats. Our forebearers knew that "keeping a Republic" meant, above all, keeping it safe from foreign transgressors; they knew that a people cannot live and work freely, and develop national institutions conducive to freedom, except in peace and with independence. In those early days the threat to peace and independence was very real. We were a fledgling-nation and the slightest misstep—or faint hearts—would have laid us open to the ravages of predatory European powers. It was only because wise and courageous men understood that defense of freedom required risks and sacrifice, as well as their belief in it, that we survived the crisis of national infancy. As we grew stronger, and as the oceans continued to interpose a physical barrier between ourselves and European militarism, the foreign danger gradually receded. Though we always had to keep a weather eye on would-be conquerors, our independence was acknowledged and peace, unless we chose otherwise, was established. Indeed, after the Second World

War, we were not only master of our own destiny; we were master of the world. With a monopoly of atomic weapons, and with a conventional military establishment superior to any in the world, America was—in relative and absolute terms—the most powerful nation the world had ever known. American freedom was as secure as at any time in our history.

Now, a decade and a half later, we have come full circle and our national existence is once again threatened as it was in the early days of the Republic. Though we are still strong physically, we are in clear and imminent danger of being overwhelmed by alien forces. We are confronted by a revolutionary world movement that possesses not only the will to dominate absolutely every square mile of the globe, but increasingly the capacity to do so: a military power that rivals our own, political warfare and propaganda skills that are superior to ours, an international fifth column that operates conspiratorially in the heart of our defenses, an ideology that imbues its adherents with a sense of historical mission; and all of these resources controlled by a ruthless despotism that brooks no deviation from the revolutionary course. This threat, moreover, is growing day by day. And it has now reached the point where American leaders, both political and intellectual, are searching desperately for means of "appeasing" or "accommodating" the Soviet Union as the price of national survival. The American people are being told that, however valuable their freedom may be, it is even more important to live. A craven fear of death is entering the American consciousness; so much so that many recently felt that honoring the chief despot himself was the price we had to pay to avoid nuclear destruction.

The temptation is strong to blame the deterioration of America's fortunes on the Soviet Union's acquisition of nuclear weapons. But this is self-delusion. The rot had set in, the crumbling of our position was already observable, long before the Communists detonated their first Atom Bomb. Even in the early 1950s, when America still held unquestioned nuclear superiority, it was clear that we were losing the Cold War. Time and again in my campaign speeches of 1952 I warned my fellow Arizonians that "American Foreign Policy has brought us from a position of undisputed power, in seven short years, to the brink of possible disaster." And in the succeeding seven years, that trend, because its cause remains, has continued.

The real cause of the deterioration can be simply stated. Our enemies have understood the nature of the conflict, and we have not. They are determined to win the conflict, and we are not.

I hesitate to restate the obvious—to say again what has been said so many times before by so many others: that the Communists' aim is to conquer the world. I repeat it because it is the beginning and the end of our knowledge about the conflict between East and West. I repeat it because I fear that however often we have given lip-service to this central political fact of our time, very few of us have *believed* it. If we had, our entire approach to foreign policy over the past fourteen years would have been radically different, and the course of world events radically changed.

If an enemy power is bent on conquering you, and proposes to turn all of his resources to that end, he is at war with you: and you—unless you contemplate surrender—are at war with him. Moreover—unless you contemplate treason—your objective, like his, will be victory. Not "peace," but victory. Now, while traitors (and perhaps cowards) have at times occupied key positions in our government, it is clear that our national leadership over the past fourteen years has favored neither surrender nor treason. It is equally clear, however, that our leaders have not made *victory* the goal of American policy. And the reason that they have not done so, I am saying, is that they have never believed deeply that the Communists are in earnest.

Our avowed national objective is "peace." We have, with great sincerity, "waged" peace, while the Communists wage war. We have sought "settlements," while the Communists seek victories. We have tried to pacify the world. The Communists mean to own it. Here is why the contest has been an unequal one, and why, essentially, we are losing it.

Peace, to be sure, *is* a proper goal for American policy—as long as it is understood that peace is not all we seek. For we do not want the peace of surrender. We want a peace in which freedom and justice will prevail, and that—given the nature of Communism—is a peace in which Soviet power will no longer be in a position to threaten us and the rest of the world. A tolerable peace, in other words, must *follow* victory over Communism. We have been fourteen years trying to bury that unpleasant fact. It cannot be buried and any foreign policy that ignores it will lead to our extinction as a nation.

We do not, of course, want to achieve victory by force of arms. If possible, overt hostilities should always be avoided; especially is this so when a shooting war may cause the death of many millions of people, including our own. But we cannot, for that reason, make the avoidance of a shooting war our chief objective. If we do that—if we tell ourselves that it is more important to avoid shooting than to keep our freedom—we are committed to a course that has only one terminal point: surrender. We cannot, by proclamation, make war "unthinkable." For it is not unthinkable to the Communists: naturally, they would prefer to avoid war, but they are prepared to risk it, in the last analysis, to achieve their objectives. We must, in our hearts, be equally dedicated to our objectives. If war is unthinkable to us but not to them, the famous "balance of terror" is not a balance at all, but an instrument of blackmail. U.S.-Soviet power may be in balance; but if we, and not they, rule out the possibility of using that power, the Kremlin can create crisis after crisis, and force the U.S., because of our greater fear of war, to back down every time. And it cannot be long before a universal Communist Empire sits astride the globe.

The rallying cry of an appeasement organization, portrayed in a recent novel on American politics, was "I would rather crawl on my knees to Moscow than die under an Atom Bomb." This sentiment, of course, repudiates everything that is courageous and honorable and dignified in the human being. We must—as the first step toward saving American freedom—affirm the contrary view and make it the cornerstone of our foreign policy: that we would rather die than lose our freedom. There are ways which I will suggest later on—not easy ways, to be sure—in which we may save both our freedom *and* our lives; but all such suggestions are meaningless and vain unless we first understand what the objective is. We want to stay alive, of course; but more than that we want to be free. We want to have peace; but before that we want to establish the conditions that will make peace tolerable.

"Like it or not," Eugene Lyons has written, "the great and inescapable task of our epoch is not to end the Cold War but to win it."

I suggest that we look at America's present foreign policy, and ask whether it is conducive to victory. There are several aspects of this policy. Let us measure each of them by the test: Does it help defeat the enemy? . . .

United Nations

Support of the United Nations, our leaders earnestly proclaim, is one of the cornerstones of American foreign policy. I confess to being more interested in whether American foreign policy has the support of the United Nations.

Here, again, it seems to me that our approach to foreign affairs suffers from a confusion in objectives. Is the perpetuation of an international debating forum, for its own sake, the primary objective of American policy? If so, there is much to be said for our past record of subordinating our national interest to that of the United Nations. If, on the other hand, our primary objective is victory over Communism, we will, as a matter of course, view such organizations as the UN as a possible *means* to that end. Once the question is asked—Does America's participation in the United Nations help or hinder her struggle against world Communism?—it becomes clear that our present commitment to the UN deserves re-examination.

The United Nations, we must remember, is in part a Communist organization. The Communists always have at least one seat in its major policy-making body, the Security Council; and the Soviet Union's permanent veto power in that body allows the Kremlin to block any action, on a substantial issue, that is contrary to its interests. The Communists also have a sizeable membership in the UN's other policy-making body, the General Assembly. Moreover, the UN's working staff, the Secretariat, is manned by hundreds of Communist agents who are frequently in a position to sabotage those few UN policies that *are* contrary to Communist interests. Finally, a great number of non-Communist United Nations are sympathetic to Soviet aims—or, at best, are unsympathetic to ours.

We therefore should not be surprised that many of the policies that emerge from the deliberations of the United Nations are not policies that are in the best interest of the United States. United Nations policy is, necessarily, the product of many different views—some of them friendly, some of them indifferent to our interests, some of them mortally hostile. And the result is that our national interests usually suffer when we subordinate our own policy to the UN's. In nearly every case in which we have called upon the United Nations to do our thinking for us, and to make our policy for us—whether during the Korean War, or in the Suez crisis, or following the revolution in Iraq—we have been a less effective foe of Communism than we otherwise might have been.

Unlike America, the Communists do not respect the UN and do not permit their policies to be affected by it. If the "opinion of mankind," as reflected by a UN resolution, goes against them, they—in effect—tell mankind to go fly a kite. Not so with us; we would rather be approved than succeed, and so are likely to adjust our own views to conform with a United

Nations majority. This is not the way to win the Cold War. I repeat: Communism will not be beaten by a policy that is the common denominator of the foreign policies of 80-odd nations, some of which are our enemies, nearly all of which are less determined than we to save the world from Communist domination. Let us, then, have done with submitting major policy decisions to a forum where the opinions of the Sultan of Yemen count equally with ours; where the vote of the United States can be cancelled out by the likes of "Byelorussia."

I am troubled by several other aspects of our UN commitment. First— and here again our Cold War interests are damaged—the United Nations provides a unique forum for Communist propaganda. We too, of course, can voice our views at the UN; but the Communists' special advantage is that their lies and misrepresentations are elevated to the level of serious international debate. By recognizing the right of Communist regimes to participate in the UN as equals, and by officially acknowledging them as "peace-loving," we grant Communist propaganda a presumption of reasonableness and plausibility it otherwise would not have.

Second, the UN places an unwarranted financial burden on the American taxpayer. The Marxist formula, "from each according to his ability . . ." —under which contributions to the UN and its specialized agencies are determined—does not tally with the American concept of justice. The United States is currently defraying roughly a third of all United Nations expenses. That assessment should be drastically reduced. The UN should not operate as a charity. Assessments should take into account the benefits received by the contributor-nation.

Finally, I fear that our involvement in the United Nations may be leading to an unconstitutional surrender of American sovereignty. Many UN activities have already made strong inroads against the sovereign powers of Member Nations. This is neither the time nor place to discuss the merits of yielding sovereign American rights—other than to record my unequivocal opposition to the idea. It is both the time and place, however, to insist that any such discussion take place within the framework of a proposed constitutional amendment—and not, clandestinely, in the headquarters of some UN agency.

Withdrawal from the United Nations is probably not the answer to these problems. For a number of reasons that course is unfeasible. We should make sure, however, that the nature of our commitment is such as to advance American interests; and that will involve changes in some of our present attitudes and policies toward the UN. Let the UN firsters—of whom there are many in this country—put their enthusiasm for "international cooperation" in proper perspective. Let them understand that victory over Communism must come *before* the achievement of lasting peace. Let them, in a word, keep their eyes on the target. . . .

Design for World Community
Adlai E. Stevenson / from *Looking Outward*

Adlai Stevenson (1900–1965) was governor of Illinois and a twice-defeated Democratic candidate for the Presidency running against Dwight Eisenhower. From the beginning of his national prominence, both friends and enemies recognized Stevenson's special powers of articulation; the intellectual community found in him a kindred spirit and mind. When John F. Kennedy became president in 1960, he appointed Stevenson as United States Ambassador to the United Nations.

The following selection is taken from a book entitled Looking Outward, *a collection of speeches made during Stevenson's tenure as ambassador. This particular speech was addressed to the International Astronomical Union at Berkeley, California, in 1961. It is characteristic of Stevenson's playful wit that he should have selected this group of far-seeing men to envision, through his own hopeful glimpses ahead into space and time, what he thought the world should be like under an advanced and progressive "United Nations system."*

In the introduction to the book, Stevenson quotes G. K. Chesterton's "satirical verses about 'The World State'" which begin, "Oh, how I love humanity," and close with "I learned, with little labor,/The way to love my fellow man/And hate my next-door neighbor!" With his usual literate grace Stevenson is able to move from Chesterton's satire to Pope John XXIII's encyclical Pacem in Terris. *Here the Pope argued specifically that the moral need for world order demanded the creation of a public authority with great power and scope. Such a public authority should have "world-wide power" and should be "endowed with the proper means for the efficacious pursuit of its objective, which is the universal good in concrete form." Like the Pope, though in more particular language, Stevenson clearly saw the UN as a step toward such a "world community": he wrote, "World society has to achieve minimum institutions of order, and the only embryo of such order is the United Nations system."*

In his speech to the astronomers, Stevenson said of the UN that it is "mankind's greatest attempt . . . to cause all men and all nations to accept the fact that there is but one world, . . . not only in science, not only in the search for truth, but in the ordering of their international lives." He saw disarmament, controlled through the UN, as the first step, and beyond this "the day when national armed forces will be done away with and only internal police units remain. . . . Then the United Nations will need its own United Nations Peace Force, capable of deterring or subduing the strongest combinations which might be raised against it."

Citing the UN Charter, Stevenson pointed to the necessary limitation on the claims of national sovereignty. He saw in the principles of the Charter, which he summarized as "community, tolerance, openness," the grounds on which the UN can and "must be built into still more—an institution which can enforce the judgments of the world community against those who threaten or break the peace." Like Senator Fulbright, he closes with a hope that "we will dare to part with habits and institutions dangerously outworn." What his conservative opponent thought of such notions and their implications we shall see in the late Senator Taft's article.

A parable for statesmen: to save mankind

. . . There was an age when it was tolerable for outworn institutions and habits of mind to persist for centuries. It took at least three hundred years for the invention of gunpowder, combined with the spreading patterns of commerce, to bring down the proud city walls of medieval Europe. But down they came in the end, and the age of national states, superseding the city-states, had begun.

Today things move more swiftly. Within ten years after man set off his first atomic explosion, the leaders of all the great powers had acknowledged that a nuclear war between any nations would be a catastrophe for *all* nations. There is now an Atomic Energy Agency which is *international*. There are strenuous negotiations for a permanent, reliable, controlled ban on nuclear weapons tests by any nation. There is a groping determination to halt the further spread of nuclear weapons to any nation. Thus atomic energy has already begun to breach some of our national walls. And no doubt the exploration of outer space will breach them further.

Certainly the consequences of space exploration, for good or evil, will be great. Dramatic improvements in weather forecasting and in worldwide communications can be more or less precisely foreseen. Science is already acquiring powerful new tools, and what the ultimate benefits to man may be, no one can tell.

We can only guess at such possibilities. But there is no guessing any more as to whether man will undertake the adventure of space exploration. Yesterday's dreams are today's facts. Scientific instruments, then animals, then men, have been hurled into space. There is no turning back; as certainly as the oceans were conquered in the century of Columbus and Magellan, new realms of space will be conquered in our century.

But in what spirit will these conquests of space be carried out, and for what purposes? Our century must answer that awesome question. For wherever man goes, though he travel to another planet, he brings with him the problem of good and evil which is his peculiar heritage. Shall space be explored for war or for peace? For national power or for the good of all men?

These questions are beyond the scope of science, but all of us, as citizens, must help to answer them. If the scientist and the engineer can create a thrust strong enough to defeat the earth's gravitation, and can plan to send groups of men into flight far beyond the earth, then it is up to us in government and diplomacy to develop a comparable "orbital velocity" of our own, great enough to lift *all* mankind beyond the dread gravitation of mistrust and war.

In the years ahead, then, international diplomacy must do far more than put out the recurrent fires of conflict. It must apply itself with massive energy to three great areas of creative effort: to disarmament, to the building of institutions to keep the peace, and to international cooperation for human progress.

All the world agrees that the arms race, especially in nuclear weapons, is anarchic, wasteful and deadly dangerous for humanity. So all agree that we must stop the race, reverse the process and disarm.

Yet it is not done. Why? Because of deep conflicts of purpose, and an even deeper mistrust. But it can be done. It involves principles which are familiar to scientists—freedom of investigation, freedom of inspection and freedom of verification. There must be, in any disarmament program, adequate inspection and verification such that each side can be quite sure, at every stage, that the other is living up to its part of the bargain.

Disarmament has been misconstrued as if it were in some way the enemy of national defense. And the idea of inspection and verification has unfortunately been misconstrued in certain quarters, as if it were in some way the enemy of disarmament. It is not. It is a necessity. The acid test of sincerity is whether one agrees to fully adequate inspection and verification. Only with these can we know that, inside the box marked "Disarmament," we will really find the reality and a peaceful world, and not something ticking away to the destruction of all of us. The same, of course, applies to the banning of nuclear weapons tests, for no permanent ban is possible without adequate inspection and verification. In years of negotiations in Geneva that has always been the key issue. And it still is.

Surely no nation today should, in the name of a selfish sovereignty made obsolete by the interdependence of us all, refuse to permit within its borders that right of adequate inspection and verification, free of veto, which alone can banish mistrust and make possible the achievement of general and complete disarmament and a peaceful world. I am glad to say that the United States has always been willing to grant such right, and I devoutly hope that the Soviet Union may show an equally real desire for disarmament and peace.

The next question is: Who is to do the inspection and verification? What sort of policeman can police the great powers?

Here we find that we cannot take even the first practical step toward general and complete disarmament and a peaceful world unless the nations are willing to build new world institutions which stand above the individual nations and act impartially for the entire human community. What is called for is an international organization within the framework of the United Nations which will see to it that no single nation fails to comply with agreed steps toward general and complete disarmament.

And if we look still further down the road, to the day when national armed forces will be done away with and only internal police units remain, then all the more will the world need institutions of international law and order. Then the United Nations will need its own United Nations Peace Force, capable of deterring or subduing the strongest combinations which might be raised against it.

That is the long-run need, but the short run makes similar demands on us. Events in the Congo have shown how vital it is that the United Nations retain and develop further the capacity to act for peace, to deploy military forces with speed and precision, and thus to uphold the integrity of vulnerable nations in emergencies where direct intervention by a great power would risk disaster. The United Nations is the world's greatest instrument, and the world community must act to uphold it, pay for it, invigorate it and support its able and courageous Secretary General.

All these things are demanded of us to save mankind from violence and war. But the community of nations should be bound together by more affirmative and creative purposes. More and more we must, as a world community, learn to practice the arts of peace cooperatively and together. And, at this fateful moment in history, when man has, so to speak, one foot already in the heavens, surely we must find ways for the powers to cooperate rather than fight in the exploration of outer space.

What good are national rivalries against the backdrop of the solar system? All the world, regardless of ideology, applauds the bravery of the first astronauts. And surely all the world would breathe easier if the conquest of space were looked on henceforward not as a means to the power and glory of particular nations or ideologies, but as one of the great adventures of the whole human race.

"Together let us explore the stars"—so said President Kennedy at his inauguration, appealing especially to the Soviet Union. A few days later he renewed this appeal in these words: "I now invite all nations—including the Soviet Union—to join with us in developing a weather prediction program, in a new communications satellite program, and in preparation for probing the distant planets of Mars and Venus."

Technology will not wait long for an answer. In just a few years there will be rocket boosters, in more than one country, big enough to launch whole teams of men on journeys to the nearest planets. Shall this too be a race for military or psychological advantage at huge and wasteful expense? Or shall it be the occasion for teamwork, ignoring ideological lines? We haven't much time left in which to decide—it is a fork in the road which will soon be passed.

We have many similar choices to make closer to home. The new nations, which have recently become independent, have an almost unlimited need for education, health, industrial development, agricultural improvement, communications and exchanges in the fields of science and culture. Shall more fortunate nations exploit those needs by offering aid only in exchange for political influence? Or shall we help because it is right to help? And shall we prefer more and more the disinterested channels of the United Nations? The path to peace must lie increasingly in the multilateral direction of the United Nations, especially with all the self-restraint and mutual tolerance which it requires.

Such are the specific challenges which face international diplomacy today and which draw still greater urgency under the accelerating pressures of science and technology: Disarmament. The building of institutions to keep the peace, both now and in a future disarmed world. International cooperation in the creative arts of peace, to abolish poverty and backwardness.

We have no choice but to meet these challenges. And, in meeting them, we shall be building together a grand design of peace, a design whose keynote is world community.

If there can be said to be a wave of the future for mankind, I believe it is in that principle of community. No one nation, no empire, no imposed system can dare to speak any more for mankind. All must be willing, if sovereignty is to make any sense in the thermonuclear age, to deny themselves some of the extravagant jungle habits which have accompanied it in times past, and to join their sovereign wills in community institutions, in common community action, and in common obedience to the community's rules.

The rules themselves already exist. They are proclaimed in one of the greatest creative acts of history, the United Nations Charter. We can attempt to restate some of them in the light of our experience since 1945 when that Charter was framed.

The Charter commands every nation not to use or threaten force against the territory of independence of another. But experience requires us to go further, for there are other means of conquest. We have seen nations and peoples subjugated by political subversion and guerrilla warfare. We have seen economic aid used as bait and club to impose political influence and subservience. We could well see the raising of new territorial claims, or even claims of possession, in outer space.

To all these exaggerations of sovereignty we must say: No, no nation, any more, by any means, direct or indirect, shall seek to extend its control at the expense of another.

A second provision of the United Nations Charter calls for international cooperation for human progress—economic, social, cultural and in the field of human rights. Much has been accomplished along those lines, but how much more could be done, both on this earth and in the spaces beyond, if all the nations would willingly pool their capacities and their efforts! The wonderful techniques of material progress should not be perverted to satisfy political or ideological ambitions. The poor and the hungry and the diseased of this world do not ask for help in the name of one "system" or another. They ask for it in the name of humanity, of the community of mankind, and it is in that name only that they should receive it.

There is a third principle of the United Nations that needs reaffirmation. It is summed up in those splendid words of the Preamble—"to practice tolerance, and live together in peace with one another as good neighbors." And tolerance is the key to peace, for there can be no peace unless there is mutual tolerance as between differing peoples and systems and cultures. Peaceful coexistence should not and cannot involve "burial" by any one of any other.

This world will always be a pluralistic world, made up of disparate beliefs and institutions, ever changing and shifting, and only in a world atmosphere of tolerance and freedom can there take place that varied experimentation and development which alone have produced human progress.

Men of science above all others should value and preach tolerance, for they have only to recall the blight that intolerance cast on Copernicus and Galileo, a blight that held back astronomy for generations, and they know only too well how the orthodoxy of one scientific era becomes the heterodoxy of the next.

The condition of tolerance is openness and the understanding that comes from openness. How can there be tolerance or understanding if great nations continue in secretive isolation from the rest of the world, rearing their children by a closed educational system and in suspicion and fear of sinister foreigners, excluding outside information, periodicals, books and broadcasts, restricting travel and hiding great parts of their territory?

Only in openness will that mistrust that poisons the world atmosphere today be dispelled, and only through open societies can there arise that tolerance that will permit all of us to live in confidence and peace with one another.

Amid the darkness of this noontime there are rays of hope that we *will achieve* an open world. It is happening, bit by bit. Recently, for example, I was happy to read the remark of the eminent Soviet astronomer, Professor A. A. Mikhailov, at a meeting in Pasadena on the astronomy of the space age. "Science is international," said Professor Mikhailov. "My hope is for the United States and Russia to share in space projects and in many other fields of human endeavor."

Community, tolerance, openness—those are the words which I would leave with you. And if they are to be made real, we all have one more great duty: to support the United Nations, which is the community's greatest symbol and greatest instrument. It is the world center of tolerance and openness. It is, as long as men are free to differ—which I trust will be forever!— a center of disciplined disagreement. No one power can dominate it, or use it to drive another to the wall. It is the greatest defense of the weak against the bullying of the strong. It is the lightning rod which prevents rampant nationalism from sparking war. And if the world is to be saved from disaster, the United Nations must be built into still more—an institution which can enforce the judgments of the world community against those who threaten or break the peace.

Now, after this exposition of our terrestrial worries, I rather wish that all of us who deal in human affairs could be astronomers and for a while deal but with the remotest celestial bodies! Sir James Jeans called astronomy "the most poetic of the sciences." Perhaps if we all practiced it, we would be filled with the wonder and excitement of discovery, with a sense of elemental majesty and beauty, with our little quarrels in better perspective, and would thus be purged of our pride and prejudice, and all the base motives which complicate and endanger our lives.

At all events, I devoutly hope that all of us in and out of the United Nations will make a new beginning; that we will dare to part with habits and institutions dangerously outworn; and that we will have the courage and determination to construct, soon enough to save mankind, a new world order more nearly worthy of the scientist and the poet, and of the best that man has in him.

Peace with Justice
Robert A. Taft/from *A Foreign Policy for Americans*

Robert Taft (1889–1953) belonged to one of the political dynasties which have been as much a part of American life as the "log-cabin" heroes. His father, William Howard Taft, was President; his son, Robert A. Taft, Jr., is currently in Congress. For many years Robert Taft was the acknowledged leader of the

Republicans in Congress and the most articulate and respected conservative spokesman in the country. Although he was often called "Mr. Republican" and was linked with conservative principles, he had his own independent integrity and intellect. For example, he supported federal housing programs and attacked the trials of Nazi "war criminals" as unconstitutional and unjust. His concern for justice as something distinct from peace and security was central to his political philosophy. The selection included here, "International Organization as a Means of Securing Peace with Liberty," is a chapter from his book A Foreign Policy for Americans.

After presenting a brief history of the support that his family and he himself gave to "international organizations to promote the peace of the world and therefore of the United States," Taft points out that he voted for the United Nations Charter despite some fundamental misgivings. For him, the real and dangerous defect of the UN Charter was that "it is not based primarily on an underlying law and an administration of justice under that law." Instead, the Charter makes its goals peace and security, and these goals, commendable as they may be, "are not synonymous with justice." Taft suggests that the UN might someday choose, as did the late Neville Chamberlain, to "take property from one nation to which it justly belonged and give it to another, because it felt that would promote world peace." As Taft himself expressed it: "I believe that in the long run the only way to establish peace is to write a law, agreed to by each of the nations, to govern the relations of such nations with each other and to obtain the covenant of all such nations that they will abide by that law and by decisions made thereunder."

Although at first glance it may appear that Taft's proposal is for a world government, it is really for a more judicially based UN. For Taft, world government was not a foreseeable possibility. First, such a government would have to rest on a united "real world public opinion" against any aggressor, and "there is no such world public opinion today." When Taft wrote these words, the Korean War—a UN-supported action—was raging; over a decade later we find in the Vietnamese War even less "world public opinion" than existed in the early 1950's.

What seemed to Taft opportunistic policy in foreign affairs indicated a repudiation of "any serious respect for law and justice" and foreboded "an arbitrary and totalitarian government at home." The President's action in Korea was, in Taft's judgment, legally questionable. Criticism should, he felt, be directed not so much against the UN as against "the limitations of the charter and our own Government for forcing the United Nations' action beyond its permanent power to perform." The Atlantic Pact seemed to him a "recognition of the impotence of the United Nations."

Taft dismisses any hopes for a world organization beyond the UN as "fantastic, dangerous, and impractical." Cultural and linguistic differences would render any attempts to speak a common political language impossible; the existence of totalitarian nations within such an organization would make it undemocratic. American sovereignty, he points out, would be destroyed and there would be no guarantee that American ideals could flourish under such a system. The real hope, according to Taft, lay in such organizations as the Atlantic Pact, in which he saw the possibility of international activities "based on law and justice . . . within the façade of the United Nations."

International organization as a means of securing peace with liberty

Entirely apart from any immediate threat of military aggression against the United States, I have always favored an international organization to promote the peace of the world and therefore of the United States. My father campaigned vigorously during World War I in behalf of a proposed League to Enforce Peace. President Wilson wrote a similar program into the Versailles Treaty in the form of the League of Nations, and I always favored strongly our joining that League. On August 26, 1943, before the American Bar Association, I urged the formation of a world-wide organization of sovereign nations, outlining the general character of that organization, and I quote from my speech:

> The plan for an enforced peace which accords most closely with the ideals of the American Republic and of the Atlantic Charter, is that for an Association of Nations to include the United Nations and the Neutrals and, after a period of probation, the Axis nations. It would be supported by covenants between sovereign nations agreeing to determine their disputes by the law of nations and judicial decision, or by arbitration. It would further be supported by covenants to join in the use of force against any nation determined to be an aggressor by the decision of some international tribunal. Frankly, this is an obligation which the American people may be loath to undertake, but I believe they will undertake it, because they know that if war is not prevented at the start, under modern conditions it is more than likely to spread throughout the world.
>
> But there are certain conditions to be insisted on.
>
> First, force should not be called for against any nation because of any internal domestic policy, except rearmament in excess of a quota imposed or agreed to. Interference in domestic policies, even such vital matters as tariffs or the treatment of minorities, would be more likely to make war than prevent it. The test is: is the subject one on which the people of the United States would be willing to have other nations interfere with our internal actions? If not, we should not attempt to impose such interference on others.
>
> Second, the covenant must be preceded by an economic arrangement fair to all nations, and by political arrangements providing for proper self-determination. The covenant, of course, must provide for the revision of boundaries and obligations, but essentially we will be asked to guarantee the status quo. We cannot make that guarantee unless the status quo is fair to all peoples and gives them a chance to live, and therefore affords a reasonable hope that peace can be maintained.
>
> Third, I believe that any obligation to use force in Europe should only be secondary, not to be effective until the peace-loving nations of Europe have exhausted their own resources. This is in accord with Mr. Churchill's suggestion of a Council of Europe under the Association of Nations. We cannot help solve the problems of Europe unless the great majority of the European nations first agree on what that solution should be.

I supported the resolution by the Republican Conference at Mackinac Island, "favoring responsible participation by the United States in a post-war co-operative organization among sovereign nations to prevent military aggression, and to attain permanent peace with organized justice in a free world." This was the language of Senator Vandenberg, and it contains the soundest, most concise statement of the proper basis of international organization.

I supported the Connally resolution adopted by the Senate of the United States on November 5, 1943. I voted for and supported the United Nations Charter in the Senate on July 28, 1945.

I was never satisfied with the United Nations Charter and stated my criticism definitely at the time. The fundamental difficulty is that it is not based primarily on an underlying law and an administration of justice under that law. I believe that in the long run the only way to establish peace is to write a law, agreed to by each of the nations, to govern the relations of such nations with each other and to obtain the covenant of all such nations that they will abide by that law and by decisions made thereunder. I criticized the Connally resolution, because it omitted any reference whatever to the establishment of a rule of law. It is extraordinary that the original Dumbarton Oaks proposals for a United Nations Charter omitted all reference to justice. The final charter, largely through the work of Senator Vandenberg, does recognize the importance and desirability of justice, but it does so only in the most general way, and the Chapters dealing with the Security Council, which form the heart of all enforcement, require the Security Council to make such decisions as will "maintain peace and security," without any reference to justice.

It is true that Article 24 contains a general provision that in discharging its duties the Security Council shall act in accordance with the purposes and principles set forth in Chapter I; and it is also true that this chapter includes justice as one consideration. But the reference to justice and international law in paragraph I of Article I and the reference to justice in paragraph 3 of Article 2 seem to be related only to the settlement of disputes by peaceful means. If the Security Council has to make a definite decision looking to the employment of force, it is done primarily on the basis of maintaining peace and security.

Peace and security are not synonymous with justice. It might well be that the Security Council, acting in full compliance with the charter, could take property from one nation to which it justly belonged and give it to another, because it felt that would promote peace. So Mr. Chamberlain agreed to the transfer of Sudetenland to Germany. By substituting the maintenance of peace and security for law and justice we authorize the basing of decisions on expediency, and for expediency there are no rules which cannot be changed by the majority to fit its desires in a particular case.

It should also be pointed out that the veto power given to prevent the Security Council from making recommendations under Article 39 or from using sanctions and force under Articles 41 and 42 completely dispels the idea that any system of universal law is being established, for surely nothing can be law if five of the largest nations can automatically exempt themselves from its application.

It is suggested that the charter can be made satisfactory by eliminating the veto power. I do not see how we ourselves can agree to eliminate our veto power, if decisions of the Security Council to use force are based on expediency rather than law. It seems to me that peace in this world is impossible unless nations agree on a definite law to govern their relations with each other and also agree that, without any veto power, they will submit their disputes to adjudication and abide by the decision of an impartial tribunal. The agreement to abide even by unfavorable decisions was the essence of the arbitration treaties which my father, when President, negotiated with England and with France. It was unfortunate that they were defeated by the Senate. Until nations are willing to enter into such an agreement, international progress toward peace is bound to fail.

Such progress is probably dependent even more on building up in the world public opinion in behalf of law and justice between nations. No matter what the covenants made, an aggressor who violates his covenants can only be suppressed if a real world public opinion unites against him, in enthusiastic military support of those who fight for peace and justice. There is no such world public opinion today, and so we find the attempt to punish aggression in Korea at best a stalemate and the attempt to punish aggression by Chinese Communists a complete failure.

I have thought that our State Department has lost complete touch with the principles of liberty and justice on which this nation was founded. Certainly those who drafted the Dumbarton Oaks proposals could not have been enthusiastic supporters of American principles. My opposition to the Nuremberg trials was based on the fact that those trials violated every instinct of justice which I have grown up to regard as fundamental.[1] Even more, by trying to clothe a matter of policy in the robes of justice, they discredited for many years the ideals of justice between nations.

We see also in the matter of our trade relations with other nations a demand by the State Department for unlimited power under the Reciprocal Trade Agreement Act and a complete unwillingness to be bound by law or standards of any kind. The brazen disregard of law in the Korean enterprise and in the setting up of an international army in Europe is further evidence that our State Department has long since repudiated any serious respect for law and justice. It is now dominated far more by the philosophy of the economic planner who feels that the Government must decree the life of its citizens and of the world on a strictly opportunistic and expedient policy. My own feeling is that this policy in the field of foreign affairs, unless restrained, can only lead to arbitrary and totalitarian government at home, as foreign affairs comes more and more to dominate our domestic activities, and to war in the world.

The net result of the terms of the charter has been to destroy the usefulness of the United Nations as far as the prevention of aggression is concerned. I pointed this out in my speech on the charter in 1945, when I said:

All the discussion about force is of minor importance because it can never be used to solve any major crisis. If the charter had been in

---

[1]See Address of Robert A. Taft at Kenyon College, October 5, 1946, on "Equal Justice Under Law."

effect, Japan would have vetoed any action against itself on the invasion of Manchuria and of China. Italy would have vetoed any action against itself on the invasion of Ethiopia. In some ways the organization would have been less effective even than the League of Nations. The charter could not use force if Russia were to invade Poland or seize the Dardanelles from Turkey. Even attacks by satellite nations of one of the great powers might be engaged in safely if a great power had agreed in advance to exercise the veto power. If one of the five great powers violates the charter, and vetoes action against its own violation, the charter is for all practical purposes dissolved in failure.

When the North Koreans attacked on June 25, 1950, it happened that Russia was boycotting the Security Council, and the resolution calling for action against the North Korean aggression was therefore passed without dissent.

On June 28, 1950, I questioned the legality of the United Nations' action, because Article 27 of the charter clearly provides that decisions of the Security Council on all matters shall be made by an affirmative vote of seven members, including the concurring votes of the permanent members. There was no concurring vote by Russia, but we overrode this objection without considering how it might be raised against us in the future. Furthermore, we took this action without considering the fact that if the Chinese Communists attacked and the Russian representative returned to the Security Council the United Nations could not follow up its action against the Korean Communists by similar action against Chinese Communists.

If the Russians had planned it that way, they could not have done better. Did they perhaps arrange the North Korean attack when they were boycotting the United Nations, so that the United Nations might take an abortive action? Did they deliberately ignore the point I have just made, relating to affirmative votes, knowing that they could later block action against China? In any event, the President committed the United States to the Korean War as an undertaking of the United Nations, deluded as to a power which never has existed under the charter. His moral position was unassailable, but he did not realize the implications of what he started.

We have tried to bypass the limitations on the power of the Security Council by asking for action by the General Assembly when a veto has been exercised in the Council. Under the charter this body has never been intended to have any power to call on governments for action or do more than recommend. It would be most unwise for us to build up such power in the General Assembly. No nation has contracted to abide by any decision of the General Assembly. There is no obligation to comply with its recommendations. Furthermore, we would only have one vote among sixty, which sometime in the future, even in the very near future, may subject us to very arbitrary treatment.

Certainly this did not excuse the long delay of the Assembly in denouncing the Chinese Communists as aggressors. Its whole dilatory action repudiates the very basic theory of the charter that the United Nations is formed to prevent aggression and maintain peace. But action taken by the Assembly today can only have moral effect.

Those who are blaming the United Nations should much more blame the limitations of the charter and our own Government for forcing United Nations' action beyond its permanent power to perform.

I believe we ought to formulate the amendments which would create an ideal organization. But for the present we can only make use of the United Nations, as best we may, as a diplomatic weapon, and through it we may hope for more general support of our position against Communist aggression. Perhaps it may assist in establishing more friendly relations with Russia. But as far as military policy is concerned I see no choice except to develop our own military policy and our own policy of alliances, without substantial regard to the non-existent power of the United Nations to prevent aggression. The very adoption of the Atlantic Pact seems to me to constitute recognition of the impotence of the United Nations.

At this point I might discuss the other alternative form of international organization which is being urged strenuously upon the people of the United States, namely, a world state with an international legislature to make the laws and an international executive to direct the army of the organization.

The theory of an international state, bearing the same relation to nations and their citizens as our federal Government bears to the states and their citizens, appears to me, at least in this century, to be fantastic, dangerous, and impractical. It is proposed that it have a supreme legislature, executive, and court. It would maintain an all-powerful military force able to dominate all nations. It would control all trade, all seaports, and all airports within the various nations. Such a state, in my opinion, would fall to pieces in ten years.

The whole idea is based on the union of the thirteen colonies in 1787. But those colonies were made up of men of similar origin, similar methods of thought, similar ideals, with similar forms of government. They lived approximately the same kind of life, with similar standards of living. Even in that case one single difference resulted in a violent civil war about seventy-five years later which almost destroyed the Union. Here we would be attempting to unite peoples who do not understand even how their new fellow citizens begin to think; we would join democracies with dictatorships, Moslem states with Christian states, the Brahmin with the Rotarian, men who talk only Japanese with men who talk only English. We would attempt to unite the most highly civilized with the aborigines, the workman who earns twenty dollars a day with the coolie who earns twenty cents a day. The difficulties of holding together such a Tower of Babel under one direct government would be insuperable.

Furthermore, if it could remain in existence at all, it would not remain democratic—if a state including dictatorships like those of Russia, Communist China, Argentina, and Yugoslavia could ever have been democratic. True freedom depends on local self-government, effective access of the people to their individual rights. Sometimes I question whether the United States has not reached the limit of size under which the people of a nation can have a real voice in its government. Certainly a world government at Geneva or Panama would listen more closely to the voice of well-organized pressure groups than to the voice of an ordinary American citizen from city, small town, or farm.

It is significant that the British Empire, because of its size, has moved toward decentralization of government and has today no over-all legislative body, no over-all executive, and no over-all police force. If Canada and Australia and New Zealand and South Africa and Eire are regarded as too diverse to be consolidated into one government, what about China, Japan, India, Russia, Switzerland, and Ethiopia?

But above all, anyone who suggests such a plan is proposing an end to that liberty which has produced in this country the greatest happiness, the greatest production, the highest standard of living the world has ever seen. He is proposing to tear up the American Constitution which has made this nation the greatest power for good in the world, setting an example of successful popular rule to the entire world. We are asked to scrap a tried plan, which up to this time has successfully maintained our liberty at home and abroad and afforded to this country the protection against invasion which is the alleged purpose of all international plans. It would subject the American people to the government of a majority who do not understand what American principles are and have little sympathy with them.

Most people who think carelessly of a world state seem to think that it would be run by the United States. But we, of course, would have a very minor voice in the character of legislation. We would be the natural target of all other nations for taxation and all kinds of economic discrimination. The controversies which would arise in trying to pass legislation would almost certainly produce hundreds of disputes which could easily lead to war between constituent states, for civil war is as possible as any other war. Most such disputes would never arise at all under a covenant between nations admitted to be sovereign in their own territory. The plan would promote war instead of preventing it.

I cannot conceive of a responsible American statesman willing to subject the great principles we have developed in this country to destruction by an alien majority. A world state might bring peace for the moment, but it would be the peace of dictatorship and in a few years would plunge us again into world-wide war. Any international organization which is worth the paper it is written on must be based on retaining the sovereignty of all states. Peace must be sought not by destroying and consolidating nations but by developing a rule of law in the relations between nations.

There are two steps which might be taken to improve the United Nations. We might press for a convention to write amendments to the charter. That would probably be blocked by Russia. We might set up an organization of nations within the United Nations under a more ideal charter. There was an opportunity to do this in the case of the Atlantic Pact, but the State Department chose to negotiate a military alliance. If all the Atlantic Pact nations agreed to a new form of international organization based on law and justice without veto, it could operate between themselves and settle all disputes among them. An example of success might lead to the new organization's becoming the real power within the façade of the United Nations.

Social Cost Accounting

Michael Harrington/from "Taking the Great Society Seriously"

Michael Harrington (1928–   ) was formerly an associate editor of The
Catholic Worker, *later became a member of the National Executive Committee of the Socialist Party, and since 1964 he has been chairman of the
board of the League for Industrial Democracy. Harrington has written two
books,* The Other America *and* The Accidental Century, *and a new
book,* Towards the Democratic Left, *is in preparation. In all of them he
shows his activist and socialist concern for civil rights and industrial democracy.
The following selections come from his article "Taking the Great Society
Seriously," which appeared in* Harper's Magazine *(December 1966).*

    *The rhetoric of President Johnson's prospectus for the Great Society
could, Harrington admits, be dismissed as "windy futurism." After all, as
he points out, we have not yet even enacted much of Franklin Roosevelt's
New Deal into reality, to say nothing of proposals for universal health insurance
made by Democratic President Harry Truman and a federal housing program
advocated by the late Republican Senator Robert Taft. To envision an America
of quality rather than quantity, of urban complexes which would fulfill "the
desire for beauty and the hunger for community," of a national style in which
leisure means imaginative development of the self and not restless boredom—
such visionary phraseology, Harrington says, is apt to strike today's young and
left-wing liberals as utopian fancies fit only for cynical mockery. To counter
such cynicism Harrington advocates what he calls a "more subversive strategy—
to take the Great Society seriously."*

    *His article then lists a number of ways to provide correspondingly
subversive tactics. He begins by appealing to the report "Technology and
the American Economy," prepared by the National Commission on Technology,
Automation, and Economic Progress—a group which has, in Harrington's
not easily shockable eyes, made "one of the most radical suggestions put forth
by a responsible body in our recent history." The Commission numbers among
its members such men as Howard R. Bowen, now president of the University
of Iowa; Daniel Bell, Columbia University sociologist; Walter P. Reuther,
head of the United Auto Workers; and Thomas J. Watson, Jr., board chairman
of IBM. The Commission calls for a new bookkeeping system in which "overviews" of allocations for social need would be made "from the point of view of
economic opportunity and social mobility." Such mobility does not, for Harrington, include our national network of superhighways. In his opinion, these
roads, especially the ones built in and around great urban centers, represent
the powerful interests of the automobile and oil industries to the detriment
of mass transit, poor people, Negroes, and the aged. In fact, Harrington
argues that the system of freeways in Los Angeles was "a major factor in the
despairing violence which broke out in Watts." The Federal Housing Administration, Veterans Administration, and the Federal National Mortgage Association have been equally guilty, he argues, of contributing to racial prejudice
and the inefficiency of urban renewal.*

    *Harrington proposes that a "Council for the Great Society be established
as part of the Executive Branch" in order to oversee plans and allocations for
making the Great Society a reality. If necessary—and it is clear that he thinks*

it necessary—the profit motive must be revised. American youth, he claims, is
already rejecting "the national idealization of personal gain." This "mythology
of profit," still "wantonly taught to innocent schoolchildren," must be done away
with—"facing up to the fact that a Great Society cannot be built on a profit
motive is an act of politics." Those whom Harrington regards as "the best of
the young" are, he argues, already committed to such political action.

In the first half of the 1960s, important people proposed that the United
States make a social revolution, but without the inconvenience of changing
any basic institutions.

The President declared "unconditional war" on poverty, and the Congress obligingly proclaimed that it was the public policy "to eliminate the
paradox of poverty in the midst of plenty." President Johnson declared that
this goal, and the abolition of racial injustice as well, were "just the beginning."
He looked toward nothing less than a Great Society, "a place where men are
more concerned with the quality of their goals than the quantity of their
goods," where leisure would mean "a welcome chance to build and reflect,
not a feared cause of boredom and restlessness," where the city would serve
"the desire for beauty and the hunger for community."

An excellent case can be made for dismissing all this talk as windy futurism.

For one thing, America has not even bothered to fulfill the hopes of
the last generation of reformers. In 1944, for instance, Franklin Roosevelt
advocated a genuine, legally guaranteed right to work; if the private sector
failed to provide a man with a job, the public sector would be obliged to
create useful employment for him. By the time a conservative Congress got
through with this fine affirmation in the Employment Act of 1946, FDR's
binding promise of work was little more than a pious wish. In the next
two decades, scandalous rates of unemployment were chronic. In the late
'forties, Harry S Truman advocated a health insurance plan to cover every
citizen. It then took twenty years of bitter struggle to gain this protection,
under Medicare, for the 10 per cent of the population over sixty-five years
old.

Perhaps the most ironic disappointment is that the United States
in 1966 had not yet constructed the number of low-cost housing units
which Senator Robert Taft, the leading conservative of his time, had targeted
for 1955.

If old-fashioned reforms have been so half-hearted, there is good reason to suspect new utopias. This is particularly true when President Johnson
suggests that fundamental transitions in American life and values are to be
achieved almost effortlessly. The corporations and the unions, the racial
majority and the minorities, the religious believers and the atheists, the
political machines and the reformers, are all supposed to unite in making
a reasonable upheaval without a trace of conflict. And in a country where
the making of money has traditionally been the most revered pursuit,
spiritual considerations are suddenly going to come first.

In short, it is easy enough to make fun of the Great Society. And it is wrong. For the new rhetoric is an admission of how deeply troubled this land is, of how much remains to be done, even if that rhetoric is inexcusably vague about how to solve the problems which it recognizes. It is an enormous gain that the leaders of the nation have admitted they are confronted with a situation which requires nothing less than new principles. That is a crucial point of departure for social theory and social innovation. And the next step is to start talking about the actual, specific details of the transition to a humane future.

It is, for instance, of the greatest significance that the government now freely admits that every big city in America is in a financial, racial, and social crisis. The present condition of our cities touches the very intangibles of the quality of our life, for here old age is lonelier, youth more rootless, the streets more chaotic.

It should be obvious that a program like the Demonstration Cities proposal fails utterly to deal with these realities. The President originally asked for $400 to $500 million a year over five or six years. Senators Robert Kennedy and Abraham Ribicoff rightly implied that this was not enough— whereupon Mayor Lindsay noted that the city of New York could easily spend $50 billion to become livable. Kennedy, adding the various estimates from American mayors of the urban need for federal funds, concluded they would total a trillion dollars. He apparently believed this figure constituted a *reductio ad absurdum,* not realizing that, since the Gross National Product should add up to well over $20 trillion during the next twenty years, this sum would not be too much more than the 3 per cent of the National Product asked for by Harry Truman in 1947 in order to rebuild Europe. There is little point, however, in arguing over figures, for Congress is clearly intent on disappointing Mayor Lindsay and Senators Kennedy and Ribicoff, not to mention President Johnson.

A new way to keep books

But instead of mocking the contrast between Presidential rhetoric and Congressional action, there is a more subversive strategy—to take the Great Society seriously.

A living precedent will illuminate the meaning of such an attitude. In recent years the American Negro outrageously demanded that this society live up to its own pieties. Words about equality and justice which had been as ceremonial as a Fourth of July speech suddenly became the programs and slogans of a militant mass movement. And all of this was not accomplished, let it be emphasized, by conciliation and good will. The dynamic was con-flict and the actual involvement of dedicated fighters who were willing to die for the literal-minded idea of freedom.

The Great Society is not going to be handed down from on high any more than the Negro has been graciously conceded his democratic rights by the white majority. A crucial paradox explains why it is necessary to expect bitter American resistance to American greatness: it is impossible really to do anything about the "quality of our goals" without a profound rearrangement in the way we order the "quantity of our goods." At times, the Presidential rhetoric seems to imply that greatness is a genteel aspiration, like planting more flowers or having more ballet. In fact, to liberate the nation's spirit will require challenging some of its most powerful material interests. And that is the political rub if one proposes to take Lyndon B. Johnson at his fine words.

In 1966 a sober government commission, composed of businessmen, scholars, civil-rights leaders, and trade unionists, proposed that the United States take specific and concrete public action to place human considerations above mere moneymaking. Perhaps it is a measure of the extent of the present crisis that it drives practical men to visions.

The report, *Technology and the American Economy*—prepared by the National Commission on Technology, Automation, and Economic Progress—called on the government "to explore the creation of a 'system of social accounts' which would indicate the social benefits and social costs of investments and services and thus reflect the true cost of a product. In such an approach, production and innovation would be measured, not simply in terms of its profitability to an individual or a corporation, but in relation to how it affects the society—of its profitability from the standpoint of the common good. There would be overviews of entire areas of social need, like housing and education, and analyses of the Gross National Product from the point of view of economic opportunity and social mobility." This information, the Commission said, would help us to calculate the "utilization of human resources in our society. . . ."[1]

This is one of the most radical suggestions put forth by a responsible body in our recent history. The idea of social costs is not, of course, a new one. But the notion of putting the government behind it, of translating it from social science into politics, is a threat to some of our most cherished injustices.

Social accounting, for instance, would inevitably attack the power of both the automobile and the real-estate industries. It would probably force the country to consider putting an effective end to both cities and states as its fundamental subdivisions. And it would most certainly promote bitter conflict between the partisans of the private interest and the defenders of the public good.

It is striking how vague government documents become when the social cost of the automobile is at issue. The Highway Cost Allocation Study presented to Congress in 1960-61 was most precise in adding up all the dollar values which federally subsidized roads added to the economy. Then, in a casual aside, the Study noted that the expressway program had also promoted the decline of the central cities of America, a deterioration in mass transit, and possibly the shoddiness of the passenger rail system as well. These enormous social costs were borne, of course, primarily by poor people, Negroes, the aged—all those who stayed behind. But they were not even considered when Congress was computing the price the nation pays for its highways.

This indifference to social costs was one of the reasons why the Council

---

[1]The report was submitted early in 1966 and is available from the Government Printing Office in Washington, D.C. Members of the Commission were Howard R. Bowen, president of Grinnell College (Chairman), Benjamin Aaron, Joseph A. Beirne, Daniel Bell, Patrick E. Haggerty, Albert J. Hayes, Anna Rosenberg Hoffman, Edwin H. Land, Walter P. Reuther, Robert H. Ryan, Robert M. Solow, Philip Sporn, Thomas J. Watson, Jr., and Whitney M. Young, Jr.

of Economic Advisers somberly warned, in its 1966 Report, that "the central core cities . . . have experienced a gradual process of physical and economic deterioration. Partly as a result of people's desire for more space and home ownership, and made possible by the development of the automobile, central cities have been losing middle- and upper-income families to the suburbs. This movement accelerated when cities became caught in a vicious spiral of spreading slums, rising crime, and worsening congestion. . . . This process created an almost impossible financial situation for many cities."

All of this is depressingly familiar. So is the Council's description of the way in which these new patterns of living have strained the urban transportation systems almost to the breaking point—and exacted a high price from the commuter in terms of wasted time and frayed nerves. Then comes the point at issue in any system of social cost accounting: "From the point of view of efficiency," the Council affirms, ". . . investments should have been made in facilities for mass transit. Instead, *for many reasons,* they have been made primarily in automobile expressways, which only increase the congestion at the center." (Emphasis added.)

It is no accident that the Council becomes so imprecise when it assigns the responsibility for the antisocial allocation of transportation funds we have made. For among the "many reasons" behind this irrational decision, the automobile industry looms large. Given the fact that seven of the ten largest corporations in the world are involved (three car makers, four oil companies) our actions are not so mysterious. . . .

Handout for the middle class

At the White House Civil Rights Conference last summer it was publicly admitted that the overwhelming bulk of federal support for housing has gone to the middle class and the rich. The poor get a highly visible, and wholly inadequate, subsidy in the form of segregated, bureaucratic high-rise projects. The well-off get an invisible and princely subsidy in the form of federal credit and tax policy, as well as through urban renewal. This system helps the middle class to maintain a certain sense of moral superiority and a loyalty to the Protestant ethic.

' The federal government generously provided much of the credit for suburbia (through the Housing and the Veterans Administrations, the Federal National Mortgage Association, and other agencies) during the very period it was supposed to be enticing the middle class back into the central city through urban renewal. There were cases, like the Title One scandal, in which speculators simply robbed the public. More often, the real-estate interests stamped the public programs with their private purposes in the full, legal light of day. As Professor James Q. Wilson of Harvard describes it, urban renewal at the local level was used "in some places to get Negroes out of white neighborhoods, in others to bring middle-class people closer to downtown department stores, in still other places to build dramatic civic monuments, and in a few places to rehabilitate declining neighborhoods and add to the supply of moderately priced housing."

Tax policy also has aided the better-off. In 1962 the value of the tax deduction on mortgage payments was roughly double the sum spent on public housing—a ratio of about $1.5 billion to $835 million. The poor got a cheap, inadequate, but highly visible, subsidy; the self-reliant and virtuous middle class received a much more munificent, but socially invisible handout.

If there were social cost accounting, however, and the public moneys were actually used to redeem the official pledges about ending poverty and building a Great Society, many of these postwar policies would have to be reversed. Public housing would no longer mean piling poor people on top of each other in segregated high-rise projects. The White House Conference on Civil Rights made a "conservative" estimate that the country needs two million new housing units a year, instead of 1.4 million now being built, and recommended that "at least half, preferably more" of the new units should be made available to low- and moderate-income families. The Conference also computed the cost of putting the poor in the private housing market through subsidies: to get all of the present families with incomes under $3,000 into decent housing would take $10 billion. . . .

Revising the profit motive

Finally, if the quality of our goals is to be placed over the quantity of our goods, then President Johnson has, perhaps unwittingly, attacked the profit motive. This may sound like a radical, even an impolite, interpretation of the premises of his Great Society; yet, paradoxically, such a recognition has an enormous political potential for national leaders in the future. The best, the most intelligent, of the American youth today are already rejecting the national idealization of personal gain. And they are the vanguard of the largest and most restless generation in American history.

Yet the mythology of profit still officially obsesses the nation; it is wantonly taught to innocent schoolchildren. An almost pathetic illustration of this devotion has been provided by the emergence of modified market principles ("Libermanism") in Russia and East Europe. The President was cheered that "Profits are coming to be understood as a better measure of productivity—and personal incentive as a better spur to effective action on behalf of the national economy." Neither Mr. Johnson, nor the editorialists who shared his jubilation, seemed to care that their free-enterprise methods were being used by totalitarian bureaucracies to make controlled economies more efficient.

Perhaps the most authoritative testimonial on the possibilities of being done with the profit motive comes from a successful businessman, a brilliant stock speculator, and a theorist who helped to save capitalism from itself—John Maynard Keynes.

In 1925 Keynes wrote, ". . . the moral problem of our age is concerned with the love of money, with the habitual appeal to the money motive in nine-tenths of the activities of life, with the universal striking after individual security as the prime object of endeavor, with the social approbation of money as the measure of constructive success, and with the social appeal to the hoarding instinct as the foundation of the necessary provision for the family and for the future." How this statement came from the pen of such a brilliant theoretical and practical entrepreneur is a fascinating puzzle in intellectual history; it is also quite relevant to the antiprofit implications of the Great Society.

Two years after this attack on the love of money, Keynes made a paradoxical distinction. There were two separate issues, he said; one concerned the efficiency of capitalism, the other the desirability of the system. "For my part," Keynes wrote, "I think that capitalism, wisely managed, can probably be made more efficient for obtaining economic ends than any alternative system yet in sight; but that in itself it is in many ways extremely objectionable." Eventually, Keynes believed, the economy would become so productive (he even imagined a zero rate of interest for capital) that society would no longer need to be immoral in order to be efficient. At that point, "The love of money—as distinguished from the love of money as a means to the enjoyments and realities of life—will be recognized for what it is, a somewhat disgusting morbidity, one of those semicriminal, semipathological propensities which one hands over with a shudder to the specialists in mental disease."

This distinction between money as means and money as end is crucial if the issues are not to be muddled. For the immediate future, and even in the visionary middle distance, almost everyone is going to devote himself to raising his standard of life and even pursuing luxuries. One accepts a modicum of self-interest and antineighborliness. But it is another question entirely that these aspects of personality should be taken as the dominant principle of a society. That, in essence, is the argument of the unalloyed profit motive.

Once upon a time there was a savage ethical theory to justify the making of money as money. It was said that profiteering—outwitting one's fellow man, getting a special advantage, buying cheap and selling dear—was necessary to evoke the extremes of entrepreneurial ingenuity and dedication. Those were the heroic, dog-eat-dog days of the business civilization. Whether this morality was really ever needed, it certainly no longer holds. Research and development are government-supported, largely carried out by scientific pieceworkers; corporations are more and more "rational" and bureaucratic—private civil services rather than robber baronies. We are at that point foreseen by Keynes where the love of money need not be acknowledged as the arbiter of society's destiny.

For the best of the young

The very best of the American young are rejecting, as Keynes did forty years ago, the "money-making morbidity." In 1964, the *Wall Street Journal* reported that 14 per cent of Harvard's senior class entered business, as contrasted with 39 per cent in 1960. In 1966 the Harris Poll surveyed college seniors for *Newsweek* and found that this trend was deepening. Only 12 per cent of the sample were looking forward to business careers—and twice as many wanted to be teachers. Harris further reported that the acceptance of business as an institution in American society declined as education increased; that those students with the most advantages were also the most alienated from the ruling economic ideology.

There was a humorous documentation of this pattern in a recent article by Roger Rapoport in the *Wall Street Journal*. A student who graduated with "the highest honors" at Michigan State University picketed his own commencement because of the presence of Vice President Humphrey, a supporter of the Administration's policy in Vietnam. This event, Rapoport wrote, was not an isolated one. Michigan State had gone out to recruit genius as it once had assembled only football teams. Because of this activist approach and generous scholarships, the University had managed to attract 560 National Merit Scholars to East Lansing. (Harvard, with the second-highest Merit Scholar total, had 425.)

But it turned out that it was precisely this intellectual elite which provided much of the impetus for campus dissidence and protest. The Merit Scholars were involved in publishing a newspaper critical of the University administration, attacking self-service laundry prices, and helping to document their own University's relations with the CIA in Vietnam. As Rapoport concluded, "the ironic situation in East Lansing points up a dilemma confronting a growing number of quality-minded universities these days."

The Michigan State experience had, of course, been presaged at Berkeley, where the student militants of the Free Speech Movement in 1965 were among the very best students on campus. All over the country one can recognize a deep current of antimaterialism and antibureaucracy among the most educated youth of the 'sixties. The brightest children of the affluent society have volunteered for dangerous civil-rights projects in the South, for community organizing in the slums of the cities, for the Peace Corps, and for VISTA.

It could be that all this is only a youthful phase. I think not. John Kennedy was among the first to understand that the youth of the 'sixties were much more readily moved by an appeal to sacrifice for the common good than by a call to scramble for private gain. In the vicious, competitive capitalist economy of the nineteenth century, it was at least possible to idealize a social Darwinist ethic. In the conglomerate enterprise of the mid-twentieth century, that is becoming infinitely more difficult.

In Thomas Mann's *Buddenbrooks,* the tough-minded merchants of the first generation were succeeded by ambiguous sons and ineffective, aesthetic grandchildren. In this country, a different case might be made: the educated grandchildren of our immigrants are becoming increasingly idealistic. If this is the trend, then facing up to the fact that a Great Society cannot be built on a profit motive is an act of politics. Such clarity will have a profound appeal to the best of the young.

There must be specific and concrete proposals to show that quality is being made sovereign over quantity. Perhaps the easiest proposal to adopt in this area is that of Kingman Brewster, who said in his inaugural address as president of Yale that social service should be given the same status in our schools now accorded to military training. The student preparing to be an officer receives allowances for schooling and for summer training. The youth who wants to be a civil-rights organizer or a Peace Corpsman, or to volunteer for any similarly useful activity, should have at least as much support.

It is not enough, in other words, to sermonize the young that they should favor a Great Society. There should be new institutions to help those who want to build a new and exciting nation. The patriotism of life should be worth at least as much to America as the patriotism of death.

Prying Beneath the Figures
John Davenport/from *The U.S. Economy*

John Davenport (1904–   ) studied economics and philosophy at Yale and since 1937 has been on the staff of Fortune, *except for a stint as editor of* Barron's Weekly. *He is currently managing editor of* Fortune.

    In his book The U.S. Economy, *Davenport expresses doubts that "the secular, democratic, and industrialized society that stretches around us" has realized "the values implicit in morality, aesthetics, and religion"—and the burden of his book is to show that intensified secular, democratic, and industrialized efforts are not apt to do so. The so-called "mixed economy," in which government, industry, and labor are to produce a kind of harmonious balance, is for him a very dubious concept because its proponents fail to consider the qualitative nature of the parts which make up the mechanism. As a result, federal action too often substitutes for action which properly is the job of "the private sector." The selections presented here are taken from the chapter entitled "Of the 'Starved' Public Sector."*

    Davenport comes down hard on governmental economists who, with their "pie charts" showing the typical allocation of the taxpayer's dollar and with their triple method of keeping books, are able to demonstrate either that "big government spending" is good for the country or, if that proof fails, that spending is inevitable. Davenport cleverly uses Harrington's chief witness, John Maynard Keynes, to support his case that governmental spending in excess of 25 per cent of the national product will lead to inflation (current federal expenditures already run to about 30 per cent). The burden of taxation undermines incentives, he says, and also produces "distorting side effects." Furthermore, should the government "one day pre-empt 50 per cent of the economy, we should have subtly collectivized the country without the advocates of socialism and statism having fired a shot."

    Although Davenport has some doubts about the present allocations for defense, space, and foreign aid, for him, domestic spending is the place where cuts would be most prudent. In 1954, he says, domestic allocations made up 30 per cent of the budget; by the mid-sixties they constituted nearly 40 per cent and would have been higher if social security were added. It is not the duty of the federal government, he argues, to do what the individual states could do as well, especially since the mere process of transferring dollars to Washington and then back to the states both shrinks their value and reduces their number.

    Moreover, he finds it subtly deceptive to argue that public needs must be fulfilled by "the public sector"; after all, such great public needs as food, clothing, and shelter, no less than luxuries, are successfully provided by the private sector. Federal expenditures in housing subsidies by the Federal Housing Administration, the Veterans Administration, and the Federal National Mortgage Association now run to over $100 billion—"a third as large as the recorded national debt." The solution to urban renewal lies not in more federal spending, he says, but in revising those distorted tax laws which now "penalize improvements on existing buildings (which, after all, house the great majority of the population)." He adds "slum-breeding rent control legislation" and "high costs exacted by building codes and the building trade unions" as other reasons for our urban problems.

The tax reforms needed for housing are only part of a general tax reform, and Davenport's thesis is that all tax reforms should be aimed at increasing "the basic motivations of the private economy on which in the end both jobs and revenue depend." If such reforms were effected, America's interests both at home and abroad would not be jeopardized and the nation would become "more puissant, productive, and free."

Of the "starved" public sector

> **"The more it snows**
> **(Tiddely pom)**
> **The more it goes**
> **(Tiddely pom)**
> **The more it goes**
> **(Tiddely pom)**
> **On snowing."**
> —A. A. MILNE, *The House at Pooh Corner*

We must now descend from the rarified atmosphere of monetary and fiscal theory to the stuffier confines of the budget bureau and the Bureau of Internal Revenue. For this pedestrian journey we shall need a guide, and Washington has long provided one. The proffered aid takes the form of a so-called "pie chart," which indicates that of every dollar the government spends the largest portion by far goes to national defense, social security, interest payments on past debt, and other "intractable" items, so that the margin for economy and economizing is practically non-existent. Armed with this device, among others, and buttressed too by the fact that these days the federal government keeps, not one set of books, but no less than three, any director of the budget worth his salt can demonstrate that even if big government spending weren't good for the country, it is all but impossible to stem the tide.

Let us admit at the outset that it has been quite a tide. The over-all figures are, of course, familiar, and yet they bear repeating at a time when it is said that the "public sector" of the American economy, or, to be blunt about it, *the government sector,* is really in a pretty starved condition—considering, at least, the needs of the nation as defined by something still more intangible, the "national purpose." In his immensely popular book, *The Affluent Society,* John Kenneth Galbraith goes out of his way to dramatize the paucity of our public facilities as compared to the luxury and waste of private economic activity. This thesis is manna to not a few politicians who in less sophisticated times might have been brushed aside as "pork-barrel" specialists. It has subtly inspired many a presidential message on the state of the nation and the state of the budget. It has even been treated with respect by a commentator of the stature of Walter Lippmann, who, as far back as the presidential election of 1960, opined that "The Republican Party under Eisenhower does not understand the necessity of greater allocation of our resources, in a growing economy, to public needs."

Unhappily, however, Mr. Eisenhower, like other Presidents both before and after him, seems to have understood this alleged "necessity" all too well. Consider the record, as told by the raw figures. In the distant years of the late 'twenties, expenditures of the federal government ran to about $2.8 billion. By 1940 the New Deal, in its role, as Mr. Roosevelt phrased it, of Dr. Beat-the-Depression, had pushed the figure up to $9.1 billion. When this doctor was dismissed and Dr. Win-the-War took over, expenditures soared up of necessity to nearly $100 billion, declining thereafter and rising again to $74 billion in 1953 under the impact of the Korean War. Then a strange thing happened, apparently unnoticed by Mr. Lippmann. Committed to economy, the Eisenhower administration did reduce military outlays somewhat in its first term in office. But in Mr. Eisenhower's second term, prefaced by a budget message wherein he stated that the people "demand, and . . . deserve" certain services, *non-military* outlays rose by 33 per cent, bringing total expenditures in fiscal 1961 to $81.5 billion. From there President Kennedy carried the ball, increasing both military and non-military outlays with impartiality and driving total outlays close to the $100 billion mark. From that politically unpalatable figure President Johnson drew back with an initial 1965 budget of "economy and progress," which held the line at $97.9 billion. . . .

It will be pointed out, of course, that while the burden of government has certainly grown, so have the shoulders of the economy. Whereas it is estimated that in 1940 total government outlays, federal, state, and local, ran to 18.4 per cent of the national product, today they run *only* to about 30 per cent—a rise, to be sure, but a smaller one than the raw figures indicate. This is an important point but not necessarily a decisive one. The English economist Colin Clark has argued—and it was an argument that impressed Keynes—that when governments take more than 25 per cent of the national product the results will be inflationary, even if the whole amount is covered by taxes. Moreover, as we shall see, taxes have been exerting a tremendous drag on the economy, undermining incentives and producing all kinds of distorting side effects. The power to tax and to spend is the power to destroy, and if government were one day to pre-empt 50 per cent of the economy, we should have subtly collectivized the country without the advocates of socialism and statism having fired a shot.

2.

Thus there is good reason to restrain expenditures and to work toward a more rational and less burdensome tax system. The place to dig in is at the federal level, where concentration of power is most dangerous in a federal republic. Unhappily, it is precisely here that the men with the pie charts have an initial advantage by being able to point out that over half of all federal budgetary outlays are for the defense of the country—an undisputed function of the central government. When one considers what the U.S. and its allies owe to our military power, one will not be inclined to stint the needs of the Pentagon. Moreover defense is highly technical, and few laymen feel competent to judge it. What the laymen can emphasize is that

defense spending of the present magnitude does constitute a difficult lump
for any free economy to digest, even though most of the great contracting
firms are privately owned and responsive to market forces. Dependence on
a single monopoly buyer exacts a hidden cost of the competitive system which
does not show up in the raw statistics. And on more than one occasion the
government has exerted its power to determine issues that have nothing to
do with preserving the safety of the country. Witness the manner in which
the Kennedy administration threatened to switch defense orders away from
steel firms that, rightly or wrongly, sought to raise prices in 1962. . . .

3.

But it is in the realm of domestic spending, which has nothing to do
with defense, space, or even foreign aid, that recent budgets have been
most vulnerable. Precisely because military expenditures are so high, it would
be only prudent to cut down elsewhere. The really discouraging thing is
that, whether Republicans or Democrats are in office, non-defense spending
continues to climb. Whereas in 1954 this spending constituted less than
30 per cent of the regular budget, it rose in the mid-'sixties to nearly 40
per cent, and to much more than that if we count in social security payments.
It is this trend which needs to be checked, if not reversed, and in doing so
we need to emphasize two basic principles.

The first is that in a federal system the central government should not
undertake duties that can be as well cared for by the individual states. Dollars are shrunk rather than enlarged by being transferred to Washington
and then back again to local communities. The second principle involves
drawing a basic distinction between the words "public" and "governmental."
Advocates of an enlarged "public sector" have subtly confused discourse
by implying that if there is a public need, then government must fill it.
But this is surely not the case. In the American, and indeed in most Western
communities, private industry meets the overwhelming body of "public"
needs, if these are defined as the provision of food, clothing, and shelter,
no less than luxuries. Moreover, there are all kinds of public services involving education, health, and welfare which are best accomplished by private associations which are neither governmental nor strictly commercial.
This free collaborative activity, plus the contribution of enterprise itself,
could be far larger than it is today if the federal government in particular
would reduce its own sprawling activity, which all too often simply jams
the system. . . .

Many other areas of the budget call for pruning, but those who would
use the shears must be expert in prying beneath the figures. Expenditures
for commerce and transportation, for instance, run to over $3 billion in the
President's administrative budget; but they are more than double that if
one adds in highway trust fund outlays. Expenditures for housing and community development still seem relatively small, but the figures that show are
only the tip of the iceberg. It is estimated that at present the total federal
involvement in housing through guaranties and subsidies runs to over
$100 billion—or a third as large as the recorded national debt. A big part

of this involvement results from the operations of the Federal Housing Administration, which, set up as a depression measure, deserves credit for setting a new pattern in home finance which private lenders have followed. It is harder to see, however, why FHA still has to insure some 15 per cent of all non-farm housing starts, why its responsibilities should be constantly expanded into other fields, and why we need in addition the parallel activities of the Veterans Administration, plus the multi-billion-dollar operations of the Federal National Mortgage Association (Fannie May), which buys up mortgages whenever it thinks the market is depressed.

Moreover, it should be noted that, having set in motion a great era of private home building, mostly in the suburbs, government administrators are now far from content with the extent of their handiwork. They are giving increased attention to what, to borrow a phrase from the late Lincoln Steffens, may be called "the shame of the cities." Urban development and the elimination of crime-breeding city slums are now the main targets, and such development involves far more than self-liquidating mortgage insurance. Forward commitments for urban renewal grants now run to over $3 billion, and, despite bitter criticism, payments for public housing, where government in effect actually owns the new facilities, have mounted in the past four years. President Johnson has repeated President Kennedy's plea for a Cabinet-level Department of Housing and Community Development, and the trend toward ever larger government involvement in this field continues.

Yet it may be doubted whether more federal spending from the top down is really the way to solve America's housing problem, such as it is. The fundamental impediments to improving the American city in particular lie in distorted tax laws which penalize improvements on existing buildings (which, after all, house the great majority of the population); in slum-breeding rent control legislation which is still on the books in New York; and in the high costs exacted by building codes and the building trade unions—to mention but a few. Many of these impediments have been built in at the state and local level, and more federal spending simply serves to divert attention from needed corrections. When all is said and done, government cannot possibly re-house America; this is the business of private industry. What governments at all levels can do is establish the framework and the rules within which private and semi-private effort can take hold. But this involves painstaking and, on the whole, undramatic reform with low vote-getting potential. It is easier, though infinitely less effective, to multiply "programs" and "plans" which will be paid for tomorrow than to face up to the realities that must be coped with today.

4.

While housing still waits for its ultimate federal coordinator, we already have a Cabinet-level Department of Health, Education, and Welfare, and the results of creating it have been, as might have been expected, a great proliferation of federal activities. Expenditures in this area—plus outlays for "labor" (manpower retraining, etc.)—run to over $7 billion per year, with the operations of the multi-billion Social Security trust funds piled on top of that. The rationale of this enormous involvement is the "strengthening of human resources," which is, of course, in the language of the times, an all-important "national purpose." Agreed. But this does not mean that reaching it necessarily depends on government. . . .

Pressure for increased federal aid to education is based on the same kind of faulty reasoning, about the shortage of both facilities and teachers. This is the theme of most recent budget messages and lies behind the drive to make a "deeper commitment" to all forms of education, including aid to the country's public school system. Propaganda for such a deeper commitment overlooks the fact that, by and large, Americans have generously supported their educational institutions, both public and private. Whereas since the turn of the century public school enrollment has more than doubled, expenditures for the schools by states and local communities have gone up over eightyfold—from $215 million in 1899–1900 to more than $18 billion in the 'sixties. As a result of this expansion, the classroom shortage in the U.S. public schools has been rapidly diminishing, and has in some communities turned into a surplus. Meanwhile, teachers' salaries have been rising proportionately faster in recent years than the U.S. per capita income or industrial wages, and the number of workers in the labor force. The fundamental need of the future is not just for more money for schools, but for more and better schooling for the money. This is an objective best achieved by keeping control of the public schools at the local community level, where their day-to-day problems are known and can be thrashed out. Intervention by the federal government cannot solve these problems, while it does raise the danger that Washington will some day try, not just to finance education, but to control it.

This danger is already apparent in the financial assistance—direct and indirect—which the federal government is now giving to higher education. Through the National Defense Education Act of 1958, Washington provides loans and fellowships to college students and makes substantial loans for college dormitories. The National Science Foundation contributes to so-called "basic research," defined as almost any kind of scientific inquiry. Such research is also financed through the National Aeronautics and Space Administration, so that the total federal money going to the colleges and universities for research of one kind or another is estimated at $1.5 billion per year. Sharp controversy about the loyalty oath and how Harvard University should use a government-financed cyclotron suggest that federal aid does bring federal influence and control. Nor will fears on this score be allayed by the suggestion that the government should be just as much interested in the teaching of the "social sciences" as it is in the teaching of the natural sciences—a statement which, if implemented, might well give increased weight, if not prestige, to the "new economics" of government spending. It would be neither foolish nor premature to believe that much government assistance to education is currently oriented in the wrong direction.

The strength of the American educational system lies in its multiplicity of means and in its diffusion of power and authority. Even in the case of primary education, the country might be better off if state and local governments, while insisting on minimal educational standards, yielded their now near-monopoly on school facilities, giving tax relief to those who choose to send their children to private schools. But while such a plan is still utopian, it is not utopian to believe that the federal government certainly should curtail rather than expand its growing power and influence at all levels of the educational process. Dollars taxed for Harvard mean fewer dollars available for private donations or for state and local use. But the argument goes beyond that. As Friedrich Hayek has said: "Nowhere is freedom more important than where our ignorance is greatest—at the boundaries of knowledge." The lasting contribution which government can make to education is to keep that freedom secure and those boundaries open.

We come, finally, to the role of government in caring for those who, whether educated or not, have lost their footing in a society which we would like to think increasingly provides opportunity for all. It was the confident hope of government officials that when the U.S. adopted the Social Security Act of 1935, providing for old age and disability insurance and giving powerful impetus to state unemployment insurance, there would be a diminution over the years of other forms of aid to the destitute, and for relief purposes. That hope has only partly been fulfilled. Federal relief, which ran high in the 'thirties, tapered off in the war years, but since then has steadily edged upward. In fiscal 1964, grants to the states for subsidiary old age assistance, aid to dependent children, aid to the blind, and for other purposes ran to some $3 billion, or over half the total relief burden. The justification for this rising commitment toward centralization is that poorer states lack the taxing potential to take care of their own. One may question this thesis. Granted that much destitution exists among the "underemployed" of the southern states, it is still true that indigent men and women may be worse off in the great cities of the richer industrial areas than on the land. Once more, dollars do not grow bigger by being taxed away to Washington to be processed and doled out again, at the risk of great political corruption. Relief of destitution should be fundamentally a responsibility of the states and local communities, where it can be integrated with the not inconsiderable and not-to-be-despised work of private charity of all kinds.

This is doubly true because Washington has pre-empted, probably permanently, the job of trying to "insure" all citizens against the hazards of old age and disability through basic social security legislation. Total payments of the old age trust fund now run to well over $16 billion per year, and will grow as population expands. The system is now so deeply embedded in the economy that it must be regarded as a permanent fixture in American life. But this surely does not mean that it should be indefinitely expanded. It must be recognized that old age benefits, as currently administered, are not in fact based on the insurance principle, but are to a large degree transfers of money from the present working population to those in retirement. Moreover, the system suffers from both its coercive character and the fact that its whole machinery is concentrated in government hands. No effort has been made to give citizens a choice between using this federal machinery or alternative private institutions. No recognition is given the man who prudently, by his own efforts, takes steps to care for himself and his family. . . .

5.

Taxes are, of course, the other side of the spending coin, and their cumulative impact has increased in direct proportion to outlays. This impact has been somewhat concealed by the withholding tax device, which is a boon to the Treasury and a kind of tranquilizer for the population. Withholding taxes for all kinds of social security alone now run to several times the *total* of all federal taxes paid at the beginning of World War II—a pointed reminder that welfare is not a free gift of a beneficent state, which in the last analysis has nothing to "give." The nation's tax load—federal, state, and local—now runs to about $160 billion; this works out to about $2,800 per household or $840 per capita.

The case for . . . reform is apparent in both the personal income tax, which now collects about 50 per cent of all administrative budget receipts, and, perhaps even more, in the corporation profit tax. Adopted in 1913, the personal income tax seemed a fairly innocuous measure, with a basic rate of only 1 per cent on the lowest bracket of taxable income and a top rate of 7 per cent. Then came the depression, and under bipartisan "leadership" the rate structure was wrenched upward to a range of 4 per cent at the bottom and a destructive 63 per cent at the top. World War II saw further rate increases and lowering of exemptions which bore down not only on the rich but also on the middle classes, while inflation increased the burden even while seeming to lighten it. In the post-war years, the harried householder running fast simply to stay in the same place became a familiar sight. In 1962, a married couple with two children who had a gross income of $7,500 in 1942 would have had to have an income of over $14,000 in order to be as well off after taxes and inflation as it had been twenty years earlier. Fortunately, people continue to move up the income ladder, to the great benefit of themselves and society. But at some point a progressive rate structure of 20 to 91 per cent was bound to weaken incentive, distort judgments, and to make the tax scoop an instrumentality for flattening out every economic recovery without necessarily covering mounting Treasury outlays. . . .

How far we should go in this direction involves partly choice of philosophy, partly more practical considerations. It has long been the contention of many eminent economists that the whole principle of progression is morally wrong, since it involves in theory and in practice a redistribution of income from rich to poor which is no business of the modern state, and that once progression is adopted there is no clear-cut *rule* to define the scope of taxation. The ideal from this point of view is a return to the rule of "proportionality," wherein the rich pay more than the poor, but all pay on the same standard. Over a century ago, the economist McCulloch argued that once this standard was abandoned, we should be left "without rudder or compass" in a sea of troubles. Considering how things have gone, it will not do to laugh off this dictum.

One need not go this far, however, to believe that the egalitarian argument for sharp progression is thoroughly suspect, and that the path of sanity lies in a continued reversal of the trends of the past thirty years. Given economic expansion and rising incomes, there should be increasing room to maneuver in readjusting rates while still meeting basic revenue needs. Some see an ideal rate structure ranging from 14 per cent to 25 per cent in the not-too-distant future. More immediately, we would be accomplishing a lot if the top limit of the personal income tax were reduced from 70 to 50 per cent—a step that is thoroughly practical when one considers that *all rates above 50 per cent have in recent years brought in less than 2 per cent* of Treasury receipts. This single statistic sheds a vast amount of light on a maze of conflicting claims and counterclaims. The fact is that the tax burden cannot be indefinitely shifted upward. It can occasionally be eased to allow the people enduring it to walk a little more upright—and a little faster.

6.

To that end, we should also press on with the further reduction of the corporation profit tax, not in the interests of "buttering up" businessmen but of creating more real output, hence income, in the economy. Once again, the recent reduction of this tax from an over-all 52 per cent to 48 per cent represents a beginning—but only a beginning, and a meager one at that. Unlike high-bracket personal income taxes, the corporate levy does cream off much revenue—some $20 billion per year—but it does so fraudulently, and in a way which dries up other sources of potential receipts. There exists ample evidence that a large part of the corporation profits tax can be and is *passed on* to the public in the form of higher prices or lower wages than would otherwise obtain. To the degree that this actually occurs, the corporation tax is a kind of concealed sales or payroll tax, whose chief virtue is its deceptiveness, hence its ease of collection. The argument that the tax is good because it restrains the "monopoly profits" of capitalism breaks down on the evidence that the man in the street, not the capitalist, pays most of it. . . .

Thus in the end true tax reform, coupled with control of the budget, offers an exciting alternative to the present dreary prospect of continued deficit finance and enlargement of the federal government's power. Whether one stresses tax reform first and curtailment of federal spending later or reverses the emphasis is to some degree a matter of political tactics. We need not indulge in futile debate about the "Puritan ethic" to resolve these claims and counterclaims. Prudence no less than vision dictates the dual course of reforming the tax structure while at the same time restricting the federal government to the tasks that it alone can accomplish, reserving the rest "to the states respectively, or to the people." The results of doing this would not be to jeopardize the vital defense of U.S. interests abroad or its needs at home. It would be to enhance a more puissant, productive, and free America.

Part III: Literature of the Liberal and Conservative Imagination

Although polemical writing sometimes attains the level of literature, as in certain works of Edmund Burke and Thomas Paine, good dramatic writing is never merely polemical. Writers who deal directly with ideas and issues are generally removed from a refined and particular awareness of human suffering and human aspirations, from the internal conflicts of character and personality, from the subjective effects of place and time. The good dramatic writer takes such matters into consideration and tempers his doctrinal convictions accordingly; if he is great, like Shakespeare, he can write scenes and speeches embodying opposite views and render them with such persuasive art that readers cannot tell where the author himself stands. Or if his own bias and judgment do emerge, they do so out of a genuine and fair presentation of the conflict, because he does not make the characters who oppose his own views mere straw men.

These observations hold true regardless of the genre. In the selections that follow, we have included the short story, the novel, and the lyric poem in modes ranging from allegory to realism. In all of these, the reader will observe how delicately the author responds to the just claims of both liberal and conservative views. In the selections by John Dos Passos, for example, the same author writes now as a liberal, now as a conservative; yet at each imaginative moment, Dos Passos retains an artistic sympathy for that which he attacks.

To deal adequately with liberal and conservative scenes, a writer often needs a broad canvas. Although we have sometimes had to make short selections from long works, we believe that the selections represent fairly the general texture of each work. The reader should see the entire canvas, however, since knowledge of the whole will affect knowledge of the part.

The riches of American literature provide many more authors than there was room to include. The selections are intended to be representative of the liberal and conservative imagination, both adequate to the doctrines and attitudes of each and competent as pieces of dramatic writing. Certain writers who might be expected in such a collection—Henry Adams, James Gould Cozzens, and John P. Marquand, or Mark Twain, Ernest Hemingway, and Arthur Miller, to name only a few from each side—were not easy to excerpt. The reader may console himself for their absence by remembering that this book is not a survey of writers but of ideas.

An Allegory of Scientific Rationalism
Nathaniel Hawthorne/"The Birthmark"

Nathaniel Hawthorne (1804–1864) was born in Salem, Massachusetts, where he imbibed Puritanism from his heritage and Romanticism from his age; the result was an artist of metaphysical and psychic conservatism. One of his ancestors was a judge in the Salem witchcraft trials; his father, a sea-captain, was drowned at sea. He attended Bowdoin, the school of Longfellow and Franklin Pierce; upon graduation, he lived with his mother and studied to become a writer. In 1839 he married Sophia Peabody and began work in a Boston customhouse; in 1841 he dabbled in the unsuccessful transcendentalist experiment at Brook Farm. When that failed, he worked again in the custom-house until 1849, when his position, obtained by patronage, was lost by the same means. He then turned seriously to producing fiction: The Scarlet Letter *(1850),* The House of the Seven Gables *(1851), a second collection of short stories (1851), and* The Blithedale Romance *(1852). Still pressed for money, he accepted, from his friend and then President, Franklin Pierce, a position in the consulate at Liverpool, where he stayed until 1858. Thereafter his life was one of wasting illness, marked only by the appearance of* The Marble Faun *(1860).*

Hawthorne's work, often strongly and even obviously allegorical, reveals little awareness of the particulars of historical events; instead, his interest in transcendentalism led him to dramatize historical events in moral and psychological terms. "The Birthmark," which follows, lacks the delicate realism of Hawthorne's greatest allegories; its technique and bias are, however, more immediately clear for that lack. In this story, Aylmer, a man of science, is wedded to a woman of transcendent beauty—except for a birthmark upon her cheek, in the shape of a tiny hand. Increasingly irritated by this flaw in human perfection, the scientist works upon his wife's feelings until she views the natural phenomenon of the birthmark as something organically evil in the very depths of her being. Together they agree that he will use his science to rid her of an imperfection both physical and moral. He is aided by Aminadab, a "human machine," a man of ugly bulk who has mechanical aptness coupled with total inability to understand the principles of his master's art. The alchemical liquor brewed by Aylmer penetrates so deeply into his wife's being that it destroys both the birthmark and her life. The "fatal hand"—his or hers?—vitiates the union of "an angelic spirit . . . with a mortal frame." To the accompanying sound of Aminadab's "gross hoarse chuckle" comes the awareness that "thus ever does the gross fatality of earth exult in its invariable triumph over the immortal essence. . . ."

Aylmer clearly represents the spirit of rationalistic liberalism seeking to establish, by scientific means, the perfectibility of man—only to find that the mysterious and "celestial" essence which he wished to perfect evaporates under his treatment. His wife becomes a perfect woman only as she dies. Had he resisted the temptation, and had he contented himself with earthly happiness, he would not have deprived himself of the divinity he longed for. Hawthorne's criticism of Aylmer's liberalism arises from an orthodox Christian conception of original sin, modified by Romantic and transcendentalist notions.

"The Birthmark"

In the latter part of the last century there lived a man of science, an eminent proficient in every branch of natural philosophy, who not long before our story opens had made experience of a spiritual affinity more attractive than any chemical one. He had left his laboratory to the care of an assistant, cleared his fine countenance from the furnace smoke, washed the stain of acids from his fingers, and persuaded a beautiful woman to become his wife. In those days when the comparatively recent discovery of electricity and other kindred mysteries of Nature seemed to open paths into the region of miracle, it was not unusual for the love of science to rival the love of woman in its depth and absorbing energy. The higher intellect, the imagination, the spirit, and even the heart might all find their congenial aliment in pursuits which, as some of their ardent votaries believed, would ascend from one step of powerful intelligence to another, until the philosopher should lay his hand on the secret of creative force and perhaps make new worlds for himself. We know not whether Aylmer possessed this degree of faith in man's ultimate control over Nature. He had devoted himself, however, too unreservedly to scientific studies ever to be weaned from them by any second passion. His love for his young wife might prove the stronger of the two; but it could only be by intertwining itself with his love of science, and uniting the strength of the latter to his own.

Such a union accordingly took place, and was attended with truly remarkable consequences and a deeply impressive moral. One day, very soon after their marriage, Aylmer sat gazing at his wife with a trouble in his countenance that grew stronger until he spoke.

"Georgiana," said he, "has it never occurred to you that the mark upon your cheek might be removed?"

"No, indeed," said she, smiling; but perceiving the seriousness of his manner, she blushed deeply. "To tell you the truth it has been so often called a charm that I was simple enough to imagine it might be so."

"Ah, upon another face perhaps it might," replied her husband; "but never on yours. No, dearest Georgiana, you came so nearly perfect from the hand of Nature that this slightest possible defect, which we hesitate whether to term a defect or a beauty, shocks me, as being the visible mark of earthly imperfection."

"Shocks you, my husband!" cried Georgiana, deeply hurt; at first reddening with momentary anger, but then bursting into tears. "Then why did you take me from my mother's side? You cannot love what shocks you!"

To explain this conversation it must be mentioned that in the centre of Georgiana's left cheek there was a singular mark, deeply interwoven, as it were, with the texture and substance of her face. In the usual state of her complexion—a healthy though delicate bloom—the mark wore a tint of deeper crimson, which imperfectly defined its shape amid the surrounding rosiness. When she blushed it gradually became more indistinct, and finally vanished amid the triumphant rush of blood that bathed the whole cheek with its brilliant glow. But if any shifting motion caused her to turn pale there was the mark again, a crimson stain upon the snow, in what Aylmer sometimes deemed an almost fearful distinctness. Its shape bore not a little similarity to the human hand, though of the smallest pygmy size. Georgiana's lovers were wont to say that some fairy at her birth hour had laid her tiny hand upon the infant's cheek, and left this impress there in token of the magic endowments that were to give her such sway over all hearts. Many a desperate swain would have risked life for the privilege of pressing his lips to the mysterious hand. It must not be concealed, however, that the impression wrought by this fairy sign manual varied exceedingly, according to the difference of temperament in the beholders. Some fastidious persons—but they were exclusively of her own sex—affirmed that the bloody hand, as they chose to call it, quite destroyed the effect of Georgiana's beauty, and rendered her countenance even hideous. But it would be as reasonable to say that one of those small blue stains which sometimes occur in the purest statuary marble would convert the Eve of Powers to a monster. Masculine observers, if the birthmark did not heighten their admiration, contented themselves with wishing it away, that the world might possess one living specimen of ideal loveliness without the semblance of a flaw. After his marriage,—for he thought little or nothing of the matter before,—Aylmer discovered that this was the case with himself.

Had she been less beautiful,—if Envy's self could have found aught else to sneer at,—he might have felt his affection heightened by the prettiness of this mimic hand, now vaguely portrayed, now lost, now stealing forth again and glimmering to and fro with every pulse of emotion that throbbed within her heart; but seeing her otherwise so perfect, he found this one defect grow more and more intolerable with every moment of their united lives. It was the fatal flaw of humanity which Nature, in one shape or another, stamps ineffaceably on all her productions, either to imply that they are temporary and finite, or that their perfection must be wrought by toil and pain. The crimson hand expressed the ineludible gripe in which mortality clutches the highest and purest of earthly mould, degrading them into kindred with the lowest, and even with the very brutes, like whom their visible frames return to dust. In this manner, selecting it as the symbol of his wife's liability to sin, sorrow, decay, and death, Aylmer's sombre imagination was not long in rendering the birthmark a frightful object, causing him more trouble and horror than ever Georgiana's beauty, whether of soul or sense, had given him delight.

At all the seasons which should have been their happiest, he invariably and without intending it, nay, in spite of a purpose to the contrary, reverted to this one disastrous topic. Trifling as it at first appeared, it so connected itself with innumerable trains of thought and modes of feeling that it became the central point of all. With the morning twilight Aylmer opened his eyes upon his wife's face and recognized the symbol of imperfection; and when they sat together at the evening hearth his eyes wandered stealthily to her cheek, and beheld, flickering with the blaze of the wood fire, the spectral hand that wrote mortality where he would fain have worshipped. Georgiana soon learned to shudder at his gaze. It needed but a glance with the peculiar expression that his face often wore to change the roses of her cheek into a death-like paleness, amid which the crimson hand was brought strongly out, like a bas-relief of ruby on the whitest marble.

Late one night when the lights were growing dim, so as hardly to betray the stain on the poor wife's cheek, she herself, for the first time, voluntarily took up the subject.

"Do you remember, my dear Aylmer," said she, with a feeble attempt at a smile, "have you any recollection of a dream last night about this odious hand?"

"None! none whatever!" replied Aylmer, starting; but then he added, in a dry, cold tone, affected for the sake of concealing the real depth of his emotion, "I might well dream of it; for before I fell asleep it had taken a pretty firm hold of my fancy."

"And you did dream of it?" continued Georgiana, hastily; for she dreaded lest a gush of tears should interrupt what she had to say. "A terrible dream! I wonder that you can forget it. Is it possible to forget this one expression?—'It is in her heart now; we must have it out!' Reflect, my husband; for by all means I would have you recall that dream."

The mind is in a sad state when Sleep, the all-involving, cannot confine her spectres within the dim region of her sway, but suffers them to break forth, affrighting this actual life with secrets that perchance belong to a deeper one. Aylmer now remembered his dream. He had fancied himself with his servant Aminadab, attempting an operation for the removal of the birthmark; but the deeper went the knife, the deeper sank the hand, until at length its tiny grasp appeared to have caught hold of Georgiana's heart; whence, however, her husband was inexorably resolved to cut or wrench it away.

When the dream had shaped itself perfectly in his memory, Aylmer sat in his wife's presence with a guilty feeling. Truth often finds its way to the mind close muffled in robes of sleep, and then speaks with uncompromising directness of matters in regard to which we practise an unconscious self-deception during our waking moments. Until now he had not been aware of the tyrannizing influence acquired by one idea over his mind, and of the lengths which he might find in his heart to go for the sake of giving himself peace.

"Aylmer," resumed Georgiana, solemnly, "I know not what may be the cost to both of us to rid me of this fatal birthmark. Perhaps its removal may cause cureless deformity; or it may be the stain goes as deep as life itself. Again: do we know that there is a possibility, on any terms, of unclasping the firm gripe of this little hand which was laid upon me before I came into the world?"

"Dearest Georgiana, I have spent much thought upon the subject," hastily interrupted Aylmer. "I am convinced of the perfect practicability of its removal."

"If there be the remotest possibility of it," continued Georgiana, "let the attempt be made at whatever risk. Danger is nothing to me; for life, while this hateful mark makes me the object of your horror and disgust,— life is a burden which I would fling down with joy. Either remove this dreadful hand, or take my wretched life! You have deep science. All the world bears witness of it. You have achieved great wonders. Cannot you remove this little, little mark, which I cover with the tips of two small fingers? Is this beyond your power, for the sake of your own peace, and to save your poor wife from madness?"

"Noblest, dearest, tenderest wife," cried Aylmer, rapturously, "doubt not my power. I have already given this matter the deepest thought— thought which might almost have enlightened me to create a being less perfect than yourself. Georgiana, you have led me deeper than ever into the heart of science. I feel myself fully competent to render this dear cheek as faultless as its fellow; and then, most beloved, what will be my triumph when I shall have corrected what Nature left imperfect in her fairest work! Even Pygmalion, when his sculptured woman assumed life, felt not greater ecstasy than mine will be."

"It is resolved, then," said Georgiana, faintly smiling. "And, Aylmer, spare me not, though you should find the birthmark take refuge in my heart at last."

Her husband tenderly kissed her cheek—her right cheek—not that which bore the impress of the crimson hand.

The next day Aylmer apprised his wife of a plan that he had formed whereby he might have opportunity for the intense thought and constant watchfulness which the proposed operation would require; while Georgiana, likewise, would enjoy the perfect repose essential to its success. They were to seclude themselves in the extensive apartments occupied by Aylmer as a laboratory, and where, during his toilsome youth, he had made discoveries in the elemental powers of Nature that had roused the admiration of all the learned societies in Europe. Seated calmly in this laboratory, the pale philosopher had investigated the secrets of the highest cloud region and of the profoundest mines; he had satisfied himself of the causes that kindled and kept alive the fires of the volcano; and had explained the mystery of fountains, and how it is that they gush forth, some so bright and pure, and others with such rich medicinal virtues, from the dark bosom of the earth. Here, too, at an earlier period, he had studied the wonders of the human frame, and attempted to fathom the very process by which Nature assimilates all her precious influences from earth and air, and from the spiritual world, to create and foster man, her masterpiece. The latter pursuit, however, Aylmer had long laid aside in unwilling recognition of the truth—against which all seekers sooner or later stumble—that our great creative Mother, while she amuses us with apparently working in the broadest sunshine, is yet severely careful to keep her own secrets, and, in spite of her pretended openness, shows us nothing but results. She permits us, indeed, to mar, but seldom to mend, and, like a jealous patentee, on no account to make. Now, however, Aylmer resumed these half-forgotten investigations; not, of course, with such hopes or wishes as first suggested them; but because they involved much physiological truth and lay in the path of his proposed scheme for the treatment of Georgiana.

As he led her over the threshold of the laboratory, Georgiana was cold and tremulous. Aylmer looked cheerfully into her face, with intent to reassure her, but was so startled with the intense glow of the birthmark upon the whiteness of her cheek that he could not restrain a strong convulsive shudder. His wife fainted.

"Aminadab! Aminadab!" shouted Aylmer, stamping violently on the floor.

Forthwith there issued from an inner apartment a man of low stature, but bulky frame, with shaggy hair hanging about his visage, which was grimed with the vapors of the furnace. This personage had been Aylmer's underworker during his whole scientific career, and was admirably fitted for that office by his great mechanical readiness, and the skill with which, while incapable of comprehending a single principle, he executed all the details of his master's experiments. With his vast strength, his shaggy hair, his smoky aspect, and the indescribable earthiness that incrusted him, he seemed to represent man's physical nature; while Aylmer's slender figure, and pale, intellectual face, were no less apt a type of the spiritual element.

"Throw open the door of the boudoir, Aminadab," said Aylmer, "and burn a pastil."

"Yes, master," answered Aminadab, looking intently at the lifeless form of Georgiana; and then he muttered to himself, "If she were my wife, I'd never part with that birthmark."

When Georgiana recovered consciousness she found herself breathing an atmosphere of penetrating fragrance, the gentle potency of which had recalled her from her deathlike faintness. The scene around her looked like enchantment. Aylmer had converted those smoky, dingy, sombre rooms, where he had spent his brightest years in recondite pursuits, into a series of beautiful apartments not unfit to be the secluded abode of a lovely woman. The walls were hung with gorgeous curtains, which imparted the combination of grandeur and grace that no other species of adornment can achieve; and as they fell from the ceiling to the floor, their rich and ponderous folds, concealing all angles and straight lines, appeared to shut in the scene from infinite space. For aught Georgiana knew, it might be a pavilion among the clouds. And Aylmer, excluding the sunshine, which would have interfered with his chemical processes, had supplied its place with perfumed lamps, emitting flames of various hue, but all uniting in a soft, impurpled radiance. He now knelt by his wife's side, watching her earnestly, but without alarm; for he was confident in his science, and felt that he could draw a magic circle round her within which no evil might intrude.

"Where am I? Ah, I remember," said Georgiana, faintly; and she placed her hand over her cheek to hide the terrible mark from her husband's eyes.

"Fear not, dearest!" exclaimed he. "Do not shrink from me! Believe me, Georgiana, I even rejoice in this single imperfection, since it will be such a rapture to remove it."

"Oh, spare me!" sadly replied his wife. "Pray do not look at it again. I never can forget that convulsive shudder."

In order to soothe Georgiana, and, as it were, to release her mind from the burden of actual things, Aylmer now put in practice some of the light and playful secrets which science had taught him among its profounder lore. Airy figures, absolutely bodiless ideas, and forms of unsubstantial beauty came and danced before her, imprinting their momentary footsteps on beams of light. Though she had some indistinct idea of the method of these optical phenomena, still the illusion was almost perfect enough to warrant the belief that her husband possessed sway over the spiritual world. Then again, when she felt a wish to look forth from her seclusion, immediately, as if her thoughts were answered, the procession of external existence flitted across a screen. The scenery and the figures of actual life were perfectly represented, but with that bewitching, yet indescribable difference which always makes a picture, an image, or a shadow so much more attractive than the original. When wearied of this, Aylmer bade her cast her eyes upon a vessel containing a quantity of earth. She did so, with little interest at first; but was soon startled to perceive the germ of a plant shooting upward from the soil. Then came the slender stalk; the leaves gradually unfolded themselves; and amid them was a perfect and lovely flower.

"It is magical!" cried Georgiana. "I dare not touch it."

"Nay, pluck it," answered Aylmer,—"pluck it, and inhale its brief perfume while you may. The flower will wither in a few moments and leave nothing save its brown seed vessels; but thence may be perpetuated a race as ephemeral as itself."

But Georgiana had no sooner touched the flower than the whole plant suffered a blight, its leaves turning coal-black as if by the agency of fire.

"There was too powerful a stimulus," said Aylmer, thoughtfully.

To make up for this abortive experiment, he proposed to take her portrait by a scientific process of his own invention. It was to be effected by rays of light striking upon a polished plate of metal. Georgiana assented; but, on looking at the result, was affrighted to find the features of the portrait blurred and indefinable; while the minute figure of a hand appeared where the cheek should have been. Aylmer snatched the metallic plate and threw it into a jar of corrosive acid.

Soon, however, he forgot these mortifying failures. In the intervals of study and chemical experiment he came to her flushed and exhausted, but seemed invigorated by her presence, and spoke in glowing language of the resources of his art. He gave a history of the long dynasty of the alchemists, who spent so many ages in quest of the universal solvent by which the golden principle might be elicited from all things vile and base. Aylmer appeared to believe that, by the plainest scientific logic, it was altogether within the limits of possibility to discover this long-sought medium; "but," he added, "a philosopher who should go deep enough to acquire the power would attain too lofty a wisdom to stoop to the exercise of it." Not less singular were his opinions in regard to the elixir vitæ. He more than intimated that it was at his option to concoct a liquid that should prolong life for years, perhaps interminably; but that it would produce a discord in Nature which all the world, and chiefly the quaffer of the immortal nostrum, would find cause to curse.

"Aylmer, are you in earnest?" asked Georgiana, looking at him with amazement and fear. "It is terrible to possess such power, or even to dream of possessing it."

"Oh, do not tremble, my love," said her husband. "I would not wrong either you or myself by working such inharmonious effects upon our lives; but I would have you consider how trifling, in comparison, is the skill requisite to remove this little hand."

At the mention of the birthmark, Georgiana, as usual, shrank as if a redhot iron had touched her cheek.

Again Aylmer applied himself to his labors. She could hear his voice in the distant furnace room giving directions to Aminadab, whose harsh, uncouth, misshapen tones were audible in response, more like the grunt or growl of a brute than human speech. After hours of absence, Aylmer reappeared and proposed that she should now examine his cabinet of chemical products and natural treasures of the earth. Among the former he showed her a small vial, in which, he remarked, was contained a gentle yet most powerful fragrance, capable of impregnating all the breezes that blow across a kingdom. They were of inestimable value, the contents of that little vial; and, as he said so, he threw some of the perfume into the air and filled the room with piercing and invigorating delight.

"And what is this?" asked Georgiana, pointing to a small crystal globe containing a gold-colored liquid. "It is so beautiful to the eye that I could imagine it the elixir of life."

"In one sense it is," replied Aylmer; "or, rather, the elixir of immortality. It is the most precious poison that ever was concocted in this world. By its aid I could apportion the lifetime of any mortal at whom you might point your finger. The strength of the dose would determine whether he were to linger out years, or drop dead in the midst of a breath. No king on his guarded throne could keep his life if I, in my private station, should deem that the welfare of millions justified me in depriving him of it."

"Why do you keep such a terrific drug?" inquired Georgiana in horror.

"Do not mistrust me, dearest," said her husband, smiling; "its virtuous potency is yet greater than its harmful one. But see! here is a powerful cosmetic. With a few drops of this in a vase of water, freckles may be washed away as easily as the hands are cleansed. A stronger infusion would take the blood out of the cheek, and leave the rosiest beauty a pale ghost."

"Is it with this lotion that you intend to bathe my cheek?" asked Georgiana, anxiously.

"Oh, no," hastily replied her husband; "this is merely superficial. Your case demands a remedy that shall go deeper."

In his interviews with Georgiana, Aylmer generally made minute inquiries as to her sensations and whether the confinement of the rooms and the temperature of the atmosphere agreed with her. These questions had such a particular drift that Georgiana began to conjecture that she was already subjected to certain physical influences, either breathed in with the fragrant air or taken with her food. She fancied likewise, but it might be altogether fancy, that there was a stirring up of her system—a strange, indefinite sensation creeping through her veins, and tingling, half painfully, half pleasurably, at her heart. Still, whenever she dared to look into the mirror, there she beheld herself pale as a white rose and with the crimson birthmark stamped upon her cheek. Not even Aylmer now hated it so much as she.

To dispel the tedium of the hours which her husband found it necessary to devote to the processes of combination and analysis, Georgiana turned over the volumes of his scientific library. In many dark old tomes she met with chapters full of romance and poetry. They were the works of the philosophers of the middle ages, such as Albertus Magnus, Cornelius Agrippa, Paracelsus, and the famous friar who created the prophetic Brazen Head. All these antique naturalists stood in advance of their centuries, yet were imbued with some of their credulity, and therefore were believed, and perhaps imagined themselves to have acquired from the investigation of Nature a power above Nature, and from physics a sway over the spiritual world. Hardly less curious and imaginative were the early volumes of the Transactions of the Royal Society, in which the members, knowing little of the limits of natural possibility, were continually recording wonders or proposing methods whereby wonders might be wrought.

But to Georgiana the most engrossing volume was a large folio from her husband's own hand, in which he had recorded every experiment of his scientific career, its original aim, the methods adopted for its development, and its final success or failure, with the circumstances to which either event was attributable. The book, in truth, was both the history and emblem of his ardent, ambitious, imaginative, yet practical and laborious life. He handled physical details as if there were nothing beyond them; yet spiritualized them all, and redeemed himself from materialism by his strong and eager aspiration towards the infinite. In his grasp the veriest clod of earth assumed a soul. Georgiana, as she read, reverenced Aylmer and loved him more profoundly than ever, but with a less entire dependence on his judgment than heretofore. Much as he had accomplished, she could not but observe that his most splendid successes were almost invariably failures, if compared with the ideal at which he aimed. His brightest diamonds were the merest pebbles, and felt to be so by himself, in comparison with the inestimable gems which lay hidden beyond his reach. The volume, rich with achievements that had won renown for its author, was yet as melancholy a record as ever mortal hand had penned. It was the sad confession and continual exemplification of the shortcomings of the composite man, the spirit burdened with clay and working in matter, and of the despair that assails the higher nature at finding itself so miserably thwarted by the earthly part. Perhaps every man of genius in whatever sphere might recognize the image of his own experience in Aylmer's journal.

So deeply did these reflections affect Georgiana that she laid her face upon the open volume and burst into tears. In this situation she was found by her husband.

"It is dangerous to read in a sorcerer's books," said he with a smile, though his countenance was uneasy and displeased. "Georgiana, there are pages in that volume which I can scarcely glance over and keep my senses. Take heed lest it prove as detrimental to you."

"It has made me worship you more than ever," said she.

"Ah, wait for this one success," rejoined he, "then worship me if you will. I shall deem myself hardly unworthy of it. But come, I have sought you for the luxury of your voice. Sing to me, dearest."

So she poured out the liquid music of her voice to quench the thirst of his spirit. He then took his leave with a boyish exuberance of gayety, assuring her that her seclusion would endure but a little longer, and that the result was already certain. Scarcely had he departed when Georgiana felt irresistibly impelled to follow him. She had forgotten to inform Aylmer of a symptom which for two or three hours past had begun to excite her attention. It was a sensation in the fatal birthmark, not painful, but which induced a restlessness throughout her system. Hastening after her husband, she intruded for the first time into the laboratory.

The first thing that struck her eye was the furnace, that hot and feverish worker, with the intense glow of its fire, which by the quantities of soot clustered above it seemed to have been burning for ages. There was a distilling apparatus in full operation. Around the room were retorts, tubes, cylinders, crucibles, and other apparatus of chemical research. An electrical machine stood ready for immediate use. The atmosphere felt oppressively close, and was tainted with gaseous odors which had been tormented forth by the processes of science. The severe and homely simplicity of the apartment, with its naked walls and brick pavement, looked strange, accustomed as Georgiana had become to the fantastic elegance of her boudoir. But what chiefly, indeed almost solely, drew her attention, was the aspect of Aylmer himself.

He was pale as death, anxious and absorbed, and hung over the furnace as if it depended upon his utmost watchfulness whether the liquid which it was distilling should be the draught of immortal happiness or misery. How different from the sanguine and joyous mien that he had assumed for Georgiana's encouragement!

"Carefully now, Aminadab; carefully, thou human machine; carefully, thou man of clay!" muttered Aylmer, more to himself than his assistant. "Now, if there be a thought too much or too little, it is all over."

"Ho! ho!" mumbled Aminadab. "Look, master! look!"

Aylmer raised his eyes hastily, and at first reddened, then grew paler than ever, on beholding Georgiana. He rushed towards her and seized her arm with a gripe that left the print of his fingers upon it.

"Why do you come hither? Have you no trust in your husband?" cried he, impetuously. "Would you throw the blight of that fatal birthmark over my labors? It is not well done. Go, prying woman, go!"

"Nay, Aylmer," said Georgiana with the firmness of which she possessed no stinted endowment, "it is not you that have a right to complain. You mistrust your wife; you have concealed the anxiety with which you watch the development of this experiment. Think not so unworthily of me, my husband. Tell me all the risk we run, and fear not that I shall shrink; for my share in it is far less than your own."

"No, no, Georgiana!" said Aylmer, impatiently; "it must not be."

"I submit," replied she calmly. "And, Aylmer, I shall quaff whatever draught you bring me; but it will be on the same principle that would induce me to take a dose of poison if offered by your hand."

"My noble wife," said Aylmer, deeply moved, "I knew not the height and depth of your nature until now. Nothing shall be concealed. Know, then, that this crimson hand, superficial as it seems, has clutched its grasp into your being with a strength of which I had no previous conception. I have already administered agents powerful enough to do aught except to change your entire physical system. Only one thing remains to be tried. If that fails us we are ruined."

"Why did you hesitate to tell me this?" asked she.

"Because, Georgiana," said Aylmer, in a low voice, "there is danger."

"Danger? There is but one danger—that this horrible stigma shall be left upon my cheek!" cried Georgiana. "Remove it, remove it, whatever be the cost, or we shall both go mad!"

"Heaven knows your words are too true," said Aylmer, sadly. "And now, dearest, return to your boudoir. In a little while all will be tested."

He conducted her back and took leave of her with a solemn tenderness which spoke far more than his words how much was now at stake. After his departure Georgiana became rapt in musings. She considered the character of Aylmer, and did it completer justice than at any previous moment. Her heart exulted, while it trembled, at his honorable love—so pure and lofty that it would accept nothing less than perfection nor miserably make itself contented with an earthlier nature than he had dreamed of. She felt how much more precious was such a sentiment than that meaner kind which would have borne with the imperfection for her sake, and have been guilty of treason to holy love by degrading its perfect idea to the level of the actual; and with her whole spirit she prayed that, for a single moment, she might satisfy his highest and deepest conception. Longer than one moment she well knew it could not be; for his spirit was ever on the march, ever ascending, and each instant required something that was beyond the scope of the instant before.

The sound of her husband's footsteps aroused her. He bore a crystal goblet containing a liquor colorless as water, but bright enough to be the draught of immortality. Aylmer was pale; but it seemed rather the consequence of a highly-wrought state of mind and tension of spirit than of fear or doubt.

"The concoction of the draught has been perfect," said he, in answer to Georgiana's look. "Unless all my science have deceived me, it cannot fail."

"Save on your account, my dearest Aylmer," observed his wife, "I might wish to put off this birthmark of mortality by relinquishing mortality itself in preference to any other mode. Life is but a sad possession to those who have attained precisely the degree of moral advancement at which I stand. Were I weaker and blinder it might be happiness. Were I stronger, it might be endured hopefully. But, being what I find myself, methinks I am of all mortals the most fit to die."

"You are fit for heaven without tasting death!" replied her husband. "But why do we speak of dying? The draught cannot fail. Behold its effect upon this plant."

On the window seat there stood a geranium diseased with yellow blotches, which had overspread all its leaves. Aylmer poured a small quantity of the liquid upon the soil in which it grew. In a little time, when the roots of the plant had taken up the moisture, the unsightly blotches began to be extinguished in a living verdure.

"There needed no proof," said Georgiana, quietly. "Give me the goblet. I joyfully stake all upon your word."

"Drink, then, thou lofty creature!" exclaimed Aylmer, with fervid admiration. "There is no taint of imperfection on thy spirit. Thy sensible frame, too, shall soon be all perfect."

She quaffed the liquid and returned the goblet to his hand.

"It is grateful," said she with a placid smile. "Methinks it is like water from a heavenly fountain; for it contains I know not what of unobtrusive fragrance and deliciousness. It allays a feverish thirst that had parched me for many days. Now, dearest, let me sleep. My earthly senses are closing over my spirit like the leaves around the heart of a rose at sunset."

She spoke the last words with a gentle reluctance, as if it required almost more energy than she could command to pronounce the faint and lingering syllables. Scarcely had they loitered through her lips ere she was lost in slumber. Aylmer sat by her side, watching her aspect with the emotions proper to a man the whole value of whose existence was involved in the process now to be tested. Mingled with this mood, however, was the philosophic investigation characteristic of the man of science. Not the minutest symptom escaped him. A heightened flush of the cheek, a slight irregularity of breath, a quiver of the eyelid, a hardly perceptible tremor through the frame,— such were the details which, as the moments passed, he wrote down in his folio volume. Intense thought had set its stamp upon every previous page of that volume, but the thoughts of years were all concentrated upon the last.

While thus employed, he failed not to gaze often at the fatal hand, and not without a shudder. Yet once, by a strange and unaccountable impulse, he pressed it with his lips. His spirit recoiled, however, in the very act; and Georgiana, out of the midst of her deep sleep, moved uneasily and murmured as if in remonstrance. Again Aylmer resumed his watch. Nor was it without avail. The crimson hand, which at first had been strongly visible upon the marble paleness of Georgiana's cheek, now grew more faintly outlined. She remained not less pale than ever; but the birthmark, with every breath that came and went, lost somewhat of its former distinctness. Its presence had been awful; its departure was more awful still. Watch the stain of the rainbow fading out of the sky, and you will know how that mysterious symbol passed away.

"By Heaven! it is well-nigh gone!" said Aylmer to himself, in almost irrepressible ecstasy. "I can scarcely trace it now. Success! success! And now it is like the faintest rose color. The lightest flush of blood across her cheek would overcome it. But she is so pale!"

He drew aside the window curtain and suffered the light of natural day to fall into the room and rest upon her cheek. At the same time he heard a gross, hoarse chuckle, which he had long known as his servant Aminadab's expression of delight.

"Ah, clod! ah, earthly mass!" cried Aylmer, laughing in a sort of frenzy, "you have served me well! Matter and spirit—earth and heaven—have both done their part in this! Laugh, thing of the senses! You have earned the right to laugh."

These exclamations broke Georgiana's sleep. She slowly unclosed her eyes and gazed into the mirror which her husband had arranged for that purpose. A faint smile flitted over her lips when she recognized how barely perceptible was now that crimson hand which had once blazed forth with such disastrous brilliancy as to scare away all their happiness. But then her eyes sought Aylmer's face with a trouble and anxiety that he could by no means account for.

"My poor Aylmer!" murmured she.

"Poor? Nay, richest, happiest, most favored!" exclaimed he. "My peerless bride, it is successful! You are perfect!"

"My poor Aylmer," she repeated, with a more than human tenderness, "you have aimed loftily; you have done nobly. Do not repent that with so high and pure a feeling, you have rejected the best the earth could offer. Alymer, dearest Aylmer, I am dying!"

Alas! it was too true! The fatal hand had grappled with the mystery of life, and was the bond by which an angelic spirit kept itself in union with a mortal frame. As the last crimson tint of the birthmark—that sole token of human imperfection—faded from her cheek, the parting breath of the now perfect woman passed into the atmosphere, and her soul, lingering a moment near her husband, took its heavenward flight. Then a hoarse, chuckling laugh was heard again! Thus ever does the gross fatality of earth exult in its invariable triumph over the immortal essence which, in this dim sphere of half development, demands the completeness of a higher state. Yet, had Aylmer reached a profounder wisdom, he need not thus have flung away the happiness which would have woven his mortal life of the selfsame texture with the celestial. The momentary circumstance was too strong for him; he failed to look beyond the shadowy scope of time, and, living once for all in eternity, to find the perfect future in the present.

The Democratic Mystic
Walt Whitman / "Eidólons"

Walt Whitman (1819–1892) described his own style as a "barbaric yawp"; that phrase itself perhaps explains why many critics, both American and European, saw in Whitman's poetry the first authentically American literary voice. His major work, Leaves of Grass, *underwent continual revision from its first publication in 1855 until his death. The revisions, however, neither altered the book's original intent nor constrained Whitman's freedom of expression: the form, free verse, was the natural embodiment of a poetic vision which sought to embrace the diversity of life with democratic zest and impartiality. He knew from the beginning that his poems would be constantly revised, for such revision was part of the organic expression of his own wholeness.*

While he was editor of the Brooklyn Daily Eagle *in 1847, Whitman was already working toward his ideals of freedom—the sanctity of the individual ego and a visionary sense of rapt identity with all people and all things. Because of his advocacy of the Free Soil Movement, he lost several jobs on newspapers and had to eke out his living by hack writing and carpentry work. During the Civil War he worked as a volunteer nurse in Washington hospitals; after the war he observed, in his clerical jobs with the government, the growing capitalistic influence on national politics.*

Whitman's unabashed acceptance of all of life—from the beautiful to the bawdy, from the delicate to the indecent—early earned him the suspicion of immorality. Stricken with paralysis in 1873, Whitman lived with his brother in Camden, New Jersey; here testimonials from Emerson and Thoreau, Burroughs and Ingersoll competed with public pressures to ban his poems. His doctrine of democratic love bore a kinship with the transcendentalist concerns for a universal oversoul, but its frank espousal of every concrete particular, from flesh to dung, tended to alienate in varying degrees many of the nineteenth-century minds who saw in his writing an indiscriminate liberalism of cosmic tolerance. It remained for the twentieth century to find in his work a genuine spokesman for a pluralistic unity.

The seventh poem in the final edition of Leaves of Grass *is entitled "Eidólons"; it expresses, in extreme form, Whitman's mystic, almost Indian, acceptance of a melting sense of identity with everything. The title comes from a Greek word which meant, in Homer, a phantom or ghost of a psyche; later it came to mean an image, and in the Septuagint and New Testament it meant an idol or god. This "old, old urge" for eidólons, for a continuous and pantheistic pantheon, includes all of the "mutable . . . materials, changing, crumbling, re-cohering." The universe exceeds, in delicacy and hugeness, the grasp of the rational mind; only "the prophet and bard" can "mediate" the experiential vision of things "to the Modern, to Democracy." Such sentiments and language explain why Whitman has become the beloved archetype of recent poets and critics like Ginsberg and Fiedler.*

"Eidólons"

        I met a seer,
Passing the hues and objects of the world,
The fields of art and learning, pleasure, sense,
        To glean eidólons.

        Put in thy chants said he,
No more the puzzling hour nor day, nor segments, parts, put in,
Put first before the rest as light for all and entrance-song of all,
        That of eidólons.

        Ever the dim beginning,
Ever the growth, the rounding of the circle,
Ever the summit and the merge at last, (to surely start again,)
        Eidólons! eidólons!

        Ever the mutable,
Ever materials, changing, crumbling, re-cohering,
Ever the ateliers, the factories divine,
        Issuing eidólons.

Lo, I or you,
Or woman, man, or state, known or unknown,
We seeming solid wealth, strength, beauty build,
But really build eidólons.

The ostent evanescent,
The substance of an artist's mood or savan's studies long,
Or warrior's, martyr's, hero's toils,
To fashion his eidólon.

Of every human life,
(The units gather'd, posted, not a thought, emotion, deed, left out,)
The whole or large or small summ'd, added up,
In its eidólon.

The old, old urge,
Based on the ancient pinnacles, lo, newer, higher pinnacles,
From science and the modern still impell'd,
The old, old urge, eidólons.

The present now and here,
America's busy, teeming, intricate whirl,
Of aggregate and segregate for only thence releasing,
To-day's eidólons.

These with the past,
Of vanish'd lands, of all the reigns of kings across the sea,
Old conquerors, old campaigns, old sailor's voyages,
Joining eidólons.

Densities, growth, facades,
Strata of mountains, soils, rocks, giant trees,
Far-born, far-dying, living long, to leave,
Eidólons everlasting.

Exaltè, rapt, ecstatic,
The visible but their womb of birth,
Of orbic tendencies to shape and shape and shape,
The mighty earth-eidólon.

All space, all time,
(The stars, the terrible perturbations of the suns,
Swelling, collapsing, ending, serving their longer, shorter use,)
Fill'd with eidólons only.

The noiseless myriads,
The infinite oceans where the rivers empty,
The separate countless free identities, like eyesight,
The true realities, eidólons.

Not this the world,
Nor these the universes, they the universes,
Purport and end, ever the permanent life of life,
Eidólons, eidólons.

Beyond thy lectures learn'd professor,
Beyond thy telescope or spectroscope observer keen, beyond all mathematics,
Beyond the doctor's surgery, anatomy, beyond the chemist with his chemistry,
The entities of entities, eidólons.

Unfixed yet fix'd,
Ever shall be, ever have been and are,
Sweeping the present to the infinite future,
Eidólons, eidólons, eidólons.

The prophet and the bard,
Shall yet maintain themselves, in higher stages yet,
Shall mediate to the Modern, to Democracy, interpret yet to them,
God and eidólons.

And thee my soul,
Joys, ceaseless exercises, exaltations,
Thy yearning amply fed at last, prepared to meet,
Thy mates, eidólons.

Thy body permanent,
The body lurking there within thy body,
The only purport of the form thou art, the real I myself,
An image, an eidólon.

Thy very songs not in thy songs,
No special strains to sing, none for itself,
But from the whole resulting, rising at last and floating,
A round full-orb'd eidólon.

The Cosmic Court Martial
Herman Melville / from *Billy Budd*

Herman Melville (1819–1891) is now regarded as one of America's greatest writers, but at the time of his death, his name had virtually disappeared from the history of American letters. Despite the publication of Moby Dick in 1851, Rudyard Kipling, for example, said in the 1890's that someone ought to write a novel about whaling. Melville's early works, like Typee in 1846, had achieved brief popularity as tales of adventure, but as his novels dug deeper and deeper into the metaphysical and psychological depths of human existence, disappointed readers turned away from him.

Born of a well-to-do New York family, Melville underwent personal and financial difficulties in the early 1830's when his father lost his money and died. From his mother and from the Dutch Reformed Church, Melville learned an austere and harsh Calvinism; the doctrine of original sin pervades all of his work despite his own skeptical agnosticism, which he found expressed, ironically, in Ecclesiastes. After a brief formal education and some experience in business and as a teacher, he went to sea in 1839. From that time on, Melville's genius principally recorded, analyzed, and reflected upon marine experiences. He served on merchant and whaling ships and on a United States man-of-war; his military experience dominates his final prose work, Billy Budd *(1891), from which this selection is taken.*

The publication of Pierre *(1851), a novel dealing with incest and suicide, marked the end of Melville's limited popularity; for the next forty years he continued to write, both prose and poetry, but his readership dwindled. Like his friend Hawthorne, Melville for many years earned a living as a customs inspector.* Billy Budd, *completed in the year of his death, remained unpublished until 1924. Since that time his reputation has grown until his work is now required reading in virtually every college in America.*

Billy Budd *deals with an innocent, almost prelapsarian, youth who is taken from a British merchant ship named* The Rights of Man, *after Thomas Paine's famous work, and impressed into service aboard a British man-of-war, the H.M.S.* Indomitable, *during the French Revolution. Budd's moral innocence is marked only by a biological birth defect—reminiscent of Aylmer's wife in Hawthorne's "The Birthmark"—which manifests itself as a stammer. He attracts the malign attention of the master-at-arms Claggart, a symbolic embodiment of evil, who seems to use his position as Budd's superior to tempt him into insubordination, with the design of destroying him. Budd's vocal impediment leads him to answer Claggart by action rather than reason; he strikes the master-at-arms dead. In the court martial that follows, Captain Vere—the etymological symbolism of the names is obvious—is torn between his love for Billy, compounded by a clear knowledge of Billy's innocence, and a sense of necessity for upholding the strictest military laws in a time of war, a war against the rationalistic liberalism of revolutionary France. Vere's impassioned defense of law and order, even at the expense of innocence, is profound, and Billy Budd's clear-voiced words from the gallows—"God bless Captain Vere"—are both an ironic forgiveness and a sincere sanction. The selection below is Vere's speech to the court.*

. . . What he said was to this effect: "Hitherto I have been but the witness, little more; and I should hardly think now to take another tone, that of your coadjutor, for the time, did I not perceive in you—at the crisis too—a troubled hesitancy, proceeding, I doubt not from the clash of military duty with moral scruple—scruple vitalized by compassion. For the compassion, how can I otherwise than share it? But, mindful of paramount obligations I strive against scruples that may tend to enervate decision. Not, gentlemen, that I hide from myself that the case is an exceptional one. Speculatively regarded, it well might be referred to a jury of casuists. But for us here, acting not as casuists or moralists, it is a case practical, and under martial law practically to be dealt with.

"But your scruples: do they move as in a dusk? Challenge them. Make them advance and declare themselves. Come now: do they import something like this: If, mindless of palliating circumstances, we are bound to regard the death of the Master-at-Arms as the prisoner's deed, then does that deed constitute a capital crime whereof the penalty is a mortal one. But in natural justice is nothing but the prisoner's overt act to be considered? How can we adjudge to summary and shameful death a fellow-creature innocent before God, and whom we feel to be so?—Does that state it aright? You sign sad assent. Well, I too feel that, the full force of that. It is Nature. But do these buttons that we wear attest that our allegiance is to Nature? No, to the King. Though the ocean, which is inviolate Nature primeval, though this be the element where we move and have our being as sailors, yet as the King's officers lies our duty in a sphere correspondingly natural? So little is that true, that in receiving our commissions we in the most important regards ceased to be natural free agents. When war is declared, are we the commissioned fighters previously consulted? We fight at command. If our judgments approve the war, that is but coincidence. So in other particulars. So now. For suppose condemnation to follow these present proceedings. Would it be so much we ourselves that would condemn as it would be martial law operating through us? For that law and the rigor of it, we are not responsible. Our vowed responsibility is in this: That however pitilessly that law may operate in any instance, we nevertheless adhere to it and administer it.

"But the exceptional in the matter moves the hearts within you. Even so too is mine moved. But let not warm hearts betray heads that should be cool. Ashore in a criminal case will an upright judge allow himself off the bench to be waylaid by some tender kinswoman of the accused seeking to touch him with her tearful plea? Well the heart, sometimes the feminine in man, here is as that piteous woman, and hard though it be, she must here be ruled out."

He paused, earnestly studying them for a moment; then resumed.

"But something in your aspect seems to urge that it is not solely the heart that moves in you, but also the conscience, the private conscience. But tell me whether or not, occupying the position we do, private conscience should not yield to that imperial one formulated in the code under which alone we officially proceed?"

Here the three men moved in their seats, less convinced than agitated by the course of an argument troubling but the more the spontaneous conflict within.

Perceiving which, the speaker paused for a moment; then abruptly changing his tone, went on.

"To steady us a bit, let us recur to the facts.—In wartime at sea a man-of-war's-man strikes his superior in grade, and the blow kills. Apart from its effect the blow itself is, according to the Articles of War, a capital crime. Furthermore—"

"Aye, Sir," emotionally broke in the officer of marines, "in one sense it was. But surely Budd purposed neither mutiny nor homicide."

"Surely not, my good man. And before a court less arbitrary and more merciful than a martial one that plea would largely extenuate. At the Last Assizes it shall acquit. But how here? We proceed under the law of the Mutiny Act. In feature no child can resemble his father more than that Act resembles in spirit the thing from which it derives—War. In His Majesty's service— in this ship indeed—there are Englishmen forced to fight for the King against their will. Against their conscience, for aught we know. Though as their fellow-creatures some of us may appreciate their position, yet as navy officers, what reck we of it? Still less recks the enemy. Our impressed men he would fain cut down in the same swath with our volunteers. As regards the enemy's naval conscripts, some of whom may even share our own abhorrence of the regicidal French Directory, it is the same on our side. War looks but to the frontage, the appearance. And the Mutiny Act, War's child, takes after the father. Budd's intent or non-intent is nothing to the purpose.

"But while, put to it by those anxieties in you which I cannot but respect, I only repeat myself—while thus strangely we prolong proceedings that should be summary—the enemy may be sighted and an engagement result. We must do; and one of two things must we do—condemn or let go."

"Can we not convict and yet mitigate the penalty?" asked the junior Lieutenant, here speaking, and falteringly, for the first.

"Lieutenant, were that clearly lawful for us under the circumstances consider the consequence of such clemency. The people" (meaning the ship's company) "have native sense; most of them are familiar with our naval usage and tradition; and how would they take it? Even could you explain to them—which our official position forbids—they, long moulded by arbitrary discipline, have not that kind of intelligent responsiveness that might qualify them to comprehend and discriminate. No, to the people the Foretopman's deed, however it be worded in the announcement, will be plain homicide committed in a flagrant act of mutiny. What penalty for that should follow, they know. But it does not follow. *Why?* They will ruminate. You know what sailors are. Will they not revert to the recent outbreak at the Nore? Aye. They know the well-founded alarm—the panic it struck throughout England. Your clement sentence they would account pusillanimous. They would think that we flinch, that we are afraid of them—afraid of practicing a lawful rigor singularly demanded at this juncture, lest it should provoke new troubles. What shame to us such a conjecture on their part, and how deadly to discipline. You see then, whither, prompted by duty and the law, I steadfastly drive. But I beseech you, my friends, do not take me amiss. I feel as you do for this unfortunate boy. But did he know our hearts, I take him to be of that generous nature that he would feel even for us on whom in this military necessity so heavy a compulsion is laid."

With that, crossing the deck he resumed his place by the sashed port-hole, tacitly leaving the three to come to a decision. On the cabin's opposite side the troubled court sat silent. Loyal lieges, plain and practical, though at bottom they dissented from some points Captain Vere had put to them, they were without the faculty, hardly had the inclination to gainsay one whom they felt to be an earnest man, one too not less their superior in mind than in naval rank. But it is not improbable that even such of his words as were not without influence over them less came home to them than his closing appeal to their instinct as sea-officers in the forethought he threw out as to the practical consequences to discipline, considering the unconfirmed tone of the fleet at the time, should a man-of-war's-man's violent killing at sea of a superior in grade be allowed to pass for aught else than a capital crime, so demanding prompt infliction of the penalty. . . .

Says a writer whom few know, "Forty years after a battle it is easy for a noncombatant to reason about how it ought to have been fought. It is another thing personally and under fire to direct the fighting while involved in the obscuring smoke of it. Much so with respect to other emergencies involving considerations both practical and moral, and when it is imperative promptly to act. The greater the fog the more it imperils the steamer, and speed is put on though at the hazard of running somebody down. Little ween the snug card-players in the cabin of the responsibilities of the sleepless man on the bridge."

In brief, Billy Budd was formally convicted and sentenced to be hung at the yard-arm in the early morning-watch, it being now night. Otherwise, as is customary in such cases, the sentence would forthwith have been carried out. In war-time, on the field or in the fleet, a mortal punishment decreed by a drumhead court—on the field sometimes decreed by but a nod from the General—follows without delay on the heel of conviction, without appeal. . . .

The Divinity of the Senses
Trumbull Stickney/"Live blindly . . ."

Trumbull Stickney (1874–1904) was the first American to receive the Doctorat ès Lettres *from the University of Paris; his brilliant promise as a classical scholar ended after only one year of teaching, when he died of a brain tumor at the age of thirty. Like Santayana, he was devoted to Lucretius and wrote a poem in honor of the Roman Epicurean. The notion that "God is dead" is not a new thing, of course; Julian the Apostate, the last pagan Roman emperor— about whom Stickney, characteristically, began a tragedy—used to wonder why Christians worshiped what he called "a dead Jew." And in Stickney's own nineteenth century, Nietzsche had proclaimed the very slogan "God is dead," a theme which recurs in many of Thomas Hardy's poems. Included here is Stickney's sonnet "Live blindly and upon the hour" which, like other of his poems, starts from the idea of a world without God and searches for a humanistic religion. In a later poem Stickney writes: "Man stood alone . . . awaiting . . . The Coming of the Lord. And behold, none/Did come."*

The particular form of religious humanism advocated by Stickney is Hellenism, the lush almost decadent Hellenism peculiar to the later nineteenth century. His sonnet begins with an echo of Jocasta's famous line in Oedipus Rex: *"It is best to live at random and as best you can." Aside from this, his poem reflects the modern mood of a conscience that feels itself in a world where God no longer lives.*

Live blindly and upon the hour. The Lord,
Who was the Future, died full long ago.
Knowledge which is the Past is folly. Go,
Poor child, and be not to thyself abhorred.
Around thine earth sun-wingèd winds do blow
And planets roll; a meteor draws his sword;
The rainbow breaks his seven-coloured chord
And the long strips of river-silver flow:
Awake! Give thyself to the lovely hours.
Drinking their lips, catch thou the dream in flight
About their fragile hairs' aërial gold.
Thou art divine, thou livest,—as of old
Apollo springing naked to the light,
And all his island shivered into flowers.
   [1898]

The Judgment of a Materialist
Anthony Hecht/"Upon the Death of George Santayana"

Anthony Hecht (1923–   ) is currently teaching at the University of Rochester (New York); he has also taught at Kenyon College, the State University of Iowa, and at Smith and Bard colleges. Winner of numerous awards for poetic distinction, he has recently introduced, with John Hollander, a new form of light verse called "Jiggery-Pokery," a double dactyl. Echoes of Greek literature, the doctrine of original sin, and medieval Catholicism frequently appear in his poetry. "Upon the Death of George Santayana," reprinted here, combines all three in an allusively orthodox indictment of the philosopher's elegant and materialistic aestheticism.

Hecht's poem refers to the closing days of Santayana's life, when the philosopher, living in a hospital managed by Roman Catholic sisters, had pathetic second thoughts about his philosophy. Santayana told reporters, on his eighty-eighth birthday, "I find things are not so simple as I had imagined, and so I am not reconciled." His last words to the young American Catholic who befriended him were, "I won't see you again. Now I am alone." He could not, even then, return to the orthodox Christianity of his birth; instead, he was willing to settle for a Greek limbo, where he could indulge in his Stickney-like Hellenism with Epicureans and Platonists. The judgment passed by Hecht on Santayana's humanism is uttered by Socrates, speaking not in a Greek but a Christian limbo, and it is couched in language reminiscent of Dante. Mere humanism, symbolized by the figure of Alcibiades, is seen as ultimately perverted and is condemned to the icy misery inflicted upon those who misuse their intellects.

"Upon the Death of George Santayana"

Down every passage of the cloister hung
A dark wood cross on a white plaster wall;
But in the court were roses, not as tongue
Might have them, something of Christ's blood grown small,

But just as roses, and at three o'clock
Their essences, inseparably bouqueted,
Seemed more than Christ's last breath, and rose to mock
An elderly man for whom the Sisters prayed.

What heart can know itself? The Sibyl speaks
Mirthless and unbedizened things, but who
Can fathom her intent? Loving the Greeks,
He whispered to a nun who strove to woo
His spirit unto God by prayer and fast,
'Pray that I go to Limbo, if it please
Heaven to let my soul regard at last
Democritus, Plato and Socrates.'

And so it was. The river, as foretold,
Ran darkly by; under his tongue he found
Coin for the passage; the ferry tossed and rolled;
The sages stood on their appointed ground,
Sighing, all as foretold. The mind was tasked;
He had not dreamed that so many had died.
'But where is Alcibiades,' he asked,
'The golden roisterer, the animal pride?'

Those sages who had spoken of the love
And enmity of things, how all things flow,
Stood in a light no life is witness of,
And Socrates, whose wisdom was to know
He did not know, spoke with a solemn mien,
And all his wonderful ugliness was lit,
'He whom I loved for what he might have been
Freezes with traitors in the ultimate pit.'

Pep and Piety
Sinclair Lewis/from *Babbitt*

*Harry Sinclair Lewis (1888–1951), a doctor's son, was born in Sauk Centre,
Minnesota, a raw frontier town from which he derived the keen sense of midwestern provincialism that was his greatest artistic asset. Although Lewis—*

a graduate of Yale—lavished a great deal of his talent on journalistic hack-work, he became in 1930 the first American to win the Nobel Prize in Literature. He wrote some two dozen novels, which in their scope and variety earn for him a legitimate claim to be America's Balzac. Main Street *(1920), his first important novel, examines the malaise of midwestern, middle-class provincialism.* Arrowsmith *(1924) treats the problems of the humane use of scientific medical research.* Elmer Gantry *(1927) unveils the meretricious evangelism of much contemporary American fundamentalist religiosity. In* Dodsworth *(1929), Lewis turned to the eastern seaboard and discovered there a spurious gentility less deserving of value even than the aggressive materialism of the west.* Ann Vickers *(1932) is a panoramic study of Christian socialism, feminism, humanitarianism, and other manifestations of liberal or radical thought. His most explicitly ideological novel is* It Can't Happen Here *(1936), a fantasy in which he imagines the ascendency of totalitarian fascism in America.* Kingsblood Royal *(1947) is a savage attack on racial prejudice.*

The selection presented here is a speech by the hero of the novel Babbitt *(1922). Quite obviously a satiric caricature of chauvinism and "boosterism," the speech reveals with devastating gusto the cultural and political bumptiousness of the growing industrial city of the 1920's. But it should not be thought that Lewis was genuinely an intellectual radical; his wife Dorothy Thompson was more nearly that. In fact, George Babbitt is not really a "Babbitt." Essentially a decent man, he has been corrupted by the heady philosophy of inexorable American progress. Discerning—and not always dimly—the blind materialism of his fellow citizens, he struggles to break out of the dollar-nexus. He fails, but the energies of his attempt are passed on at the end of the novel to his son Ted, for whom he sanctions a freer life. What is clear is that Babbitt's illiberal republicanism is inextricably bound up with his genuine conservative virtues: industriousness and fidelity to family, community, and church.*

It is a tribute to the evenness of Lewis' political and social vision that, though distinctly liberal in his views, he could not be claimed by any doctrinaire ideology; his characters, because of a generous infusion of human sympathy, rarely sink to the level of mere caricature. At the same time, it is a measure of his ideological limitations that we are not able to construct from his works, even by implication, a coherent social philosophy peculiarly his own.

Mr. Lucas Prout and Sound Business defeated Mr. Seneca Doane and Class Rule, and Zenith was again saved. Babbitt was offered several minor appointments to distribute among poor relations, but he preferred advance information about the extension of paved highways, and this a grateful administration gave to him. Also, he was one of only nineteen speakers at the dinner with which the Chamber of Commerce celebrated the victory of righteousness.

His reputation for oratory established, at the dinner of the Zenith Real Estate Board he made the Annual Address. The *Advocate-Times* reported this speech with unusual fullness:

"One of the livest banquets that has recently been pulled off occurred last night in the annual Get-Together Fest of the Zenith Real Estate Board, held in the Venetian Ball Room of the O'Hearn House. Mine host Gil O'Hearn had as usual done himself proud and those assembled feasted on such an assemblage of plates as could be rivaled nowhere west of New York, if there, and washed down the plenteous feed with the cup which inspired but did not inebriate in the shape of cider from the farm of Chandler Mott, president of the board and who acted as witty and efficient chairman.

"As Mr. Mott was suffering from slight infection and sore throat, G. F. Babbitt made the principal talk. Besides outlining the progress of Torrensing real estate titles, Mr. Babbitt spoke in part as follows:

"'In rising to address you, with my impromptu speech carefully tucked into my vest pocket, I am reminded of the story of the two Irishmen, Mike and Pat, who were riding on the Pullman. Both of them, I forgot to say, were sailors in the Navy. It seems Mike had the lower berth and by and by he heard a terrible racket from the upper, and when he yelled up to find out what the trouble was, Pat answered, "Shure an' bedad an' how can I ever get a night's sleep at all, at all? I been trying to get into this darned little hammock ever since eight bells!"

"'Now, gentlemen, standing up here before you, I feel a good deal like Pat, and maybe after I've spieled along for a while, I may feel so darn small that I'll be able to crawl into a Pullman hammock with no trouble at all, at all!

"'Gentlemen, it strikes me that each year at this annual occasion when friend and foe get together and lay down the battle-ax and let the waves of good-fellowship waft them up the flowery slopes of amity, it behooves us, standing together eye to eye and shoulder to shoulder as fellow-citizens of the best city in the world, to consider where we are both as regards ourselves and the common weal.

"'It is true that even with our 361,000 or practically 362,000 population, there are, by the last census, almost a score of larger cities in the United States. But, gentlemen, if by the next census we do not stand at least tenth, then I'll be the first to request any knocker to remove my shirt and to eat the same, with the compliments of G. F. Babbitt, Esquire! It may be true that New York, Chicago, and Philadelphia will continue to keep ahead of us in size. But aside from these three cities, which are notoriously so overgrown that no decent white man nobody who loves his wife and kiddies and God's good out-o'-doors and likes to shake the hand of his neighbor in greeting, would want to live in them—and let me tell you right here and now, I wouldn't trade a high-class Zenith acreage development for the whole length and breadth of Broadway or State Street!—aside from these three, it's evident to any one with a head for facts that Zenith is the finest example of American life and prosperity to be found anywhere.

"'I don't mean to say we're perfect. We've got a lot to do in the way of extending the paving of motor boulevards, for, believe me, it's the fellow with four to ten thousand a year, say, and an automobile and a nice little family in a bungalow on the edge of town, that makes the wheels of progress go round!

"'That's the type of fellow that's ruling America to-day; in fact, it's the ideal type to which the entire world must tend, if there's to be a decent, well-balanced, Christian, go-ahead future for this little old planet! Once in a while I just naturally sit back and size up this Solid American Citizen, with a whale of a lot of satisfaction.

"'Our Ideal Citizen—I picture him first and foremost as being busier than a bird-dog, not wasting a lot of good time in day-dreaming or going to sassiety teas or kicking about things that are none of his business, but putting the zip into some store or profession or art. At night he lights up a good cigar, and climbs into the little old 'bus, and maybe cusses the carburetor, and shoots out home. He mows the lawn, or sneaks in some practice putting, and then he's ready for dinner. After dinner he tells the kiddies a story, or takes the family to the movies, or plays a few fists of bridge, or reads the evening paper, and a chapter or two of some good lively Western novel if he has a taste for literature, and maybe the folks next-door drop in and they sit and visit about their friends and the topics of the day. Then he goes happily to bed, his conscience clear, having contributed his mite to the prosperity of the city and to his own bank-account.

"'In politics and religion this Sane Citizen is the canniest man on earth; and in the arts he invariably has a natural taste which makes him pick out the best, every time. In no country in the world will you find so many re-productions of the Old Masters and of well-known paintings on parlor walls as in these United States. No country has anything like our number of phonographs, with not only dance records and comic but also the best operas, such as Verdi, rendered by the world's highest-paid singers.

"'In other countries, art and literature are left to a lot of shabby bums living in attics and feeding on booze and spaghetti, but in America the successful writer or picture-painter is indistinguishable from any other decent business man; and I, for one, am only too glad that the man who has the rare skill to season his message with interesting reading matter and who shows both purpose and pep in handling his literary wares has a chance to drag down his fifty thousand bucks a year, to mingle with the biggest execu-tives on terms of perfect equality, and to show as big a house and as swell a car as any Captain of Industry! But, mind you, it's the appreciation of the Regular Guy who I have been depicting which has made this possible, and you got to hand as much credit to him as to the authors themselves.

"'Finally, but most important, our Standardized Citizen, even if he is a bachelor, is a lover of the Little Ones, a supporter of the hearthstone which is the basic foundation of our civilization, first, last, and all the time, and the thing that most distinguishes us from the decayed nations of Europe.

"'I have never yet toured Europe—and as a matter of fact, I don't know that I care to such an awful lot, as long as there's our own mighty cities and mountains to be seen—but, the way I figure it out, there must be a good many of our own sort of folks abroad. Indeed, one of the most enthu-siastic Rotarians I ever met boosted the tenets of one-hundred-per-cent pep in a burr that smacked o' bonny Scutlond and all ye bonny braes o' Bobby Burns. But same time, one thing that distinguishes us from our good brothers, the hustlers over there, is that they're willing to take a lot off the snobs and journalists and politicians, while the modern American business man knows how to talk right up for himself, knows how to make it good and plenty clear that he intends to run the works. He doesn't have to call in some highbrow hired-man when it's necessary for him to answer the crooked critics of the sane and efficient life. He's not dumb, like the old-fashioned merchant. He's got a vocabulary and a punch.

"'With all modesty, I want to stand up here as a representative business man and gently whisper, "Here's our kind of folks! Here's the specifications of the Standardized American Citizen! Here's the new generation of Americans: fellows with hair on their chests and smiles in their eyes and adding-machines in their offices. We're not doing any boasting, but we like ourselves first-rate, and if you don't like us, look out—better get under cover before the cyclone hits town!"

"'So! In my clumsy way I have tried to sketch the Real He-man, the fellow with Zip and Bang. And it's because Zenith has so large a proportion of such men that it's the most stable, the greatest of our cities. New York also has its thousands of Real Folks, but New York is cursed with unnumbered foreigners. So are Chicago and San Francisco. Oh, we have a golden roster of cities—Detroit and Cleveland with their renowned factories, Cincinnati with its great machine-tool and soap products. Pittsburg and Birmingham with their steel, Kansas City and Minneapolis and Omaha that open their bountiful gates on the bosom of the ocean-like wheatlands, and countless other magnificent sister-cities, for, by the last census, there were no less than sixty-eight glorious American burgs with a population of over one hundred thousand! And all these cities stand together for power and purity, and against foreign ideas and communism—Atlanta with Hartford, Rochester with Denver, Milwaukee with Indianapolis, Los Angeles with Scranton, Portland, Maine, with Portland, Oregon. A good live wire from Baltimore or Seattle or Duluth is the twin-brother of every like fellow booster from Buffalo or Akron, Fort Worth or Oskaloosa!

"'But it's here in Zenith, the home for manly men and womanly women and bright kids, that you find the largest proportion of these Regular Guys, and that's what sets it in a class by itself; that's why Zenith will be remembered in history as having set the pace for a civilization that shall endure when the old time-killing ways are gone forever and the day of earnest efficient endeavor shall have dawned all round the world!

"'Some time I hope folks will quit handing all the credit to a lot of moth-eaten, mildewed, out-of-date, old, European dumps, and give proper credit to the famous Zenith spirit, that clean fighting determination to win Success that has made the little old Zip City celebrated in every land and clime, wherever condensed milk and pasteboard cartons are known! Believe me, the world has fallen too long for these worn-out countries that aren't producing anything but bootblacks and scenery and booze, that haven't got one bathroom per hundred people, and that don't know a loose-leaf ledger from a slip-cover; and it's just about time for some Zenithite to get his back up and holler for a show-down!

"'I tell you, Zenith and her sister-cities are producing a new type of civilization. There are many resemblances between Zenith and these other burgs, and I'm darn glad of it! The extraordinary, growing, and sane standardization of stores, offices, streets, hotels, clothes, and newspapers throughout the United States shows how strong and enduring a type is ours. . . .

"'Yes, sir, these other burgs are our true partners in the great game of vital living. But let's not have any mistake about this. I claim that Zenith is the best partner and the fastest-growing partner of the whole caboodle. I trust I may be pardoned if I give a few statistics to back up my claims. If they are old stuff to any of you, yet the tidings of prosperity, like the good news of the Bible, never become tedious to the ears of a real hustler, no matter how oft the sweet story is told! Every intelligent person knows that Zenith manufactures more condensed milk and evaporated cream, more paper boxes, and more lighting-fixtures, than any other city in the United States, if not in the world. But it is not so universally known that we also stand second in the manufacture of package-butter, sixth in the giant realm of motors and automobiles, and somewhere about third in cheese, leather findings, tar roofing, breakfast food, and overalls!

"'Our greatness, however, lies not alone in punchful prosperity but equally in that public spirit, that forward-looking idealism and brother-hood, which has marked Zenith ever since its foundation by the Fathers. We have a right, indeed we have a duty toward our fair city, to announce broadcast the facts about our high schools, characterized by their complete plants and the finest school-ventilating systems in the country, bar none; our magnificent new hotels and banks and the paintings and carved marble in their lobbies; and the Second National Tower, the second highest business building in any inland city in the entire country. When I add that we have an unparalleled number of miles of paved streets, bathrooms, vacuum cleaners, and all the other signs of civilization; that our library and art museum are well supported and housed in convenient and roomy buildings; that our park-system is more than up to par, with its handsome driveways adorned with grass, shrubs, and statuary, then I give but a hint of the all-round unlimited greatness of Zenith!

"'I believe, however, in keeping the best to the last. When I remind you that we have one motor car for every five and seven-eights persons in the city, then I give a rock-ribbed practical indication of the kind of progress and braininess which is synonymous with the name Zenith!

"'But the way of the righteous is not all roses. Before I close I must call your attention to a problem we have to face, this coming year. The worst menace to sound government is not the avowed socialists but a lot of cowards who work under cover—the long-haired gentry who call them-selves "liberals" and "radicals" and "non-partisan" and "intelligentsia" and God only knows how many other trick names! Irresponsible teachers and professors constitute the worst of this whole gang, and I am ashamed to say that several of them are on the faculty of our great State University! The U. is my own Alma Mater, and I am proud to be known as an alumni, but there are certain instructors there who seem to think we ought to turn the conduct of the nation over to hoboes and roustabouts.

"'Those profs are the snakes to be scotched—they and all their milk-and-water ilk! The American business man is generous to a fault, but one thing he does demand of all teachers and lecturers and journalists: if we're going to pay them our good money, they've got to help us by selling effi-ciency and whooping it up for rational prosperity! And when it comes to these blab-mouth, fault-finding, pessimistic, cynical University teachers, let me tell you that during this golden coming year it's just as much our duty to bring influence to have those cusses fired as it is to sell all the real estate and gather in all the good shekels we can.

"'Not till that is done will our sons and daughters see that the ideal of American manhood and culture isn't a lot of cranks sitting around chewing the rag about their Rights and their Wrongs, but a God-fearing, hustling, successful, two-fisted Regular Guy, who belongs to some church with pep and piety to it, who belongs to the Boosters or the Rotarians or the Kiwanis, to the Elks or Moose or Red Men or Knights of Columbus or any one of a score of organizations of good, jolly, kidding, laughing, sweating, upstanding, lend-a-handing Royal Good Fellows, who plays hard and works hard, and whose answer to his critics is a square-toed boot that'll teach the grouches and smart alecks to respect the He-man and get out and root for Uncle Samuel, U.S.A.!'"

Henry Ford and Walter Reuther
John Dos Passos/from *The Big Money* and *Midcentury*

John Roderigo Dos Passos (1896–   ) was born in a hotel room in Chicago, the illegitimate son of attorney John Randolph Dos Passos. The year of his birth marked William McKinley's victory over William Jennings Bryan: the triumph of capitalism and gold over agrarianism and silver. Dos Passos' childhood was itinerant and insecure. After attending Choate School—under the name of John Roderigo Madison—he graduated cum laude *from Harvard in 1916. During World War I, he served in the French and Italian ambulance services. Abandoning painting for literature, he began writing in earnest at the end of the war.*

*In his first three novels—*Three Soldiers *(1921),* Streets of Night *(1923), and* Manhattan Transfer *(1925)—he chronicles the decline of Rooseveltian and Wilsonian reformism and idealism after World War I. In his greatest work,* U.S.A.*, a trilogy written between 1929 and 1936, Dos Passos— after a visit to Russia—began to work out his ideological position more systematically. The result was a lengthy historical novel which, while distinctly liberal and leftist, disassociates itself from Stalinist communism. In a second trilogy, written between 1939 and 1949, entitled* The Grand Design*, Dos Passos reveals his opposition to the collectivism and statism which sometimes appeared as tendencies in* U.S.A.

But one should not suppose that Dos Passos is an ideological turncoat; he has constantly searched for a polity that guarantees the sanctity of the individual, whether that sanctity be threatened by big business, the state, or the labor union. His support of Senator Barry Goldwater for the Presidency in 1964 and his recent identification with the American Right make it clear that he considers big government the greatest current menace.

The selections printed here are biographical sketches—"Tin Lizzie" from The Big Money *(1936), the final novel of the trilogy* U.S.A.*, and*

"Social Engineer" from Midcentury *(1961), a novel which won the Pulitzer Prize. In "Tin Lizzie" Dos Passos presents a thumbnail biography of Henry Ford, a man whose personal and political history is very nearly as complex as Dos Passos' own. A believer in a fundamentalist Protestant ethic for himself and for his workers, Ford was one of the industrialist giants who gave impetus to the mass production and urbanization which undermined that ethic. Suspicious of all visionary ideologies, Ford nevertheless joined ranks with pacifists in a comically pathetic attempt to end World War I. The very apostle of industrial progress, Ford died an antiquarian anachronism, shrunken by fear of the angry mobs set loose in a depression that he could not understand. Here Dos Passos dramatically demonstrates the inability of old-style simplistic capitalism to deal with the social problems which it created.*

The second selection, "Social Engineer," is a capsule sketch of Walter Reuther's remarkable career as a labor leader. Starting with many of Ford's fundamentalist social and religious assumptions, Reuther traveled the opposite political direction. Inspired by Eugene V. Debs' and Norman Thomas' doctrine of the socialist perfectibility of man, Reuther dreamed of a working man's utopia, hated Nazis, visited Russia, and then returned home to fight the class war against Ford's brutally anti-union "Service Men." But when the fight was won, the habits of violence and power, according to Dos Passos, enslaved Reuther; the injustices which he suffered earlier at the hands of the capitalists were returned in kind. For Dos Passos, then, arrogant labor, no less than arrogant business, threatens the freedom of the individual. Yet the portraits reveal, as good art often does, a compassionate understanding of both men.

"Tin Lizzie" / from *The Big Money*

"*Mr. Ford the automobileer,*" the featurewriter wrote in 1900,

"*Mr. Ford the automobileer began by giving his steed three or four sharp jerks with the lever at the righthand side of the seat; that is, he pulled the lever up and down sharply in order, as he said, to mix air with gasoline and drive the charge into the exploding cylinder.... Mr. Ford slipped a small electric switch handle and there followed a puff, puff, puff.... The puffing of the machine assumed a higher key. ... She was flying along about eight miles an hour. The ruts in the road were deep, but the machine certainly went with a dreamlike smoothness. There was none of the bumping common even to a streetcar.... By this time the boulevard had been reached, and the automobileer, letting a lever fall a little, let her out. Whiz! She picked up speed with infinite rapidity. As she ran on there was a clattering behind, the new noise of the automobile.*"

For twenty years or more,

ever since he'd left his father's farm when he was sixteen to get a job in a Detroit machineshop, Henry Ford had been nuts about machinery. First it was watches, then he designed a steamtractor, then he built a horseless carriage with an engine adapted from the Otto gasengine he'd read about in *The World of Science,* then a mechanical buggy with a one-cylinder fourcycle motor, that would run forward but not back;

at last, in ninetyeight, he felt he was far enough along to risk throwing up his job with the Detroit Edison Company, where he'd worked his way up from night fireman to chief engineer, to put all his time into working on a new gasoline engine,

(in the late eighties he'd met Edison at a meeting of electriclight employees in Atlantic City. He'd gone up to Edison after Edison had delivered an address and asked him if he thought gasoline was practical as a motor fuel. Edison had said yes. If Edison said it, it was true. Edison was the great admiration of Henry Ford's life);

and in driving his mechanical buggy, sitting there at the lever jauntily dressed in a tightbuttoned jacket and a high collar and a derby hat, back and forth over the level illpaved streets of Detroit,

scaring the big brewery horses and the skinny trotting horses and the sleekrumped pacers with the motor's loud explosions,

looking for men scatterbrained enough to invest money in a factory for building automobiles.

He was the eldest son of an Irish immigrant who during the Civil War had married the daughter of a prosperous Pennsylvania Dutch farmer and settled down to farming near Dearborn in Wayne County, Michigan;

like plenty of other Americans, young Henry grew up hating the endless sogging through the mud about the chores, the hauling and pitching manure, the kerosene lamps to clean, the irk and sweat and solitude of the farm.

He was a slender, active youngster, a good skater, clever with his hands; what he liked was to tend the machinery and let the others do the heavy work. His mother had told him not to drink, smoke, gamble, or go into debt, and he never did.

When he was in his early twenties his father tried to get him back from Detroit, where he was working as mechanic and repairman for the Drydock Engine Company that built engines for steamboats, by giving him forty acres of land.

Young Henry built himself an uptodate square white dwellinghouse with a false mansard roof and married and settled down on the farm,

but he let the hired men do the farming;

he bought himself a buzzsaw and rented a stationary engine and cut the timber off the woodlots.

He was a thrifty young man who never drank or smoked or gambled or coveted his neighbor's wife, but he couldn't stand living on the farm.

He moved to Detroit, and in the brick barn behind his house tinkered for years in his spare time with a mechanical buggy that would be light enough to run over the clayey wagonroads of Wayne County, Michigan.

By 1900 he had a practicable car to promote.

He was forty years old before the Ford Motor Company was started and production began to move.

Speed was the first thing the early automobile manufacturers went after. Races advertised the makes of cars.

Henry Ford himself hung up several records at the track at Grosse

Pointe and on the ice on Lake St. Clair. In his .999 he did the mile in thirty-nine and fourfifths seconds.

But it had always been his custom to hire others to do the heavy work. The speed he was busy with was speed in production, the records, records in efficient output. He hired Barney Oldfield, a stunt bicyclerider from Salt Lake City, to do the racing for him.

Henry Ford had ideas about other things than the designing of motors, carburetors, magnetos, jigs and fixtures, punches and dies; he had ideas about sales;

that the big money was in economical quantity production, quick turnover, cheap interchangeable easilyreplaced standardized parts;

it wasn't until 1909, after years of arguing with his partners, that Ford put out the first Model T.

Henry Ford was right.

That season he sold more than ten thousand tin lizzies, ten years later he was selling almost a million a year.

In these years the Taylor Plan was stirring up plantmanagers and manufacturers all over the country. Efficiency was the word. The same ingenuity that went into improving the performance of a machine could go into improving the performance of the workmen producing the machine.

In 1913 they established the assemblyline at Ford's. That season the profits were something like twentyfive million dollars, but they had trouble in keeping the men on the job, machinists didn't seem to like it at Ford's.

Henry Ford had ideas about other things than production.

He was the largest automobile manufacturer in the world; he paid high wages; maybe if the steady workers thought they were getting a cut (a very small cut) in the profits, it would give trained men an inducement to stick to their jobs,

wellpaid workers might save enough money to buy a tin lizzie; the first day Ford's announced that cleancut properly-married American workers who wanted jobs had a chance to make five bucks a day (of course it turned out that there were strings to it; always there were strings to it)

such an enormous crowd waited outside the Highland Park plant

all through the zero January night

that there was a riot when the gates were opened; cops broke heads, jobhunters threw bricks; property, Henry Ford's own property, was destroyed. The company dicks had to turn on the firehose to beat back the crowd.

The American Plan; automotive prosperity seeping down from above; it turned out there were strings to it.

But that five dollars a day

paid to good, clean American workmen

who didn't drink or smoke cigarettes or read or think,

and who didn't commit adultery

and whose wives didn't take in boarders,

made America once more the Yukon of the sweated workers of the world;

made all the tin lizzies and the automotive age, and incidentally,

made Henry Ford the automobileer, the admirer of Edison, the bird-lover,

the great American of his time.

But Henry Ford had ideas about other things besides assemblylines and the livinghabits of his employees. He was full of ideas. Instead of going to the city to make his fortune, here was a country boy who'd made his fortune by bringing the city out to the farm. The precepts he'd learned out of McGuffey's Reader, his mother's prejudices and preconceptions, he had preserved clean and unworn as freshprinted bills in the safe in a bank.

He wanted people to know about his ideas, so he bought the *Dearborn Independent* and started a campaign against cigarettesmoking.

When war broke out in Europe, he had ideas about that too. (Suspicion of armymen and soldiering were part of the Mid-West farm tradition, like thrift, stickativeness, temperance, and sharp practice in money matters.) Any intelligent American mechanic could see that if the Europeans hadn't been a lot of ignorant underpaid foreigners who drank, smoked, were loose about women, and wasteful in their methods of production, the war could never have happened.

When Rosika Schwimmer broke through the stockade of secretaries and servicemen who surrounded Henry Ford and suggested to him that he could stop the war,

he said sure they'd hire a ship and go over and get the boys out of the trenches by Christmas.

He hired a steamboat, the *Oscar II,* and filled it up with pacifists and socialworkers,

to go over to explain to the princelings of Europe

that what they were doing was vicious and silly.

It wasn't his fault that Poor Richard's commonsense no longer rules the world and that most of the pacifists were nuts,

goofy with headlines.

When William Jennings Bryan went over to Hoboken to see him off, somebody handed William Jennings Bryan a squirrel in a cage; William Jennings Bryan made a speech with the squirrel under his arm. Henry Ford threw American Beauty roses to the crowd. The band played *I Didn't Raise My Boy to Be a Soldier.* Practical jokers let loose more squirrels. An eloping couple was married by a platoon of ministers in the saloon, and Mr. Zero, the flophouse humanitarian, who reached the dock too late to sail,

dove into the North River and swam after the boat.

The *Oscar II* was described as a floating Chautauqua; Henry Ford said it felt like a Middle-Western village, but by the time they reached Christian-sand in Norway, the reporters had kidded him so that he had gotten cold feet and gone to bed. The world was too crazy outside of Wayne County, Michigan. Mrs. Ford and the management sent an Episcopal dean after him who brought him home under wraps,

and the pacifists had to speechify without him.

Two years later Ford's was manufacturing munitions, Eagle boats;

Henry Ford was planning oneman tanks, and oneman submarines like the one tried out in the Revolutionary War. He announced to the press that he'd turn over his war profits to the government,

but there's no record that he ever did.

One thing he brought back from his trip

was the Protocols of the Elders of Zion.

He started a campaign to enlighten the world in the *Dearborn Independent;* the Jews were why the world wasn't like Wayne County, Michigan, in the old horse-and-buggy days;

the Jews had started the war, Bolshevism, Darwinism, Marxism, Nietzsche, short skirts and lipstick. They were behind Wall Street and the international bankers, and the white-slave traffic and the movies and the Supreme Court and ragtime and the illegal liquor business.

Henry Ford denounced the Jews and ran for Senator and sued the *Chicago Tribune* for libel,

and was the laughingstock of the kept metropolitan press;

but when the metropolitan bankers tried to horn in on his business

he thoroughly outsmarted them.

In 1918 he had borrowed on notes to buy out his minority stockholders for the picayune sum of seventyfive million dollars.

In February, 1920, he needed cash to pay off some of these notes that were coming due. A banker is supposed to have called on him and offered him every facility if the bankers' representative could be made a member of the board of directors. Henry Ford handed the banker his hat,

and went about raising the money in his own way:

he shipped every car and part he had in his plant to his dealers and demanded immediate cash payment. Let the other fellow do the borrowing had always been a cardinal principle. He shut down production and canceled all orders from the supplyfirms. Many dealers were ruined, many supplyfirms failed, but when he reopened his plant,

he owned it absolutely,

the way a man owns an unmortgaged farm with the taxes paid up.

In 1922 there started the Ford boom for President (high wages, waterpower, industry scattered to the small towns) that was skillfully pricked behind the scenes

by another crackerbarrel philosopher,

Calvin Coolidge;

but in 1922 Henry Ford sold one million three hundred and thirtytwo thousand two hundred and nine tin lizzies; he was the richest man in the world.

Good roads had followed the narrow ruts made in the mud by the Model T. The great automotive boom was on. At Ford's production was improving all the time; less waste, more spotters, strawbosses, stoolpigeons (fifteen minutes for lunch, three minutes to go to the toilet, the Taylorized speedup everywhere, reachunder, adjustwasher, screwdown bolt, shove in cotterpin, reachunder, adjustwasher, screwdown bolt, reachunderadjustscrewdownreachunderadjust, until every ounce of life was sucked off into production and at night the workmen went home gray shaking husks).

Ford owned every detail of the process from the ore in the hills until the car rolled off the end of the assemblyline under its own power; the plants were rationalized to the last tenthousandth of an inch as measured by the Johansen scale;

in 1926 the production cycle was reduced to eightyone hours from the ore in the mine to the finished salable car proceeding under its own power,

but the Model T was obsolete.

New Era prosperity and the American Plan
(there were strings to it, always there were strings to it)
had killed Tin Lizzie.
Ford's was just one of many automobile plants.
When the stockmarket bubble burst,
Mr. Ford the crackerbarrel philosopher said jubilantly, "I told you so.
Servés you right for gambling and getting in debt.
The country is sound."
But when the country on cracked shoes, in frayed trousers, belts tightened over hollow bellies,

idle hands cracked and chapped with the cold of that coldest March day of 1932,

started marching from Detroit to Dearborn, asking for work and the American Plan, all they could think of at Ford's was machineguns.

The country was sound, but they mowed the marchers down.
They shot four of them dead.

Henry Ford as an old man
is a passionate antiquarian
(lives beseiged on his father's farm embedded in an estate of thousands of millionaire acres, protected by an army of servicemen, secretaries, secret agents, dicks under orders of an English exprizefighter,

always afraid of the feet in broken shoes on the roads, afraid the gangs will kidnap his grandchildren,

that a crank will shoot him,

that Change and the idle hands out of work will break through the gates and the high fences;

protected by a private army against

the new America of starved children and hollow bellies and cracked shoes stamping on souplines,

that has swallowed up the old thrifty farmlands
of Wayne County, Michigan,
as if they had never been).
Henry Ford as an old man
is a passionate antiquarian.
He rebuilt his father's farmhouse and put it back exactly in the state he remembered it in as a boy. He built a village of museums for buggies, sleighs, coaches, old plows, waterwheels, obsolete models of motorcars. He scoured the country for fiddlers to play oldfashioned squaredances.

Even old taverns he bought and put back into their original shape, as well as Thomas Edison's early laboratories.

When he bought the Wayside Inn near Sudbury, Massachusetts, he had the new highway where the newmodel cars roared and slithered and hissed oilily past *(the new noise of the automobile)*
>moved away from the door,
>put back the old bad road,
>so that everything might be
>the way it used to be,
>in the days of horses and buggies.

"Social Engineer" / from *Midcentury*

Walter Philip Reuther was born into the vanguard of the labor movement. His father Val Reuther was president of the Ohio Valley Trades and Labor Assembly. His grandfather helped organize the Brewery Workers.

Valentine Reuther was a sober literate German-American working man. He preached responsibility. He made his children pay attention in school. He raised his boys to be leaders of labor.

The mother was a devout Lutheran. Sunday mornings they went to church. The father was a devout Socialist. Sunday afternoons they debated the issues. It was a close knit family. They studied social problems together. Val Reuther urged his boys to read. He sent them to the public library to bone up on contested points.

The Reuther home was a warm seminar of the hopes of a new world to come. The Reuthers were working people, they were poor but they knew they were the salt of the earth. A certain amount of poverty must be borne with pride, as a badge. Under socialism they would come into their own.

That was what Debs told the working people crowding into labor temples and union halls during his presidential campaigns. When socialism won at the polls and the trade unions took over the factories, the old Adam would slough off meanness and greed. Freshfaced and rosy as on the sixth day of creation mankind would inaugurate the cooperative commonwealth. A vote for Debs was a vote for man's perfectibility. Val Reuther brought his boys up in reverence for Eugene V. Debs.

The Reuther boys were all bright, but Walter was the redhead. He had a winning way, and a knack with words.

At fifteen because money was short he left highschool and went to work for a corrugating plant. The plant went on a seven day week. Sunday work meant giving up the discussion sessions at home and it was a damned outrage besides. Walter had been raised to give vent to his opinions. He did.

Tried to talk up a union. Fired. No more jobs at home in Wheeling for radical young Walter Reuther.

The automobile industry was booming in Detroit. Ford's five dollars a day attracted up and coming metal workers like bees to a clover field. Walter left home for Detroit and got himself hired at the Briggs body shop. Then he switched to Ford's where he became foreman of a tool and die room. He studied nights to finish highschool and started a college course at Wayne University. He organized a Social Problems Club. He campaigned for Norman Thomas in 1932. The Young People's Socialist League. A vote for Norman Thomas was a vote for the perfectibility of man.

Agitators were no more tolerated at Ford's than at Wheeling Steel. Walter Reuther's radical talk caught up with him. He was asked to step up to the pay window. No more working at Ford's.

Jobs were hard to come by. It was the deep dark of the Depression. A third of the population of Detroit was out of work. American capitalism seemed on its beam ends.

The Reuther boys were frugal fellows. They'd saved up a little dough. Nothing doing at home: why not see the world? Walter and Victor pooled their savings and decided on a trip to the Soviet Union to see how the working class was doing in the only country governed in its name.

While they waited for the Russian bureaucracy to furnish them with a visa they toured Europe on bicycles. They stayed in youth hostels. They visited factories and union halls. They pedaled out to the village near Stuttgart where their mother was born. They turned up in Berlin the day of the Reichstag fire.

Nazism made Walter Reuther's hackles rise. He was still German enough to feel it close to. The Reuther boys were full of anti-fascist zeal when they climbed on the long slow dingy train to Moscow. The Soviet Union was the workers' republic, socialism in our time. Why wouldn't their blood tingle?

Walter got himself a job as diemaker in the truck factory Ford's people had designed for the Russians at Gorki on the Volga. He was made foreman, only there they called it "leader of a labor brigade."

The Russian language was a maze. Soviet life was confusing. "Who are we to criticize? The Russians have to do things their own way."

The people were full of cordial curiosity about their American comrades. The girls were caressing. Here was a great nation relentlessly pursuing the ideals the Reuther boys had been brought up in from the cradle. Why shouldn't they write enthusiastic letters home?

After sixteen months, before they'd had a chance to learn, through Stalin's purges, the bloody underside of soviet socialism, the Reuthers left by the Transsiberian for home. After all they were Americans. It was American socialism they were dedicated to build.

On the way home they peeked into China, had a glimpse of India, spent a few weeks in Japan.

Back in Detroit, since he was still blacklisted as a radical, Walter went to work for General Motors under an assumed name. He married a red-headed girl who had been active in the Teachers' Union and started seriously organizing the West Side local of the United Automobile Workers. When his local sent him to a convention in South Bend he had a time convincing the chair that Walter Reuther and the other guy were one and the same.

Never again was there any doubt who Walter Reuther was.

Elected to the international board he opened a tiny office at 5th and Michigan Avenue. He was a labor organizer now full time. He started with seventyeight members. After the sitdown at Kelsey Hayes there were thirty thousand paying dues. Unionization was an avalanche. The agitators found themselves trying to hold their workers back until they could train up the organizers to service them. Even the Communists had their hands full.

The Reuther boys were campaign strategists. The class war was developing military tactics: strike where the enemy least expects it.

The automobile workers fought Harry Bennett's Service Men and the local cops and threats of fine and imprisonment.

and broken heads and bloody noses,

with organization and oratory at all night meetings, and soup kitchens and hospital units,

and baseball bats on the picket line: the battle of the Dearborn drawbridge.

This was the contest the Reuther boys had been training for all their lives.

Industrial Michigan was in insurrection. Good kind liberal Frank Murphy, who wanted to be the working man's friend, couldn't very well help calling out the state militia. From the Olympian heights of Washington Franklin Roosevelt talked the national interest: a plague on both your houses.

John L. Lewis, institution-building in the CIO, bustled with beetling brows between the White House and the UAW, blustered, bullied; squeezed every last dribble of drama out of the scene when he ostentatiously boarded the night train for Detroit to take over the sitdowns:

"Let there be no moaning at the bar," he boomed somewhat out of context to the reporters, who dutifully copied out these sibylline words for the morning papers, "when I put out to sea."

Franklin Roosevelt and John L were working at cross purposes, but between them they convinced the automobile industry that unions were here to stay. Ford's reversed its policy overnight. Harry Bennett agreed to negotiate. The National Labor Relations Board held an election in which the UAW won 58,000 out of 80,000 votes cast. Ford's signed, agreed to the union shop, the checkoff, overtime pay, seniority, grievance machinery, everything all down the line.

Harry Bennett did have one last word: the pluguglies of Ford's Service Department had acted like "a lot of tough bastards," he admitted, "but every goddam one of them is a gentleman."

The United Automobile Workers became the largest union in the world. The local at Ford's #600 (dominated by the Communists to be sure) was the largest single local in the world.

Through years of strategy and strikes and long night sessions at the bargaining table, Walter Reuther gained influence in the UAW. His brothers backed him. Victor documented his theories and did his paperwork. For the

Reuthers Walter was the front man, the sweetfaced redhead with the winning way.

First he had to team with the Communists against Homer Martin's AF of L administration. Factions in the union came and went. The UAW was a sure enough industrial democracy. Teaming now with one group, now with another Walter Reuther forged ahead.

He never had much sympathy with the Communist bigots. He'd been raised a social-democrat. He had faith in selfgovernment.

He liked to quote John Stuart Mill: "If all mankind, minus one, were of one opinion and only one person were of the contrary opinion, mankind would be no more justified in silencing that one person, than he, if he had the power—would be justified in silencing mankind." This didn't quite apply to scabs.

Walter Reuther was an idealist with an institution to build. Building institutions takes special skills. Walter was a quiet family man of blameless life who drank only milk and didn't gamble and never smoked and who didn't give a damn about money and style. He was so convinced of the probity of his own intentions that he never could believe in the probity of people who had other ideas.

Organizing the nation for global war Franklin Roosevelt took the laborleaders into camp. War Production Board, War Manpower Commission, Labor-Management Production Committees. Alphabet enough for everybody on Olympus except for John L. Lewis who sulked. Walter Reuther learned his Washington.

The truce with industry ended with the shooting. Now, their treasuries swollen with wartime dues, the labor unions demanded their place in the sun. Walter Reuther could debate with management on equal terms.

He had become famous for his coolness at the bargaining table. Always neat, his associates marveled that even in the hottest weather he had the look of just coming out from a cold shower. Where other men got drunk with power, Walter Reuther took it in sips, coolly, like a glass of milk.

At last at the national convention in Atlantic City in March of 1946 his long climb ended with his election as president of the UAW-CIO. His first act was to introduce his old father to the delegates. It was a great day for the Reuthers.

Although the Communists had been with Reuther at first they turned on him savagely. A man makes enemies when he climbs to power. His campaign against gambling in the plants had antagonized the gangsters and the fast buck boys. One night when, coming back tired from the office, he sat drinking a glass of milk in the kitchen of his "modest workingclass home" someone shot at him through the window with a sawed off shotgun. He was dangerously hurt and carries the scars on one arm to this day.

A year later an almost identical attempt was made to kill his brother Victor. Vic came away with his life but lost an eye. In spite of rewards posted and hullabaloo from detectives and district attorneys no one was ever able to discover who arranged these shootings.

Violence.

Institutions are built on zeal.

They are also built on fear. The Reuthers came to feel that to question the UAW's mission to organize every bunch of metal-workers they could lay their hands on was treason to the working class and unAmerican besides. Democracy was when the men voted the way the Reuthers wanted them to vote in a union election.

When they struck Kohler's works that make bathtubs in Sheboygan the Reuthers were hurt and pained to discover that quite a large body of working people didn't want to be serviced by their organization.

This time the storm troops were on the union side. "No one has a right to scab," said the UAW officials the way Harry Bennett at Ford's in the old days used to say "No one has a right to strike."

When the Congressional Committee presided over by Senator McClellan questioned Walter Reuther about the fanatical boycott of Kohler products and the beatings of nonstrikers, the wrecking of automobiles, the throwing of acid, the spraying of paint into livingrooms, rocks thrown and foul vituperation of working men's wives and children over the telephone, he answered with his usual righteous coolness and a trace of his small winning smile: "I believe that when a company deliberately and willfully embarks upon a labor policy designed to break a strike and destroy a union, that it must assume the prime moral responsibility for anything that happens."

The Politics of Relativism

Robert Penn Warren / from *All the King's Men*

Robert Penn Warren (1906–   ) was born in Kentucky, educated at Vanderbilt, the University of California, Yale, and Oxford. Despite this cultural variety, his attitudes have remained steadfastly southern. In 1930, he collaborated with John Crowe Ransom, Donald Davidson, Allen Tate, and eight other southerners, in writing I'll Take My Stand, *a book of essays defending the southern way of life and indicting northern industrialism. Penn Warren later defended segregation, a position which he has moderated considerably in recent years.*

After some early fine poetry, Night Rider *(1939), Penn Warren's first novel, appeared. This story of violent and lawless lust for power among southern tobacco farmers immediately marked his interest in the character of men as it is revealed in political crisis. At* Heaven's Gate *(1943) is also a study of power and egotism, though this time the scene is shifted to circles of high finance. The most compelling of Penn Warren's power-hungry men is Willie Stark, a hero of* All the King's Men *(1946), a novel which won the Pulitzer Prize. Since 1946, Penn Warren has published one allegorical and two historical novels. Although the political content is considerably lessened, the theme of individual responsibility which marked his earlier work is still central. In fact, the whole canon of Penn Warren's work seems to be based on a true—nearly Christian—humanism significantly adjusted to the writer's almost Calvinistic insight into the pervasiveness of human corruptibility.*

The selection printed here is from All the King's Men. *The novel, based loosely on the career of Huey Long, governor of Louisiana from 1928 to 1931 and then U.S. senator until his assassination in 1935, dramatizes the political career of Governor Willie Stark, "the Boss," which ends with his assassination by Dr. Adam Stanton. Willie is not simply a fascistic demagogue. His shocking moral relativism and political brutality are complicated by an almost orthodox Calvinism: "Man is conceived in sin and born in corruption and he passeth from the stink of the didie to the stench of the shroud." As Willie says, he attended Presbyterian Sunday School when they still taught some theology. Furthermore, Willie has a fierce family loyalty and a cutting disdain for the self-righteous privileged classes who have long controlled the state with a corrupt political machine. It is difficult to disentangle his genuine reformism from his cynical use of public projects to manipulate his constituency, the upstate red necks.*

In the following scene, the narrator of the novel, Jack Burden, a disillusioned member of the old aristocracy who has joined Willie politically, recounts Willie's meeting with Dr. Adam Stanton, who has agreed to manage a huge new public hospital for the governor. Willie gives the idealistic and naïve aristocrat a lesson in theology and political philosophy. The two men, with their symbolic names, confront each other across a chasm of opposing political and social assumptions. Drawn together briefly by a shared concern for suffering humanity, they will inevitably destroy one another.

The big black Cadillac, the hood glistening dully under the street lamps— as I could see even from the back seat—eased down the street, making its expensive whisper under the boughs which had new leaves on them, for it was early April now. Then we got to a street where there were not any nice trees arching over.

"Here," I said, "that place on the right, just beyond that grocery."

Sugar-Boy put the Cadillac up to the curb, like a mother laying Little Precious down with a last kiss. Then he ran around to open the door for the Boss, but the Boss was already on the curb. I uncoiled myself and stood beside him. "This is the joint," I remarked, and started in.

For we were going to see Adam Stanton.

When I told the Boss that Adam Stanton would take the job and that he had sent me a message to arrange things, the Boss had said, "Well." Then he had looked at me from toe to crown, and said, "You must be Svengali."

"Yeah," I had said, "I am Svengali."

"I want to see him," the Boss had said.

"I'll try to get him up here."

"Get him up here?" the Boss had said. "I'll go there. Hell, he's doing me a favor."

"Well, you're the Governor, aren't you?"

"You're damned right I am," the Boss had said, "but he is Doc Stanton. When do we go?"

I had told him it would have to be at night, that you never could catch him except at night.

So here we were, at night, entering the door of the crummy apartment house, climbing the dark stairs, stumbling over the kiddie car, inhaling the odor of cabbage and diapers. "He sure picked himself a place to live," the Boss said.

"Yeah," I agreed, "and lots of folks can't figure out why."

"I reckon I can," the Boss said.

And as I wondered whether he could or not, we reached the door, and I knocked, entered, and confronted the level eyes of Adam Stanton.

For a half moment, while Sugar-Boy was easing in, and I was shutting the door, Adam and the Boss simply took each other in, without a word. Then I turned and said, "Governor Stark, this is Dr. Stanton."

The Boss took a step forward and put out his right hand. Perhaps I imagined it, but I thought I noticed a shade of hesitation before Adam took it. And the Boss must have noticed it, too, for when Adam did put out his hand, the Boss, in the middle of the shake, before any other word had been spoken, grinned suddenly, and said, "See, boy, it's not as bad as you thought, it won't kill you."

Then, by God, Adam grinned, too.

Then I said, "And this is Mr. O'Shean," and Sugar-Boy lurched forward and put out one of his stubby arms with a hand hanging on the end of it like a stuffed glove, and twisted his face and began, "I'm pl-pl-pl-pl—"

"I'm glad to know you," Adam said. Then I saw his glance pick up the bulge under Sugar-Boy's left armpit. He turned to the Boss. "So this is one of your gunmen I've heard about?" he said, definitely not grinning now.

"Hell," the Boss said, "Sugar-Boy just carries that for fun. Sugar-Boy is just a pal. Ain't nobody can drive a car like Sugar-Boy."

Sugar-Boy was looking at him like a dog you've just scratched on the head.

Adam stood there, and didn't reply. For a second I thought the deal was about to blow up. Then Adam said, very formally, "Won't you gentlemen have seats?"

We did.

Sugar-Boy sneaked one of his lumps of sugar out of the side pocket of his coat, put it into his mouth, and began to suck it, with his fey Irish cheeks drawn in and his eyes blurred with bliss.

Adam waited, sitting straight up in his chair.

The Boss, leaning back in one of the overstuffed wrecks, didn't seem to be in any hurry. But he finally said, "Well, Doc, what do you think of it?"

"Of what?" Adam demanded.

"Of my hospital?"

"I think it will do the people of the state some good," he said. Then added, "And get you some votes."

"You can forget about the vote side of it," the Boss said. "There are lots of ways to get votes, son."

"So I understand," Adam said. Then he handed the Boss another big chunk of silence to admire.

The Boss admired it awhile, then said, "Yeah, it'll do some good. But not too much unless you take over."

"I won't stand any interference," Adam said, and bit the sentence off.

"Don't worry," the Boss laughed. "I might fire you, boy, but I wouldn't interfere."

"If that is a threat," Adam said, and the pale-blue blaze flickered up in his eyes, "you have wasted your time by coming here. You know my opinions of this administration. They have been no secret. And they will be no secret in the future. You understand that?"

"Doc," the Boss said, "Doc, you just don't understand politics. I'll be frank with you. I could run this state and ten more like it with you howling on every street corner like a hound with a sore tail. No offense. But you just don't understand."

"I understand some things," Adam said grimly, and the jaw set.

"And some you don't, just like I don't, but one thing I understand and you don't is what makes the mare go. I can make the mare go. And one more thing, now we are taking down our hair—" The Boss suddenly stopped, cocked his head, leered at Adam, then demanded, "Or are we?"

"You said there was one more thing," Adam replied, ignoring the question, sitting straight in his chair.

"Yeah, one more thing. But look here, Doc—you know Hugh Miller?"

"Yes," Adam said, "yes, I know him."

"Well, he was in with me—yeah, Attorney General—and he resigned. And you know why?" But he went on without waiting for the answer. "He resigned because he wanted to keep his little hands clean. He wanted the bricks but he just didn't know somebody has to paddle in the mud to make 'em. He was like somebody that just loves beefsteak but just can't bear to go to a slaughter pen because there are some bad, rough men down there who aren't animal lovers and who ought to be reported to the S.P.C.A. Well, he resigned."

I watched Adam's face. It was white and stony, as though carved out of some slick stone. He was like a man braced to hear what the jury foreman was going to say. Or what the doctor was going to say. Adam must have seen a lot of faces like that in his time. He must have had to look into them and tell them what he had to tell.

"Yeah," the Boss said, "he resigned. He was one of those guys wants everything and wants everything two ways at once. You know the kind, Doc?"

He flicked a look over at Adam, like a man flicking a fly over by the willows in the trout stream. But there wasn't any strike.

"Yeah, old Hugh—he never learned that you can't have everything. That you can have mighty little. And you never have anything you don't make. Just because he inherited a little money and the name Miller he thought you could have everything. Yeah, and he wanted the one last damned thing you can't inherit. And you know what it is?" He stared at Adam's face.

"What?" Adam said, after a long pause.

"Goodness. Yeah, just plain, simple goodness. Well you can't inherit that from anybody. You got to make it, Doc. If you want it. And you got to make it out of badness. Badness. And you know why, Doc?" He raised his bulk up in the broken-down wreck of an overstuffed chair he was in, and leaned forward, his hands on his knees, his elbows cocked out, his head outthrust and the hair coming down to his eyes, and stared into Adam's face. "Out of badness," he repeated. "And you know why? Because there isn't anything else to make it out of." Then, sinking back into the wreck, he asked softly, "Did you know that, Doc?"

Adam didn't say a word.

Then the Boss asked, softer still, almost whispering, "Did you know that, Doc?"

Adam wet his lips and said, "There is one question I should like to ask you. It is this. If, as you say, there is only the bad to start with, and the good must be made from the bad, then how do you ever know what the good is? How do you even recognize the good? Assuming you have made it from the bad. Answer me that."

"Easy, Doc, easy," the Boss said.

"Well, answer it."

"You just make it up as you go along."

"Make up what?"

"The good," the Boss said, "What the hell else are we talking about. Good with a capital G."

"So you make it up as you go along?" Adam repeated gently.

"What the hell else you think folks been doing for a million years, Doc? When your great-great-grandpappy climbed down out of the tree, he didn't have any more notion of good or bad, or right and wrong, than the hoot owl that stayed up in the tree. Well, he climbed down and he began to make Good up as he went along. He made up what he needed to do business, Doc. And what he made up and got everybody to mirate on as good and right was always just a couple of jumps behind what he needed to do business on. That's why things change, Doc. Because what folks claim is right is always just a couple of jumps short of what they need to do business. Now an individual, one fellow, he will stop doing business because he's got a notion of what is right, and he is a hero. But folks in general, which is society, Doc, is never going to stop doing business. Society is just going to cook up a new notion of what is right. Society is sure not ever going to commit suicide. At least, not that way and of a purpose. And that is a fact. Now ain't it?"

"It is?" Adam said.

"You're damned right it is, Doc. And right is a lid you put on something and some of the things under the lid look just like some of the things not under the lid, and there never was any notion of what was right if you put it down on folks in general that a lot of them didn't start squalling because they just couldn't do any human business under that kind of right. Hell, look at when folks couldn't get a divorce. Look at all the good women got beat and the good men got nagged and couldn't do any human damned thing about it. Then, all of a sudden, a divorce got to be right. What next, you don't know. Nor me. But I do know this." He stopped, leaned forward again, the elbows again cocked out.

"What?" Adam demanded.

"This. I'm not denying there's got to be a notion of right to get business done, but by God, any particular notion at any particular time will sooner or later get to be just like a stopper put tight in a bottle of water and thrown in a hot stove the way we kids used to do at school to hear the bang. The steam that blows the bottle and scares the teacher to wet her drawers is just the human business that is going to get done, and it will blow anything you put it in if you seal it tight, but you put it in the right place and let it get out in a certain way and it will run a freight engine." He sank back again into the chair, his eyelids sagging now, but the eyes watchful, and the hair down over his forehead like an ambush.

Adam got up suddenly, and walked across the room. He stopped in front of the dead fireplace, with old ashes still in it, and some half-burned paper, though spring was on us, and there hadn't been any fire for a time. The window was up, and the night air came into the room, with a smell different from the diaper-and-cabbage smell, a smell of damp grass and the leaves hanging down from the arched trees in the dark, a smell that definitely did not belong there in that room. And all of a sudden I remembered once how into a room where I was sitting one night, a big pale apple-green moth, big as a bullbat and soft and silent as a dream—a Luna moth, the name is, and it is a wonderful name—came flying in. Somebody had left the screen door open, and the moth drifted in over the tables and chairs like a big pale-green, silky, live leaf, drifting and dancing along without any wind under the electric light where a Luna moth certainly did not belong. The night air coming into the room now was like that.

Adam leaned an elbow on the wooden mantelpiece where you could write your name in the dust and the books were stacked and the old, dregs-crusted coffee cup sat. He stood there as though he were all by himself.

The Boss was watching him.

"Yeah," the Boss said, watchful, "it will run a freight engine and—"

But Adam broke in, "What are you trying to convince me of? You don't have to convince me of anything. I've told you I'd take the job. That's all!" He glared at the bulky man in the big chair, and said, "That's all! And my reasons are my own."

The Boss gave a slow smile, shifted his weight in the chair, and said, "Yeah, your reasons are your own, Doc. But I just thought you might want to know something about mine. Since we're going to do business together."

"I am going to run the hospital," Adam said, and added with curling lip, "If you call that doing business together."

The Boss laughed out loud. Then he got up from the chair. "Doc," he said, "just don't you worry. I'll keep your little mitts clean. I'll keep you clean all over, Doc. I'll put you in that beautiful, antiseptic, sterile, six-million-dollar hospital, and wrap you in cellophane, untouched by human hands." He stepped to Adam, and slapped him on the shoulder. "Don't you worry, Doc," he said.

"I can take care of myself," Adam affirmed, and looked down at the hand on his shoulder.

"Sure you can, Doc," the Boss said. He removed his hand from the shoulder. Then his tone changed, suddenly businesslike and calm. "You will no doubt want to see all the plans which have been drawn up. They are subject to your revision after you consult with the architects. Mr. Todd, of Todd and Waters, will come to see you about it. And you can start picking your staff. It is all your baby."

He turned away and picked up his hat from the piano top. He swung back toward Adam and gave him a summarizing look, from top to toe and back. "You're a great boy, Doc," he said, "and don't let 'em tell you different."

Then he wheeled to the door, and went out before Adam could say a word. If there was any word he had to say.

Sugar-Boy and I followed. We didn't stop to say good night and thanks for the hospitality. That just didn't seem to be in the cards. At the door, however, I looked back and said, "So long, boy," but Adam didn't answer. . . .

Between Aquinas and Dewey
Mary McCarthy / from *The Groves of Academe*

Mary McCarthy (1912–   ) describes herself as a "Libertarian Socialist"; the complex phrase—perhaps obliquely reminiscent of Metternich, who said he was a "conservative socialist"—reveals something of her independent and yet doctrinaire attitude. Married four times, once to literary and social critic Edmund Wilson, she has written dramatic criticism for such unorthodoxly left-wing journals as the Partisan Review *and has produced a series of novels acidly describing the vagaries of intellectual life in America. Although her recent novel,* The Group *(1963), is her most popular work, the selection included here is from* The Groves of Academe *(1952). In this novel, she deals specifically with life on the campus—of one of those advanced and experimental liberal arts colleges for which America is famous. Presumably the book reflects some of her experiences as a girl at Vassar and in later life at Sarah Lawrence and Bard.*

So much is being satirized in the novel that it is difficult to classify the author simply as either liberal or conservative. The machinative complexity of the plot, with its surprise ending, enables her to mock progressive education and the professional liberalism of the faculty as well as the conservative elements in the administration and elsewhere. Despite her own Catholic upbringing, she does not use her satire to sustain any orthodoxy. Lacking a formulated ideology of her own, she often seems to satirize things for the sake of wit. Her eye and ear for the idiocies and idiosyncrasies of the contemporary scene are extremely alert; and she indulges them. What saves her work from being an ephemeral pastiche is the conviction, felt by the reader, that Miss McCarthy is honestly concerned with finding the truth. No matter how acerbic the satire is, the author is never merely malicious; instead she tempers her

*witty acidity with a sympathy for both sides—the liberal and the conservative—
so that imaginary Jocelyn College contains a core of integrity under its façade
of poses. "These men of conscience and consistency" fight over the spellings
"catalogue" and "catalog" not simply because they are petty pedants—though
they are that, too—but because in the semantic labyrinth of academe the most
trivial detail may conceal a philosophy and a movement.*

*Like the faculty and the administration, the students receive their share
of satiric exposure. Yet among the types, the unconventional Blancas and the
bourgeois Allysons, "badly prepared, sleepy, and evasive," there are always
"a handful of gifted creatures who would redeem the whole." After six months
at Jocelyn, the students "felt that they had 'seen through' all attempts to educate
and improve them, through love, poetry, philosophy, fame . . ."—and yet
they could still, from time to time, be moved "to wonder and pent admiration at
the discovery of form and pattern in history, or a work of art or a laboratory
experiment." These balanced notions indicate the author's biting sympathy;
perhaps her native Catholicism shows up, vestigially, in her satiric sorrow that
a humanistic utopia is not possible.*

Ancient history

Jocelyn College, on this mid-morning in January, as Henry Mulcahy
trod softly through its corridors, had a faculty of forty-one persons and a
student body of two hundred and eighty-three—a ratio of one teacher to
every 6.9 students, which made possible the practice of "individual instruction" as carried on at Bennington (6:1), Sarah Lawrence (6.4:1), Bard (6.9:1),
and St. John's (7.7:1). It had been founded in the late Thirties by an experimental educator and lecturer, backed by a group of society-women in
Cleveland, Pittsburgh, and Cincinnati who wished to strike a middle course
between the existing extremes, between Aquinas and Dewey, the modern
dance and the labor movement. Its students were neither to till the soil as at
Antioch nor weave on looms as at Black Mountain; they were to be grounded
neither in the grass-roots present as at Sarah Lawrence nor in the great-
books past as at St. John's or Chicago; they were to specialize neither in verse-
writing, nor in the poetic theatre, nor in the techniques of co-operative
living—they were simply to be free, spontaneous, and coeducational.

What the founder had had in mind was a utopian experiment in so-
called "scientific" education; by the use of aptitude tests, psychological
questionnaires, even blood-sampling and cranial measurements, he hoped
to discover a method of gauging student-potential and directing it into
the proper channels for maximum self-realization—he saw himself as an
engineer and the college as a reclamation project along the lines of the
Grand Coulee or the TVA. The women behind him, however, regarded the
matter more simply, in the usual fashion of trustees. What they wanted to
introduce into their region was a center of "personalized" education, with
courses tailored to the individual need, like their own foundation-garments,
and a staff of experts and consultants, each with a little "name" in his field,
like the Michels and Antoines of Fifth Avenue, to interpret the student's
personality. In the long run, these views, seemingly so harmonious, were

found to be far apart. The founder had the sincere idea of running his college as a laboratory; failure in an individual case he found as interesting as success. Under his permissive system, the students were free to study or not as they chose; he believed that the healthy organism would elect, like an animal, what was best for it. If the student failed to go in the direction indicated by the results of his testing, or in any direction at all, this was noted down and in time communicated to his parents, merely as a matter of interest—to push him in any way would be a violation of the neutrality of the experiment. The high percentage of failure was taken to be significant of the failures of secondary education; any serious reform in methodology must reach down to the kindergarten and the nursery school, through the whole preparatory system, and it was noteworthy, in this connection, that the progressive schools were doing their job no better than the old-fashioned classical ones. Indeed, comparative studies showed the graduates of progressive schools to be *more* dependent on outside initiative, on an authoritarian leader-pattern, than any other group in the community.

This finding convinced the trustees, who included the heads of two progressive schools, that the founder was ahead of his time, a stimulating man in the tradition of Pasteur and the early vivisectionists, whom history would give his due. He left the college the legacy of a strong scientific bent and a reputation for enthusiasm and crankishness that reflected itself in budgetary difficulties and in the prevalence of an "undesirable" type of student. Despite a high tuition and other screening devices (a geographical quota, interviews with the applicant and with the applicant's parents, submission of a photograph when this was not practicable, solicitation of private schools), despite a picturesque campus—a group of long, thick-walled, mansarded, white-shuttered stone dwellings arranged around a cupolaed chapel with a planting of hemlocks, the remains of a small, old German Reformed denominational college that had imparted to the secluded ridge a Calvinistic sweetness of worship and election—something, perhaps the coeducational factor, perhaps the once-advertised freedom, had worked to give the college a peculiarly plebeian and subversive tone, like that of a big-city high-school.

It was the mixture of the sexes, some thought, that had introduced a crude and predatory bravado into the campus life; the glamour was rubbed off sex by the daily jostle in soda-shop and barroom and the nightly necking in the social rooms, and this, in its turn, had its effect on all ideals and absolutes. Differences were leveled; courses were regarded with a cynical, practical eye; students of both sexes had the wary disillusionment and aimlessness of battle-hardened Marines. After six months at Jocelyn, they felt that they had "seen through" life, through all attempts to educate and improve them, through love, poetry, philosophy, fame, and were here, it would seem, through some sort of coercion, like a drafted army. Thronging into store or classroom, in jeans, old sweaters, caps, visors, strewing cigarette-butts and candy-wrappers, they gave a mass impression that transcended their individual personalities, which were often soft, perturbed, uncertain, innocent; yet the very sight of an individual face, plunged deep in its own introspection, as in a blanket, heightened the crowd-sense they communicated, like soldiers in a truck, subway riders on their straps, serried but isolated, each in his stubborn dream, resistant to waking fully—at whatever time of day, the Jocelyn students were always sleepy, yawning, and rather gummy-eyed, as though it were seven in the morning and they unwillingly on the street.

Yet this very rawness and formlessness in the students made them interesting to teach. Badly prepared, sleepy, and evasive, they *could* nevertheless be stirred to wonder and pent admiration at the discovery of form and pattern in history or a work of art or a laboratory experiment, though ceding this admiration grudgingly and by degrees, like primitive peoples who must see an act performed over and over again before they can be convinced that some magic is not behind it, that they are not the dupes of an illusionist. To teachers with some experience of the ordinary class-bound private college student, of the quiet lecture-hall with the fair duteous heads bent over the notebooks, Jocelyn's hard-eyed watchers signified the real. Seeing them come year after year, the stiff-spined, angry only children with inhibitions about the opposite sex, being entrained here remedially by their parents, as they had been routed to the dentist for braces, the wild-haired progressive-school rejects, offspring of broken homes, the sexually adventurous youths looking to meet their opposite numbers in the women's dormitories, without the social complications of fraternities and sororities or the restraints of grades, examinations, compulsory athletics, R.O.T.C., the single well-dressed Adonis from Sewickley with a private plane and a neurosis, the fourteen-year-old mathematical Russian Jewish boys on scholarships, with their violin cases and timorous, old-country parents, hovering humbly outside the Registrar's door as at a consular office, the cold peroxided beauties who had once done modeling for Powers and were here while waiting for a screen-test, the girls from Honolulu or Taos who could "sit on" their hair and wore it down their backs, Godiva-style, and were named Rina or Blanca or Snow-White, the conventional Allysons and Pattys whose favorite book was *Winnie-the-Pooh*—seeing them, the old-timers shook their heads and marveled at how the college could continue but in the same style that they marveled at the survival of the race itself. Among these students, they knew, there would be a large percentage of trouble-makers and a handful of gifted creatures who would redeem the whole; four out of five of these would be, predictably, the scholarship students, and the fifth a riddle and an anomaly, coming forward at the last moment, from the ranks of Allysons or Blancas, like the tortoise in the fable, or the sleeper in the horse-race, a term which at Jocelyn had a peculiar nicety of meaning.

And over the management of these students, the faculty, equally heterogeneous, would, within the year, become embroiled, with each other, with the student-body, or with the President or trustees. A scandal could be counted on that would cause a liberal lady somewhere to strike the college from her will: a pregnant girl, the pilfering of reserve books from the library, the usual plagiarism case, alleged racial discrimination, charges of alcoholism or homosexuality, a strike against the food in the dining-room, the prices in the college store, suppression of the student paper, alleged use of a course in myth to proselytize for religion, a student demand that a rule be laid down, in the handbook, governing sexual intercourse, if disciplinary action was to be taken against those who made love *off* the college premises and were observed by faculty-snoopers. No truly great question had ever agitated the campus since the original days of the founder, but the ordinary trivia of college life were here blown up, according to critics, out of all proportion. There had been no loyalty oath, no violation of academic freedom, but problems of freedom and fealty were discovered in the smallest issue, in whether, for example, students in the dining-hall, when surrendering their plates to the waiters, should pass them to the right or the left, clockwise or counterclockwise; at an all-college meeting, held in December of this year, compulsory for all students, faculty, and administrative staff, President Maynard Hoar had come within an ace of resigning when his appeal for moderation in the discussion had met with open cat-calls from the counterclockwise faction.

Thus the college faced every year an insurrectionary situation; in the course of twelve years it had had five presidents, including the founder, who was unseated after only eleven months of service. During the War, it had nearly foundered and been saved by the influx of veterans studying under the GI bill and by the new plutocracy of five-percenters, car-dealers, black-market slaughterers, tire-salesmen, and retail merchants who seemed to Jocelyn's presidents to have been specially enriched by Providence, working mysteriously, with the interests of the small college in mind. These new recruits to the capitalist classes had no educational prejudices, were extremely respectful of the faculty, to whom they sent bulky presents of liquor or perfume, as to valuable clients at Christmas-time; they came to the college seldom, sometimes only once, for Commencement, passed out cigars and invitations to use the shack at Miami or Coral Gables *any time at all*— this benign and preoccupied gratitude, tactfully conscious of services rendered, extended also to friends and roommates of the poorer sort. Several years after graduation, little shoals of Jocelyn students would still be found living together co-operatively, in Malibu or St. Augustine—occasionally with an ex-teacher—sharing a single allowance under the bamboo tree.

Hence, though the college was in continual hot water financially, it had inevitably grown accustomed to close shaves and miraculous windfalls. Only the bursar seriously worried about balancing the budget, and his worries were accepted tolerantly—this was his *métier*. The faculty now took it for granted that fresh students would appear every fall out of nowhere, from the blue sky of promoters' ventures, a strange new race, or stock issued by a wildcat bank, spending what would appear to be stage-money; and the yearly advent of these registrants in defiance of the laws of probability created in the staff a certain sense of displacement or of nonchalance or autarchic license, depending on the individual character. Careless of the future, fractious, oblivious of the past, believing that the industrial revolution was an actual armed uprising of the nineteenth century, that oranges grew in Norway and fir trees on the Nile, these sons of shortages and rationing seemed to have sprung from no human ancestry but from War, like the dragon's teeth sown in the Theban meadow. And the faculty which was teaching them their Cadmean alphabet fell to some extent under their influence; they too became indifferent to the morrow and forgetful of past incentives. There was a whiff of paganism in the air, of freedom from material cares that evoked the South Sea islands even in the Pennsylvania winter; more than one faculty-member, washed up on this coral strand, came to resemble, in dress and habits, the traditional beachcomber of fiction.

But the absence of pressure from without, the unconcern of parents and inertia of alumni groups, produced at the same time an opposite and corrective tendency. The faculty contained a strong and permanent minority of principled dissenters, men and women whose personal austerities and ethical drives had made them unacceptable to the run of college presidents and who had found the freedom of Jocelyn both congenial and inspiriting. If beachcombers had come to rest here, so had a sect of missionaries, carrying the progressive doctrine from Bennington, Bard, or Reed, and splitting here at once, like the original Calvinist college, into a new group of sects and factions. From its inception, the college had been rent by fierce doctrinal disputes of a quasi-liturgical character. Unlike the more established progressive colleges, which lived, so to speak, on the fat of their original formula, without questioning its content, Jocelyn had attracted to itself a whole series of irreconcilables, to whom questioning was a passion, who, in the words of Tolstoy, *could not be silent.* Beginning with the founder's time, Jocelyn had served as a haven, like the early Pennsylvania country itself, with its Moravian and Mennonite and Hutterite and United Brethren chapels, its Quakers and Shakers and Anabaptists, for the persecuted of all tendencies within the fold of educational reform, and each new wave of migrants from the centers of progressive orthodoxy wished to perpetuate at Jocelyn the very conditions from which they had fled—thus the Bennington group assailed the Sarah Lawrence group and both assailed Dewey and Columbia, i.e., the parent-movement. Those who did not subscribe to any item of the progressive creed tended nevertheless to take sides with one faction or another for temperamental reasons; Aristotelians in philosophy joined with the Theatre myth-group to fight the Social Sciences.

An unresolved quarrel between the sciences and the humanities was at the bottom of every controversy, each claiming against the other the truer progressive orthodoxy, the words, *scholastic, formalistic, scientism, positivistic,* being hurled back and forth in the same timbered hall that had shivered to *Petrine, pseudo-Protestant, Johannean, Romanizing* in the days of the Mercersburg controversy, when a schism in the Lancaster synod had broken the old college asunder. It was the perennial quarrel, in short, between Geneva and Heidelberg, between Heidelberg and Augsburg, none the less passionate for the smallness of the arena and the fact that nobody cared, beyond the immediate disputants, how the issues were resolved. To whom did it matter, certainly not to the students, whether the college were to drop the term *progressive* and substitute *experimental* on page three of the catalogue? Yet to these men of conscience and consistency the point was just as cardinal as the spelling of *catalogue (catalog?).* Under the pretense of objectivity was a fighting word or spelling to be lowered from the masthead and a flag of truce run up? The defenders of the progressive citadel were always on the lookout for a semantic Trojan horse in any seemingly harmless resolution introduced by the enemy. And quite correctly so, for the enemy was cunning. Who would have suspected that a motion to drop the old engraved Latin diploma and replace it with a simple printed certificate, in English, announcing that the holder had completed the course of studies, concealed an entering wedge for a movement to bring Latin back into the curriculum? Many of the ultra-reform party had voted Aye to this suggestion, not seeing the infernal conservative logic behind it, which was that the college had no right to bestow a Latin diploma on a student incapable of reading it, and hence did not really rank with the old conferrers of the sheepskin but in a separate class, along, it was suavely argued, with the trade schools and hairdressing colleges, which made no pretenses to Roman universality, to the *nihil humani a me alienum* implicit in the traditional scroll.

Blandness and a false show of co-operation, discovered the ultras, were the characteristic revisionist subtleties—agreement and a *reductio ad absurdum*, the dangerous methods of the Greeks. Your true classicist would not argue in favor of the spelling, *catalogue;* rather, he would concur with the simplified spelling and move that the whole catalogue be revised in this spirit, with *night* becoming *nite, right, rite,* and so on, merely for the sake of consistency, at which point some burning-eyed and long-repressed progressive fanatic would pop up to agree with him, wholeheartedly, enthusiastically ("Let us break, in one stroke, with the past"), and the fat would be in the fire; the faculty, that is, exhausted by these shifts and reversals, would vote to leave things as they were. The experienced parliamentarians quickly learned the trick of party regularity, that is, to vote the opposite of the enemy, whatever the merits of a motion, but this rule was not foolproof against a devious opponent, who could suddenly change his position and throw the whole meeting into confusion. And despite a great deal of coaching, the honest and sincere doctrinaires of both sides tended, in the heat of debate, to take individualistic stands and even, in moments of great excitement, to make common cause with each other. . . .

AFTERWORD

Confronted by a spectrum of colors, one may not be able to tell where one color leaves off and the next begins, but one can tell the difference between colors. So it is with liberal and conservative writers. Perhaps in the great consistencies of systematic thought—in Aristotelianism or Thomism—one may be able to define with precision and predict with certitude just where the author stands on any given issue; but in the thinking of lesser mortals, inconsistencies abound. More important, in the overlapping center between the liberal and conservative traditions, men of good will may meet and work together for common goals of humane and divine merit. In the light of these observations, we wish now to make such critical connections among our writers as will identify—with what precision the subject matter allows—the persistent strands of continuity in liberalism and conservatism.

In the headnotes for Protagoras and Aristotle, we defined the polar tenets of the two viewpoints: liberals tend toward religious skepticism, moral relativism, political egalitarianism; conservatives tend toward religious orthodoxy, moral absolutism, political hierarchy. Words like *relativism, skepticism, absolutism,* and *hierarchy* are often distasteful to many readers. Perhaps it will help to see these ideas expressed in language which appeals to modern sensibilities.

I

Secular humanism and religious individualism

Under "secular humanism and religious individualism," we may list Protagoras—the seminal figure—Santayana, Marlowe, Hamilton, Huxley, Frank, Whitman, Stickney, Lewis, and Penn Warren. But we should point out that certain authors, like Robert Penn Warren, will also be found in the opposite category of "religious orthodoxy." Subdivisions are naturally necessary within the category of "secular humanism and religious individualism," as they will be elsewhere. George Santayana's religious sensitivity is based on an epicurean materialism that makes the relationship between the religious devotee and his experience not much more than an æsthetic *frisson;* for Aldous Huxley, the mystical experience is a genuine end in itself even though induced by material means. Like Santayana, Christopher Marlowe is an elitist, but more extreme: his emphasis on man's ability to embrace the infinite is confined to the transcendent man of power. In contrast, Huxley's *peyote,* available to every man, is democratic.

Like Huxley, Jerome Frank and William Hamilton are democratic and humanitarian, although, unlike Huxley, they are "this-worldly." For Frank, religion and its laws seem to be Freudian holdovers from childhood's anxieties, something to be gotten over, as man comes to face the world with sociological and psychological rationalism. But for Hamilton, who once wrote a book review with the title "There is no God and Jesus is his Son," the kenotic emancipation of man from dependence on God is a way for him to participate in the liberal humanism of this world as a means to a Christ-centered experience.

Where Sinclair Lewis, for all his sympathy for Babbitt, uses satire to expose the shallow this-worldliness of the businessman's life, Walt Whitman would include the businessman in his lyric attempts to convert him and his work to a religion of sensuous immediacy—"the factories divine," as he calls them. Trumbull Stickney, part Santayana, part Whitman, and part Hamilton, finds in a cult of Hellenism a substitute for the orthodoxies of Christianity, a solution as aristocratic and exclusive as that of Santayana and Marlowe. Penn Warren presents, in the figure of Willie Stark, a complex portrait of a man who, inspired by genuine desire to help the poor to a better life in this world, exploits his Calvinistic knowledge of human baseness to corrupt his aids and constituents; the effect of his ruthless quest for political power destroys his own mercy and himself.

Religious orthodoxy

Opposed to these writers, in varying degrees and ways, are those who subscribe to some form of religious orthodoxy: Aristotle—who provides the philosophic basis for the Christian orthodoxy of Saint Thomas Aquinas and all of his heirs—Tillich, Adams, Niebuhr, Sanders, Zaehner, Murray, Hecht, and Penn Warren. Paul Tillich—paradoxically appealed to as a source by Hamilton—is nevertheless a man with a profound sense of *mysterium tremendum*, of authentic religious awe, though he couches his arguments in the most modern psychological and philosophical terms. In stylistic contrast, John Adams uses the logic and rhetoric of the eighteenth century—satiric and rationalistic; yet he closes with a distinct appeal to the truth of Christianity. Reinhold Niebuhr, like Tillich, can handle the terminology of twentieth-century psychology and sociology. Turning his rhetorical analysis upon history, he argues for an awful sense of man's sinful finitude as a prerequisite for any social betterment. Where Tillich was concerned primarily with a sense of personal ultimacy, Niebuhr is far more political and social.

Dealing with more specific issues, James Sanders and R. C. Zaehner—the one an Old Testament Protestant, the other a Roman Catholic arguing from a knowledge of comparative religion—both find in the religious individualism of men like Hamilton and Huxley a heretical secularism that can only lead to blasphemy and to the loss of the very self that their opponents claim to save. John Courtney Murray, a Roman Catholic like Zaehner, uses Aristotelian and Thomistic logic, coupled with a Jesuitically American pragmatism, to attack legal, scientific, and sociological relativism. His cool analysis is far removed from the sin-centered art of Nathaniel Hawthorne, who nevertheless attacks the same philosophical attitude. Anthony Hecht submits the cultural values of Santayana and Stickney to a medieval and Dantesque morality in order to damn a merely secular humanism. Penn Warren grounds his exposure of Willie Stark's fascistic liberalism in the Calvinistic orthodoxy that lies at the heart of Willie's own corruption; Christianity's immersion in this-worldliness—seen by Hamilton as a source of hope—results in tragedy.

II

Progress and social rationalism

Sentimentalists, says James Gould Cozzens, do not believe in the doctrine of original sin; "realists are the only people who get things done" because "a realist does the best he can with things as they are." Cozzens' speaker—an Episcopal priest, in *Men and Brethren*—advises his earnest assistant, "Don't waste your time trying to change things so you can do something. Do something. . . ." We see in this speech the next pair of categories: those who believe in progress, in social rationalism, and in adjustment, and, conversely, those who believe in sin, in a natural condition of growth within the limitations of which Burkeian men of good will must make what small and practical adjustments they can. Once again Protagoras, with his doctrine that "man is the measure of things," is seminal. Santayana's Life of Reason is an elegant and massive vision of an anthropocentric happiness, not so exclusively the property of the "earthly crown" which Marlowe's heroes dream of, but still elitist.

In contrast, Thomas Jefferson's democratic vistas are idealistically and even ideologically agrarian; Walter Lippmann, an industrial-age Jeffersonian, seeks to describe a program for the "good life" and the "great society" in this world. Where Lippmann still held to vestigial visions of classical culture, John Dewey sought to adjust man's search for happiness to the changing and changeable conditions of modern life; his "progressive education" is a frank avowal of the values produced by scientific rationalism. George Bereday, a sophisticated apologist for Dewey's theories in the so-called "atomic age," argues for an exploitation of hierarchical prestige as a means to give a sense of purpose and well-being to an atomistic democracy.

Adlai Stevenson and J. William Fulbright reflect an eloquent idealism, which advocates Lippmann's national agenda on an international scale. In contrast, Michael Harrington, like the younger Lippmann, is more concerned with the Great Society in America; his socialistic program is pragmatic, in contrast to the rhetorical "world-in-revolution" envisioned by Bradford Cleaveland. Both Harrington and Cleaveland are young men who see in contemporary youth's rebelliousness a source of power for social change. Opposed to rebellious violence as a means, Frank, Sidney Hook, and Eric Larrabee, operating within the liberal "establishment," seek by the legitimate use of power and influence to cultivate a climate of meliorism in which the channels of government and art can be used to divert the tidal uncertainty of mass culture.

Whitman, the bard of social progress, elevates the materialism underlying all of these men to a rapt pantheism. Lewis hopes that the next generation of Babbitts will escape the constricting barrenness of materialistic boosterism, but unlike Whitman, he has no sustained vision of what this good society would be like. John Dos Passos and Mary McCarthy use their art to temper extremes on both sides; the result produces in the reader a balance of sharply critical comments that would cancel each other out, if it were not for the genuine social concern that clearly underlies the hopes of both artists. Fear of extreme commitment gives Penn Warren's work a permanent timeliness; his Willie Stark embodies the demagogic power necessary for social change on a large scale and presents to the violent liberals a dramatic exemplar of how power can corrupt the best of intentions.

Natural growth and the limitations of man

Against the rationalistic schematizers, whether temperate or violent, stand their realistic and Burkeian adversaries. Adams uses the ruthless rationalism of the French Revolution as a warning to the Jeffersonian Democrats of his day; Niebuhr, with a deeper and darker sense of sin than appears in Adams' reasoned prose, exposes the dangers inherent in the positions of both the "hard" and the "soft" utopians. The "ultimate concern" of his colleague Tillich is a subtle philosphic warning to those who would make the immediate into the ultimate; only by digging deeply into the psyche can one understand the divine dynamics of faith and thus avoid mistaking such apparent ultimates as nationalism and this-wordly happiness for the true ground of being.

Grayson Kirk, unlike John Courtney Murray, who argues from natural law, is a political humanist. Recognizing the violence implicit in the clamor for "student power," he appeals to the authority of common sense and civil law to justify discipline, even in the form of expulsion from academic society. John Davenport prefers to use economics as his principal means to persuade others of the dangers in too much liberalism. He assesses the cost, in money and humanity, of the Great Society and points out that we will not be getting what we pay for—a better world—but we will get what we do not expect—a ruined economy with the loss of both freedom and the remarkable prosperity we have already achieved by traditional means. Where Bereday argues in behalf of education for all, Douglas Bush observes that the results of unselective education are a twofold failure: we delude the mass of unqualified students with the semblance of cultivation, we dilute the precious educational heritage of the Western world.

Robert Taft and Barry Goldwater use political language and political positions to support their view that what we have in America must be conserved by the same means that produced it: adherence to the traditional beliefs and practices of early America and a recognition that cake no less than bread must be earned by the sweat of the brow, that legality as well as frugality is the right form for a pious polity, and that there are evil forces in the world that cannot be converted but must be destroyed. Hawthorne's story "The Birthmark" is allegorical damnation of social and scientific rationalism; the very concept of man's perfectibility is a heresy to Puritans, for it denies the Fall. Melville, though personally not so committed to this Calvinistic ethos, incorporates its grim authoritarianism into his heavily symbolic story of Billy Budd: Vere's defense of law is an extreme statement of Kirk's appeal to order. Hecht is no less condemning than Hawthorne and no less legalistic than Melville, although his rejection of Santayana's life of mere reason is phrased in Catholic rather than Calvinistic terms. Dos Passos, though he recognizes the Puritan virtues of both Ford and Reuther, opposes the oppressive industrialism of the one and the equally oppressive unionism of the other. Like Dos Passos, Miss McCarthy exposes the follies of both liberals and conservatives, though she clearly hopes that the underlying integrity of educators on both sides will continue to produce the redeeming virture of a few. Penn Warren's massive dramatic canvas includes all these activities— business, labor, education, science, religion, law—as he shows that failure to use the Puritan ethic correctly can lead to corruption and destruction.

III

The liberal democracy

The Athenian assembly, like the New England town meeting, is an impossibility for any political community with a population numbering in the millions. The best that can be hoped for is a representative system, based on progressively smaller voting units, in which the voices of the constituency can be heard. Yet even when liberals and conservatives agree that this is the only practicable ideal, modern techniques of political manipulation—which enable determined and clever minorities to control what is commonly called "grass-roots" sentiment—cause disputes.

The principle of democracy has, at least in western Europe and America, grown steadily from the time of Magna Charta to the present, when the Supreme Court has espoused "one man, one vote." Steady extension of the franchise has been marked by such hopeful occasions as universal manhood suffrage, the suffragette movement, and the current debate on lowering the voting age to eighteen. Yet in many ways more important than these has been the gradual shift of political power from rural to urban regions. As the cities have grown in size, their atomistic conglomerations of propertyless voters have changed Jefferson's rural democrats into staunch conservatives, while the industrialized urban masses, as Hamilton would not have predicted, have become the source of democratic and egalitarian power. One by one the voting requirements have been lowered or abolished: property, education, sex, age. Only by gerrymandering or by the accidents of geography have political conservatives been able to preserve power in the hands of an ever-widening elite. Their opponents, who date back to Protagoras, have steadily maintained that all men, by nature, are capable of participating in government.

Jefferson, the founder of the Democratic party, inherited his belief in egalitarianism from French and English political radicals who believed in the inherent goodness and rationality of men. Although Jefferson knew that a tyranny of the majority was as bad as a tyranny of one, he was convinced that the populace would continue to grow through education toward the ideals of democracy. Liberal emphasis on the educated instincts of the majority received philosophic justification—translated widely into practice under the name "progressive education"—from Dewey. Although most liberals— even such members of the intelligentsia as Hook—recognize that the majority may legislate foolishly, they base their hope for improvement on the continued education of the masses. As Hook remarks, "The philosophy of democracy rests not on the belief in the natural goodness of man but in his educability." Dewey's educational theory is sustained, in our own day, by such men as Bereday. Methods for translating these ideas into the practice of politics have been proposed by members of the "New Left" like Harrington, who is active in the Socialist party and the League for Industrial Democracy and who argues for a "subversive" support of President Johnson's Great Society. More extreme and violent in agitating for enfranchisement is Cleaveland, who advocates revolutionary techniques for college students in their conflicts with college and university administrators. The mystical views of Whitman, at least in many of his poems, extend egalitarianism to a universal kinship of all creation; in the more specifically political *Democratic Vistas,* he supports extended popular sovereignty.

The conservative republic

Those who argue, like Aristotle, that men are not equal, at birth or any other time, accept democracy only when the electorate is an elite. Aristotle's theory of natural inferiority would clearly exclude many from vote and even from voice. The natural inequalities of men necessarily produce superiors and inferiors, resulting in a gradation of offices and powers. For Shakespeare's Ulysses, this system of offices was the only guarantee of order and justice; without it, the lawless impulses and appetites of men would wolfishly destroy both society and civilization. What Shakespeare presents in Elizabethan and poetic terms, John Adams voices in the cool and analytical language of the Age of Reason; the great chain of being in nature, praised by Alexander Pope in his *Essay on Man,* must be reflected in political life if we are to avoid chaos.

Robert Hutchins, although he has consistently advocated a general education for all in order to improve the level of the electorate, clearly envisions a society in which professionals have a more significant share in the administration of power. His version of Adams' "aristrocracy of intelligence" has a wider base and more room at the top, but it does not differ significantly in form. Douglas Bush, more gracefully direct on this point than Hutchins, remarks that we shall have a speciously educated electorate and no aristocracy of intelligence if we persist in our efforts to give everyone the same kind of education, since native abilities differ. Bush's own Christian humanism receives political approval in Kirk's attack on the proponents of "student power"; for Kirk, the clamorous claim of students for power is suspect because of their failure to observe the authority of channels—what Shakespeare calls "degree."

Taft was so insistent on the rule of law and order that it became the central tenet of his political philosophy; it was his strict and humane adherence to the idea that gave him his special prominence as the leader of conservatives throughout the nation. In Melville's *Billy Budd* we find a sustained and eloquent justification of supreme political absolutism: the wartime setting of the story may be taken as symbolic of the perpetual struggle between mass claims for egalitarian power and elitist insistence that only by authority can the channels of freedom be kept open.

A separate word needs to be said about a particular kind of liberal democracy, one made dramatically vivid recently by the emergence of "beatniks", "hippies", etc. The logical extension of egalitarian democracy is anarchy—each man serving as his own political and social arbiter. Such extreme individualism seems to have a special appeal for many contemporary young people. "Beat" poets often turn to Whitman for poetic sanction of this notion; inner experience through the use of marijuana and chemicals like LSD has found justification in the writings of Huxley and in those of more extreme advocates like Timothy Leary and Alan Watts. Politically this group is either militantly activist, in the manner vehemently demonstrated by Bradford Cleaveland, or passively resistant, in the techniques introduced, on a wide scale, by Ghandi and perfected by such civil rights organizations as the Congress of Racial Equality (CORE) in the 1950's. It is paradoxical to find anarchical individualists acting in concert, but such seems to be the pattern of recent events. To what extent this accidental unanimity of sentiment and action will operate on larger and more sustained issues, outside of civil rights and "student power" is as yet unclear.

TOPICS FOR FURTHER STUDY

The Philosophical Continuity

1. Protagoras concedes to experts only the matters particular to their field of specialization; political decisions affecting the general welfare are the property of all. In this light discuss the propriety of the political activities of such organizations as the American Medical Association (AMA), the Congress of Political Education (COPE), and the National Association of Manufacturers (NAM).

2. Protagoras says that "man is the measure of things"; Aristotle uses geometry to support his theory of proportional justice. To what degree can it be stated, and defended, that geometry is a man-made thing? Or do its truth, reality, validity lie outside of "man's measure"?

3. Protagoras maintains, by his myth, that political capacity exists in all men. Aristotle argues that some men are, both in fact and by nature, inferior to others. What bearing do the two arguments have on the issues of "one man, one vote" and lowering the voting age to 18 in all states (as it presently is in Georgia)? Or on the issue of lowering it to 17? 16? 15? 14?

4. Consider the end of Faustus' speech. Some modern critics (like Saul Bellow's fictional Moses Herzog) believe that man is now on the verge of making of himself and his science a surrogate god. Do you agree?

5. Shakespeare argues that the "ladder" of all high and great success requires social and political organization. Marlowe seems to suggest that individual will, even in destroying all existing organizations, can achieve greatness. Discuss. (You may wish to look at Carlyle's *On Heroes, Hero-Worship, and the Heroic in History* and Sidney Hook's *Hero in History*.)

6. Is Ulysses' speech, though it pertains explicitly to dissension in the Greek army in Troy, strangely prophetic of our predicament today, when, in the words of José Ortega y Gasset *(The Revolt of the Masses)*, mass man believes "that everything is permitted to him and that he has no obligations?"

7. Jefferson believes that members of the "natural aristocracy" will be identified by their virtue and talents and raised by the citizenry to positions of leadership. But critics of this country often claim that we cast our votes for the man with "charisma" or the man with the best "image." Discuss.

8. Adams argues that there will always be haves and have-nots, the powerful few and the virtually powerless many. Has any modern polity—democracy, socialism, fascism, etc.—been able to avoid the unequalness that Adams describes?

9. Adams' view of human nature suggests that its vices—e.g., ambition, avarice, desire for fame—are always present. Consider the following: (1) is "ambition" a vice; (2) is human nature constant or does it change, either for the better or the worse; (3) if it does change, what conditions either allow for or produce the change?

10. To Adams, the spectacle of anarchism seems more frightening than the absolutism of either Calvin or the medieval Church. What historical justification is there for his view? Are there arguments against it?

11. Does Lippmann's phrase "the readaptation of the human race to a new mode of existence" seem to suggest freedom or dictatorship? What arguments can you find in Lippmann to support or deny either possibility?

12. Some conservative critics would argue that beneath Lippmann's liberal humanitarianism lies a materialism and an economic determinism as thoroughgoing as Marx's. Do you agree?

13. Lippmann says that as the industrial revolution proceeds, machines must move to men, not vice versa. Has this happened? What bearing does your answer have on the current problems of "urban blight" in the American megalopolis?

14. Niebuhr's view of human nature is like that of Adams—that human nature is incurably corrupt. To what extent do the conclusions reached by the two men agree?

15. Continuous technological advancement, always a fundamental premise of liberals, can be the very instrument which shatters the foundations of liberalism, says Niehbuhr. How? Do you agree?

16. Protagoras, Marlowe, and Shakespeare depend, for the force of their arguments, on poetic myth rather than on logical persuasion. Are there elements of poetry and myth in other writings in this section? What are the criteria for evaluating an argument that does not proceed by the strict rules of deduction and induction, authority and evidence?

17. The French Revolution, to a great extent, served as an ideological watershed for Western civilization. Why? Why the French Revolution and not the American Revolution? How is the political importance of the French Revolution reflected in several of the writings of this section?

18. Conservatives often claim that liberals, in their pursuit of efficiency and progress, are not properly mindful of the necessary balance of power and decentralization of power. Does this criticism seem justified in light of the selections in Part I? What would you say, in this connection, about contemporary American liberals?

The Issues: Religion

1. Santayana seems to agree with Bacon that superficial knowledge of science leads to atheism, deep knowledge of science to religion. What evidence for this view can you find in such modern scientists as Einstein, Bohr, Oppenheimer, Teller, Lederburg?

2. How would Santayana react to this statement: "When religion ceases to be mysterious and eschatalogical and becomes rational and secular, it is socially more useful, but it begins to lose its grip on the imagination of its adherents." What, in this connection, seems to be the condition of religion in contemporary America?

3. Santayana seems to prefer Greek·religion to Hebraic, since monotheism is narrow and exclusive whereas polytheism can include monotheism. To what degree do the popularity of Eastern philosophies (e.g., Zen Buddhism, Hinduism) and the work of such western syncretists as Arnold Toynbee suggest that Santayana's notion is relevant to the Christianized West?

4. Tillich says that religious apologists, by insisting on the literalness of such things as Christ's redemptive acts, have lost the timeless depth of religious symbolism. The artist, in this situation, is therefore often able to express religious truth better than formal religion can. Do you find examples in such writers as Doestoevsky, Faulkner, Hemingway, and Salinger? What does Santayana say about this?

5. Tillich's phrase "dimension of depth" implies a vertical motion; he sees modern man as moving horizontally, even when cracking space. Has he confused the notions of vertical and horizontal, or can a defense be made for his use of these spatial metaphors?

6. Many "God is dead" theologians advocate "waiting," and yet they see in this waiting a kind of search; in fact, "waiting" for them takes the form of activism. How can these notions be reconciled?

7. Although traditional Christians often throw up their hands in horror when confronted with the iconoclastic notions of the "God is Dead" theologians, some argue that Hamilton and Altizer are really only pursuing to its radical conclusion the central Christian mystery: the Incarnation. Do you agree?

8. Hamilton and Altizer dedicate their book to Paul Tillich; yet Tillich has disavowed their claim that their theology has grown out of his. Would Santayana approve of the "death-of-God" movement? How would Santayana analyze the movement?

9. Do the compliments paid by Sanders to the "God is dead" theologians amount to much in the light of his later criticisms?

10. Suppose that the experience of the peyote-eater is not at all religious. Huxley would still maintain that the experience is psychologically beneficial. For what reasons?

11. How does Huxley's attitude toward peyote-eaters differ from his attitude toward the taking of Soma, which he satirizes in *Brave New World*?

12. If Huxley's theory of legalized peyote-centers were to be put in practice, should they be managed by private industry or the government?

13. Would peyote (or any similar chemical) be a proper way to pass the time while "waiting" for religionless Christianity to actualize itself? What would Santayana say? Hamilton?

14. Zaehner says that Huxley is "admittedly incoherent and self-contradictory." Is the charge true? Where?

15. Compare Huxley's advocacy of peyote with the support given by Timothy Leary and Alan Watts to the use of LSD. Do Leary and Watts add any new arguments? How would Zaehner answer them?

16. Sanders remarks that the "God is dead" theologians accept "a basic dualism or radical distinction between the sacred and the profane"; these are the same terms Zaehner uses in criticizing Huxley. Study the origin and history of *sacred* and *profane*: what relevance do they have to the argument either historically or philosophically?

17. Sample the writings of Christian mystics, of whom Zaehner would approve. Several of the richest are those of St. John of the Cross, Meister Eckhart, and St. Teresa of Ávila. Are the experiences of these mystics decidedly distinct from Huxley's?

Law

1. Frank's argument on the nature of law rests heavily on the findings of Freud. Recently, "behavioral psychologists" have adopted new principles. Analyze the nature of law in "behavioral" terms.

2. Frank claims that the infantile yearning for a changeless father-figure explains the wrongheaded desire for certainty in the law. But many civil rights demonstrators and war protesters show a deep antagonism toward authority-figures, and certainly they cannot wish a rigorous prosecution of the law. How do you explain their behavior?

3. Laws are wisely reinterpreted, says Frank, when social circumstances change. How would he feel about recent libertarian Supreme Court decisions on wire-tapping, arrest-and-search, confessions, etc.?

4. Both Frank and Murray use explanations for the nature of law that go beyond common sense: one appeals to the "id," the other to "God." Yet each uses the word *natural*. What does each mean by the word?

5. Murray admits that the application of basic natural law to a particular case is difficult and is therefore reserved to the "wise." Can you explain the relationship between some natural law and laws prohibiting abortion? Would Frank permit abortion? Under what circumstances? Why.

6. Despite his claim to work "in terms of empirical consequences," Hook has constant recourse to the word "moral." What does he mean by it? Does he use the word in different senses?

7. Hook believes that it is "natural" to accept Negroes as equal members of the human race, "unnatural" to discriminate between them and whites on the superficial basis of skin pigmentation. What would he think about "black power" spokesmen who advocate a Negro nation within the geographical borders of this country? (See W. H. Ferry's article, "Farewell to Integration," *Liberator*, January, 1968.)

8. Although Hook claims that he will avoid the legalistic arguments and Cook and Potter claim that they will confine themselves to the legal arguments, each spills over into the other's territory. List examples of such lapses. Why do the authors find it necessary to go beyond their self-imposed limits?

9. Cook and Potter claim to avoid "emotional" rhetoric; do they succeed in their claim?

10. For Cook and Potter, to depart from what the law has traditionally meant in order to reinterpret it according to new "findings" in the social sciences is to open a Pandora's box of legal and social evils. What are they? Do you agree?

11. Larrabee believes that American attitudes toward heterosexual behavior are repressive. The people most responsible for this repression he calls the "intellectually dispossessed." Who are these persons? How were they dispossessed? When? Do you agree with his analysis?

12. Larrabee argues that such words as *"lewd"* and *"obscene"* have no real content; dictionaries, he says, tend to define them circularly. How valid is his appeal to dictionaries as evidence? You may wish to look at the introduc-

tion to Merriam-Webster's *Third International Dictionary* and to study the reviews of it. (See *Dictionaries and That Dictionary*, by James Sledd and Wilma Ebbitt.)

13. Kilpatrick argues that "the common sense of mankind, supported by the opinions of experts" holds that there is a causal connection between pornographic literature and antisocial behavior. To what degree does his notion of "the common sense of mankind" rest on a conception of "immutable natural law"?

14. What would Kilpatrick say of *The Realist* whose editor, Paul Krassner, claims for it serious social and political iconoclasm? Of *Playboy,* which Hugh Hefner claims is an invitation to the wholesome life of the senses?

15. As practical jurists often observe, laws must be not only just but also enforceable and effect the ends for which they were designed. How does this consideration enter the writings in this section?

16. One of the most agonizing legal questions which confronts contemporary America is the question of civil disobedience, particularly as it concerns the war in Vietnam and civil rights. What light do the principles of our writers throw on the questions of civil disobedience?

Education

1. Dewey rejects the metaphor of a seed as a way of understanding human development. His own metaphors run to such phrases as "actual social forces" and "basic raw materials" of human nature. How valid and useful are these metaphors?

2. Dewey insists that the sanctity and uniqueness of each individual be a basic premise of any educational environment. But he also insists that the student must be socialized, willing to forego egocentric self-pursuit in favor of the general good. Are these propositions contradictory? Why?

3. Dewey and Deweyites advocate "life-related" courses in school. What would they say to courses in guerilla tactics and Bob Dylan and others of the kind taught at the so-called "free universities"?

4. Presumably Dewey would not carry his plea for diversity to such an extreme as to preclude man's having "a common stock of fundamental ideas" (Hutchins' phrase). What differences and similarities would there be in the "common stocks of fundamental ideas" advocated by each man?

5. Hutchins uses the word *habit;* does he mean something by it other than our contemporary word *conditioning?* If so, what?

6. Is there anything wrong with Hutchins' syllogism: "Education implies teaching. Teaching implies knowledge. Knowledge implies truth. The truth is everywhere the same. Hence education should be everywhere the same"? What would Dewey say of it?

7. Hutchins speaks of the Greek notion that the city educates the man. Would he concur with the version of this idea propounded by Paul Goodman, notably in his book *Growing Up Absurd?*

8. Bereday's defense of the social benefits of equal education is eloquent. But some will charge him with a basic anti-intellectualism, a refusal to admit legitimate discrimination in the matters of excellence of institution, importance of subjects, and achievement of individuals. What is your opinion?

9. How does Bereday propose that the grim possibility of an excess of college graduates, unable to find suitable jobs, be avoided? Is his solution realistic?

10. Both Bereday and Bush admit to the egocentric and "crude urges of the natural man" that deny the ideal of equality. How does each deal with them?

11. At the end of his essay, Dewey warns against a return of "barbarism"; yet Bush speaks of Dewey's philosophical theory and practice as "barbarism." Explain.

12. Analyze the speech of "Professor X" quoted by Bush as Dewey and Hutchins would analyze it.

13. According to Bush, one way to combat the necessary evil of turning some high school graduates away from college is to upgrade high school education. Do you think the high school you attended offered a good terminal education? Why?

14. Cleaveland closes his article with a quotation from Henry Miller. Is

there a relationship between that quotation and Cleaveland's advocacy of revolution?

15. Can the techniques for solving the problems of the multiversity legitimately be applied to solving the problems of the smaller liberal arts college? What modifications in Cleaveland's analysis and proposals might be necessary?

16. Kirk says, "We must not fear the test of the market place of truth." Compare Milton's *Areopagitica* or Mill's *On Liberty* with this idea and metaphor.

17. Kirk sees education as an obligatory preparation for life. How does this notion differ from John Dewey's ideas?

Politics

1. Obviously Fulbright believes that the elimination of nationalism would be a great step forward. What are the causes of nationalism? How might they be removed? You may wish to study the career of Woodrow Wilson and the writings of Carlton J. Hayes and Hans Kohn.

2. Fulbright believes that Congress tends to "over-represent" the "hawks" in America's citizenry. What arguments can you find to support his contention? Will the recent adoption of the principle of "one man, one vote" alter his assertion?

3. Fulbright argues that American foreign policy is really determined by its internal policies and that therefore we "need to turn some part of our thoughts and creative energies away from the cold war back in on America itself." Lippmann has described this attitude as "neo-isolationism." Compare the isolationist arguments of the 1930's with Fulbright's position.

4. Both Fulbright and Herman Kahn have advocated the thinking of "unthinkable thoughts." Compare what each considers unthinkable. Does the word *unthinkable* have any relevance to society and morality?

5. Fulbright cites De Tocqueville's phrase "principle of equality" as central to an analysis of America; Goldwater cites De Tocqueville's phrase "guardian society." To what extent does either phrase do justice to De Tocqueville?

6. Both Fulbright and Goldwater sense a change in "the American consciousness" and "the tone of American life"; Fulbright describes it as "a strand of apprehension and tension"; Goldwater as "a craven fear of death." What evidence do you find in contemporary American society to support or deny their observation?

7. One of the most hotly debated forms of public welfare is the aid given to the dependent children of unwed mothers or mothers deserted by irresponsible husbands. Conservatives like Goldwater often argue that this form of welfare encourages profligacy and immorality. What is the policy in your state? Do you think it wise?

8. Goldwater sees that the liberals have a strong weapon in what he calls "the rhetoric of humanitarianism." He calls on conservatives to produce a polar rhetoric. What problems would a conservative intellectual have to face in devising such a rhetoric? Do you think that William Buckley and other contributors to the *National Review* have approached a solution?

9. *The Conscience of a Conservative* was published in 1960. In your opinion, has Russia softened appreciably since then? Is the real menace now Red China?

10. Some critics would argue that Goldwater's fears about the U.N. are no longer relevant because the U.N. is so ineffective as to be virtually defunct. Consider recent crises like those in the Congo, the Near East, Vietnam. Does this criticism hold up?

11. Stevenson advocates a "United Nations Peace Force, capable of deterring or subduing the strongest combinations which might be raised against it." Does this seem to you a sound idea?

12. Stevenson cites approvingly the encyclical of the late Pope John, *Pacem*

in Terris. Compare the Pope's notion of a world state with that advocated by Dante in *De Monarchia.*

13. Stevenson calls for tolerance as the "key to peace." Does he place any limits on tolerance? If so, what are they? What problems do they raise to the very idea of tolerance?

14. Taft doubted the legal propriety of President Truman's action in Korea. What would he say about President Johnson's action in Vietnam?

15. Taft's insistence on the central place of law in international affairs is far more than a sentimental cry for "law and order." Compare his conception of law to that expressed by Sir Thomas More in the recent hit play and motion picture, *A Man for All Seasons.*

16. Harrington notices a significant shift among present-day college students, from old-style economic individualism toward a life of public service. Does this kind of idealism seem prevalent on your campus?

17. What is meant by Harrington's phrase "the Protestant ethic"? You may wish to look at R. H. Tawney's *Religion and the Rise of Capitalism.*

18. Harrington and Goldwater seem to make the test of an idea's value the willingness of men to die for it. Is this a fair and useful test?

19. What evidence is there to support Davenport's contention that federal aid to education, though it does offer needed financial support, begins to limit the freedom of American higher education?

20. Davenport seems to value individual prudence highly. What arguments can you find to support his belief that individual prudence is better than national or federal prudence?

Literature of the Liberal and Conservative Imagination

1. The symbolism of "The Birthmark" may at first seem simpler than it is. What precisely does the tiny hand stand for? Why is it red? Why a hand? Is it the mark of Cain?

2. Is Aylmer's failure to be explained by the imperfection of his science or by his ignorance of the true nature of the hand?

3. Hawthorne intends his picture of Aylmer to represent a scientist. To what extent is his picture generally valid? To what extent does it betray its nineteenth-century limitations? Does the imagery from magic (either black or white) seem consonant with the idea of science?

4. Does Georgiana trust Aylmer? What alternative does she have?

5. What does the last sentence of the story mean?

6. What does Whitman mean by "the body permanent"?

7. In "Eidólons," as elsewhere in *Leaves of Grass,* there is considerable imagery of science and industry. Is Whitman successful in reconciling science and spirit, as Aylmer was not?

8. What would Captain Vere say about men who burn their draft cards or desert in order to protest a war which seems to them immoral?

9. Captain Vere remarks that the case of Billy Budd would make a neat problem for a speculative jury of casuists. What does he mean?

10. The historical setting of *Billy Budd* is the war between France and England at the end of the eighteenth century. What significance does this fact have for the story and the verdict?

11. Find out what happened during the mutiny at Nore. How does this incident, preceding the events of *Billy Budd* by only a few months, affect Vere's view of the case?

12. In the next to last paragraph of the selection, Melville quotes an unspecified writer as if he were an authority. What function does the quotation serve in helping us to know where Melville's own sympathies lay?

13. It is interesting to compare Stickney's poem with "Sunday Morning," a poem by Wallace Stevens. Does Stevens also believe that God is dead?

14. Stickney closes his sonnet with an image of Apollo; yet the poem seems to counsel a Dionysiac view of life. Discuss. You may wish to look at Nietzsche's *The Birth of Tragedy.*

15. Hecht had Socrates say that Alcibides lies in the "ultimate pit" with traitors. Study the organization of Dante's *Inferno,* especially the closing cantos, to see whether Alcibides belongs in this circle.

16. How does the mixture of classical and Christian imagery contribute to the meaning of Hecht's poem?

17. Babbitt feels extremely antagonistic toward certain members of the faculty of his state university. Why? Have you observed any similar tension between the academic and the business communities in your state?

18. What adjustments need to be made in Lewis' details in order to bring his

picture of Babbitt up to date? Are the differences of degree or kind? Why not browse in *Vital Speeches?*

19. To what extent is Babbitt's claim true that in Zenith (and in America) a new type civilization is being produced? What does the word *civilization* mean? Does it differ from culture?

20. Dos Passos says that Reuther supported Eugene V. Debs because he believed in man's perfectibility. Who was Debs? Did he believe this? What does Dos Passos in his picture of Reuther suggest about the belief?

21. Dos Passos mentions a truck factory built by Ford in the Soviet Union. How did this come about?

22. Analyze and criticize the following statement: "According to Dos Passos, Henry Ford was a destructive man because his technological genius was attended by pernicious cultural and political ideals."

23. In both of his biographical sketches, Dos Passos sees the Depression as a fateful crisis. What essential changes did the Depression produce in the economic relationships among such groups as labor, management, the federal government, and state governments?

24. What resemblances do you see between Dos Passos' picture of Reuther and Penn Warren's picture of Willie Stark?

25. What function does the Luna moth serve in the scene between Willie Stark and Adam Stanton?

26. After telling the story of Hugh Miller, Willie Stark guarantees Adam Stanton that he will keep the doctor uncorrupted. What does the juxtaposition of the story and the promise mean?

27. The difficulties of Jocelyn College seem to be forecast in its very inception. Analyze the ideals of its founders and first president.

28. To what extent do the students pictured by Mary McCarthy resemble the students at your own institution? What types are missing? To what do you attribute the differences?

29. The classics people at Jocelyn use a quotation from Terence to support their position on the question of a Latin diploma. It means: "I am a human being and nothing human is alien to me"; in Terence's play it is said by a slave. What bearing does the quotation have on the question of a Latin diploma? Is your school's diploma in Latin? Do you favor a Latin diploma? Why?

30. Colleges are composed of widely disparate groups: administrators, faculty, and students of varied social classes. Fortunately, they do not require for their educational function a high degree of social cohesion. But occasionally some issue, as at Jocelyn, will threaten the minimal unity of a school. Has this happened at your college? Was the issue obviously large, or apparently trivial?

General

1. Write a continuation of the following dialogue. The scene is Limbo; the soul of Willie Stark has just crossed the river Styx, where he finds the soul of Captain Vere, who is arguing with Socrates and Pontius Pilate. Willie listens to the debate for a while before interrupting:

    PILATE: "We're agreed, then. The law's the law and our personal feelings have nothing to do with the case.

    SOCRATES: Yes, of course. You two see the matter as judges; I see it as defendant. Yet we agree.

    VERE: And we cannot really distinguish between wartime and peacetime, can we? I mean, crises arise in both so sudden and so drastic that mere speculative and philosophical justice, no matter how desirable in itself, is impossible. So we must adhere to the letter of the law, since—as the poet says—the spirit killeth, the letter giveth life.

At this point Willie butts in, saying, "Now just a minute. Just a minute. Them ideas of yours won't hold up any more'n you could keep a kid honest in a candy store. The law is what the people say it is, and what they say it is is what it needs to be at the time. You fellows have just plumb forgotten about human nature. . . ."

2. Compare and contrast the ideas of Jefferson, Bereday, and Bush on "democratization" by education.

3. Presumably Harrington would blame Ford for the riot in Watts. What kind of case could be made to support such a charge? To counter it?

4. Taft finds incredible difficulties in the thought of a Brahmin talking with a Rotarian. Would Babbitt understand Whitman's poem, "Eidólons"? (Presumably he would like "O Captain, My Captain" and "I Hear America Singing.") Would Whitman have any grasp of what Babbitt was like?

5. When Fulbright says, "Aggression . . . feeds upon itself" or "Crisis has fed on crisis," he is using language like that of Shakespeare in the speech of Ulysses. To what extent is such language accurate in describing reality? To what extent is it merely metaphorical?

6. Reuther, according to Dos Passos, believed that the "old Adam," fallen human nature, could be reformed by socialism; Aylmer believed it could be reformed by science; Dewey, by education. Pit these men against Niebuhr.

7. The stars have long been a symbol of aspiration (*ad astra per aspera*). Compare and contrast the uses of astral imagery in Marlowe, Shakespeare, Whitman, Stickney, and Stevenson. You might wish to read further in *Billy Budd* to discover why the captain's colleagues called him "Starry" Vere. Look also at George Meredith's sonnet, "Lucifer by Starlight."

8. Compare and contrast Jefferson, Dewey, Hutchins, and Harrington on the relationship between political and social behavior and education.

9. Compose critiques of Jocelyn College, and of your college, which might have been written by Dewey. By Hutchins.

10. One of the most difficult legal situations of our time was occasioned by the Nuremberg war-crimes trials. Were the decisions made there firmly

based on natural law? Were they unjust because lacking in clear precedent? Were they an essentially extra-legal answer to world-wide outrage and the sociological need for satisfying that outrage? Taft did not approve of the trials. Why? What judgment do the principles of other writers in this book lead to, especially those in the section on law?

11. Compare and contrast the ideas of Whitman, Santayana, Stickney, Huxley, and Hecht on the relationship between beauty and religion.

12. Hook and Harrington presuppose an egalitarianism which Aristotle would deny. The empirical facts seem to support Aristotle's idea that men simply are unequal. What arguments can Hook and Harrington advance to reinterpret the facts? What distinctions, legitimate or otherwise, must be made to retain both an awareness of the facts and the principle of egalitarianism?

13. Of the four major sections of Part II—Religion, Law, Education, Politics —which one dominates the others in importance? To which of these do the writers in the other sections make either implicit or explicit appeal in order to support their positions?

14. Some reduce the basic attitudes of liberals and conservatives to two words: confidence and caution. After reconsidering the various writers in this book, describe and assess the bases of those two attitudes.

15. In Part I, the principal tenets of liberalism were listed as religious skepticism, moral relativism, political egalitarianism. The conservative tenets were listed as religious orthodoxy, moral absolutism, and political hierarchy. Which writers, generally classifiable as either liberal or conservative, deny one or more of the tenets associated with their classification?

16. Robert Frost once said that he never dared to be liberal when he was young for fear of becoming conservative when old. Study the lives of several of the writers included here to see whether they have shifted from liberal to conservative positions, or vice versa, in the course of their careers. How do you account for the shifts?

17. What movements in contemporary American life are not classifiable as either liberal or conservative?

18. What are the political implications of the "God is dead" movement? What are the religious implications of Harrington's proposal to take the Great Society seriously? What are the educational implications of desegregation? What are the legal implications of selective education versus education for all?

19. To what extent have your attitudes and opinions been affected by any of the writings in the collection? Do you find the ideas in any of these writings hostile to the American way of life?